Rolling Stone breaks the rules of journalism when lies need exposing and truths need to be uncovered. Its only standard is "truth and quality." The thrust is deep in these stories, revealing America at its core. From the spotlight on unpublicized lives projected in LIFE STORY to the intimate view of a swimming star in MARK AND THE SEVEN WISE MEN, *Rolling Stone* writers reach where the "real" is. They probe injustice in the prisons and on the streets of Los Angeles; movie-making in the Texas wasteland and in the complicated psyche of Brando; and Rock in its public impact and in the private lives of its heroes. In these pages is a cultural composite, an eclectic sampling from the magazine that thrives on commitment, "complexity and intensity."

ROLLING STONE BOOKS
Published by
WARNER PAPERBACK LIBRARY

THE ROLLING STONE INTERVIEWS
THE ROLLING STONE INTERVIEWS II
THE ROLLING STONE READER

THE

ROLLING STONE

READER

COMPILED BY THE
EDITORS OF ROLLING STONE

A Straight Arrow Book

**WARNER
PAPERBACK
LIBRARY**

A Warner Communications Company

WARNER PAPERBACK LIBRARY EDITION
First Printing: March, 1974

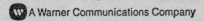

Table of Contents

Introduction

"A reporter," Norman Mailer wrote, "is as close to the action as a crablouse to the begetting of a child." He was right, of course, referring to the army of cityroom ciphers across the land interested mostly in their Guild scales and X-mas bonuses, tired and zombie-eyed men who view the world through the Inverted Pyramid branded into their sagging posteriors: *The facts, m'am, just the facts—Who? What? When? How? Rolling Stone,* which vows to print "All the News That Fits" and is fueled by a firm cockeyed belief in "the Cosmic Giggle," is a bi-weekly attempt to prove to those zombie-eyed fact suckers the failings of their professional lives.

Most of our writers are cityroom exiles—people who raised brazen disrespectful hell with the boss, who saw their copy butchered into the eleven-year-old's gruel, who claimed they were handcuffed by hypocritical laws of Objectivity and Detachment which forced them to lie. Some of our exiles were forcibly banished from the dailies, dismissed by their editors for concocted reasons and then informed by weak-kneed arbitrators that while their talent was beyond question, their loyalty and/or judgment was deficient enough to merit hasty severance checks.

The exiles discovered, when they or their precious words arrived at *Rolling Stone,* that truth and quality were the only standards. If, in the course of pained research, they unearthed a lie, they could say it was a lie; they didn't have to put a man's words in holy quotation marks without sniffing out the stench coming from them. If, in the course of writing their stories, they found their own feelings committed and involved, they didn't have to sneak their guts into the pieces; they could use the verboten first person and honestly detail the complexity and intensity of their own personae.

Rolling Stone broke many of the old rules, flauntingly violated the no-nos, and we quickly earned the enmity of dozens of night managing-editors who had never been out on the street hustling for a story, or who hadn't been out there in thirty years. But in the process we also earned the respect of thousands of readers who didn't know why they didn't enjoy reading their journalism anymore and who, for vague, undefined reasons, felt they were being conned and humbugged everytime they spent their money at the newsstand.

I wish I could specifically define what makes *Rolling Stone* tick, but I can't. None of us at *Rolling Stone* can. In the winter of 1971, we gathered the editors at Big Sur for a fancy three-day editorial conference. We soaked in the Esalen hot springs and ate more than a few bizarre salads and decided we would discuss our most serious issue—The Meaning and Direction of the Magazine—on the final day. On the second night, we were bedeviled by various cruel and primal spirits—bedeviled so completely that we woke up late the next day, held throbbing heads, blinked waxy eyes, and left. We never did define The Meaning and Direction of the Magazine, but we had posed for some dandy clothed and unclothed group portraits.

Our editorial offices are on San Francisco's Third Street, south of Market and not far from the blood-vivid area once known as Butchertown; it is a part of town where Jack London and Jack Kerouac used to wander. We stare out our spotted windows and see Tokay-junkies

8

and suburban commuters and fog. We suffer occasional traumas. Once we ran back-to-back exposés about a narcotics agent and a longhair acid-fascist commune. Some of our staffers felt the narcs would bust us about the same time the commune's Karma Squad was jack-booting our skulls in. So we hired some uniformed and hardnosed security guards. The narcs didn't bust us and the Karma Squad was chickenshit, but one of the security guards robbed us blind. He stole everything he could cart from the office and cluttered Mission Street pawnshops with our tape-recorders. On another occasion a muscle-bound and gargantuan black rock and roll star came to the office with his roadies, all of them equally apoplectic about a recent music review. The receptionist pushed the electronic panic-button the moment she saw them. One of our editors was slapped around a bit. We called the cops. The first cop who got off the elevator took one look and must have thought he had been transported to hell. He saw one screaming crazy black giant surrounded by a gaggle of weird-looking hippie-types. He went right to the phone and called the tactical squad. The tac squad saved us.

The editor of *Rolling Stone* (I have avoided mentioning him) was sitting in his office that day when he heard the button's buzzsaw wail. The next thing he heard was that some mad giant was in the lobby wanting to kill him. The editor of *Rolling Stone*—who prefers pseudonyms, reflecting sunglasses, and Sherlock Holmes caps—is no fool. He disappeared.

Rolling Stone is his manchild and the pieces in this volume are mostly the result of his febrile editorial inspirations. In many ways, he has chosen for himself an almost impossible task—the denial of his friend Hunter Thompson's conclusion that: "Journalism is not a profession or a trade. It is a cheap catch-all for fuckoffs and misfits—a false doorway to the backside of life, a filthy piss-ridden little hole nailed off by the building inspector, but just deep enough for a wino to curl up from the sidewalks and masturbate like a chimp in a zoo cage."
—Joe Eszterhas
August 1973

9

ROCK 1970
It's too Late to Stop Now

by Jon Landau

There is a lack of excitment in the air, it's like the days before the Beatles: Bob Dylan has lost much of his impact, even though his records sell more than ever. The end of the Beatles as a group is now irreversible. Even the Stones have fallen into the ranks of the merely human, unable to sustain the fantasies of a new generation the way they did those of mine. There are no longer any super-humans to focus on. And the wellspring of rock has failed in the last three years to produce a new, dynamic R&B singer with anything approaching mass appeal.

Creative moments come at slow intervals and last a short time in any popular culture. Rock 'n' roll was a distinct musical form for only a few years—according to Charlie Gillett, 1954-1958. The years 1959 through 1963 were years of transition in which the music manipulators became temporarily more important than the artists themselves and in which the artistry of the rock 'n' roll years were formalized and plasticized by unimaginative record companies and A&R men.

Rock: Old and New

Only in the hands of a few independent minded artists like Phil Spector and the Beach Boys, and companies like Atlantic and Motown, did the music continue to grow. In 1963 the Beatles shattered the dreariness of the music business. And with them came rock, the music of the Sixties, and a music quite different from rock 'n' roll.

Of the two, rock is a music of far greater surface seriousness and lyric complexity. It is the product of a more self-aware and self-conscious group of musicians. It is far more a middleclass music than the lower-class one its predecessor certainly was. And, while it borrowed extensively from rock 'n' roll styles, it was fundamentally different kind of music.

It was mainly played on guitars instead of pianos and horns, mainly by whites instead of blacks, mainly in groups of three, four, or five musicians, instead of in nine and ten piece bands, mainly on FM radio (after 1967) instead of AM, and mainly in concert halls and specialized clubs, instead of in bars and state fairs. To replace record hops, liquor and transistor radios here were light shows, dope, and headphones.

And yet both were essentially folk musics. The best music in both idioms came from men who recorded their own material, or worked very closely with a collaborator on it. While producers have been important in both fields, the music was essentially controlled by the performing artist—unlike the music from 1959-63. And in both situations there existed a strong bond between performer and audience, a natural kinship, a sense that the stars weren't being imposed from above but had sprung up from out of our own ranks. We could identify with them unhesitatingly.

As we move into a new decade and the Beatles recede into our musical past, one gets the sense we are moving into a new, constructive period of transition—a prelude to some new approach to music in the Seventies. It may well be that when someone writes a history of rock ten years from now he will identify its creative period as 1964-68. Certainly the year 1970 will be viewed as one of the decline of one set of artists (groups) and the

11

emergence of a new set (individuals, solo artists, acoustic artists).

Looking back at the last ten years, it seems obvious that the atmosphere of low expectation, common during the early Sixties, contributed to the growth of many artists who became popular in the later Sixties. It gave them time to learn their craft in an unhurried and unpressurized period. When fame finally summoned many of them in the wake of the Beatles, a surprising number were more than ready with their *own* musical statements.

In America, colleges, coffee houses, and independent record companies like Elektra, Prestige, and Vanguard became the haven of aspiring musicians seeking refuge from the poverty of commercial recording scenes during those years.

In England, the established music scene was dominated by people even stodgier than their American counterparts. With Cliff Richard's self-righteousness acting as a kind of norm of acceptability, few new groups were even given an opportunity to record. And yet, despite its inaccessibility through records, increasingly well-educated British young people turned away from pop and found a haven in small clubs where groups like the Stones, Animals, and Mayall's various bands played blues and early American rock 'n' roll.

As in the States, the commercial potential of this new thing was ignored by established companies which in turn gave musicians a chance to grow without being hustled into record contracts prematurely. The Beatles themselves were the classic example. It is therefore not surprising that when the Beatles proved the commercial viability of rock in 1964, there were so many groups prepared to follow through with their own distinctive music.

The British Invasion

The Beatles established rock with the finality that Presley had established rock 'n' roll. In their wake came two types of groups: the forerunners of mid-Sixties FM rock, who included the Yardbirds, Them, the Pretty Things, Manfred Mann, the Who, the Animals, and the Stones; and the rest—the pop establishment's attempt to update itself without accepting the cultural changes implied in the styles of the more adventurous and innovative groups. These children of Cliff Richard included Billy J. Kramer and the Dakotas, the Searchers, Freddie and the Dreamers, Herman's Hermits, and Gerry and the Pacemakers. Through the mid-Sixties these two different styles achieved high levels of popularity.

So many of the most popular groups of the late Sixties came from England because in that country they could remain shielded from American audiences until they were well prepared. American groups had to make their debuts and mistakes in front of the audience that counted most. In addition, English groups have been more obviously theatrical, the usual explanation for it having to do with English vaudeville traditions.

American groups were often natural but less interesting on stage. Mick Jagger's command of the stage may have been programmed but it was perfect. Jim Morrison's more spontaneous, debauched style was merely vulgar. English groups were comfortable with their popstar identities. American groups would be considered *dressed up* if they appeared in something other than jeans. These days American groups are more show conscious while the English popstars have taken to jeans.

Through the mid-Sixties, American rock was defining its own ambience and style. Through the flirtation with folk music in the early Sixties many musicians found a unique source out of which to mold a new kind of rock, something distinct from what British bands were offering. Foremost among these were the Byrds, who transformed Dylan into rock more extensively than Dylan ever did himself. Their special talents allowed them to combine the prettiness of popular folk music with the drive and strength of rock rhythm. The results were usually among the best rock of the period.

The Buffalo Springfield had a similar talent and were more adventurous as song-writers, as well. Veering more to the pop side of the music were the Mamas and Papas and Simon and Garfunkel, both of which became masters of the art of studio recording. While a bit too polished and successful to be called an underground group, the Lovin' Spoonful kept more of an informal image than any

13

of their fellow groups. Somewhat less talented than the others, they were often the most spirited. And like the others, they enjoyed huge AM successes in 1965 and 1966.

Most of these groups were concerned with attaining conventional success. In later years their music would appeal to the FM audience, but for the time being they committed themselves to the pop process. Other groups less concerned with (or less capable of) obtaining conventional success were creating a true underground: the Paul Butterfield Blues Band, the Blues Project, and, eventually, the San Francisco groups. That city's musical development proved to be a fascinating story in its own right.

The San Francisco Era

During the early and mid-Sixties San Francisco had the advantage of being shielded from the music business people of Los Angeles and New York. Because there were no firm practices already accepted on how to handle popular music, people there were free to invent their own. Ballrooms emerged as rock's first answer to folk clubs, discotheques, and civic auditorium concerts with poor sound and lighting. The Fillmore eventually served as a model for every rock club in the country, and it is interesting (maybe even absurd) to recall that there was little regular presentation of rock in New York City until Graham decided to open the Fillmore East.

In companionship to Fillmore, KMPX started a new form of FM radio in San Francisco which quickly spread to other big cities. In two years time FM became more important than AM in affecting album sales and, more importantly, in successfully providing rock audiences with a style of radio and an outlet for music which suited their needs. The mass acceptance by rock audiences of FM, with its superior fidelity and variety, make it clear that the Seventies will see the further demise of AM programming. In cities like Boston (WBCN) and Detroit (WABX and WKNR) as well as on the West Coast, FM stations have already destroyed the primacy of AM radio for good. A new federal regulation requiring all 1971 cars carrying radios to have both AM and FM bands will hasten the process considerably.

In the mid-Sixties San Francisco was the only city to develop a consciousness about the importance of rock. That cultural awareness was the cushion for all other developments. Rock was not only viewed as a form of entertainment; part of that collective outlook held that music was the essential component of a "new culture." The almost religious fervor that surrounded rock in 1966 and 1967 was occasionally frightening. Like the infatuation with drugs, there was a sense of discovery going on that made it seem like nothing could ever be better and that nothing would ever change. Things were so good, who could ever get tired with them.

Moby Grape was the best performing band to come out of San Francisco, although few people in their native city recognized it. Perhaps because there was a little too much Hollywood in the group for the new audiences and new performing style. Their first album for Columbia was by far the best first album from a San Francisco group. Regrettably, with so much talent in the group, they went the way of all hypes and spent three years trying to catch up with an unbelievably inflated press.

Janis Joplin, who came to national attention in the summer of 1967, was typical of a number of San Francisco musicians who had immigrated from Texas and the Midwest.

The two most important groups to come out of the city were the Jefferson Airplane and the Grateful Dead. Together they defined an American style of improvised music that was quite different from the blues bands (Butterfield) that preceded them and the English groups (Cream) that would come after them. The Airplane on record confined themselves to an elongated fabric of folk-rock. Live, however, they jammed often and at length. Unlike British groups, their jams seldom centered around blues but instead displayed a more intellectual and complex approach that was loud but not hard. The Dead did involve itself more with blues and, later on, country, but they too specialized in cerebral improvisation.

Both bands have grown considerably since they first became popular. *Volunteers* was an undeniably powerful statement about America after Chicago while the Dead's "Casey Jones" shows them ready to adapt to anything.

15

Both groups are something of a national institution and are the closest thing American bands come to permanence.

The Invention of the Underground

In the wake of the success of San Francisco groups, American businessmen saw the potential in this new approach to popular music, dubbed it "Underground Music" and started responding to what had already become a fact of life for hundreds of thousands of young people. In three years' time it would number in the millions.

During the late Sixties, literacy, the first sign of civilization, struck rock hard, first in the form of Crawdaddy and Richard Goldstein's writing in the *Village Voice,* and then in the pages of *Rolling Stone.* Dissemination of news and publicity to the new audience became an amazingly efficient process, thereby accelerating the pace of change within the business itself.

All of these new conditions helped to make possible the second coming of British rock groups, the British underground acts. In 1966, a harbinger of the future occurred. Having missed the boat in San Francisco, Atlantic records decided it had to expand from its R&B base and sign some of the English groups. This led to meetings with Robert Stigwood, the notorious English impresario. Stigwood offered Atlantic a package of two groups. One was put forward as the new Beatles, the latter was forced upon the company as part of the deal. The former was the BeeGees; the latter was Cream.

Cream legitimized the whole new development with unimaginable force. In New York a new booking agency, Premier Talent Associates, evolved to specialize in British groups and following the pattern of Cream's success helped establish the modern concept of a tour. It entailed extensive promotion of new releases on a regional basis. In each of the major markets of the country the group would appear at the local club, usually getting FM airplay (where they would often turn up to do interviews), coverage in the local underground press, and word of mouth publicity from those who saw them.

This last was ultimately decisive. The tie-in between new releases, FM airplay, and appearances in selected markets was successfully used to build Jeff Beck, Jethro Tull, Joe Cocker, and Led Zeppelin. It became a formula still rigidly adhered to today.

As in the late Fifties and early Sixties, towards the end of the decade the formula seemed to be taking precedence over creativity. A group of people emerged, sometimes producers, sometimes managers, sometimes engineers, who understood rock well enough from a technical point of view to manipulate it with above average success. Technological changes within the recording process itself helped to make this possible.

During the late Sixties eight- and 16-track tape recorders became the standard of the industry. These machines not only improved the quality of recorded sound but made it easier to program. Producers and engineers, increasingly the equivalent of movie director and editor (or cameraman) have greatly increased their roles in the recording process. The negative consequence is a potential reduction in spontaneity and feeling. Over-dubbing as a recording technique has virtually eliminated the need for musicians to play together at all. Mixing, in turn, offers vast opportunities to affect the sound of the record after the actual recording has been done. Together they make it possible to formalize and standardize recorded sound to a higher degree than ever before.

The British Groups

Cream more than any other group established the importance of improvisation and instrumental facility as bases for new rock. They had no talent for and did not rely on singing or song writing. The core of their live performance material was blues although Cream was not merely a blues band—at their best they combined that musical form with rock in an expert and exciting way. At their worst, they indulged in a narcissistic display of technical virtuosity. Among other things, they institutionalized rock "jams" and long cuts, and they may well have pulled it off better than anyone who has tried them since.

Jimi Hendrix was the other major artist who helped elevate the importance of instrumental rock. While Cream maintained a detached image of themselves as craftsmen, Hendrix flaunted his decadence and outrageousness in an almost vaudevillian style. And even more than Clapton, he challenged people with his extensions of the guitar into all sorts of realms that had been overlooked, ignored, or undiscovered.

The children of Cream and Hendrix—Jeff Beck, Ten Years After, Led Zeppelin, Grand Funk, and Mountain —were outgrowths of blues bands and used blues as the framework for developing individual styles. Beck was perhaps the first to take the more exhibitionistic elements of the approach and turn it into a virtual parody of improvised music. Ten Years After's Alvin Lee followed Beck with a primitive form of show-offishness that created brief moments of excitement and long hours of tedium.

Led Zeppelin has by now become the most popular of all the late Sixties British bands. Like their predecessors, they build their style on doubling bass and guitar figures, thereby creating a distorted emphasis on the bottom sound range. It is a completely physical approach to sound that usually works better live than on records. Zeppelin's demeanor, like that of most of these groups, was loud, impersonal, exhibitionistic, violent, and often insane. Watching them at a recent concert I saw little more than Plant's imitations of sexuality and Page's unwillingness to sustain a musical idea for more than a few measures.

I got a sense that the real mood of the band is ennui. I sat there thinking that rock could not go on like this. There are those who are prepared to buy it now, but there is no future in it, and that is why groups like Zeppelin take it all in now. They have no place to go, no place to grow into, no roots anywhere. And so they were in front of 15,000 people, going through the motions— their "act"—in order to pick up a paycheck. 15,000 people sat through it all hoping that somehow their expectations would be fulfilled. They weren't because in the words of a fine Bob Dylan song, "nothing was delivered."

The changes of the late Sixties were illustrated best at the three major festivals that took place between 1967 and 1969. The Monterey International Pop Festival signaled the decline of the then existing rock establishment and legitimized the underground. Out of Monterey came Jimi Hendrix, Janis Joplin, and the Who, as well as increased mass acceptance of some San Francisco bands and Otis Redding. These relatively new names entirely overshadowed the AM stars: the Association, Simon and Garfunkel, Scott McKenzie, and even the Mamas and Papas. One could witness the underground culture at a point of transformation into a mass culture.

The Woodstock Music and Art Fair, held only two summers later, signified the ultimate commercialization of that same culture. A fitting end to the Sixties, it showed the country just how strong in numbers the rock audience had become, and just how limited its culture was. It was the last assembly, if not the only one, of virtually every name of any consequence to have emerged since Monterey and was held in front of the largest audience ever assembled. After it there was no place left to grow, no way for things to get any bigger, nothing that could be more exciting or gargantuan.

The energy and intensity of interest could only be imitated cheaply then parodied, and from bathos it went through pathos to tragedy: at Altamont, the anticlimax of it all, an audience once naively optimistic turned rancid with cynicism, a cynicism that was but a reflection of the stars whom they admired.

The vibrations that emanated from the Stones' free concert showed at least a healthy sign that people had not forgotten how to be critical of both themselves and those whom they admire. And yet somehow one realized it couldn't be made up: Altamont showed everyone that something had been lost that could not be regained.

This past summer saw exploiters and manipulators trying to pull off Woodstocks all over the country. The incompetence of Woodstock, an incompetence (and the resultant spontaneity) which was worshipped in the media, could not be institutionalized as a fixed part of the program by the new promoters.

The rock business has had a bad case of elephantiasis and everything that had been swept under the rug was now coming into the open: the greed, the hustle, hype, and above all, the lack of a long range commitment to the music or the audience on the part of many groups, managers, agents, and record companies. More and more, it looked like people trying to take the money and run.

19

And when decadence comes into the open, decline cannot be far behind.

Presley was forced to look at his reflection in the face of Frankie Avalon. The Stones saw themselves parodied by the Doors. And Bob Dylan must have tired long ago of that sincerest form of flattery, imitation.

The Heavies of 1970

Cream created the instrumentally oriented trio and then had to watch it come back to them in the form of Jeff Beck, Zeppelin, and finally (one hopes, finally) Grand Funk Railroad. In these last three there is a chronological pattern moving from bad to worse. With Grand Funk we finally reach sort of nadir with the expectation that people must inevitably turn their attention elsewhere.

Zeppelin and lately Grand Funk, stand as the current word in English hard rock (despite the fact that Grand Funk is an American band). Blood, Sweat and Tears are the opposite of Zeppelin's parody of sexuality. This group is the slick, castrated, middle of the road rock that only Columbia could do justice to in its marketing. Andrew Sarris, in one of his more charitable moments, said of director Stanley Kramer, "He will never be an original, but time has proven that he is not a fake." No one will ever say the same for Blood, Sweat and Tears.

Creedence probably sells more records than anyone else these days and are uniformly respected for their diligence and taste, as well as their ability to make catchy 45s. They may well be the best popular band in America, but if rock was where it should be that statement would be ludicrous. When a competent and talented, but unspectacular band such as this represents the height of the scene, something has surely gone wrong.

Crosby, Stills, Nash, and Young may never perform together again. They were the latest contribution to the soft sound within the rock heirarchy. While gifted in any number of areas and capable of doing spectacular live shows, their records have been contrived without direction. The sense of an organic unit working tightly together seldom intrudes. Which is why it is so easy to believe talk about their breaking up.

The Who were one of the truly inspired groups of the

mid-Sixties. After expending so much energy just getting known in this country, they have finally reduced what was once a blazingly exciting concept into their own set of rules and formulas. *Tommy* has made the Who a permanent institution, and wonderfully so. Unfortunately, it seems that their most innovative days are behind them.

The Band, like Creedence, seems to have almost everyone's respect and have created one unquestioned masterpiece, *The Band*. However, they have not ignited the massive enthusiasm common to some of the biggest bands precisely because of their conservative, thoughtful approach to performing. Also, there is no single personality upon whom public interest has focused. On *Stage Fright* they show signs of believing their own publicity a bit too much with the result that they are trying to sound wise before their time and have become too tight as well. They will continue making important music, but they are in many ways an isolated phenomenon.

Of all the major groups of the Sixties still performing, Sly and the Family Stone is among the best musically. His influence on contemporary music has yet to be fully understood. He is the only major rock figure who has a deep following with both whites and blacks. He completely reshaped the content of R & B following the death of Otis Redding and the eclipse of Stax records. Motown, the greatest hit factory in the land, is currently in hot pursuit of his style. Unfortunately, his personal problems have complicated what could still be one of the most rewarding careers in the recent history of popular music. However, it is fair to say that his influence will last longer than anyone now imagines.

Such are the heavies in 1970. Omitted are Santana, Traffic, Jethro Tull, Ten Years After, the Doors, Steppenwolf, Three Dog Night and so many other names that could be pulled off the Billboard chart or a good agent's client list. But it is a fair cross-section: British and American, hard and soft, East Coast and West, and even a black man.

Every group on the list contains at least one exceptional musician. Each one's music is stylistically well-defined. And yet something fundamental is missing. Certainly

21

there are no names to equal Dylan, the Stones, or the Beatles. With a possible exception or two, there are no legends, no passion, no glamor, and no stars. And while a lot of the music is good, not too much of it is interesting and very little of it will have any impact beyond the lifespan of the group itself. For me, most of the names on the chart already conjure images of the past. The future lies mainly with an altogether different group of artists.

The Return of the Solo Artist

Rock in the late Sixties was, ultimately, a harsh music. It most often communicated frenzy, confusion, anxiety, depression, and anger. It often failed to give expression to the tender emotions. And among its most positive accomplishments were the acceptance of long rock improvisations and the breakdown of the three-minute rule for recorded music.

By the end of the Sixties counter-trends, often springing from within these very groups, began to emerge. As the harsher forms became increasingly repetitious and unimaginative, musicians flirted with country music, old rock and roll, and new styles of production and arranging, often involving the use of a greater variety of instruments than are associated with rock bands. The solo artist, a concept that had all but been abandoned with the decline of the folk revival of the early Sixties, was revived by the likes of Delaney and Bonnie, Leon Russell, Dave Mason, Neil Young, Rod Stewart, Elton John, Van Morrison, Eric Clapton, Joni Mitchell, and James Taylor. This group of artists is almost as diverse in character as any listing of rock groups, but there are important distinctions to be made. In general, they are a more reflective, relaxed, sometimes even pastoral, group of artists. The elimination in many instances of the banks of amplifiers and the breaking of the group bond returns the accent to a single person's feelings and thoughts. In many ways it allows for a far greater range of emotional expression. The soloists are without a doubt the new *auteurs* of popular music.

As yet only three have achieved economic parity with the larger rock bands: Joe Cocker, James Taylor, and

Neil Young. Cocker stands like a storm in the middle of this new sea of tranquility, a magnificent anomaly. His tour last spring with the Leon Russell group of musicians was an exciting and sometimes spectacular event, as it matched one of the fine vocalists of the moment with what was at the time the best performing band in rock. The results, captured to a surprisingly accurate degree on *Mad Dogs and Englishmen,* gives us one of the few truly joyful albums of the year as well as an inspiring bit of contemporary musicianship, from beginning to end. The Cocker tour not only had musicianship and artistry, but a grapes and wine decadence and glamor that was inspiring in itself. He and his colleagues carried on like true stars: they oozed with confidence and self-assurance.

It was all so refreshing, and yet inherent in its very over-large structure was its own inevitable self-destruction. It had one great quality that had been missing from so much of the music of the last two years: spontaneity. And yet one could see a hint of desperation underneath the smiles that seemed to say, "Get it while you can."

The backbone of Cocker's tour was composer-singer-pianist-arranger-producer Leon Russell. Russell worked regularly and especially on the Cocker tour with a fabulous group of West Coast musicians and free lancers that included drummers Jim Gordon and Jim Keltner, bassist Carl Radle, guitarist Don Preston, and hornmen Jim Price and Bobby Keys. Many of these same men had toured earlier with Delaney and Bonnie, a white country soul duo with a distinctive style. Out of that association came organist Bobby Whitlock who was now joined with Radle and Gordon to form the Dominoes in Eric Clapton's new band, Derek and the Dominoes. Many of these same musicians accompanied Russell, Clapton, and Dave Mason on their solo albums.

Russell himself is a genuine talent. His "Shoot Out On the Plantation," "Hummingbird," and "Delta Lady" are among the finest songs of recent years. His piano playing, with its flashes of Earl Hines, is about the best to be heard these days and while his singing is erratic, it is also intensely personal.

Eric Clapton was a leader of the band scene in the

Sixties and has taken a larger role with his new group than he ever did with Cream or Blind Faith. Not yet accomplished as a singer or as an arranger, he still ignites occasional sparks that make it clear his best days are still ahead of him.

Delaney and Bonnie are talented musicians who have yet to find themselves. Each of their five albums, especially *From Delaney to Bonnie,* has had its moments, but never enough of them. Dave Mason is bound to be one of the really bright faces of 1971. His first album displayed excellent songs and arrangements from beginning to end. His only shortcoming is an apparent tendency towards cuteness.

Sensing the danger of over-production, many of the new solo artists have reacted the opposite way. Traveling alone or with small groups, they are more concerned with feelings of intimacy, naturalness, warmth, and honesty. They seldom try to intimidate, overwhelm, or to energize an audience physically.

Of the soloists to appear so far, James Taylor is probably the most influential and most talented and certainly the most popular in this vein. He is establishing the style of the genre in the early Seventies.

Contemplative, reflective, natural to an often painful degree, unpretentious, not inordinately humble, he comes before audiences as Dylan did in the early Sixties and asks people to accept him for what he is. He refuses to try too hard but will always meet his audience half way.

The music of *Sweet Baby James* is embellished in a subtle way that leaves him in the foreground. What solos there are are thoroughly de-emphasized as the lyrics and voices are once again made central. "Country Road" is an almost perfect song, with its deceptively simple beginning, its barely noticeable syncopation on the chorus, and its clear lyric line. However, at the end of the album Taylor reminds us over a delightfully rocking Russ Kunkel on drums, that "Oh, my soul, I'm sure enough fond of my rock and roll."

Neil Young reflects a different mood than Taylor, a mood much more enriched by sophistication. Taylor's music is often painful; Young's is confused. His new album *After the Goldrush* is one of the best to be released this year and should serve to further define the contemplative approach just emerging. His languid and plaintive style is obvious emotionalizing at its best. His "Oh Lonesome Me" is a minor masterpiece.

Rod Stewart is different from both Taylor and Young because his background is so closely tied to the British rock band scene. Even now he continues to lead a schizoid existence. On the one hand he records and tours with a fine little British funk group, the Small Faces. On the other he has released two superb solo albums which comprise a much more intimate and personal statement. *Gasoline Alley* is an exceptionally brilliant piece of work which shows Stewart blending all manners of folk and rock styles into a very cohesive statement of himself. Particularly startling are his superb renditions of Elton John's "Country Comfort," his own "Gasoline Alley," and his stylized rendition of Eddie Cochran's "Cut Across Shorty." At time he blends the styles of Sam Cooke, Bob Dylan and Ewan McCall, but on *Gasoline Alley* he has emerged as a true original.

Van Morrison will undoubtedly be one of the major figures of the Seventies. *Moon Dance,* one of the major releases of recent years, was a work of brilliant originality. It combined a soul-styled approach to melody and arranging with a simple and personal style of lyric writing. Morrison's voice—his phrasing, timing, tone quality, and diction—are close to the summit of rock singing from any period of time. The richness of feeling in his work should set an example for every practicing singer-songwriter.

Elton John bears some resemblance to Morrison in his use of some soul devices in his composition. He has a fine voice and has thus far collaborated with an excellent lyricist, Bernie Taupin. The production on his first album was big but John used it to his own best advantage. An excellent pop piano player, his music has a depth missing from most group rock. His two best songs, "Country Comfort" and "Border Song," have been covered beautifully by Rod Stewart and Aretha Franklin respectively.

Some of the new solo artists are reminders of their own past. Figures like John Sebastian were closely tied to the first folk revival of the early Sixties and are now completing some kind of musical odyssey. Through the years Sebastian has learned how to play on people's sentimentality and desire for tranquility in an almost cynical way. While his voice is rather meagre he has developed a cult based on his capacity to accept virtually anything as being groovy, warm, and loving.

Randy Newman, Harry Nilsson, and Neil Diamond, in increasing order of commercial musical styles, all offer something more substantial in the solo vein. Joni Mitchell has developed the ability to express the mood of frustrated intellect in a time when thought is so under-valued to an ever-expanding degree. Melanie has emerged as the female counterpart to Sebastian in sentimentality. Carole King has come out from behind her writing career and is a beautiful pianist, arranger, and singer. Her legendary talents as a songwriter are now revealed as but a part of an unbelievably whole musician. And Laura Nyro, one of the most talented but confused artists of the period, may find the new mood of the audience more sympathetic to her erratic but superb talents than that of the Sixties was.

The dozens of solo artists will begin to have larger show business potential than do rock groups. Johnny Cash has sold more albums than anyone else last year as he parlays his legendary background into a model for the nation's most primitive forces. Tom Jones and Glen Campbell have cleaned up in the old Sinatra market. And, in what is probably the most revealing fact of all, Elvis Presley found this year to be the right one to wage a full-scale comeback attempt. For what time could compare to the present for the return of the most stylized, personalized, and possibly the most talented, of all the rock stars.

In the range of the popular solo artists, seen as a group, certain traits are clearly manifested.

There is also a greater focus on songs and singing than on any form of virtuosity, particularly instrumental virtuosity, which is a quality that few of them possess. And because the work of so many of these artists is so percise and compressed, it is often best presented through records rather than live appearances. In fact what has happened, as it always has when popular music is at a crossroads, is a return to the basic facts: the singer and his song.

As the image of this type of performer jells, we can expect an increasing number of press releases that jabber about honesty, restraint, quiet, countriness, and reflectiveness. And while the approach of these artists is easily parodied, those adjectives fairly describe the best of them. Before their day is over we are in for a lot more of them than anyone has already imagined. On the basis of the evidence thus far, can anyone doubt that this is a reason for some excitement and enthusiasm over the future of our music.

Thus, the most easily identifiable major shift of early 1970 is that the R&R band scene introduced in 1963 by the Beatles and which dominated pop music through 1969 is in the initial stages of decomposition.

The Black Music Scene

The black music scene has not gone untouched. The popular stars of the last few years have all gone into decline and no replacements are on the horizon. Aretha Franklin stopped making personal appearances though she is making a comeback. James Brown has lost some of his overwhelming drawing power at the box office, and Motown performers continue to be locked into their plastic nightclub performing style. Only the incredibly popular Jackson 5 come before us with something wholly original to say.

In recording, the most stunning fact of recent years has been the decline of Stax records. When Stax left the Atlantic fold, the rights to Otis Redding and Sam and Dave, reverted to Atlantic Records. Since that time they have discovered they suddenly were without major stars. Perhaps the lone and not particularly strong exception is Isaac Hayes, whose sentimental, talky "soul" versions of pop hits has connected with the black middle of the road audience, one of the few things keeping the company going.

Atlantic's black music has gone into something of a decline as well, as Wilson Pickett no longer turns out hit after hit; and many of those he does are not close to

27

his great era. Aretha has been fair to middling, although it now looks like she is on the comeback trail with her fine version of "Don't Play That Song" and "Border Song." Sam and Dave have tragically parted company while people like Percy Sledge are in danger of drifting into obscurity. Joe Tex has started imitating Isaac Hayes to no avail and singers like DeeDee Warwick just aren't distinctive enough. Only Clarence Carter keeps churning it out, and his records are straight pop AM radio pieces by now. The problem at Atlantic revolves around the lack of a contemporary, original style of recording what used to be called soul artists, and in the failure to develop new personalities.

Those two problems do not plague Motown at the moment and they are justifiably as hot as ever. They have already developed the major new soul group of the Seventies, the superb Jackson 5. Norman Whitfield continues to turn out contemporary, Sly-influenced, repetitious rhythm records on people like Edwin Starr and the Temptations. Stevie Wonder has recently developed into not only the brilliant singer heard on "Signed Sealed and Delivered," but with that record and the Spinner's "It's a Shame" a fine producer as well. The latter is the best single to come out of the company in recent months.

It is important to remember in discussing the work of black artists that they are dealing with an increasingly homogenized market in which the old class of R&B and soul records is merging more and more with the basic pop market. Secondly, it is a music still basically oriented to the 45 and AM radio. Consequently, the immediate pressure to find big stars is not as great as the need to find songwriters and producers who can turn out consistently commercial singles. No one has greater success in developing such production teams than Motown, but towards the end of the Sixties the team of Kenny Gamble and Leon Huff seemed like a good pair of challengers.

Gamble and Huff, who are based in Philadelphia, are independent producers who have worked with the Intruders, the O'Jays, Dusty Springfield, Archie Bell and the Drells, and Jerry Butler. Their two albums with Butler, *Ice on Ice* and *The Iceman Cometh,* represent some kind of zenith in the pop production of soul artists. Their integration of strings, horns, choirs and timpani into unbelievably well-recorded arrangements of their own melodic and lyrically sensitive songs was often astounding. Unfortunately, they and Butler have parted ways and the potential of their work may never be realized. Without Butler, whose singing is possibly the most sophisticated in all of pop music today, their productions lost their focus. Often they sound contrived and the worst of it is beginning to sound like a parody of their earlier work. Like so many producers before them, they have reduced what was refreshingly original to something trivial through repetition. The fire is gone and only another "Western Union Man," "Never Gonna Give You Up," or "Only the Strong Survive" is going to light it again.

As an offshoot of the Gamble and Huff development, other producers using the same studio and band have made interesting records in Philadelphia. Of them, the best are done by the Delphonics, who are the masters of the trendy "sissy soul" sound. Masters of falsetto harmony, they have produced a succession of fine pop records culminating in their last hit, "Didn't I Blow Your Mind This Time."

Of the other independent producers, the American studio in Memphis has gone into an entirely pop bag and have been almost unbearably successful at it.

Rick Hall scores with occasional hits, but nothing new of consequence has emanated from there beyond his superb record of Carter's "Patches." The other studios in the south, with the exception of Atlantic's Criteria in Miami, have been cool.

While it may be sacrilegious to say it, the most influential black artist of recent years, with the possible exception of Jimi Hendrix, has undoubtedly been Sly and the Family Stone. In the early R&B days it was not uncommon for songs to have one chord. Sly has revitalized that concept and recharged it with contemporary rhythms and a group singing approach that is pure delight. His versatility and capacity to synthesize seems almost endless.

Both the singing and the rhythm have been completely absorbed by Motown, with the Temptations making greater use of the former and the Jackson 5 modeling themselves on the latter. Without "Dance to the Music" there never would have been "I Want You Back." His influence has been vast. Even Lulu has cut her Sly imitation of "Hum A Little Song From My Heart."

The Jackson 5 stand as something of a phenomenon amidst all this. The voice of 12-year-old Michael Jackson is so fresh and pure that it would sound good singing anything. As it is they give him the absolute best R&B being composed today and provide him with the best vocal and instrumental arrangements anyone has heard anywhere lately. The only thing keeping the Jackson 5 from establishing a new hegemony over the entire R&B scene is their youthfulness.

As with white groups, recounting the names and companies and hits only serves as an ultimate reminder of the lack of cohesiveness on this scene. The major problem is how to deal with the black record buying public when it has merged so tightly with the AM pop market. Will black record buyers ever start buying albums in preference to 45s? And are well-produced records more important than the perennial need for major personalities? On this last point, the stark fact is there are none. Sly came close but he blew it. Isaac Hayes is a fad. The Motown artists are all too limited on stage. Only Jerry Butler has real possibilities, and thus far it hasn't happened. There is no James Brown or Otis Redding to set it all right these days. There is no one with a personal vision to offer this time around. No matter how good some of the records are, the black scene remains business as usual right now. In many ways it is a cynical business indeed.

The Big Three

Through most of the Sixties three figures conjured up the mood of the music: The Beatles, the Rolling Stones and Bob Dylan. Not only was their music important but they fulfilled the mythic need for leadership in the period. Every era requires strong innovators and personalities to give glory to the movement; revered figures who achieve universal respect and can be held up as models to aspiring musicians as well as to audiences: heroes. And perhaps the thing that tells us most about the changes going on in rock are the changes that overcame the heroes of the Sixties.

While an enormous financial success, the Stones tour of 1969 will ultimately account for their decline as a Pop myth. They simply could not live up to their own introduction: "The greatest rock and roll band in the world." People enjoyed themselves but they knew it wasn't that different, that much better, that much more exciting. As Michael Lydon noted, at each concert there was more applause at the beginning of the first number than at the end of the last.

And yet the Stones knew that if they hadn't toured they would have suffered *more* precisely because it had been so long since they had communicated in the flesh and there were millions of kids who wanted to see them who hadn't even heard "Satisfaction" when it was released in 1965. Even God has to deliver a miracle from time to time just to keep the customers satisfied. Indifference is the enemy of all deities, religious or secular.

Dylan's dilemma is much deeper. The source of the rock intelligence, the originator of the contemporary rock lyric, the synthesizer, the opera singer, the solo artist, the true outsider: he has so much to live up to, so many expectations to fulfill.

And yet, like the Stones he has been caught by his past. *Self Portrait* was such a disaster precisely because it wallowed in the past. *New Morning* was a refreshing step away from the emptiness of its predecessor but not quite a large enough one. Dylan's problem is one of time. He is older than most of us and it's beginning to show in his music. That isn't necessarily bad, but who can say that it is necessarily good. He has been around long enough to see an approach that he gave definition to in the early Sixties revived in the early Seventies: The force of a single personality. The question facing him is whether or not the students still need their teacher.

And the Beatles: as Dylan traversed the line from underground folk hero to national and international rock star, the Beatles went from international rock stars to underground folk heroes. They played all roles to all people and were ultimately accepted by the Queen and Timothy Leary, AM and FM, black and white, and by musicians of all types and in every field. Their separation, when it finally occurred, was a result of the inability of so much talent to be contained within the limits of a group. And yet it is certain that no single member of the group on his own will enjoy anything approaching the popularity or influence of the Beatles as a group.

The Fate of Rebelliousness

The Beatles when they began were superb exponents of a simple adolescent rhythmized form of popular music whose life style addressed itself to its audience's needs as perfectly as Presley had to his. And like Presley they achieved unanticipated and incalculable popularity in a brief period of time. With success undoubtedly weighing heavily on them, they did not chance to move into an openly rebellious stance, preferring instead to play the part of a flea riding an elephant. Their rebelliousness, while entirely real, was always gentle and they preferred to kneel rather than fight.

By comparison, the Stones were a more violent and openly defiant group. The media could never adjust to them and as a result a young audience could feel that they belonged to them and them alone. The Stones did not share themselves with adults in witty and clever movies. Parents would find themselves saying about the Beatles: "Well, they are cute." When Jagger finally made it to the screen in *Performance,* the adjective most commonly used to describe him was "loathsome."

The Stones music was blues-based instead of pop-based. There was no chance of them recording "A Taste of Honey" or "Till There Was You." They seemed to be flaunting their anger when the Beatles sometimes seemed to be concealing it, and as a result the audiences learned to love the Stones in a quite different way than they did the Beatles.

Dylan, the American, stood apart from groups and came before his earlier audiences as a self-proclaimed phophet. His anger was the most blatantly obvious of the three, as his tone, his lyrics, and his music were all designed to express it explicitly. Many songs from his earliest period were filled with hatred ("Masters of War") and his political anger often carried over into other areas ("Ballad of a Thin Man") in his later works, only to mellow by the time he arrived at *John Wesley Harding*.

What rebelliousness there was in all three entities is tamed today. Little they do appears outrageous any longer, and in the case of Dylan and the Beatles (except for John Lennon), that appears to be the way they want it. Having grown older, they seem to have grown wiser and are less intensely engaged in the conflicts that dominated their earlier music. It all sounds very mature, in fact quite often too mature, too self-accepting, too accepting of things as they are.

Only the Stones continue to play with defiance, but after their last American tour it's hard to take that too seriously. Rather one gathers that the Stones harp on the past in their live presentation because they have no place else to go with it. If Jagger is not outrageous, what then is left of the Stones? Unlike Dylan they cannot cope with, or do not have, the luxury of change at that level. Their music, however, continues to grow, often dramatically so. It is just that the context now seems to be more theatrical than life-like.

Awe Replaces Enthusiasm

The truth of the matter is that the names of the Sixties have become anomalies. No one looks to them for direction, no one copies them and few are still influenced by them. Despite the high level of its musical content, *Let It Bleed* had virtually no effect on pop music today. Jimmy Page and Robert Plant are more to be emulated by every flourishing high school band in the country than Mick and Keith. While there are still those who imitate the old Dylan—Arlo Guthrie is perhaps foremost among them—who has been affected by the Dylan of *Self Portrait?* And with the exception of Badfinger and other isolated instances, the last group to strive for the Beatle style was the Bee Gees. The work of the rock triptych is consumed and passed over with reverence and awe but not with the enthusiasm of past years.

None of this is meant to imply that the individuals involved will no longer create great music. They surely will. Rather it is in their relationship with an all-adoring public that change is most visible. Their music has changed—whether for better or worse—and with those changes their audience has too. Whatever happened to Bob Dylan, the Rolling Stones and the former members of the Beatles in the Sixties, it will not be the shape of things in the Seventies. They were once more than musicians. They were once Gods.

The alternatives are not well defined, and there is confusion at all levels of the music industry about the direction music is taking. For the men who stage live shows, now often unable to afford the superprices of the supergroups, the question of the day is where the stars of tomorrow are coming from. The clubs and medium-sized concert halls are in trouble.

"Who are the big groups to emerge over the summer?" asked an agent in one of the largest independent booking agencies. The answer was none. Club owners are now headlining acts they might well have passed over for second billing a year ago. Some clubs have closed, others closed for the summer, and in many cities where music is being presented regularly, business is very, very soft.

Because of the current economic recession customers seem to be concentrating more money on fewer attractions, whether buying records or tickets. As a result, a handful of acts have become incredibly popular, while it has become harder than ever for a middle-level band to get along or a new band to get off the ground.

For the past two and a half years, since the success of *Sgt. Pepper,* the album sweepstakes has begun to look like the singles game, with many companies shotgunning it: releasing large numbers of albums on the assumption that something will catch on. While they may have been right in the short run, in the long run they have saturated the market, making it harder for talented new musicians to break through the mass of pap at the rate of 150 new albums released *every* week along with 200 new singles per week.

The Rat Race

It's now widely assumed that sooner or later the audience will be unable to absorb any more of a particular kind of music, and everyone in the business is searching desperately for what's coming next. If someone *were* to find the next thing, though, it's inevitable that he would rush it too fast, and record it to death before it had a chance to grow into anything at all.

Once there were dozens of talented musicians who only needed to get inside a studio to do something interesting, now there are few who don't get a chance to record something years before they are prepared for it. There was a time when going to see a band play on a weekend could be something to look forward to for days. Now it can often be an invitation to depression.

Rock and roll is madness and the method that has been imposed on it is too rational, too business-like, and too orderly, and if something doesn't break loose soon, it will kill off what energy is left for a good long time.

Rock, the music of the Sixties, was a music of spontaneity. It was a folk music—it was listened to and made by the same group of people. It did not come out of a New York office building where people sit and write what they think other people want to hear. It came from the life experiences of the artists and their interaction with an audience that was roughly the same age. As that spontaneity and creativity have become more stylized and analyzed and structured, it has become easier for businessmen and behind-the-scenes manipulators to structure their approach to merchandising music.

* * *

The process of creating stars has become a routine and a formula as dry as an equation. But thankfully, if history is any judge, it is only a matter of time before adhering to that equation will reach a point of diminishing returns and those who stick to it will pay the consequences. For while equations don't change the audiences, musicians, and music, do.

A cycle is coming to an end. Rock's first phase, which truly began with "I Want to Hold Your Hand," ended with the break-up of the Beatles. And amidst the economic tightening in the industry, and the changing character of the audience, something new is forming. Whether or not it will lead to something basically different than the music of the last six years cannot be discerned as of yet, but the change is now.

There is a new audience that grew up on the music of the Sixties that is going to require and demand a music for the Seventies. No one yet knows what that audience will want or what the musicians will give them. But one thing is certain: that audience *will* have music. For whether we know it or not, we are all committed to music. And whether we believe it or not, it is too late to stop now.

LIFE STORY
An Experiment in Participatory Journalism

edited by David Felton
and Cindy Ehrlich

When nearly five months ago we put out a call for "autobiographic mass feedback," we were hardly prepared for what followed. I'm not sure what we had in mind, exactly. We were intrigued by a readership that seemed, from letters to the editor and other correspondence, unusually articulate and imaginative. We thought they might have some good stories to tell from their personal lives, stories normally bypassed by the practices of conventional, event-oriented journalism.

We were right, of course, but there was no way to predict the level of adventure, humor and tragedy reached by the 17 published here (and, I should add hastily, by some 200 more of the 1,067 stories sent in.) We printed only 17 simply because there was no more room. We originally selected nearly twice that number, but finally decided, rather than mutilate each piece, to drop the others, including the work of several "tentative winners" already contacted by telegram. We're presently exploring possibilities for publishing the rest.

I guess the stories printed here do represent what we

felt were "the best," but it's hard to say precisely why. It was more a gut thing than any predictable quality; one way or another we reacted more emotionally to these 17 stories than to the rest. I suppose we were looking for "originality," but only in a journalistic sense. We were after good stories rather than good writing, originality not merely of expression or thought, but of event and predicament—sometimes even the originality of a person's insight about his lack of originality.

In presenting these extremely personal works, we tried to keep editing at a minimum. We cut some words and lines, when they seemed too irrelevant or distracting, but we substituted none of our own. Generally we changed punctuation only to prevent confusion and corrected spelling only when it was obviously mistaken and inconsistent with the rest of the work. When the authors supplied titles, we used them as is; when they didn't, we supplied them by using quotation marks and quoting directly from the work itself.

Every word of every story sent was read at least once. Every story was "logged" with comments and saved; those with stamped return envelopes will be returned, the others will be filed, for a while at least.

The order in which these stories appear has nothing to do with their quality; it just seemed like a nice, readable order. A thorough reading, I assure you, will be worthwhile.

When we called this "an experiment in history and journalism" five months ago, it probably sounded pretty presumptuous. You know how crazy we all get when we're dealing with the unknown. And while I'm not sure of their historical value (or of the value of history, for that matter), as pieces of journalism these stories are as moving as any I've read. They're real stories, with real direction, insight and movement. And, like any good journalistic work, they're particularly dramatic because they're true.

—DF

F. Alan Shirk,
Fleetwood, Pennsylvania:

Will You Still
Love Me Tomorrow?

I am an American. I know that because I am not Chinese, German, Japanese or Nigerian. I heard somebody say once that America is a place where people ask you how you are and never wait to find out. I guess I would agree with that, but I'm getting off the subject.

I was born on October 16th, 1942, at 5:47 PM in Reading, Pennsylvania, which, in case you didn't know, is pretty well in the heart of the conservative Pennsylvania Dutch country. That makes me a Libra, and for the last 29 years, I've been waiting for the good Libra horoscopes in the newspaper to come true.

Raised in the typical middle class fashion, my life has turned out to be disgustingly ordinary. I assume I belong to that great mass of men leading lives of quiet desperation, as Thoreau says. But only because I have not yet found another way.

Let's see . . . I spent seven years in the Scouts, joined a Reformed church, received a couple of perfect attendance certificates during formal schooling, smoked my first cigarette in the fifth grade, chugged my first quart of beer at 15, learned to dance in 7th grade (The Crazy Otto was the initial favorite), acquired an early knowledge of the birds and the bees in 6th grade (verbal only), appeared once in a police station after a Halloween raiding party, learned to drive with a stick '53 Plymouth Cranbrook, received letters from Arlene Sullivan and Justine Corelli of American Bandstand, went steady and got my first kiss in 9th grade, memorized the lyrics of the greatest rock and roll, bought a picture of Elvis Presley at the Reading Fair in 1957, moved into the brainiest class in high school, flubbed miserably in athletics, got A-stars on all my Latin quizzes, placed my hand inside a girl's brassiere in 10th grade (she was wearing it), learned to dance the Chicken, Stroll, Strand, Bop and Lindy, never got into a fight and graduated in 1960. Five days later I shot myself in the leg accidentally with a .22 pistol during a camping trip.

Armed with this experience and well wishes from my family, I marched off to Penn State as a future electrical engineer. But my non-technical mind would not absorb theories of statics, electromagnetics or calculus, and I nearly flunked out. I switched to English. At Penn State, I was swallowed up in the masses, but I had my first sexual experience, learned who the Moonglows were, joined a fraternity and began molding myself for acceptance. I kept a diary and was spurred on in my writing by some favorable comments from John Barth and Paul West. I drank a lot, studied little, but learned a lot.

I find myself still unable to disassociate myself from the longing for a return to the peace and freedom I experienced in the Nittany Valley. Born too soon, as I drove down College Avenue for the last time in 1965, I witnessed the beginning of the great awakening. A Vietnam War protest on the Penn State campus.

I jumped into the real world as a news reporter at $75 a week. My wife, my son and I moved into our first apartment. Now I would settle down and work for that house in the suburbs and financial independence, looking forward to 65. I spent 4½ years on two eastern Pennsylvania newspapers covering everything from cops to concerts. The experience turned me quite cynical. Yet, I could not put down the radical idealism that churned in my guts.

Partially for money and partially for the promise of doing more, I took a job as a public relations man for a public utility. Needless to say, the last two years in this position have been utter frustration, headaches and upset stomachs. Watching my utility peers pay lip service to the individual and freedom, I am an outcast because I wear no American flag pin in my lapel. I have simply done my job and have tried to make the place more human. Getting nowhere fast, it becomes harder each day to sit idly by and watch the bungling and ineptitude that pervades. But that's another story.

Selfishly, I seek to find some way in which I can help to make things better. The most satisfaction I've gained in recent years has been managing a baseball team of 13- to 15-year-old kids. I'm no Danny Murtaugh, but no one expects me to be.

The best job I've ever had was mopping floors in a State College Bar for 27 bucks a week. But knowing how I feel, I don't think I could escape to something like that again.

So, here I am. Still a radical idealist (more convinced after reading Alinsky's interview in *Playboy* that people must do more than just talk about the bullshit). I'll soon be 30, but I feel like I'm still 16. (I get carded yet when I go into bars.) My Salvation is the Grateful Dead or the Stones on a headset and a few bottles of apple wine. I'm taking guitar lessons because I want to know more about music. I have a home in the country (a palatial two-acre estate). I have a fine woman to share the days with. I have two beautiful sons. I want to write a novel and make a movie.

But you know, I can't enjoy it because I can't divorce myself from what is going on.

I wrote a letter to the *Wall Street Journal* once asking that a foundation be set up to finance people who want to drop out but can't afford it. I'd like to see America, but you can't see much on two weeks' paid vacation.

I believe in my heart that we will persist. But it's a question of how we'll persist. I really want to help, but I don't know how.

And what I'd like to know is, should I sell my house and move north, or should I stay and fight, because, after all, I am what I am.

Karin Sjilds,
Occidental, California:

1969 Abortion

I had full conscious realization the moment I conceived and I knew I didn't want a baby. New York City had ruined all aspects of my health. My friends got together $200 for me and I returned to D. C. to look for an abortion. I was staying at the Free Press house and there was a hip (?) doctor hanging out there. I asked him if he could find me a good abortion and he said, "Sure—it costs $600." I told him I only had $200 and he said I had to have $600. So I found a funky one for $200. Michael drove me over to a ghetto development apartment and I went in alone as arranged. A young black woman met me and took my money. Then she inserted a rubber catheter into my uterus which would begin the labor-like expulsion of the tiny fetus.

I went home and waited. Mary stayed with me. The contractions began and they hurt a lot. In the middle of this, some friends from New York came in and tried to whisk me away to California. I tried to explain the situation. I went in the bathtub and out came, it seemed like, all my insides—and a tiny peanut-sized person. I was sad and glad—confused, I guess. Everyone fell asleep; I stayed awake all night with the most excruciating pains and feelings. The pain lifted me up to another place, it was so heavy.

In a couple of days I developed a bad fever and infection after being turned away from one hospital (there questioned by police whom I lied blatantly to), admitted to one and operated on. I ran away, to my friend's house in the country, and was glad to be alive, as spring awakened all life around me.

1971 Birth

Up in the tiny attic my friend, David, was reading from an old book of Aesop's fables to me. It was too dark to walk home, so I was sleeping there, at the house in the oak tree. We curled up and said good night. I stared out at the winter trees and puddles reflecting moon. Something strange was happening inside me. I felt excited and then I knew.

We stumbled out into the cold moonlight. My baby was going to be born soon.

Contractions were coming on and off for a day. By

1 or 2 AM the next morning I was getting impatient. Doris, my friend and midwife, had told me if I got to this place to drink a cup of Blue Cohosh tea. I drank about half a cup and in about five minutes labor had begun to establish its rhythm—regular strong contractions began. I got on the bed and Bill went and got midwife and friends—about six or seven including two children and a dog.

My house is small and rustic. From the bed you can see miles of hills and canyons stretching to the ocean, old redwoods, cows and fog. In the beginning of labor I lay in bed watching the clouds, conserving my energy for the "labor" to come. This is why I never considered giving birth anywhere but home, if possible. I wanted to be comfortable with friends and close to the natural rhythms of the earth and air. The clouds were beautiful, changing and rolling in waves along the hills.

Now as I entered real labor, the hard work began and I became pure animal energy life force earth breath. Feeling my body breathing and moving. I got to a really stoned place where perceptions of people and situations were crystal clear and where all sociable manners and bullshit disappeared. Contractions changed. Bill brought a movie camera. Mary was taking stills. Labor progressed as fast as I could handle it. As soon as I really got tired of one stage (or type) of contractions, I slid into another. Someone gave me some grass, then some tea. I threw up. I laughed. I cried. Then concentrated on my insides.

At last I reached the final stage—the pushing part. It was like a storm hitting my body. Waves and thunder and rolling ocean. It really freaked me. After each contraction push, I said, "I can't take one more," and one more kept coming. Here is where friends helped the most —one on each side, holding my legs and giving good energy. Reverent faces. Also reminding me to relax between each stormy contraction.

Now each time the lips parted the baby's head came down, then retreated. David came inside from the porch and said each time the baby's head appeared, the clouds parted and the moon appeared, then retreated. Soon the light of the new day showed some people sleeping, others waiting. I could really feel the baby near the opening, moving down and myself stretching open.

"Isn't he there yet, isn't he coming out?" Needing constant reassurance now. Doris could see the bag of water bulging out, so she broke it with scissors and it sprayed her. Great release of pressure. Now the top of baby's head was staying in the tight ring of flesh. Doris —"One more push." I grunted as loud as I could (this opened me up) and felt a pop release of pressure and gush of flesh and liquid. Everyone was crying as the rest of the body slid out in one orgasmic rush.

I wouldn't look at the baby until he was all the way out, his cord still attached to the placenta inside me. When I did look at this naked slippery person I fell deeply in love. Our eyes met and we drank each other in. Bill cut the cord and Doris wrapped him and handed him to me. I held him but I was so wasted I handed him to his father. Then I pushed the placenta out into a pot. It looked magnificent—purple and red and turquoise. Then me and Bill and the baby crawled into bed together, and everyone left except Rebecca who stayed behind to steam the placenta which I ate and shared with friends. It was wonderfully replenishing and delicious. We lay in bed the rest of the day watching the clouds, feeling tired and joyous.

Michael Mulvihill,
Morgantown, West Virginia:

"Koop-da-Grace"

Well, it was half-time, we were down by 20 or so. The first half we played a zone and this forward was pumping in everything he threw up. Fifteen-foot jumper —good. Twenty-foot jumper—good. Man, he must have swished eight in a row from the corner.

Billy Morris was his name, a future all-leaguer, must have been averaging at least twenty points a game.

Coach walks into the locker room, half-time, and says, "Well, we're gonna have to stop that guy in the corner.

44

What's his name? The forward, you know, the guy who keeps hitting. Who is that guy?"

Wow, the coach doesn't even know the guy's name—one of the best players in the league—"We're gonna have to start coming out on that guy," he says.

Well, this time we were down by 30 at half-time. We were getting blown out of the gym as they say.

Ol' Coach marches into the locker room, Knute Rockne etched on his face. "We'll put on the press," he announces. "A steal here, a steal there and we'll be back in the ball game!"

Rolling eyes are falling onto the floor. Is this guy for real? Everybody tries to keep a straight face—want to play in the next game.

"If we can," he shouts, "get back into the ball game and pull off an upset—It'll be the koop-da-grace of our season!"

Koop-da-grace! Oh my god! I glance to the corner, Steve is holding his stomach and biting his lip. Dave is doubled over, trying not to fall off the bench. I'm coughing, trying to muffle my laughter.

After the pep talk, Steve, the team captain, walks up to the coach. Coach puts his arm on Steve's shoulder and asks, "Steve, what do you think?"

Steve says, "Coach, it's pronounced, coo-de-gra, not koop-da-grace." Coach ponders over the statement for a moment and says, "Thanks Steve, thanks for telling me in private."

That did it. I mean, Jesus Christ, "A steal here, a steal there, and we'll be back in the ball game!" And, "Who is that guy?" And, "Koop-da-grace." I mean, there just had to be something else.

Oh, I was born in Omaha, Nebraska, raised in New York and played high school basketball for three years —didn't go out in my senior year.

Wayne Ross,
Cambridge, Massachusetts:

"Formerly Demented Wayne"

My name is Wayne; formerly demented Wayne. How I became demented and where I am now is pretty much the story of my life.

I am a Pisces with Aquarius rising, Aquarius moon, and four planets (Moon, Sun, Mercury and Jupiter) in the first house.

From childhood I remember a few happy times but mostly fear. I was scared shitless of adults and teenagers because they had power and I had none.

My father is a brittle, lonely, alienated man. His frequent and ever-increasing temper outbursts oppressed everyone in the house.

He liked to move every two years, and being in the Navy made it easier for him. We lived in Boston, then Colorado, then Boston, then Texas, then New Jersey.

In New Jersey he went to Spain and left us behind. My mother told my teachers that they could treat me as their son. I was beaten by all of them and resented it fiercely.

There was a clique of arrogant middle-class greasers in my class who lived down the street from me. I earned their contempt because I didn't like to fight and was poorer than they were. They liked to humiliate me, beat on me, and throw rocks at me. Once they even chased me into a tree and stoned me for an hour. I just wanted to be their friend.

My mother was flipping out, drinking more each day. Grinding poverty began setting in. I desperately needed human contact and yet feared everyone.

My father came back and after horrible beatings and a near murder they broke up.

After three more years of New Jersey's torture we moved to Dorchester, trying to live with my father again. My mother left and I began sniffing glue daily.

My pain, paranoia and hatred became overwhelming.

I became a greaser—fighting at the least excuse. I became extremely arrogant. I hated everyone in the world, myself most of all. I wanted to kill everybody. Hatred became my bedmate and life.

I was arrested for swearing at a girl, spent three weeks in the Youth Service Board, and was sentenced to 2 YEARS probation by Judge Troy. I wanted to beat him to death but instead kicked over 200 gravestones. Troy sentenced me to 5-7 YEARS in jail, this time I appealed. I was on appeal for about eight months, then was put on probation.

In March of '68 I tried to join the Marines because I wanted to get out of school and kill communists. They refused me on psychiatric grounds. Hurt and angry, I decided to join the hippies, and went to Project Place.

I violated my probation by fleeing to Canada and got caught at the border. I was sentenced to 35 days observation at Metropolitan State Hospital in May. Once out I was put on probation. I violated it by trying to kill myself with 30 mgs. of scopolamine, a very toxic dose (this was the eighth attempt). The court committed me to Boston State Hospital until my eighteenth birthday. I began writing poetry more often, and was discovering myself through poetry.

In November I decided to kill myself with dope—it would take a long time, I could change my mind if I wanted to, and I would have a blast doing it. I was in utter agony. The hospital was a nightmare of neglect, callousness and arrogance. I didn't want to live, yet I didn't want to die.

The court freed me from probation in March of '69 and I promptly escaped. I nearly killed myself with speed and nearly every other drug imaginable.

Then I met Melissa. Bang—my life turned around. I stopped shooting and fell madly in love with her. From then on my life was one ego trip after another. First we were acid heads, then we got into white magic with a very powerful friend. We were planning to wipe evil off the earth, and all the time we were so oppressive and blind to it, it's hard to believe.

Melissa and I flipped out and ran to Dorchester, both of us psychically exhausted. I worked in a rubber stamp

47

factory and embraced Neo-Christianity. I became a preacher (not ordained). In May we moved to a different part of Dorchester and slowly began starving to death (I couldn't find a job). I embraced logic as the instrument to save the world. In November we moved to a beautiful rural commune in North Heath, Mass. Melissa by now needed an operation on her overactive thyroid. She went to Maine to live with her parents while I worked in Boston and lived with my mother.

I embraced revolution and wanted to kill "capitalist pigs" such as Rockefeller.

Melissa came back in March and we lived with a friend who was into radical therapy, and I became a psychologist. We moved to Cambridge and started doing yoga. We also got into Trout Fishing in America, a sort of free school. I read Adelle Davis and started teaching nutrition, and finally gave that up too.

My number of head trips is amazing. Every time I get into one Melissa says, "Wayne, you're doing just what you did before," and I always say "I am not!" Finally I am listening to her.

Yoga is helping me to see every way that I oppress people, and at the same time shows me my God-self.

David Perdue,
Berkeley, California:

"Back to Kentucky"

Dear Virginia,

How's the Berkeley weather holding up as Christmas draws near? My trip to Kentucky has been interesting, and I've enjoyed it as much as I've hated it. The people back here have freaked out on my long hair and beard. Whenever I walk downtown or on the mall, I get all sorts of double takes, angry stares, or out and out scowls. Even the young kids (the hope of the future) give me a hard time, pointing and giggling at me. It's really a culture shock for them, and for me, too.

My parents have been acting pretty cool, though. They were really surprised when I showed up the other night. It's been over three years since I "left home." Anyway my mom says, "It's a great surprise and the best Christmas present I could have hoped for."

I haven't done much since arriving, mostly just talking to my family, telling them what I've been doing in California for the last three years. But the other night my dad piled the family in the car—my mom, my sister, my brother, and me—and drove us around town showing me all the new buildings and making comments about changes that have happened since I left. Some parts of the town I hardly recognized.

As we were driving, we passed the house of an old friend of mine, Bill Castor, who I haven't seen in a long time. My mom suggested that I stop in and say hello and Merry Christmas to him and his parents, since we'd been best of friends before I'd left home. I said all right, so my dad let me out.

I hesitantly went up to the door and rang the bell. It appeared that no one was home and there didn't seem to be any lights on inside. Just as I began to leave, Bill's mom came to the door. I hadn't seen her in over four years, so I felt sure she wouldn't recognize me. But to my amazement, as I stood on the shadowy, unlighted front porch, she peeked out the window, opened the door, and said, "Da-a-a-vid, well bless my heart, how ya' doin'? Come on in, right this minute." I told her I could only stay a minute, that I'd just come by to say hi to Bill before I left to go back to California in a few days.

Without hearing a word I said, she sent me back to the car to bring in the rest of the family. Mr. Castor came out in his house coat and slippers to greet us. He shook my dad's hand energetically, hugged my mom and sister, and led us all inside. These people are full-blooded Kentuckians and fairly old—in their late 50s —so I thought that with my long hair and beard and all that trip, they'd at best be formally receptive to me, especially judging from the reception I'd received from the rest of the town so far. But they were so happy, and they kept saying that they were real glad to see me. Bill hadn't come home from the University of Kentucky yet, but they promised that "the minute he gets

49

home we'll have him call you." They made up some hot chocolate and began telling stories about Bill, my brother, Doug, and me when we were kids.

Mrs. Castor, looking older than her 57 years (she always looked old to me, even as I remember her when I was a kid), sat on the arm of the chair I was sitting in, with her arm around my shoulder, and said, "The funniest thing I ever remember David saying was when he, Doug, and Bill were down at the schoolyard playing baseball one night about 6:30 and Doug looked at David, remembering that they were supposed to be home at 6:00. He said, 'Dave, we'd better get on home, we're already half an hour late now.' And David turned away from him and replied, 'Oh come on now and finish the game! Dad can't spank us no harder for being half an hour late as he can for being an hour late.'"

This broke up my whole family, especially my dad. Mr. Castor, sitting in a chair to my right, still laughing, said, "Yeah, and I remember," coughing and then taking a drag on a cigarette, "when we were to drive Dave, Doug, and Bill down to Madisonville to see a football game," taking a deep breath, "and David came out to the car, and Doug was still inside talking to you, Jack," as he looked over at my Dad and smiled, "'cause you'd just had a new gas lamp put in your front yard the day before. It hadn't been in for 24 hours when Doug broke the glass passing a football to Dave. Well, we were sitting there in the car waiting for Doug," coughing again, this time standing up, slapping both knees with his hands as he bent over to sit down, laughing, breathing heavily, "and finally he came out and got in the backseat of the car, and David leaned over and in a low voice said to Doug, 'What'd he say, what'd he say to ya'?' And Doug mumbled back, 'Dad said he was surprised that the lamp glass lasted as long as it did.'" Mr. Castor slapped his hands on his knees again and coughed, trying to laugh.

We stayed about 20 minutes more, listening to more stories and drinking hot chocolate. I thought as Mr. Castor walked us out to the car that this visit to their house had made my trip back to Kentucky worthwhile. As we drove back home, my eyes watered, and I felt nostalgically happy. Those people have always treated me so good. I'm not sure if those stories about Doug, Bill and me are true or not. They could be false, as likely as not, since the Castors are storytellers and tend to invent and exaggerate, but it doesn't really matter. I felt really good.

When we got home, my mother told me that Mr. Castor had lung cancer and was expected to live not longer than two years.

Well, I should be leaving here in a couple of days after Christmas. I'll be flyng into Oakland airport. I'll call you the night before I leave and tell you which flight I'll be arriving on so you can pick me up.

Love,
David

Richard Curtis,
Santa Cruz, California:

"How I Got Out"

In June of '65 I graduated from high school, but in May of '65 I had already joined the Army, because my father had convinced me that it was the only thing to do.

My very first impression of the Army was that it was ridiculous. Nothing was based on logic. In basic training, at Fort Dix, N.J., they has us digging holes and filling them up again, on the theory that idle hands are the Devil's workshop. And I was bored. The only thing the Army taught me was how neat it was to go to bed with boys. And lieutenants. That's how I got out.

After basic training, I wanted to take a class in photography, but they talked me into taking cryptography (top secret) instead. One Wednesday I skipped class, which is a definite no-no, and hitchhiked to New York to buy a few things for my plan to get out of the Army—things like male nude magazines. But I got nervous and figured that wasn't the way to get out. So I decided to kill myself.

I went to the base library and studied some books on handwriting and suicide notes. I learned all about suicide notes, and I wrote an absolutely perfect one, which I mailed to my lieutenant.

That evening during dinner, I was called to my lieutenant's office in the barracks. He wanted to know why I had skipped class that day. I told him I had gone to New York to buy some magazines. When he asked what kind, I didn't know what else to say, so I said, "Magazines of naked boys." He asked me if I was gay. I didn't know what he meant by "gay," but when he explained, I told him I had a boyfriend on base. Then he said I could go.

The next day I was called back to my lieutenant's office. There were two officers there with pencils and note pads, taking down everything that was said. I sat down. They said they wanted to know the details of what I did with this other boy. I was scared shitless and didn't know what to say. So they suggested a few things that men might do together sexually, and asked me if I had done them. I said yes to all of them! The officers made me sign what they were writing, and I was free to go.

That afternoon, they held an inspection in our barracks. They never inspected more than one or two lockers, so you never knew who was going to get it. Today they checked mine first. They found a portrait of my sister, and I had a hell of a time trying to convince them that it was not a picture of my girlfriend. Fortunately we look a lot alike. Under the picture they found the magazines I had bought in New York but had decided not to use, which they took with them.

In the office again next day, they wanted to know about the suicide note they had just received. I insisted I hadn't written it. They let me go, but I heard nothing in the next couple of days, and I was very unhappy. I thought I had failed.

I knew I had to do something, so that night, instead of going back to the barracks, I just started walking along the road. Suddenly there was a patrol car behind me telling me to stop. I kept on walking with my hands in my pockets; they kept telling me to stop. I thought to myself, "Well, here goes," and fell down flat on my face in front of the car. The police jumped out of the car, rolled me over, and ask me what was wrong. I said nothing, but played dead, keeping my eyes open. (I felt very bad, because I could see their faces, and I realized that they were just two young dudes who were really concerned about me. But I still played dead.)

They called for an ambulance, and I was rushed to the emergency ward of a hospital nearby. One of the guys wrote on a report that I looked almost dead. (This was released to the press, and my obituary appeared later in my hometown paper.)

At the hospital I was given a spinal tap and kept completely naked in front of a roomful of concerned people while they tried to figure out what had happened to me. After some hours, I said, "Rape," in a strained voice, and started to cry. After another hour they managed to get it out of me that I had been raped by two guys. They gave me a shot and put me in bed.

They left me alone for two days until I had recuperated, and sent me back to my barracks, where I was called into the office again. They had analyzed and verified my suicide note. They were still looking for my rapist. They decided I was truly homosexual and couldn't be in the Army. Next day I was sent to Valley Forge General Hospital in Pennsylvania, the out-patient hospital of the Army, where within a month, thanks to my good behavior, I was ward head.

On the 1st of March, 1966, I was released from the hospital and from the Army. Because they are obligated to pay your bus fare home, they asked me where I wanted to go. I said, "San Francisco." I went to San Francisco to become a hippie.

Jesse Bear James,
Somers, New York:

The Story of A Loner's Life

"As soon as we are born we are given a name by our parents to be just like them when we grow up. We are give a name because we can't make up one that young, so when you are old enough you should make up

53

your own to whatever you want; if you don't you are a prisoner of the name you have till the day you die."

When I was about seven years old and spending time in White Plains, visiting relatives every weekend or so, I always had this thing for looking out windows when I got bored. One Friday they went out and I was looking out of the window. There was this lady hanging up laundry from a basket on the side of an apartment building, to a clothesline. Then a man came out from another apartment bulding and grabbed her and started choking her, and hitting her. He then dragged her behind the apartment building. I didn't think much of it then. I thought the guy was Santa Claus then because he had a scarf covering his face.

Me and this guy named Bob Pecora used to shoot arrows at each other; they were pointed but we didn't pull the bows all the way back. I don't know why we did it. It was a real long time ago. I used to have a lot of friends then, I remember that. We lived nearby some woods in a development and I used to play baseball a lot and build tree houses. I always used to sell things in school, comic books, candy, records, anything just about. I thought about selling myself to a pawn shop in '68 just to see what it would be like. I never did it though.

Around '66 I met this girl named Lisa; that was when I changed from greaser. I started letting my hair grow long, then, but my super-straight parents didn't like it. So they decided to cut it, and they did. I was going with Lisa for about six months, and we broke up. My hair had gotten back to the way it was, and I was on the basketball team. They told me to cut it or I couldn't play. So I quit. I started a fire on the lake where Lisa lived and broke into their house.

I had a lot of friends then so I really didn't have time to be lonely. I stayed in my room sometimes. We moved from there in '67 and my parents decided to give our cats away, and they did, and ever since that day I've hated their guts and I swore revenge someday.

In April of '67 I met this guy named Tor, and one day we were at his house— he had moved in where Lisa lived cause she had moved a couple of miles away. Tor's

54

sister was named Lisa, too, and she was there. Tor wanted her to strip for me, but she didn't want to. We went into her room and I held her down and Tor took off her clothes. She just stood there with her eyes staring at us. What a cunt, and only 11 years old. Then her father came down the driveway; she put her clothes back on. I had met her father and he didn't like anybody with long hair. He was like a Nazi general who didn't know that the war was over.

Around September or so a guy named Bob Weth and me used to hang out together after school sometimes. He made his own guns and was a marksman. One day I was at his house and he was shooting at me with a pellet gun or something. We went hunting once and he got mad cause he couldn't find anything to shoot; so he told me to run and I started running cause he wasn't joking. He didn't hit me but he got awfully close. He loved guns more than anybody I'd ever seen.

In September of '68 my parents cut my hair for the last time. I beat up my mother and threatened to kill her if she ever tried it again.

I met this guy when school opened in '68 named Jonathen Dering. We became good friends, and one day we went to see the Airplane and Spooky Tooth in Central Park. I was going to put gasoline in my parents room for cutting my hair, lighting it when they were sleeping. A couple of months later I woke up and found out that John Dering was dead. A bus had crushed his car and him in it. This was in June '69 and my hair had grown back to my shoulders again, and I started going to the city a lot to hang out at the Fillmore East. John, Lee, Pete, Jimmy, and Steve and me, we went down to a concert; sometimes different combinations of us went down.

In '69 I met this girl named Carol in school and she was unbelievably beautiful. We were going together for a while and having great times together. We went down to the Fillmore, Madison Square Garden and other places, and we'd sleep in Grand Central and talk to the old ladies. We used to sit above the people on the higher level and make believe all the people were sharks, and we were on an island.

Then around March '70 I got kicked out of school,

cause I had a wine bottle of whiskey and I was smoking a cigarette and I was stoned in class. I had a steak knife and I ran it across my wrists, on the top of my wrist, that is; and I was laughing and all the people were staring at me, or some of them, anyway. The next day I ran through the halls screaming and the principal was running after me, and he caught up to me in art, and I started smiling. He was mad as hell, he threatened me, and that's how I got kicked out of school. I did it cause me and Carol had broken up and I just went nuts. They took me to see a psychiatrist, and I walked out and slammed the door in his face.

About a week later I went to live in the East Village and I started snorting heroin to try to forget Carol, but I couldn't. We ate spaghetti and had jelly sandwiches and drank wine all the time; that's all we ever did, or hang out in the Village. I got mugged in the park, and held up on the street and beaten over the head. So after two weeks I decided this wasn't the East Village I had known, so I moved out. When we had heroin, it was usually in the morning. This guy used to come over like a milkman and we'd snort together or apart. I got real sick one night and fell unconscious and didn't wake up till the night. I thought I was going to die from it then.

I still hadn't forgotten that girl, so I came home and stayed in my room and house for six months without ever going out. I went outside three or four times in the backyard to keep my sanity—if I hadn't already lost it. I wrote some songs with a borrowed guitar when I could a while later. I also wrote a book about a beatnik worm and a hippie turtle. I didn't have any friends, so I took to Charles Manson and made him as my friend. I bought his album, and saved everything in the newspapers about him. I would take out pictures or just clips of people who were murdered and put my friends in their places—rather, the people I once knew who were once my friends. I wanted to be just like him, too.

I saw Carol again because she was wondering what had happened to me, as were some others. I saw her for about a month, and then she told me she didn't want to see me any more cause she loved a guy named Ritchie and he would get mad. But before that we went down to the city; I hoped it wouldn't happen again, but it did. She even admitted it was her fault for what she did to me. She started crying in the movies and saying how sorry she was when we were in New York City. Loneliness had made me a madman.

I've gotten away from Charles Manson, and it's been a year since then, and she's married. I'm still a loner. I stay in my room except on Saturdays, and I'm trying to get married or trying to find someone to live with. I don't know how much longer I can do it. The only reason I'm alive is that I believe I can make a record with my songs: if I didn't I'd be dead most likely. I've been a loner for a long time and it turns you into things you don't want to be, but it just happens that way. I've lived with so much pain inside me. I've seen a lady get killed and cut in half in White Plains and just too much. That's all I've got to say, thanks for listening.

Ms. Pat Rutter,
West Creek, New Jersey:

Me!

I had a lonely childhood; where I lived there were no other children my age that lived near—only a cousin or two, but they were quite a few years younger than me. The town I lived in was rather small and it always seemed to me that all possible playmates lived so far away. My parents were quite strict and it was only after much persuading that I obtained permission to go out of the yard. This staying home has its effects on me even now. I spend much time at home, reading, cooking and writing.

When I started school, I went to a very old school house not far from where I lived. It had three classrooms, two baths and a kitchen. I was a painfully shy little tyke with ankle socks and a permanent.

My teacher for the next three years was in a class all by herself. She was an old woman, say in her late 60s. The only reason they kept her was that no one else would teach three classes in the same classroom, for not much pay. She abused the children, the worst being eating cokes and doughnuts while teaching the class, or hitting them.

The principal was also different. She had a drinking habit and it wasn't an odd sight to see her sit in the car, get juiced, and come in to get all her students cokes so they wouldn't tell on her.

My childhood passed rather uneventfully, getting only pimples and a complex to remember it by. Sort of a keepsake.

Around this time I discovered religion. My parents got very religious all of a sudden, and started going to church. I hated it at first; we never went before, so why start now? I finally converted to the Baptist faith. I wasn't no zealous convert who went around preaching hell, fire, and brimstone.

My teen years weren't much different from my young years. I was still shy and found it so hard to talk to anyone. So my parents and a couple of helpful teachers took me to a psychiatrist. In my opinion I saw nothing wrong with me, but then, what I felt didn't count. Those teachers who didn't even know me convinced my parents that something was wrong with a person who didn't like to talk to people.

Analysis didn't help me; I was defensive and wouldn't respond to any of the questions or "games" they planned. The only thing that really happened to me at that time was when I was given some pills that had side effects on certain types of people. But the good doctors didn't tell my mother that. I went into convulsions and wasn't almost admitted to a hospital because it was the middle of the night.

In spite of my trip into analysis, I was still shy and spent much time at home reading a great deal. I read many religious books such as *Pilgrim's Progress* and the Bible. I took organ lessons on which I played classical and religious music. Even though I was a Beatle fan, I never played rock and roll on the organ.

School was one tiring ordeal. I hated school. Staying home became a favorite pastime of mine. I only felt safe within the confines of the house. I spaced the days I was absent so as to not arouse any suspicion.

I did have some tragic experiences. One which always stands out in my mind was when my brother was killed in Vietnam. His death is constantly before me as I look back at all the things I could have done for him but didn't. Only those who have went through that know how it really feels!

When you are a teenager you are supposed to date. I never did, and for a long time thought it was my looks. Now I am no beauty, but after seeing some of those who even wound up married I know now it wasn't my looks.

Graduation from high school finally came. The happiest time of my life. After a few months, I got a job typing at Spencer Gifts. It wasn't very exciting sitting there typing all day so I quit. My main ambition is to write. I used to write stories, and my seventh grade English teacher told me that I was college material and had real talent. Imagine!

Right now, however, I have went through so many personal changes. My religious life is nil. It left me with so many unanswered questions that it no longer seemed real—only a ritual you go through every Sunday.

I still stay at home. I read still, mainly books and magazines and newspapers. I cook but don't gain weight. Writing and politics take up most of my life. So here I be, a dateless 18-year-old who wonders if she will be doing the same thing when she is 30.

Mrs. Barbara Walker,
Moline, Illinois:

My Life and Pleasures

Can you imagine a mother of five girls an avid rock lover? I believe I have all the loves and joys possible to a woman of 33. As of the present, I am a homemaker and Brownie Scout teacher, along with the role of motherhood and wife. I also, more or less, plan the songs and music to be used in a local Rock Band. I am literally tone-deaf, but occasionally play the tambourine with groups.

Music has been my whole life for as long as I can remember. At two years old, I used to sit by my record player for hours on end. All of my life I wanted to be a drummer. But, to my parents' belief, it wasn't lady-like! I took piano, accordian, and organ lessons, but wasn't satisfied. My girls are all musically inclined, and would rather listen to Alice Cooper than watch television. My nine-and 13-year-olds play the guitar, and my six-year-old has a four-piece drum set. We also have bongos, a conga drum, tambourine, harmonica, bleach bottles, etc., and really "get it on" to the music with our own little rock session. I believe our whole life revolves around music, everything from Grand Funk and Janis Joplin to Neil Young.

Kids from all over come over to jam with us, or just to rap with us. My husband will be 40 years old next month. Kids find it so hard to believe that people our age can be so far-out! We never miss Rock Concerts or Rock Festivals, and really dig all the Hippies, Long-Hairs, and Heads. I think we have a very close-knit family and a very rich and meaningful life.

This sounds as if all my life revolves entirely in just listening to my records and tapes. True, to a certain sense. But, while music is on, I make good use of my time. I love arts and crafts of all kinds, and I am always making something. I have refinished furniture, re-upholstered furniture, engaged in candlemaking, ceramics, plastic resin, macrame, embroidery, string art, batic, glass staining, flower arranging, felt and art foam projects, papier mache, collages, and tie-dyeing, among others. I even tried my hand at drawing. But, I found I'm not too artistic. Our whole family engages in making Christmas decorations and gifts for friends. You wouldn't believe our basement and garage—boxes and sacks galore! I would like to have a head shop and craft shop someday.

As for my other hobbies, I believe cooking is my main one. I have seven recipe boxes, plus 63 cookbooks, all of which I use avidly. I love to read, as you might surmise from our four bookcases full of books. My main interests are of the sinister, nightmarishly haunting type science fiction, "adult only" books, mysteries, the Black Arts, and Astrology.

We also like outdoor sports, such as swimming, water skiing, sledding, roller and ice skating, or a ride in the country on our 750 Norton. I believe this just about sums up my life: a busy one of motherhood, rock music, arts and crafts, cooking, reading, and outdoor sports with our five daughters. What more fulfillments in life could one woman ask for?

Jon Locke,
Chattanooga, Tennessee:

"God Bless Us Everyone"

So I balled this chick everyday until I had enough. She yelled at me a lot—a beauty queen she was.

I learned then that I couldn't lead a girl into my trip. A cute 16-year-old picked me up at local Teen Club and sucked me as I drove her car. I thought that was cool. I went to other girls—cashing in my karma all along the way.

I had not balled until I was 29 years old, it was fun and crazy. I worked in a Phoenix Dope Rehab house, you know. And I would turn on and ball my "clients." You know the scene. I was supposed to be a kind of guru—long hair and all. I was amazed at how God was giving me all I wanted (even more) on the material plane. I couldn't even think. Then there were army tanks on McCallie Ave. and a race riot. So I started thinking and quit all the psychedelic running around. I went the Jesus trip and shaved and got "cleaned up" and went to work.

I don't mind. I've got a 3.5 Highest Honors in Nuclear Physics degree, so I like my mind and I see girls as complex wiring networks. I see God as the absolute—I have seen God. That is my salvation and my hang-up; I scream to you from a burning mind. I had schizophrenia at 19. So what! So freak out. I did the Big Sur, California, Janis Joplin in concert thing. Blew the works, *et al.*

Worked for a year in Yogananda's Monastery on Mt. Washington, Los Angeles. Got horny after nuns and figured it was time to leave.

Yes. This body has been blessed to feel Bliss. By Grace of Guru and God (what's the difference?) I was given a taste of ever new joy, as high as acid, only I could still drive a car and go to school—but it lasted three weeks night and day. Even watched myself dream and sleep. "Ready to wake up now, body?" "OK. Sure."

Astral projection was nothing.

I can say I have tasted what every man is seeking. That is my Honor and I live by it today. God bless us everyone.

Tina Dawson,
Helena, Montana:

Life (Mine)

I was born in some hospital in Helena, Montana, on December 7, 1956. I wasn't due until February but my maw got bloated so I had to come out. Doc almost lost both of us, maw had an infection. I have a brother and a sister, both nine and seven years older. If any of you people out there ever have any kids, have them about two years apart because far apart really screws 'em.

Anyway, I don't really remember much up until I was about five. The thing I remember then is that my family went to Great Falls for the state fair and my sister took me in the witches' house where you ride around in a car in the dark and things pop out at you. I was really scared and was screaming bloody murder at the top of my lungs. I don't know how I survived.

Then came the greatest event in everybody's life: school! First year I had a real nice lady teach. One day I was running down a real small slope to my neighbor's house and I slipped and twisted my ankle. My dad carried me to the house. I had to wear my red slippers with the flowers to school. I rode to school one morning with my parents 'cause of my foot. The janitor let me in because nobody else was there. So I sat in my seat and when the teacher came in she said, "What are you doing here so early?" She sounded so mad, and I thought she'd be glad to see me. I started crying. Nobody is ever glad to see me.

Another time in first grade I thought I'd be real brave and climb up the long green slide where people slide down. So I started climbing up and got a few steps, when whack! The mean old second grade teacher told me to get off of there. I ran up to my teacher and told her what had happened. She said I knew better than to do that and to not climb that way again. I had expected sympathy. The adult world is so confusing.

In second grade my teach was a little old lady; she was OK. One day after school another girl and I were erasing the boards and on each side of the room on a board the teach had written QUIET! and we weren't supposed to erase them. She went out of the room for a minute so we decided to help her and on every board a couple of times we wrote QUIET! She came back in the room with some important person. When he left she started cussing us out 'cause she was embarrassed. Heck, we thought we were doing her a favor. Nobody appreciates anything I dream up.

In either second or third grade I embarrassed myself so bad I thought I'd die. I went to the lavatory and did my thing and came back to the room. The teacher went out and then came back. She asked, "Who plugged up the toilet in the girl's bathroom?" Nobody raised their hand. Then she thought for a moment and then looked at me. "You were in there last. Did you plug it?" I nodded "yes" and she told me to go find the janitor. Now the janitor is a really sweet old guy but can you imagine a little second or third grade girl going up to a tall man and telling him that you plugged up the toilet? I think I cried then too.

In fourth grade we had a pretty nice teach but she was kinda screwy. In fact, we got on her nerves so much she collapsed. One day a girl went up to ask her something just before lunch and the teacher just looked at her and fell over out of her chair onto the floor. The ambulance came and took her away to a hospital for about a week. Then she came back OK.

Sixth grade was a little better than average year. We had a great big snowfall that year and the schools were closed for a day or two. About ten of us kids would wade through the drifts to school and jump rope and goof around. We also had a graduation. Boy that was neat then but seems funny now. We had a big buffet dinner with our parents in the lunch room and after dinner us kids sang some songs. We sang "Born Free" and a few others and were going to do "Sounds of Silence" but we couldn't quite get together.

Seventh and eighth were bummers. Now ninth has come around and it's gettin' to be another bummer. School didn't used to be so bad but when you're about to flunk in something . . . I know now how dropouts feel. I can't stand going to school with freshmen and sophomores. I feel I'm more mature than they and they seem like such kiddies. I can really get it together with people around in their 20s and so on, except for some old folks, more than I do with my own age group. I'm always very friendly toward anybody that old foggies call "hippies," whatever they are. I just feel like we're all brothers and should be friends.

I don't really know what I want to do with my life yet, but I know one thing I want is to somehow help people. I'm kinda thinking about maybe being a nun but I don't know what's going on.

I know that this sounds very droopy and uncheerful, but really, how many of you sweeties out there had a happy adolescense? I know of quite a few people who about literally died at that time. I am just waiting for the day when I can get out of this hell. After I get my diploma I'm leaving this place and if I can help it I'm never coming back. There are too many people in this town who would like to see me destroyed, including me. My summer school teacher told me last summer that I am a paranoid. I think I probably am, but then people act that way, so . . . I get very depressed easily and feel sorry for myself, as you can probably guess.

Everybody wonders why there are so many "freaks" and "weirdoes" running around. It's because of their shitty parents. If there weren't any bastards to say, "Oh, you're so ugly and can't do a damn thing and you're just

64

a piece of shit," and make you think you're a piece of nothing, then maybe we wouldn't have so many lost souls. If you don't mind me using the term "hippies": there are so many "hippies" with long hair and beards that are really just human beings. Sweet, kind, skin people. In my opinion there is no such thing as a "hippie." The term isn't even in the dictionary. I have a friend who, according to my mother, is a "hippie," but maw doesn't even know what a hippie is. I love every "hippie" in the country. Just because they have long hair they are prejudiced against them. They haven't done anything, but somebody has to be a scapegoat for the old people who can't account for themselves.

So goes my life which I don't value too much cause I ain't much to value, but anyway here it was!

Douglas Fiske,
Encinitas, California:

Poem

I was barrel assin' down the freeway
In this big, long Cadillac
When all of a sudden
The mother broke down
And I wound up on a country road
In front of this huge sign
It said: Stop. Proceed with Caution.

Clyde Kimball,
Madison, Wisconsin:

Cross Country Adventure

I drove into Denver on Interstate 80 West at 7:00 A.M. The traffic got progressively heavier as I neared the city. The roads got progressively worse. Industrial fumes choked me, dirtied my windshield, and with grime on my windshield and sun in my eyes, visibility was extremely poor. The traffic was thick. One curve was like an

Indianapolis bank turn with 50 mph warning signs. An oil slick at this spot would slide anyone off the road into oblivion. The roads had deep ruts etched into the paving —enough to throw cars when their wheels got into them.

I was extremely tired—I had driven from Madison, Wisconsin, with no sleep. I drove ahead of a snow, ice, and wind storm which closed Iowa traffic shortly after I got through the blizzard. My windshield had a crack from a thrown stone. Gusts of 60 miles per hour were pressing on the glass. I hoped Detroit knew what it was doing when it built the car. I was also aware that if cars didn't break, the automotive industries' profit would be cut in half. So I was completely paranoid—this was more hazardous than Washington crossing the Delaware.

I was anxious to get to my friend Greg's house, but I wasn't sure I could make it. The highway signs were nearly invisible—small and glaring—and generally appeared too late for me to turn without smashing into several lanes of cars. Some drivers were ignoring everyone else.

I pulled up to a curb and walked into the house. Greg was in bed with a woman. They both looked at me, unsurprised, and asked, "What brings you here?"

I told them I was on my way to California to copyright some songs. I took a bath and slept several hours.

When I woke up there were screaming sirens coming from ambulances stationed next door to Greg's. Reed Ambulance gets a lot of business; their windows show off pictures of destroyed cars and occupants. I can see why so many die—unaware drivers, poor roads, and Mother Nature's basic imbalance which affirms we all must go sometime. I wasn't sure if the pictures were a warning to drive carefully, or if the city was showing off their kills like trophy hunters.

Greg and I went to my car, whereupon I tied a red balloon to my antenna to look inconspicuous among civil service cars. People would glance, see a red bubble off the top of my wagon, and give me the right of way or get turned on by the sexual hue. My only fear was the police—I felt they may want to pop my bubble.

I had had to get money wired from my parents, so

I called my mother from Safeway. We went in for food. Black children asking for cigarettes and a hungry old man looking for food in the delicatessen. I offered him something and got a flat refusal—too much pride to accept a handout. I told him wasted food could be collected from schools and restaurants and redistributed to starving people and pets through the church—true religious morals.

We went back to Greg's, played guitars, and in walked Matey, another local. He was not surprised to see me either. He wants to play drums, but can't afford to buy a set with the job he's got. He's a dishwasher at a restaurant that throws out untouched food. It's great food for insects and bacteria, even though people continually starve. Matey, Greg, and many others involved in fine arts need places to meet, to arrange and produce material where neighbors can't be disturbed. As it is, they get off work too late to play without disturbing the peace. More on these matters later.

We drove Matey to work and on the way I tried to call my mother about the money—I used four methods of long distance, heard several suspicious clicking sounds, and verbally threatened the FBI. I would arrest them for illegal wiretapping. No use, the phone was dead, the operator couldn't be reached. I ran across the street to Target shopping center and dialed the operator angrily.

"Now listen to me carefully," I growled through clenched teeth, "Alexander Graham Bell designed this system as a public service for use by the people. If you don't let this call through you are violating the law and I will have you arrested."

"Yes sir," she replied.

My mother's voice said, "I already sent the money," and I thanked her graciously. I apologized to the operator and went to the Western Union Telegraph office.

While waiting in line I told an ex-GI to carry his wallet in the pocket over his heart so he's free to ward off pickpockets. His face lit up like a faithful military man when I demonstrated how to hit and kick those who attempt to take your money. I wonder if the VC is after only enough money for survival of their people, or if they're defending their wealth with war, like Americans. I'll never know why countries won't share everything and realize that we're all equal, just like the Bible says.

I took my money and went to a gas station where I got an oil change and a new tire. The old oil was drained as waste. The gasman and I agreed the oil could be refined and re-sold. The carbon could be used for pencil leads. This could prevent undersea drilling and oil slicks. An older man helped me pick a retread with the words "hazard tire" printed on a yellow tag. I wondered if this was the manufacturer's guarantee the tire would blow out or if it was simply saying "not safe." I commented tires could be made of metal, nylon, fiberglass, and rubber. I bought a retread in Idaho that was made of sawdust and rubber—definitely unsafe.

While I was paying the man, I talked with girls talking about music. One had hair like George Washington's appears on the dollar bill. I told her, "People respect this paper with a picture of a man on it who has hair longer than you or I as if it were a god. I have hair shorter than either you or George, but even I am hassled by people for something as ridiculous as style."

"It is silly," she said. When I asked her who her musical favorites were, she said CSN&Y.

"Beatles?" I asked.

"Definitely," she said, "but they'll never get together again."

I heard they might. They ought to, they produced *Sgt. Pepper*—*the* classic record of the century.

I noticed the Denver police have blue flashing lights on their cars, so I attached a blue balloon above the red one for driving security. I showed Greg a song I wrote, got names and specialties from several people, and left.

Upon attempting to leave town, I was caught in a complex labyrinth of one-way streets. I wondered if the police and traffic departments had set it up so out-of-towners would get caught making mistakes and be ticketed (to the glee of the money-hungry city). It was like a test in which rats attempt to reach their feed without getting electrical shocks from a mad scientist. I was determined to make it through so I could warn the people of these perils.

I pulled up to an intersection which had a bottle placed on the crosswalk stripe. I wondered if they wanted me to run over it and pop my tire or if I was merely supposed to knock it over and alert them with the clatter. "Right turn only" was posted so I swung left, around the bottle, and took a right. Another right, and another in a poor section. Another stop a block away from the bottle. At this intersection was a beer can in the same position the bottle was in on the other corner. I carefully swung around it, fearing it was either a bomb or a noisemaker. I went another block, took a right and came to a five way street. One turn sign pointed an arrow labeled "no." Another said "OK." OK to turn or OK to get a ticket? I took the OK turn, got on 125N and headed north.

Naively I assumed I was safe. Twenty-five overlooks the city. It was like driving on the backbone of a gigantic, primitive beast, many lights glaring, guard rails glimmering like rows of teeth. A sports car passed me like a predator from the jungle, darting around and running people off the road. I held tight to the wheel, not believing the road conditions. It would be great for auto testing grounds, but it is wholly unsafe for the public.

I figured if I followed the locals they would guide me past the dangerous spots. Not true—some places there were no safe spots. There is one hole the length and width of a full size station wagon. It sinks two to three inches below the rest of the paving. The car drops in and pops out—enough to scare the hell out of anyone.

Then on the other side of the road, just over the rise—a spectacular jump, suitable for race drivers, ski jumpers, and joy riders. A lot of fun. Trouble is when your car comes down to the pavement, the nose nearly hits the ground. If your shocks are bad it can throw you off the road. In fact mine need replacing after the ride. North again, there are ripples on the surface that collect oil—avoid 'em, they make your tires slick.

Truck ahead of me dragging chains. Earlier a wrecker hung a ball and hook over the top of my car—it was very ominous. I got through the ruts and holes, and on up a hill to a bridge on the crest. Smooth paving led to the bridge, but the bridge was rutted, pitted, and of a different texture than the road itself. The downgrade was as smooth as the upgrade, but I can now see why the ambulances are so busy.

Lyn Weiner,
San Francisco, California:

Lyn Weiner's Diary 1953

Jan. 1. Well, it's 3:00 AM. I got home from a New Year's Eve Party not too long ago. It was fair. My birthday was last night. It was at exactly 17 minutes of ten. I was 14 years old.

Jan. 10. Today I saw a picture of Robert Wagner. Boy, how can people be so lucky to be so pretty. (He is a new up-coming movie star.) Some people are so successful and others just fail in life. I guess I'm talking a little deep. But I just would like to know just what life is all about. Is it a game? I just don't understand. Here I am in punko Pottstown wasting my time, while someone in New York is getting much more out of life than I'll ever get here. Oh, I just can't express myself. I guess I'm just feeling a little low but I really would like to start all over again somewhere like California or New York. Oh, I'm just sick of this town!

Jan. 17. Boy, did I ever have a good time at the dance tonight! I'll tell you every detail. First as soon as we got there, Neil Block asked me to dance (a big shot from Norristown). I then looked for Irv. He was there! I danced the next dance with him, and all the dances after that. We got them to have a statue dance—that is when the music stops, you must stand perfectly still and not move a muscle. Well, first five then 10 people were eliminated until there were only 2 couples, one of which was us. They had to play about three records till they found the winner, which of course was us. (We made up our minds to win.)

Jan. 20. Today President Eisenhower was inaugurated. We saw it all on TV in school. They had two TV sets

70

in the cafeteria, two in the auditorium and two in the gym. Pretty neat, huh?

Jan. 29. There is a dance at school tomorrow but I'm not going. Never have any fun anyway. I remember when I was in the 7th grade I thought, well it won't be long now—next year and after that maybe I'll get dances and what happens? I get into the 9th grade and I'm just as ignored as I was in the 7th grade.

Jan. 30. Walked home with my girlfriend Teddy today and we talked about kissing. We both think that it's terrible and we both have been kissed, so we know what it's like. Ugh! We had a very interesting discussion, *if you know what I mean.*

Feb. 12. Today was very unfortunate for me! Alyce and I had a little quarrel. This is how it all started. We were in our home room the last period for a study hall. I went up to the pencil sharpener, and on passing her desk, I noticed her pocketbook was on the floor; so I being always very devilish picked it up and took it back to my seat with me. It was open so Alyce came back and said, "Get out of there!" I never was in it. She took it and I said (of course like a dope) "I bet something's missing." Well, something was—her hankie. Naturally she thought I had it. Who wouldn't? So she took my History Book and I got that back, so then she took my precious ear muffs so I took her scarf. I got my ear muffs back and gave her the scarf. Now everyone believes I took her hankie.

Feb. 21. Well, we couldn't get rides to the big dance in Phoenixville. I cried all night. I even had the days marked off in my notebook. In the four weeks I've been waiting, I went to one movie. All the rest of my time was spent in the library making up reports, or watching TV. I am not going to go to one single dance ever again (unless a Jewish party), no more movies (unless *Peter Pan*), and I won't wear lipstick anymore. That's just the way I feel. I have nothing to look forward to except more waiting till the next dance and reports for History.

Feb. 22. My cousin Jay is coming to supper and then I hope to go to the movies with him to see *Dangerous When Wet* with Esther Williams and Fernando Lamas. Oh, incidentally, those things about the movies, dances and lipstick I said, I didn't mean it. I even have on lipstick right now.

March 4. Exciting news! Josef Stalin is in critical condition. (He is a cruel dictator and the leader of communism in Russia.) He had a hemorrhage of the brain or something of that effect. I wonder if he will die.

March 5. I just got back from the hairdresser's. A special bulletin was announced over the Groucho Marx show at the hairdresser's—Stalin is dead. (I don't know whether to be glad or sorry.)

March 16. Well, we got our report cards today—brace yourself. I got as follows: English-B, Algebra-A, Latin-A, History-A. I made the *A Honor Roll!* Boy oh Boy! I'm happy *but,* they will have to go down. They can't go anywhere else.

April 24. We had sewing today and I got scolded for not paying attention. Boy, now I hate sewing all the more.

May 8. Well, I just do about everything wrong in sewing. I didn't match any of my seams and for the third time I put my facing on wrong. There'll be nothing left of the blouse when I'm finished.

June 9. Tonight was The Graduation Pageant. I was one of the "Four Freedoms." You know, freedom from want, fear, speech. I was from fear. It was a scene in which everyone held their positions and didn't even bat an eyelash.

July 18. Had a very interesting and educational time tonight! There was a dance and Roy came about 10:30 in dungarees. But I didn't mind. He said he was so very tired so we sat out on the deck under the stars. Oh, how I like him now. After we sat for a while he tried to kiss me—several times, but I was afraid. Finally, he asked me what was wrong. I wouldn't tell. Finally I (of all things) started to cry. I blurted out to him that someone kissed me once before and I didn't like it. He said that I should speak to my mother about this but I said I already had and she said she didn't *blame* me for not liking it.

Aug. 11. Brother, today was honestly the most boring day of my life. This afternoon, my cousin Patty and I made cupcakes. Mine didn't turn out so good, in fact, they didn't turn out period. At about 9 I went into the bathroom to look out the window at some kids. I leaned (only *leaned* mind you) on the towel rack when lo and behold it came out of the wall. Boy, I sure am unlucky.

Oct. 17. Well, today was the big day—Gail Pollack's hayride. Here are the highlights. About 60 of us went all the way out in the sticks, and there were these two big wagons chuck full of hay and each one was drawn by four black horses. It lasted for three hours not counting the dance afterwards. I was supposed to sit with Elliot but there wasn't any room where he was sitting. (Oh, I suppose I could have squeezed in.) Anyhow, I sat on the opposite side, with George.

Nov. 2. Today all the girls remarked with emphasis how well George and I look together and how nice we dance together and blah blah this and blah blah that.

Dec. 31. Tonight I went to the YMCA First Annual New Year's Eve Dance. It was nice. I danced a lot with Dick Markowitz (who I believe was drunk—but then a lot of them were). Why, oh why, do boys have to drink??? Then a bunch of us went to Donna's. She had some wopper of a party. She had refreshments and dancing plus the King's Men (a band) were there and a whole slew of other kids. Neat! There was supposed to be a party at Harold Hoffman's tonight but it was canceled. I wouldn't have gone anyway. All the little seventh and eight graders were invited. Forgot to mention, Dick kissed me at 12 tonight. After all, it *was* New Year's!

Michael Ignatieff,
Cambridge, Massachusetts:

"No Roads Back"

i

Maybe you understand only at the very end. Perhaps when you die, you go to a room and they give you a shell or a leaf or some music which you can hold in your hand like a carving. There are others there, people

73

who died at the same time, but in the light you cannot see them. And they are also given a shell or a leaf or something else from the life they have left.

And as you feel the ribbed shell or the leaf or hear the song in the carving, you realize that these things are your *life* and that you have been brought here to hold your life in your hands and to understand it at last.

But maybe it won't be like that, and all you will see is your life disappearing like a stranger's face in the window of a passing train.

ii

Most of them died before I was old enough to know them: Grandmother, Grandfather, Principal Grant, Uncle Nick and the others.

Heli, Nick's widow, told me once one night when we were lighting the candles at her house, "You talk like he did, you know." But I don't know, I don't understand, because she lost him, we lost him, 20 years ago, when I was still too young to remember. So now, at 24, I am like a man I never knew. Yet he is still with us. When I pass the place near the Hart House Tower where they told me he fell, suddenly on a day in 1952, I often think of him.

My Dad says I look like my grandmother, but I don't know, she died three years before I was born. I am a Mestchersky, he says. Mestchersky was her name before she married Paul Ignatieff, who was my grandfather, and who was Minister of Education under the last Czar. My father was the youngest of their five sons and he was born in St. Petersburg in 1913. He was too young to remember the night when the Bolshevik committee came to the summer house in Kislovodsk and took his father away in a car. He has clouded memories of his father's later release and the family's escape to Constantinople on a British ship. He was told the stories and he has told them to me, but sometimes I wonder whether he really knows what they mean to him now, a middle-aged civil servant 3,000 miles from the land of his birth. There are evenings at home when I think I can see him

looking at the portrait of the little boy in the blue sailor suit, painted 50 years ago in St. Petersburg, and wondering whether it is really him.

I think the Revolution broke his childhood apart and now there are no roads back for him, or for me.

iii

No that is not quite true. My mother's mother was still alive when I was a little boy.

I first remember my mother taking me to see her when I was six or seven. I held mother's hand as we climbed the stairs to the red lacquered door at 7 Prince Arthur and I was a little afraid of the old lady who bent over to kiss me. I couldn't understand how anyone could be my mother's mother. How could anyone be so old?

She was a clever and commanding woman in her 70s. She was the kind of grandmother who thought it was foolish to make a fuss over a child simply because it was small, but later, when I was ten, I found out that she was one of the few people prepared to take a little boy seriously. When I stayed for week-ends at her house, I would go into her bedroom on Sunday mornings and sit on her bed and we would eat Ryveeta biscuits and butter from a service on her lap and have thoughtful conversations. We would read the newspaper together, or rather, she would read it and ask me what I thought. She was a beautiful woman. As she lay there, propped up on her pillows, the long grey and black hair that she let down at night and the ravage of her age gave her a sad and queenly dignity.

Her house was a dark place. The light fell brown like stout through the tendrils and roots of the water plants she grew in tall Atlas battery jars on the window sills. Her husband, Principal Grant, had been a scholar and the only disorder still allowed in that house of polished wood and old carpets were the books in his study: teetering towers of them stacked on the floor, thumbed and marked with paper slips and notes which have such pathos for me now because only my grandfather understood them, and he has been dead 35 years, and all the

75

labyrinthine paths he cleared in those books are grown over again and lost.

The house had many treasures: the stamping machine that printed 7 Prince Arthur Avenue in embossed letters on her blue vellum envelopes; grandfather's small brass snake whose wriggles provided a place to moor his pens; and, of course, the little boxes where she put things that were most precious. One of these boxes was made of mother of pearl which made it seem like a little square of blue water. Inside it were tiny agates that glowed like cranberries in the soft light of the sitting room. She let me hold them in my hand. In another box like that she had fragments of bombs dropped by the Zeppelins on London in the First World War. They were savage and jagged pieces of bored metal, and she said, "Hold them in your hand," and I looked up at her when I took them in my palm because they had such a sinister heaviness.

There were other memories of war in that house, and I think it was then that I first wondered whether I would be brave in a war. I have talked to my mother about this. She worked in military intelligence in England during the Second War and she knew the men who parachuted into France to help the Resistance. I have met some of those who survived. I once told my mother that I envied them, and envied her for having known them in that brave time. She looked at me and said sadly no no it was a terrible time we lost so many of the people we loved.

In that house, on the mantelpiece, there was a scrap of crimson silk pressed between two pieces of glass. I asked my grandmother what it was and she took it down and gravely told me. When she was married and living in England during the First World War, she knew a young man who came to the house for the teas she gave. He was very shy. He used to wait in the hall until she coaxed him into taking her arm and coming in to meet the other guests. Then I remember her pausing and I looked up at her and she was thinking. "He died very bravely in the war," she suddenly said after a minute. They found a crimson flag near where he fell in no man's land in the Somme or at the place with the beautiful name, Passchendaele, and they sent it back to her so she could remember him.

There was another treasure in her house: the animals. Once or twice she took them out of the bottom drawer of the cabinet behind the sofa and placed them on the old carpets. They were gaunt and strange carvings: giraffes, leopards, buffalos, zebras, crocodiles and lions. They were a hundred years old, she told me, and her father, Sir George Parkin, had got them from the tribes in South Africa when he was there in the 1880s. They had a magic in their inert eyes and cold black bodies and I would watch them in the dark room and be a little afraid.

I had only a few years with my grandmother, when I was old enough to talk to her and she was still well.

Then there came a Sunday when I was 11 or 12 and I went with my Aunt Charity to have Sunday lunch with her. I suddenly realized that she was no longer able to recognize me. Charity and I kept talking across the mahogany table and eating our lunch, but I could see her slipping away from us, grain by grain, staring sad and broken at the hotel wall outside the dining room window.

One day they told me she had died and we went down to the Church to be with all the people who had loved her, and a man by the altar with velvet gloves poured a tiny vial of ashes out on a coffin and I wept.

My childhood was over: she was dead and soon her house was sold and the treasures were dispersed.

Lita Verhaegen,
Crows Landing, California:

My Life

Everyday I think about writing down my autobiology, but I can never think of what to write because I feel it's not too exciting. I'm a housewife, I do yoga, I go for beautiful country air bicycle rides in the early afternoon, I cook for my husband who is a farmer of some sort. He planted our garden which provides me with all the

77

fresh vegetables I want, he also planted 2 Cherry Trees, I Bing the other Tartarian, I Plum tree and a Peach tree. He also planted lawn in front of our house and on the side. The side of the house really should be the front because the sun hits the "side" all the time (when the sun is out) where everything is always green. I take care of our 2 dogs who really have their shit together. Blue was here when we moved in and Puppy is his son, which both of them look alike. They are pals through thick and thin. I also take care of 3 cats. I really don't take care of them, they use me only for my nice warm cozy place.

My social life isn't much more exciting, though I've gone to some good concerts at the Winterland, where I always end up having a great time. You really can get loose there, it's like a big playground free with live music and sometimes good light shows. But one can't always go to concerts; one can, but it kinda gets expense after awhile. We go to all the shows that are worth seeing and even to the half-ass ones just to go to the show. We entertain in a reasonably amount. We through a Eclipse Party and watched the moon go over the sun or the sun go over the moon and we had a real good time.

I just live for everyday, taking care of the house, learning to cook more and better dishes, going for bicycle rides, washing clothes only because the sun is out, exercising constantly and my yoga. I have a book called *Be Young with Yoga* which I devour. It has helped me so much that I'll never be without it again. I now walk more gracefully, have more poise and balance and I'm shaping into a woman very nicely. Only at 19, I know I've come along ways, but I'm still not ripe yet; that should take some care in the coming years.

Another past time that I always do is that I'm constantly looking and reading my recipes over and over again hoping that someday I'll be cooking that dish. The only basic baking I've done is with Yeast. So far, I've made Whole Wheat Bread, Cinnamon Buns and English Muffins. Out of the 3, the English Muffins were the best. Though the Cinnamon Buns were alright and the Whole Wheat Bread didn't rise the Muffins had distinction. I'm going to try it again with those muffins because they weren't quite cooked all the way through. And I limited my baking only for the weekends.

You now know what Lita Verhaegen does everyday at her home in Crows Landing, California. Where the air is always fresh (and I mean "fresh") where you can always hear the birds singing in the morning as the Sun moves across the sky and where you can see all of universe with it's shinest and most brightness stars ever around. I suppose my life really isn't that boring after-all, so here is my contribution to you, My Life. Whoopee!

Charles W. Olmstead,
Lompoc, California:

"Dearest Mother and Father,
It Is My Assignment to Inform You,
That Your Son Has Died in Vietnam"

I was born on September 4th, 1947, in Birmingham, Alabama, to parents with high plans and visions of a wholesome and promising future for their first born. Had I known then about the burdens and disappointments that lay ahead, I undoubtedly would have never agreed to entering physical life; I surely would have shined on and passed the invitation to this tragic comedy.

Nevertheless, I had no say in the matter. Not being born a child genius, I had to go through the motions of experience before I finally realized where I was; and by then I was long past that umbilical border and point of no return. As everyone, I was a victim of "like it or lump it."

I was raised in Norwood, Pennsylvania, more or less; at least I have a lot of good memories coming from there —root beer, fire engines and the Fourth of July, grandparents, cousins, and Dickie, this retarded boy who lived down the block. I loved Dickie. People hassled him because he walked sort of loose and didn't speak clearly. Dickie was retarded but not dumb; he taught me how to rip off newspaper machines with clotheshangers and chewing gum. He couldn't make it in standardized schools, but I know if he's alive today he can make it on the street. Perhaps he was a foreshadowing of days to come—Dickie was my first lesson in survival when survival looks slim.

My father was a lifer in the Army. He did a term in the Navy and then got out only to find he couldn't "make it" outside with a family, so he re-enlisted in the Army as a career. My father and I were stumbling blocks for one another. Had I not been born perhaps he could have "made it" as a civilian, and had he not been an Army lifer perhaps I'd have never followed his Army issue foot steps. But so goes the game of "like it or lump it."

For close to 17 years we lived in one Army post after another—Fort Campbell, Fort Lee, Robinson Barracks in Germany, back to Fort Lee then to Fort Knox. We were in and out of Army run schools and never kept friends for more than two years at a time; the pace was extremely hectic and very untogether—too many loose ends. The Army way of life and its restrictions were, to say the least, insane. A kid that lived next door to us at Fort Knox had to shine his fathers boots and brass *before* he was allowed to do his homework at night. On week-ends his room was *inspected* in relation to Army standards; upon failing one such inspection he was restricted to "quarters" for the week-end. If he ever expected to have any freedoms he complied with his fathers orders, he learned to shine boots and brass, he learned to pass those jack-ass inspections, in short he learned ahead of time how to be a soldier.

Soon our redemption was nigh. We were at Fort Ord, California, and my father was finally retiring; we moved to Lompoc, California. Leaving that armed force environment gave me a feeling that could closely resemble how the Israelites felt when they left Egypt. I was 16, stereo-typed and sterilized, and I'd never been to bed with a woman. Upon the sudden release, I went crazy from the fresh air and new freedoms. I quit school and started getting rowdy. Like many of us, I "thought" I was in love and even planned to get married (I was 18 now).

Suddenly a lot of new pressures started closing in.

My folks were unhappy and worried about my future. I was reminded daily that I was a bum and a no-count because I quit high school. My fiancee's parents stressed these same points and assured me that I'd never marry their sanitary napkin as long as I was a drop-out and working at Al Vidos car wash. My father was chanting "join the Army, you'll be drafted anyway" and my mother and fiancee's parents were harping about going back to school.

I actually didn't want to do either of the two, so I did the stupidest most possible thing. An Army enlistment officer (who everyone knows by now are the greatest straight-faced liars in the art of un-truth) layed the old soft sell on me about how I could join up and finish high school in the Army and kill two birds with one stone. "And besides," he added, sounding much like someone I knew, "if you don't enlist you'll be drafted anyway." At the time I had no moral concepts or understanding of what I was actually doing; I was 18 and in a big rush, a blind rush, to attain those pre-set standards of living that make a person acceptable in this country —a car, money in the bank, my own home, etc. etc.

It would take no amount of guessing as to where I would end up once in the Army. I should of known all along but I think everyone is such a sucker once in their life. All of a sudden there I was in Vietnam with the 11th Cavalry, running around the jungle like a bunch of morons that don't know where they are, why they're there and where they're going. Fortunately there was one mainstay in Nam that could ease the tension in the "where-in-the-fuck-are-we?" existence, GRASS! "Oh lovely flower and herb of tranquility, that brings rest to tension and peace midst the war."

I spent seven months in Nam before I was wounded and shipped back to the States. I'd seen much and learned a lot in such a short time; all my old concepts turned to dust and were replaced by new ideas. It was a complete transition, as the "other" me had died and a new, or at least different, person had come home. I felt this metamorphosis strongly and while in the hospital in Japan just prior to going stateside I wrote this feeling in prose . . .

Dearest Mother and Father,
It is my assignment to inform you,
that your son has died in Vietnam.
Oh don't be alarmed . . . he's alive,
but the son you knew died,
when his mind went above,
and beyond the call,
of duty.
When his mind went above,
and beyond the whip,
of blind obediance.
When his concept of humanity went above,
and beyond the ideas
of white racist Americans.
When his morality and love of God went
    above,
and beyond the graven image,
of that old tattered flag in the attic.
When his love went above,
and beyond the crust
of your warm apple pie.
When his consciousness went above
and beyond the sickening duties and
    insanity
of war.

> In Peace, your son.

I remained hospitalized for half a year at Fort Ord, California, where doctors told me I'd be medically discharged. As it turned out, they were only lying again. In my own mind I was changed, a totally different person, and this new person was in no way, shape or form about to support the government and the armed force that was directly responsible for the thoughtless murder of Asian civilians, women and children alike, not to mention the deaths of thousands of American men senselessly used as a cover up for this capitalist war. It all stunk to me now, where I had at one time ignorantly accepted it.

I knew I couldn't go into some Army colonel and try to explain how I had had a change of heart and mind. I also knew that the man I was now would never go back to duty or any other forms of service towards this system. So I did what was left to do; I deserted.

I remained a deserter until I was apprehended some six months later. I was sentenced to six months at hard labor in the Fort Ord stockade where I saw men beaten and abused and exploited to no end. I saw a young man shot to death trying to escape. His offence? A.W.O.L. A congressional investigation followed when over 200 men reported that the guard never hollered halt nor fired a warning shot. He just simply blew the guy's heart out.

The guard, by the way, was given a 30 day leave and was reassigned.

Upon my release I married the woman I met during my desertion. I was reassigned to Fort Lewis, Washington, where my wife and I moved and lived off post. I made a valiant but unsuccessful try in coping with being in the Army, but my conscience would not allow it. I began having nervous breakdowns that soon developed into mild amnesia. I was put under psychiatric observation and it took only two meetings to convince the shrink that I was not really capable of remaining in the service. I was a mental disaster at age 22.

He immediately recommended me for separation from the service. This is where I was fucked over beyond reason. The final decision was in the hands of my company commander, who denied permission to have me removed from duty—his reason being that he thought I was capable of doing my job and saw no reason to let me go. At the time I *had no job* or particular duty because I was under psychiatric care, and I have two men who could testify to the fact.

But here's the clincher. Three days after my company commander told the doctor of his refusal, on grounds that I was capable for duty, I put in for a pass. My company commander denied the pass. And on the pass form there's an area for remarks on reasons as to why he denied the pass; in the block he wrote, "This man is under psychiatric care and is not capable of having a pass or leaving the area because of amnesia problems"—a *direct* contradiction of what he told the doctor three days prior. I kept a copy of this pass with his remark and signature and sent it along with a letter to Congressman

Teague. The result? Nothing. Later I was threatened to be put in the stockade the next time I had (as my company commander put it) "one of those so-called blackouts."

It was rather apparent that I was up against the wall. There was no one to turn to for help, not even a Congressman (pawn). I wasn't about to hang around and wait for the day when I'd have a mental blackout and wake up in prison. There was only one path left to take. Desertion.

My wife and I split to California and stayed in a Christian commune for four months until again I was apprehended. Only this time, being a lot more desperate, I escaped in three days. This time we ran to Seattle hoping to get established later in Canada. We were there about five months until someone snitched and I was captured again.

This is where my story draws to an end. The same day I was caught I escaped by diving through a window at the M.P. station at Fort Lawton. I was chased after dark through the surrounding woods. It was pitch dark, and in the chase I blindly ran over the edge of a 250-foot cliff, severing my spine and paralyzing me from the chest down for the remainder of my life. I was given an Undesirable Discharge on March 11th, 1971, after spending six months on my back at Madigan Army Hospital.

As for now, Amy and I are living on welfare and I am not eligible for Veterans benefits so we just get by with the essentials. But what counts is we're happy. I'd certainly rather be paralyzed for the rest of my life than give this system and this Army five minutes of my time. It's really sort of ironic and even funny how the Army chased after me for so long trying to sink their filthy hooks in me, and when they finally got me I just sort of self-destructed right in their hands like that tape on *Mission Impossible*. The real gas is that I didn't self-destruct completely.

There is still enough left of me to fight. I've still got my mind and my hands and a pen. I've written anti-war and pro-life articles for underground papers in Seattle, New York and Boston. I'm currently writing poems and articles for Vietnam Vets Against the War of which I am a member, and as far as life goes, God gives us all the power to love it, *and* one another, despite the lumps; besides, if we all really got it together, couldn't those lumps be hammered out?

George Jackson: Death on the Yard

by Tim Findley

The chubby little bailiff growled about the nuisance of it all as he took down names of reporters and let them out through the door in the bullet-proof glass partition.

"Nobody's gettin' back in unless I got their name," he muttered, glaring especially hard at the newsmen with long hair. He knew he wouldn't believe anything he saw about it on the tube tonight or in the papers tomorrow. He was just going through another one of those formalities for the sake of people he didn't like or trust.

On the other side of the glass, Dan Siegel stood in the aisle looking pissed at everybody, especially the little stream of reporters coming out and down the aisle, headed for a recess news conference outside the courtroom.

"I hope you do better on this than that story you had in today," he snarled, half threatening, at the last reporter out. The former student body president at U.C.-Berkeley, like a lot of other people in the spectator section of the court, was mad as hell about the page one account of San Quentin prison authorities' version of George Jackson's death.

Siegel not only didn't believe it, but considered it just one more calculated extension of the plot to kill George Jackson and bring down oppression on everybody in and out of prison who was fed up with Amerikan oppression and dared say so. If a story about how the prison guards say Jackson died was to run at all, Siegel and others felt, it ought to make it clear that prison authorities were lying. The Barb did that, the Tribe did that. Every publication that knew in advance that everything the prison people said was a lie did that. Only so far, there wasn't any proof that they were lying, just a lot of more or less rational speculation that the guards murdered George Jackson and that anybody who wasn't a pig and could think at all knew that. In fact, you didn't even have to be able to think much. If you weren't a pig, you just believed what everybody in the Soledad Brothers Defense Committee said happened, and called anybody who questioned it a pig. That's the way truth is arrived at. The chubby bailiff figured things about the same way, except he called everybody who questioned the prison authorities' version a bastard or a nigger.

"Hate vibes? You get hate vibes here?" Joy Marcus said at a rally outside the San Quentin gates a couple of days later.

Everybody was chanting, "We lo-uve George Jackson, We lo-uve Ruchell Magee."

But when that got worn out, everybody switched to "Three dead pigs ain't ee-nuf."

Hate vibes.

You're part of the solution, or you're part of the problem—you're with us or you're a pig. The only thing in between is keeping your mouth shut and staying out of it.

Same thing on the other side—you question some big ugly holes in their story and you're a commie creep who ought to be taught a lesson.

"PIG."

"NIGGER."

Everybody gets his rocks off calling somebody else names that mean essentially the same thing.

There's maybe less than a hundred people who really know the truth about what happened August 21, and probably none of them know all of it.

Officer O.G. Miller knows some of it. O.G. drew the gun tower that rain-puddled day back on January 13, 1970, when Soledad Prison opened up its new exercise yard outside "O" Wing adjustment center. An inmate crew had just finished painting its walls deep green the day before, a few hours before the rain doused

86

the Salinas Valley where Soledad sulks and chokes on its gutful of 2400 prisoners.

The "yard" is more like a pit. It's built into the space between "O" wing and the prison hospital, both of them branching off like crossbars on the long central pole of Soledad's main line. At the open end is a wall topped with barbed wire, good for handball, or for lining someone up to shoot them from the gun tower that perches at the other end of the small yard.

Sitting with a gun is usually one of the more boring jobs in the normal drudgery of being a correctional officer. New or "fish" bulls do it a lot as part of their orientation. Other officers draw it on rotation, and sometimes the older officers, or the ones the inmates most despise, prefer it up there. Inmates didn't like O.G. Miller. He'd had some trouble in the last year when he yanked one inmate drunk on prison-made pruno out of his cell and ran into a number of other inmates coming back from a movie. Miller had to blow his whistle and fight his way out of that one.

"O" wing is Soledad's prison within prison. Inmates, or as most of the heavier dudes would rather be called, "convicts," get sent there on "115's"—violations of prison rules that range from sticking a shank in somebody to having an extra sandwich in your "house" or cell. There isn't any definite time set for when you get out of the adjustment center—"hole" as it is more aptly and customarily referred to in the joint. Like California's indeterminate sentence law, there is no definite limit to how long you are to be punished. That is decided by a disciplinary committee comprised of the program administrator for the hole, maybe a couple of guards, and a correctional counselor (who is usually a former guard who switched to civilian clothing). So, sometimes, an inmate does a long stretch in the hole—maybe years. To imagine what the hole looks like, check out the local SPCA or a pet shop sometime. Rows of cages. At Soledad, barred doors reinforced with heavy, finger-cutting stretched steel mesh. The only thing the inmates get that the animals don't is a bunk, sometimes just a thin mattress on a concrete slab, and a combination toilet and sink. If everything is going just right, the inmates

87

in the hole are let out of their cells one hour a day to walk around on the narrow tier for exercise. The rest of the time, they sit in the cells and, like one dude said, "masturbate a lot." But the tedium and pressure of being locked down like that has to vent itself somewhere, and in Soledad and other joints, it often did so in almost constant screaming of racial epithets at other inmates. A few white inmates in the hole even carved swastika tattoos on their chests and called themselves Nazis. When they got a chance, they tried to "kill themselves a nigger." And when the blacks got a chance, they might get themselves a Nazi.

A lot of what is radical prison reform today began behind that situation. People who came out of the joint said guards and prison officials aggravated racial discord to make it easier on themselves. If the inmates fought each other, they'd never get it together enough to threaten the outnumbered guards. That was also the official reason for opening the new yard—an effort to cool racial tensions by providing an outlet in exercise.

So O.G. Miller took his post in the gun tower that day they opened the new yard. Inside "O" wing, they let the inmates out one at a time. Each man was given a skin search—get naked, open your mouth, lift your arms, bend over and spread your cheeks so the guards can look up your ass. And the guards made it very careful —letting out first a white inmate and then a black inmate, keeping the odds even. The white dudes went to one side of the yard and the blacks to the other side.

Miller sat up there with his .30-.30 watching it all. There were only 16 men in the yard when it started— a little over half the total due to come out. Miller said a "racial brawl" broke out—just what everybody was afraid of, authorities said later.

Miller said he blew his whistle once and then fired a warning shot, chipping a gouge into the newly painted green wall.

Then he fired again and again and again.

Earl Satcher, a black inmate who has spent more than five years in one hole or another in the California prison system, finally stopped it, running into the crowd of men with his hands raised and shouting:

88

"Cool it, cool it, this is just what the pigs want!"

But three men were already dead or dying and a fourth wounded. The three dead were all blacks, and, curiously, they were men considered among the key leaders of blacks in Soledad at the time. William Nolan, in fact, was considered among the heaviest dudes in Soledad. Cleveland Edwards and Alvin Miller, the other two dead men, were his close followers. Edwards was shot and killed as he ran to help the already mortally wounded Nolan. Nolan was also one of several inmates who had recently been arguing that the racial fights in the prison were being used by guards to keep inmates from rebelling against their mutual oppressors.

The wounded man was Billie Harris, a well-known prison Nazi. Authorities said he was hit by a ricochet.

Just two days short of the first anniversary of that incident in the "O" wing yard, while Harris was still doing time in the Soledad "hole," somebody shoved him into the showers, beat him, and stabbed him. He survived again.

Many inmates in Soledad felt immediately that the shooting in the yard was a set-up, designed primarily to get Nolan. Authorities said the shooting was regrettable, but necessary. And to back up their story, they invited an investigation by the Monterey County district attorney's office. It took three days for the district attorney to agree that it had been regrettable, but necessary.

It was so regrettable, in fact, that the D.A. called a news conference to say so.

In the bench-filled concrete rooms off Soledad's main line, inmates sat that evening and watched the latest news. And they booed bitterly under the glaring eyes of the guards when they heard how regrettable it had been.

John V. Mills probably never knew any of the truth about it. Even though he had been working there almost a year, the 26-year-old Mills was barely more than a "fish" guard. He still pulled odd-houred shifts in various spots in Soledad. The quiet-spoken and slightly built young officer had not yet found his own permanent niche in the prison. Not all guards are hated by inmates. Some of them are just seen as doing their time in a lousy job. The ones inmates hate are guards who go out of their way to make it hard on a convict. Maybe only because he hadn't been there long enough and wasn't sure of himself, and maybe because he understood something of the plight of the inmate, Mills didn't hassle people. Even some of the toughest inmates there at the time remember Mills as a docile guy who said very little —if indeed, the inmates remembered him at all.

The regular third-watch officer in "Y" wing was off that night, so Mills pulled another odd shift in a relatively unfamiliar wing of the prison.

It was sometime before the 11 PM lock-up. Mills was on the floor of the three-tiered wing, its iron steps marching up in the middle of the room to the darkened top tier where inmates with good records gain more privacy. The stairs partially concealed the four or five tables in the center of the wing with their coarse-cloth tops worn threadbare by countless domino matches.

The joint was getting ready to lock down for another night. Nobody was out on the main line; even the officers in the hallway were chatting around "control," the little bay window behind which switches can be pulled to shut off the line into three parts and release tear gas beneath the floor.

In the wings, inmates with enough good time had their own keys to their "houses." All the cells would be locked with a single bar at the lock-up, but until then, an inmate decided for himself whether his door was locked or open.

All Mills had to do was be there and keep an eye out for trouble. Usually, it was a boring job with much of the time spent in rapping with inmates or leaning back against the square-paned glass that looks out to the flat-colored mainline. The smells of concrete and wax, layers of strong soap and more wax, a heavy dull odor that somehow gets into everything, including the food. At night, people would be showering, or at the tables, or just leaning on another inmate's door, bull-shitting away another night before lock-up. Sometimes it's better to just rack out early and see if you can sleep into the next boring day of your time.

Mills had a whistle—they cost 50 cents and officers pay for them themselves. It is their only means of warning and, ultimately, protection. But he was slugged insensible and grabbed around the throat from behind, probably before he could think fast enough to remember where his whistle was. There was little noise as Mills was dragged up the iron stairs to the third tier, and many inmates in the wing probably did not even notice it. On the third tier, the only sound was a fleshy thunk of fists going into Mills' face, and a few moments later the whapping sound of him being beaten with his own flashlight.

Mills' body was edged over to the rim of the catwalk below the iron railing, lifted slightly, and shoved over the edge. It smacked heavily into the second tier railing and bounced off, twisting slowly and slapping dead on the concrete floor.

"Lock up! Lock up!" some inmate on the first tier who saw the body land shouted, and the doors to "Y" wing's "houses" went closed and cold before he could finish the words.

When a suspicious officer came in a few minutes later from the main line, he couldn't see Mills until he walked around the stairs. Filling with dread at the sight of the bloody body, and fearful for himself, he bent down to examine Mills and saw the note near his body.

"One down, two to go."

Mills was the first correctional officer to be killed at Soledad prison since it was built in 1952. Within a year there were three, and within 14 months, there were four.

When three inmates were charged with Mills' murder, the reports came out with special little flourishes. George Jackson, doing one-to-life on a robbery conviction in Los Angeles County. Fleeta Drumgo, doing six months to fifteen years for burglary in Los Angeles County. John Clutchette doing six months to fifteen years for burglary in Los Angeles County.

But that was just the simple background; thrown in as well were the interesting little items, like that one about Jackson which said he was known in the joint as "Karate Jackson." He wasn't, and prison authorities later denied they said he was. But Jackson was known for his skill in karate. In fact, he used to teach it informally in the prison yard.

The guards didn't like that, and more than once warned him to stop the lessons. Jackson, according to men who did time with him, had a reputation for being quick-witted and well-informed, especially about politics and organizing. He was known as a leader, but among more than a few inmates, he also had a reputation as a bully —a low rider who could shove people around just to prove his authority.

Fleeta Drumgo probably had more real friends because he seemed less threatening. With his small, almost delicate features and a manner given more to good-natured jiving than rhetoric, Drumgo had a reputation as someone who wouldn't knowingly hurt anybody.

John Clutchette was a more or less average con who didn't get in anybody's face very often. He was doing his own number, and, in prison lingo, he was getting "short." Clutchette had a parole date in April of that year. Had he not been busted for Mills' murder, he'd be on the streets today.

The racial turmoil at Soledad had been in and out of the headlines even before the January 13 incident, and groups of concerned reformers had already moved to point out the brutal inequities of the hole and the in-difference of the complicated prison system as being responsible for making California prisons not only a breed-ing ground for crime on the outside, but themselves the worst localized spots for crime in the state. While the rate of violent crimes was climbing steadily on the out-side in the last years of the Sixties, it was soaring at an even faster rate inside the state's toughest joints.

The prisons blamed that on the state's probation subsidy program—a program whereby counties are paid a state and sometimes federal subsidy to help keep a convicted felon on the streets under a parole program, or at least in a county jail nearer his own home. The probation pro-gram was largely a paper one, with not much supervision of the probationer and even less in the way of services and assistance to the convicted felon. But it kept more men out of prison—enough so that by 1970, the state said only 10 percent of the convicted felons were actually going to prison. Those that did go were the armed robbers, the murderers; the violent ones, the prison said. The guys who used to bring some balance to what authorities call the "mix," the bad check writers and the clever con artists, were going on parole. The guys who really went to prison, officials often complained, were really violent types who needed close watching and strict, tough walls.

The guys who went to prison in 1970 were more than 30 percent black.

The term "Soledad Brothers" just seemed to materialize naturally. For one thing, it was a lot easier than making clumsy repeated references to Jackson, Clutchette and Drumgo. But before long, it became clear that "Soledad Brothers" meant primarily George Jackson.

Jackson's entire mature life had been sliced up by a microcosm of some of the worst evils of California prisons, all tuned in and focused on Jackson's history with the state's institutions.

At 19, he was busted along with two others for a $70 gas station robbery. Jackson later copped out to driving the getaway car—a deal which usually brings a break. The break was that he was charged with second degree robbery and given a sentence of one year to life. The standard time a man serves in a California prison on a one-to-life sentence like that is usually about two and a half years. Then he's usually given a parole.

Jackson did almost 11 years.

"He just had a fat mouth," said one prison authority. He became known in prison as a militant and a tough guy—the kind who angers the righteous sensibilities of the eight-member Adult Authority. The Adult Authority is appointed by the governor. All are former peace officers—an FBI agent, a former chief of police, a couple of district attorneys, a former detective—men with that kind of background.

Their job is to fix a man's sentence at a specific time and decide when he is given parole. An inmate sees a panel of Adult Authority members for about five minutes once a year. They look over his prison record, ask him if he's sorry he committed the crime, if he can admit he did it, if he's well enough adjusted to get back on the bricks. Then they send him back to his cell to await the verdict.

The Adult Authority never did fix George Jackson's sentence, and it turned out to be life.

When the long, intricate courtroom procedures involving the Soledad Brothers got under way, they used to bring the three inmates into court in tight shackles. A chain was bound around their waist and linked to their handcuffs, and then looped down to hobble their ankles. The three sort of shuffled and clattered into court. And the courtroom procedures went slowly. From the start, radical-minded attorneys from San Francisco pointed at the bigotry and bias in Salinas where the courts had jurisdiction over nearby Soledad. As the early months trailed on and the numbers of spectators supporting the Soledad Brothers in court increased, Monterey County authorities finally, and with what appeared to be almost relief, granted a change of venue to the already overburdened courts of San Francisco. The Soledad Brothers were moved from the hole in "O" wing, to the hole in San Quentin—just downstairs from the prison's overflow death row population.

Before August 21, the efforts of Soledad Brothers attorneys had succeeded in disqualifying a total of four judges from the case on grounds that they would be biased in the matter or personally prejudiced toward the defendants.

Young Jonathan Jackson, George's 17 year-old-brother, was in court each time. He was the first to snap up with a militant fist in salute as he watched his brother come in in chains.

In August of 1970, Jonathan led what was up to then the most dramatic and among the most bloody attempted convict break-outs in California history. Jonathan, a judge, and two inmates were killed when two correctional officers opened fire as Jonathan tried to drive an escape van out of the Marin County Courthouse grounds. Angela Davis, who had become an attorney's investigator and a rallying figure in the Soledad Brothers case, was later accused of supplying the guns for Jonathan's bizarre move.

Most of that incident is well known, but a couple of

things usually go unnoticed. When Jonathan and three convicts led their hostages out of the courtroom that day, instead of walking directly out the entrance to the courthouse, they turned right—into a blind hallway that ended at the entrance to the press room. The press room door was locked. But later Jonathan shouted to a photographer, "We want the Soledad Brothers free in two hours."

"If I'd known ahead of time, I would have stopped him," George Jackson said a week later and almost a year to the day before his own death. "I know these guards here. I knew they'd shoot. I knew they'd kill Jonathan."

Now, in rallies and speeches and dialogues and rap sessions, the Soledad Brothers and Angela Davis and all political prisoners—victims, not villains, of the society —became inseparable causes. The pressure was on to reform prisons—not just pressure from radicals or inmates, but from straight lawmakers and the press and even from some prison people themselves.

About 150 bills on prison reform were proposed in the state legislature in the last year. The Department of Corrections successfully opposed every one, saying that traditionally prison reform has best been left in the hands of prison people.

Indeed, California's prisons were known more for their contradictions than their consistent brutalities. There were bitterly cruel adjustment centers in at least four of the 13 prisons, but there were innovative conjugal visiting programs in three of those same joints. There were buildings in use as cell blocks that were built in the 1870's, but there were two major prisons without any wall at all that were considered models of enlightened penology.

To aggravate the contradictions, prison authorities were not just hassled by pressures of radical reformers. A revolt was building inside the ranks of correctional officers at the same time. In all the years from 1953 until January, 1970, there had been only four correctional officers killed on duty. But between January, 1970, and August 1, 1971, there were five. The officers were mad —mad at the prison administration for not providing what they considered necessary new safety procedures and for becoming "too soft" on inmates. Mad, especially, at the new waves of attorneys they suspected of stirring up the new, dangerously radical mood of inmates. (One group of officers at Soledad even tried to lay direct blame for three killings there on the California Rural Legal Assistance program—a program that provides legal aid largely to victimized farm workers.)

The officers are among the lowest paid of state employees. Their ranks include a number of retired military men to whom the meager salary of a correctional officer rounds out their retirement benefits. They feel a kinship with hardhats and cops, but they also felt that theirs is a special and significant profession all its own. For that reason, they dislike being called "guards," and hate it even more when more and more inmates call them "pigs."

Partially in response to this, prison authorities began to keep a closer watch on attorneys and attorneys' investigators who visited inmates—especially radical "celebrity" inmates in the new politics of prison reform. There were repeated spates of hunger strikes and general strikes at various prisons behind a series of demands, usually beginning with a change in the indeterminate sentence and including better treatment in the adjustment centers. When they happened, prison authorities began to make more and more little comments about radical attorneys "stirring up" the inmates.

The courts were getting angry, too. In April, during another Soledad Brothers hearing, someone in the spectator section tried to pass George Jackson a leaflet of some kind. A guard yanked it away from Jackson, and Jackson swung on the guard. In an instant, two other men leaped over the rail. There was a brief scuffle—won by reinforced squads of guards.

Jimmy Carr, a close friend of Jackson's went to county jail as a result of that incident. His name was all but forgotten until about three months later.

For Jackson, and for the other Soledad Brothers, it was a time of soaring and slumping contradictions. George's book, *Soledad Brother: The Prison Letters of George Jackson,* was well received and even winning wide acclaim.

Like What You've Read? The Best Is Yet To Come.

ROLLING STONE is a lively, innovative magazine covering the full spectrum of popular culture and the personalities that make it happen. Newsmaking, provocative interviews ranging from Paul McCartney and Ray Charles to Daniel Ellsberg and Truman Capote. Features on everything from Inside the Dylan Tour and Who's Who on the Watergate Committee to the Corporate Structure Surrounding The Grateful Dead and a Very Candid View of Hugh Hefner—not to mention the most quoted record reviews in the business and an industry inside second to none. ROLLING STONE: informative, controversial and always readable.

You can enjoy the luxury of having ROLLING STONE delivered right to your door and save a substantial amount of money by starting a subscription. A 1-year (26 issues) subscription costs $12.00—a $7.50 savings off the newsstand price—and guarantees that you won't miss even one great issue. Be thrifty, enjoy home delivery and get "all the news that fits" too by starting your ROLLING STONE subscription today.

Enter my subscription to ROLLING STONE for 1-year (26 issues) at $12.00 (a $7.50 savings off the newsstand price).

□ Payment Enclosed   □ Bill Me Later

›Name⎯⎯⎯⎯⎯⎯⎯⎯⎯⎯⎯⎯⎯⎯⎯⎯⎯⎯⎯⎯⎯⎯⎯⎯⎯⎯

Address⎯⎯⎯⎯⎯⎯⎯⎯⎯⎯⎯⎯⎯⎯⎯⎯⎯⎯⎯⎯⎯⎯⎯⎯

City/State/Zip⎯⎯⎯⎯⎯⎯⎯⎯⎯⎯⎯⎯⎯⎯⎯⎯⎯⎯⎯⎯⎯
                                                              0923

This offer applies to U.S., APO & FPO only. For foreign and airmail rates, please write to the address on this card.

The pressures for prison reform were at an all-time peak. The trial was delayed and delayed as attorneys won small but potentially significant points about bigotry and the dehumanization of prison.

But the San Francisco courtroom had also been converted to a little Bastille all its own. A unique bullet-proof shield was built to separate spectators from the court. Armed deputies waited out of sight, but ready, at the hearings.

In prison, there were inching improvements, but raging discontent. There was frequent talk that radical inmates were being "set up" to be killed. In the joint, it is not necessary for a guard to kill an inmate he wishes to see dead. All he need do, if the inmate is well known enough, is allow him some freedom among certain inmates who can be relied upon to strike at him for the mere opportunity of gaining a reputation.

And for the officers, it was a time of genuine, knot-tight tension. On July 21, San Quentin officer Leo Davis was standing guard in a quiet hospital corridor over an inmate who had supplied some important information on one of the guard killings at Soledad. Davis was killed by at least two inmates trying to get at the "snitch."

All of it was bringing a ponderous mood of tension into August and the expected opening of the Soledad Brothers trial at mid-month.

George Jackson's last published writing was in the June issue of *The Black Scholar,* an issue devoted entirely to "The Black Male." Jackson's piece was a scholarly one dealing with revolution and the necessity of a "collective sense of community" for those oppressed. It dwelt in part on the recent crisis in the Black Panther Party between Eldridge Cleaver and Huey Newton, and criticized Cleaver for failing to see the need for separation "between military and political cadre, between military and political action." In concluding, Jackson said he had written Cleaver asking the self-exiled former convict to show proof he was not "a compulsive disrupter or agent provocateur." Cleaver replied, Jackson said, with burning invective "—in short, a vendetta." Then Jackson's article took on a sharp threatening tone to Cleaver, warning that 7000 miles and the prison walls were not enough to protect Cleaver from "my special brand of discipline . . . . The substructured prison movements are gaining momentum."

Jackson's concluding paragraph sounded like an ominous invitation.

"My trial is set for early August, 1971, there'll be a hearing in between of course, if they are at all like the last you'll get to see my special bastardized style of martial arts; I'm working hard to stay in form also. I wasn't at my best last showing. I'll clean them all next time they attack—attend. Let me see your style."

The hearing he referred to was set for August 23.

* * *

For nearly eight years of his 10 years in prison, George Jackson had been in one or another "hole" in the joint—and for all the period since Mills was killed, he'd been held in the tightest security. George Jackson knew all about skin searches—for years he went through at least two of them a day. He knew well the difficulties of smuggling something past such a search.

In mid-afternoon of Saturday, August 21, he took his last skin search. Attorney Stephen Bingham had been kept waiting at the San Quentin gate for more than three hours, but finally, Associate Warden James Park relented and allowed him permission to visit with Jackson.

A woman later identified as Vanita Anderson who gave her address as the Oakland headquarters of the Black Panther Party was forced to wait outside the visiting area for Bingham. She complied, handing Bingham his briefcase to take into the visiting room.

The metal detector—convicts call it a "snitch box" —sounded its little electronic bleeps as Bingham went through. The attorney explained to the guard that it was his cassette tape recorder, a routine tool of attorneys. The officer followed his routine also, taking out the battery pack of the recorder to see that nothing was hidden behind it, and allowing Bingham to go into the separate visiting room once reserved only for Death Row inmates.

From this point on, the sequence becomes a question of who is telling the truth.

Prison authorities said Bingham had a 9mm Spanish Astra M-600 hidden in the gutted-out tape recorder. In their reconstruction of the events, they said Bingham passed the weapon and a wig he had hidden elsewhere to Jackson. Jackson, they said, placed the automatic in the wig and pulled the arrangement down over his own full natural.

An Astra M-600 is eight and one-eighth inches long —not a small gun. The *San Francisco Chronicle* tried with a black model and an Afro wig to conceal an identical weapon, with the handles removed as authorities said they were. It didn't work. Even when the model had the gun fairly concealed, it wobbled when he moved and he instinctively put his hands to his head. But maybe there was some trick to it.

Jackson had to walk about 50 yards out of the visiting area and through the pleasantly landscaped mall that fronts on the prison chapel and is used as a deceptive showpiece for casual visitors. Officer Frank DeLeon, a veteran guard who happened to draw that Saturday shift, walked with him as an escort. Out the iron-doored gate and under No. 1 Gun Tower, past the glassed, unarmed enclosure of Four Post, and into the entrance to the adjustment center at the north end of the drab-colored building. On arrival, Jackson would have to go through another skin search in a rectangular room occupied by the officers and separated from the other inmates of the adjustment center by a barred sally port.

Part of the procedure in a skin search is to rub your hand through an inmate's hair to see if any small weapon might be concealed there. But officers later admitted that they were reluctant to do so to militant blacks who resented white guards' hands on their proud naturals. So, often, the procedure broke down into one of having the inmate rub his own hand through his hair, or, more likely, dragging his comb through his hair. Assuming

99

the gun was securely hidden beneath a wig, it might have been missed.

But authorities said one officer spotted something in Jackson's hair.

"What's that, a pencil?" they reported the officer as saying.

At that, according to authorities, Jackson whipped out the pistol and barked, "This is it." They were the same words his brother used in the Marin County Courthouse a year earlier.

Jackson, authorities said, surprised the guards even before he slapped one of two ammunition clips into his weapon. Where the clips were hidden was never made clear.

Inmates tell it differently. Through attorneys who interviewed some of the other 28 inmates in the adjustment center that day, they said it was a guard who pulled the gun on Jackson—apparently intending to kill him and other inmates who were ordered out of their cells by the guards.

As the inmates were directed to one side of the wing, attorneys reported, Jackson yelled at an inmate, "Get down, get down." The guard turned his attention for a moment, and Jackson wrestled the gun from him.

Jackson, according to the inmates' account, realized it was him the guards wanted. He reportedly said, "Well, they want me," and dashed out into the mall to his death.

"Getting outside the adjustment center was the only way to save the lives of the others inside," said Ruchell Magee's attorney, Phillip Ryan. "They [the guards] could not justify going in and machine-gunning down the men inside with Jackson dead in the courtyard."

There are some things hard to visualize in life and therefore easy to pass over. One of them is the agony of years in a single concrete cell. The day-by-day buildup of frustration, loneliness, fear, anger. The sworls of your finger tips to take up interest in the endless hours. The jaw-tightening bitterness. The numbing despair.

Try to feel it. Try to let it soak down and boil inside. And then imagine a moment when somebody opens your cage and there is a chance, however slim, however fleeting, at freedom. And if not freedom, then at least revenge.

The authorities said Jackson ordered his captive guards —three of them—to open the cells on the first tier of the adjustment center, and shouted to the inmates, "We've got to do it now."

In the adjustment center that day was the kind of "mix" that scares hell out of corrections authorities. Not only were the Soledad Brothers there, but so was Ruchell Magee, one of the inmates Jonathan Jackson sought to free. So was Hugo Pinell, an inmate accused of killing one of the three dead guards at Soledad. So was Johnny Spain, a friend of Jackson's from Soledad, brought up to San Quentin only two or three months before.

Now try to imagine the other thing.

Put your finger on your throat and feel the soft, easy pumping of the jugular vein. Feel how vulnerable it is, see how reluctant you are to press hard on it.

It's the way they kill pigs in the stockyard. They say it doesn't hurt much, but the pigs squeal and kick with terror. Even after they lose consciousness, they jerk and jolt against their bounds, fighting, screaming for life. It's only part of it to die that way. The other part is to kill that way. To be indifferent to the gruesome last few minutes while the blood spurts in a torrent out on the concrete floor.

Five men—three officers and two white "tier tenders" (inmates given some degree of freedom in the adjustment center)—died, or at least started to die that way that Saturday. The principal weapon, authorities said, was a razor blade attached to a tooth brush. Two of the officers, including Frank DeLeon who had escorted Jackson from the visiting room, were also shot in the back of the head. According to authorities, five of the dead were dragged to Jackson's cell and thrown in there in a pile. They said there were wide streaks of blood down the tier hallway. One officer, whose throat was also cut, survived, authorities said, because he was thrown in the cell first and the others tossed in on top of him.

Nobody noticed he was still alive until after it was all over.

The bodies of the officers, authorities said, had been stripped of clothing. They speculated that it would be used as part of the escape attempt.

Authorities said it was 2:50 PM, a relatively quiet time on a Saturday in the "joint." One of the at least four daily "counts" takes place at 2:30 PM. Inmates all over the prison line up in front of or in their cells, and guards take a nose count to be sure everyone is there. Chow in the adjustment center usually comes about 2:30 PM—that's one reason why visits with adjustment center inmates are supposed to end by that time.

The authorities said all seemed quiet until an officer noticed some flashes of movement in the adjustment center. An officer on the second tier had, meantime, heard what he thought to be strange noises. The first guard went to investigate the movement, authorities said, and as he peered in an inside door in the adjustment center, a shot tore through the window and past him. He ran back for the yard, furiously blowing his whistle. On the second tier, the other guard was now sure he'd heard a strange noise; his alarm went in almost simultaneously.

That, authorities said, is when George Jackson suddenly bolted out the door, running hard across the mall in the general direction of an alley way that dead-ends in a 20-foot-high, barbed wire-topped wall. Behind him came Johnny Spain, but nobody else.

George Jackson was hit twice by gunfire from Tower One over the main gate and a gun railing near the alley way. One shot hit him in the top of the head, and his body lay face down in a pool of blood far short of the wall. Spain, authorities said, dived into some bushes and froze.

Inside the adjustment center, two live guards were still being held as hostages. Both were bleeding from the neck, and prison officials said one inmate had given up on the razor blade and was jabbing and digging for one of the guards' jugular vein with the file end of a pair of finger nail clippers.

Officers armed with machine guns and rifles burst into the adjustment center.

"We've got hostages," an inmate reportedly shouted.

"That doesn't matter," an officer shouted back and sprayed a wall with bullets. The two hostages ran out. The glimpse of freedom was over, and the inmates were ordered to take off their clothing and lay face down and nude in the mall.

By this time, Associate Warden Park had turned in a county-wide alarm. The prison was ringed with scores of police, some oddly dressed in off duty uniforms—tennis shorts, loud sports shirts, blue jeans. All were heavily armed and waiting.

The inmates lay face down on the turf for more than six hours. Some of them were hog-tied, their wrists to their ankles; others were shackled.

Alan Mancino, one of the inmates nude on the grass, tried to stand up at one point. A rifle blast struck near him, grazing his leg, authorities said, with chips of cement.

There were rumors of another gun in addition to the 9mm Jackson carried with him in his last sprint for freedom, and authorities began an intensive search of the adjustment center.

They did not find another gun, but they did discover an assortment of ammunition—a 4.10 shell, a .38, a .22—all hidden in hollowed out bars of soap or squares of processed cheese. A zip gun barrel was also found. And on both Jackson's body and hidden in the adjustment center, authorities said they found small vials of what was later identified as a plastique-type explosive. A couple of days later, authorities said they found an Afro wig stuffed down a toilet in one cell.

The adjustment center inmates lay there on their faces, not knowing what to expect. There were five dead men inside and three others wounded, and behind them, they could hear one of the wounded officers begging to be given a gun.

Medical attendants pushed the bodies of the dead officers on gurneys out of the adjustment center and through San Quentin's upper yard, down the middle of the quadrangle of cell blocks. And some inmates cheered.

Outside the wall, Associate Warden Park was talking

to the press. Television viewers that night would see, and ignore, a rarity on their tubes. For once, the TV people did not bleep out the swear words. They came out just like Park said them when he blamed the incident on "these bullshit dilettante revolutionaries."

It was all part of an elaborate escape plan aided by people on the outside, Park said.

And that went by people a little too fast, too.

* * *

Warden Park knows much of the truth about what happened. The question is, how much of it has he told?

From the variety of ammunition found inside the adjustment center, it was early concluded by prison authorities that there was an escape planned, though probably not for that Saturday. Jackson, the theory went, was forced to step up his plan by the unexpected discovery of the gun.

A few days later, we learn from a newspaper source very close to the FBI, that there was, indeed, an escape plan, and that a map of it had been discovered in a pocket of a pair of trousers Jimmy Carr, George Jackson's old friend from Soledad, had sent to the cleaners. Furthermore, authorities said there had been a note smuggled out to George's sister, Penny, instructing her to smuggle in explosives in tubes inserted in her vagina. There had been an incident two weeks before, the authorities said, when Penny came in with two children. One of them, her nephew, lit up the snitch box as he went into the visiting room. The boy pointed at the buckles on his shoes, officials said, but they searched him and found a toy gun hidden in his pants. Miss Jackson complained that it was simple harassment of the children, but authorities said they thought it was some sort of trial run.

The theory that George Jackson wrestled a gun away from a guard about to kill him and other adjustment center inmates requires a good deal of blind faith in the tellers. First of all, even assuming a guard would take the extraordinary risk of smuggling a gun into prison and even into the adjustment center, he would still be outnumbered if, as the inmates say, he let them out of their cells. He might kill Jackson, but with only one gun he would surely seal his own fate as well.

Frankly, the guards could find simpler ways of doing in an inmate they wished dead.

There is a theory that Jackson never made it back to the adjustment center—that he was shot as he left the visiting room. If so, that doesn't explain how the officers died in the adjustment center, and certainly not how two of them were shot in the back of the head.

John Clutchette went to a visit with his mother, Mrs. Doris Maxwell, shortly after Jackson went to his visit with Bingham. Mrs. Maxwell remembers George stopping at their visiting room and saying hello to her as he was led back—a strange act for a man smuggling in a gun and an even stranger thing for his escort guard to permit. Mrs. Maxwell, in fact, believes she was the last visitor to leave the prison that day, another strange fact, since authorities let the visit go on longer than usual—longer than the normal 2:30 cut-off time, she said. The guard who escorted John Clutchette back to the adjustment center was one of those wounded.

George Jackson died of a bullet that hit him in the top of the head, coursed down in front of his spine, shattered two ribs, and exited from his lower back. The wound is inconsistent with the angles of fire at a running man from the two gun locations around the mall. It seemed likely that Jackson was first hit in the ankle, and then hit again with the fatal shot as he struggled to his feet.

He was running for a wall he could not possibly have scaled. A wall that does not lead to freedom, but merely to a slice of no-man's land between the yellow stone wall and the fenced perimeter of San Quentin. Even prison authorities conceded that if Jackson was running for that wall, he knew he was committing suicide.

There are likely to have been inmate witnesses to the shooting as well as officers, since the mall is a site of frequent activity, and since four buildings, in all of which there might have been inmates, look out on the mall. But so far, no inmate witnesses have been identified, save those in the adjustment center.

But authorities have worked hard to establish that

the incident was an aborted escape attempt—they point to the note, the map, the ammunition, and to Penny Jackson's earlier visit.

All of those clues, however, were apparently discovered before August 21. In fact, authorities said they had identified Jackson as the leader of a clandestine revolutionary group of convicts months earlier.

If that is so, did they suspect something was coming? And if they did, what were they waiting for? Perhaps to see who would bring in the gun? Perhaps to see who on the outside was involved? Whose plan, in that case, went awry? The plan to escape—or the plan to halt the escape?

Steve Bingham might know something about it, but neither he nor Vanita Anderson have been seen since that Saturday.

Alan Mancino might know something, too, but he has been spirited away from San Quentin to the Nevada State Prison for safekeeping—they say he is talking. If the authorities knew about a planned break, did they just learn of it from outside sources, or was there a snitch inside the adjustment center? Did Mancino try to stand up out of fear of the guards that day, or out of fear of the other inmates?

There is a good deal of it that everybody should know. They should know that one of the principal culprits was the prison system itself—that whatever the motive, what happened August 21 was the manifestation of an ugly failure of the American system of justice.

The two black dudes who walked into Ingleside Police Station in San Francisco a week later and blew the chest off Sergeant James Young knew that much. They probably didn't know much more of the truth about it, even though they righteously believed they did, because it was clearly done to "avenge" George Jackson.

But it's almost certain that Sergeant Young didn't know even as much about it as they did.

He just died.

And counting from that gloomy day at Soledad in January, 1970, he was the 14th person to be killed behind this particular sticky web of half truth and doubt

—and the first of those to die outside the secret-shielding walls of prison.

Hate vibes.

HOMETOWN FOLKS
Letters from American
Political Prisoners

by Timothy Ferris

Silence is the subtlest penalty of imprisonment. Like most people on the outside, we did not realize how hard it was to get in touch with prisoners until we tried to write to some of them. We sent personal letters to more than 300 inmates in institutions all over the country, inviting them to contribute to this article. Nearly half our letters were returned, some accompanied by tortuously worded forms from prison officials expressing logic that could have come from Kafka. The Federal Correctional Institution—as it is called—at Danbury, Connecticut, advised that "the reason your letter was opened was due to the fact that you failed to place your name and return address on the envelope in which your letter was contained." The return address was in fact printed on the envelope.

Most prisoners are limited to a list of "approved correspondents" with whom they can exchange letters. Almost always this list is restricted to family, friends, attorneys, and officials of the prison system. If a prisoner lists, say, the editor of the *New York Times,* the news director of WKCR radio, the US ambassador from

108

Equador or the Pope, prison officials can simply say no.

Regulations vary widely from state to state, but most have in common that they are couched in humanitarian terms while equipped with an escape clause vague enough to allow prison officials to restrict correspondents virtually at will. In federal prisons, inmates are allowed to write to people outside their immediate family only if "it appears that such correspondence will not adversely affect the inmate's chances of rehabilitation or that it will not be detrimental to the well-being of the inmate or his correspondent," whatever that means. New Mexico allows acquaintances on the list if "a bona fide friendship exists and the correspondence is for a legitimate purpose."

Censorship of the mail typically is justified on principles equally vague. Texas regulations require that "inmates shall limit their letters to matters of personal interest to friends and relatives." In New York, a prisoner's letter can be handed back to him if, as the rule puts it, "You did not stick to your subject."

When it comes to the press, prison authorities draft rules like men bailing out a sinking ship. Many states —as large as New York and as small as Vermont—simply prohibit inmates from communicating with news media. If a prisoner leaks information to a newspaper without permission he can be punished, whether the information was true or not. Other more "liberal" states allow letters to newspapers and magazines, but censor them. Pennsylvania prison authorities are not permitted to censor inmates' personal mail (except on a spot check basis), but when it comes to the media, letters "shall be censored" if they are "clearly misleading" or perhaps just "potentially misleading" in the opinion of the authorities.

Recently, journalists in several states have filed suits which may force the US Bureau of Prisons to liberalize its regulations about correspondence and visits with journalists. The Department of Justice is working on new rules, and if they prove sufficient to evade the suit many states may follow their example.

Many prisons censor publications with as free a hand as they restrict correspondence. Oregon bans "publications which excite, encourage and/or promote violence or disorder," a provision which sounds reasonable enough but which in practice can be used to stop anything from a daily paper on up. In Hawaii, prisoners may not be exposed to "comics, risque magazines or pocketbooks of a derogatory nature." The man in charge of mail at Wyoming State Penitentiary refused to allow an inmate to receive *Rolling Stone* or the *Whole Earth Catalog* because, he said, "You're here for rehabilitation, not to read about hippies."

Books prohibited in New York state prisons include the *I Ching,* Martin Sostre's *Letters From Prison,* and Hunter Thompson's *Hell's Angels.*

The cases which appear here were assembled over a period of three months primarily through the help of the prisoners themselves. Our purpose is to allow them to communicate. They are in no way meant to represent all prisoners; each case is different, and we heard from no one who claimed to speak for anyone but himself.

The very nature of prison regulations distorts the sample. A disproportionate number of the prisoners we heard from were white, middle-class men in medium or minimum-security institutions, where mail regulations are more liberal. Most of them are accustomed to writing letters and are well aware that prison conditions for them are not what they are for some others. For, say, a black man educated in ghetto schools and county jails and now locked in solitary in some federal prison, the obstacles to communication with anyone outside can be almost insurmountable. In a sense, then, these cases represent the luckier recipients of political justice in America.

Few women are represented, partly because of the law's strange courtliness toward them (prosecutors and judges often let women dope offenders go and jail their men), partly because the draft laws do not address themselves to women, and partly because this sociey imposes stronger moral sanctions against women in prison than against men, so that each is more likely to feel ashamed.

Nor can we hear from the dead: Anthony Jones, 19 years old, an asthmatic who died after being forcibly administered four heavy doses of Thorazine in a so-called School for Boys in Illinois. Philip Lassiter, a victim of sickle cell anemia at a Virginia prison farm, who screamed in his cell day and night for almost a week before he died. Willie Stewart, a frail 17-year-old boy who succumbed under the harassment of guards before he could complete a one-day sentence at Cummins Prison Farm outside Little Rock, Arkansas. Lloyd Lott, 20 years old, who did time at Parchman Prison in Mississippi, was released, and shot himself when it appeared he would be sent back again.

Who is a political prisoner? For the purpose of this article we have included not only prisoners whose alleged crimes were political in nature but prisoners whose due process was, at some point, warped because of their social or political background. On this matter, Angela Davis, destined to be one of America's most celebrated political prisoners, says the following in her recent book *If They Come in the Morning:*

In this country . . . where the special category of political prisoners is not officially acknowledged, the political prisoner inevitably stands trial for a specific criminal offense, not for a political act. Often the so-called crime does not even have a nominal existence. As in the 1914 murder frame-up of the IWW organizer, Joe Hill, it is a blatant fabrication, a mere excuse for silencing a militant crusader against oppression. In all instances however, the political prisoner has violated the unwritten law which prohibits disturbances and upheavals in the status quo of exploitation and racism. This unwritten law has been contested by actually and explicitly breaking a law or by utilizing constitutionally protected channels to educate, agitate and organize the masses to resist.

A deep-seated ambivalence has always characterized the official response to the political prisoner. Charged and tried for a criminal act, his guilt is always political in nature. This ambivalence is perhaps best captured by Judge Webster Thayer's comment upon sentencing Bartholomew Vanzetti to 15 years for an attempted payroll robbery: "This man, although he may not have actually committed the crime attributed to him, is nevertheless morally culpable, because he is the enemy of our existing institutions."

During the months that we worked to contact these prisoners, people all over the country contributed their efforts with startling readiness. We owe thanks especially

111

to Keith Stroup of the National Organization for Reform of the Marijuana Laws, to the American Civil Liberties Union, and to Andrea Wyatt, poet, songwriter and founder of the First National Bail Fund of America.

—*Timothy Ferris*

Refusing to Kill

1. The government shall decide who may lawfully be killed and who may not. **2.** Anyone who kills someone the government has not said it is all right to kill is guilty of murder. **3.** Anyone who won't kill someone the government says it is all right to kill is guilty of Refusing to Kill. **4.** Anyone who interferes with the government in telling its citizens who to kill is guilty too. **5.** Anyone who abets or encourages someone who has Refused to Kill is guilty of Conspiracy to Refuse to Kill. **6.** Some offenders may choose certain alternatives to killing, such as helping the sick. Some may not. It shall be determined by a panel of men who think the government is right. **7.** Penalty. Offenders are to be locked up for the period of time they would otherwise have spent killing.

* * *

Larry Zink burned his draft card February 13, 1969 at a student-faculty meeting at the University of Nebraska, where he was studying electrical engineering. He asked others to join him; none did.

He refused induction, was arrested for burning his card and sentenced under the Youth Corrections Act to "zip-six" an indeterminate term of up to six years. Last March he entered prison at Springfield, Mo., was transferred to El Reno, Oklahoma ("the cesspool of the federal prison's youth division," says Zink), and finally entered the minimum-security Federal Correctional Institution in Seagoville, Texas, outside Dallas.

"My reasons for becoming involved with resistance and antiwar activity were more philosophical than political. I could find no value higher than life to justify the taking of another human life. For this reason I felt I could not continue to be silent while this country carried out mass slaughter of human life and the destruction of the Vietnamese culture. . . .

"In all three of the prisons I have been in I have found the idea of rehabilitation to be a cruel joke. The libraries are, for all practical purposes, non-existent. The educational facilities at first glance look fair, but few of the teachers have any college education, much less a degree. . . . I can't think of a single privilege, whether it be liberal mail rules or honor housing, the main purpose of which is not control of the inmates. Even basic things that one on the street would take as a right, like a little privacy, on the inside must be obtained by playing the sick games and trying not to lose one's self-respect in the process. . . .

"Although my immediate oppressors are the people in the Bureau of Prisons, I can't lay much of the responsibility on their shoulders, but must place it where it belongs, on American society. It is the citizens of this country who force the prisons to operate on their small budgets, and their attitude of 'I don't want to be bothered with it,' which allows these conditions to continue.

"As for me personally, I guess it can best be summed up by stating that I don't regret taking the steps that led me here, and I would probably do it again. . . .

* * *

Karl Meyer has a wife, three children and a 14-year record of resisting federal taxes because their revenue is "overwhelmingly devoted to warfare." From 1968 to 1970, Meyer paid no tax at all—he filed deduction claims covering all his income—and last April he was sentenced to two years in the Federal Correctional Institution at Sandstone, Minnesota.

"As I was led from the courtroom to begin serving two years, I had only time to wave briefly to my seven-year-old son, William. In the marshal's lockup I broke down and cried. But this time has not in any way broken down our commitment to respect and defend our life and the lives of others. . . .

"I do believe that we should all strive to live in a simpler way. If we work part-time for wages and live on less than taxable incomes, we will have extra time to grow, create and do more things for ourselves, or to

113

offer our work as a gift to people in need of it. Even if we work full time for taxable wages, but successfully resist collection of the taxes, we should still live simply in order to share our surplus money with others who are in need. I have done this all my adult life and intend to go on with it.

"There is one main thing that the government asks of ordinary people to support its military policies: Just go along and pay your taxes. And because that is the main thing asked of us, that's one thing we will never do."

* * *

Richard Fox was locked up in Seagoville last October on a "zip-six" sentence for failing to report for his pre-induction physical or for induction itself.

"When I first awakened at age 22, I had dropped out of college, was married and living in the Sangre de Cristo mountains of northern New Mexico. My wife Mimi and I were living in an old, smoky and magic tipi while the cabin was being built. We had found our way back to a home and a way of living we'd always wanted. Hard work was all it cost us.

"I wrote my draft board and explained that I was a pacifist and why, and that I would leave them alone, and expect the same.

"Throughout the winter tension and friction between the people on the land we shared grew and spread to the local residents. In the spring men came with guns and killed a friend. The land purchase failed, so we left to find land of our own and start again. For two years we moved from place to place, working a while then leaving. . . . Eventually we worked our way to California and the mountains east of San Bernardino. By this time Mimi was pregnant, so we stayed, and Jedediah was born there in November 1970. In December I received a letter of induction. I remember thinking how clean the snow looked as I crumpled the notice into the trash.

". . . In February my parents contacted us and said they'd been notified by the FBI that I should turn myself in and apply for CO status. They said that they had to tell where we were living. I said I understood and not

114

to worry, but I did; we had no money and the truck was acting up and Jed was only a few months old. So I drove down the mountain and turned myself in. All my questions concerning applying for CO were ignored. . . . Six weeks later, agents came and busted me in my parents home in El Paso, where it all had started. . . ."

* * *

"My name is Mike McClain. I'm currently serving three years in Seagoville on the charge of mailing obscene matter. After receiving numerous warnings and notices to come and be drafted, I decided it would be keen to let my local draft board know exactly how I felt about their army, so I sent them a graphic picture of my dick.

"Needless to say, they didn't find it humorous, and I soon after came home to find two FBI agents waiting with a warrant. The trial was a farce: The judge sitting upon his throne, rather bored, a huge emblem embedded in the wall behind him, and behind the wall behind that, cages holding some of the finest people I'd met. . . . I got three years.

"[At Seagoville] I have felt negative pressure put on my projects to get prisoners together to play music. It really threatens them, because it's organized, self-sustaining activity that they can't control short of stopping it entirely. I really enjoy doing it, not so much because I love it and they hate it, but because it is a positive way to maintain my soul, which they try so desperately to take away. That's all prison can do to you—rip off your spirit. The time in itself would not be so painful. It's all the other shit you have to contend with: 'rehabilitation,' 'adjusting' so you'll no longer be a thorn in society's side; mental shock treatment, honing down all the peaks and filling in the valleys, shaping you into another helpless ball-bearing for their insane machine. Censored mail both ways, censored books and magazines (*Rolling Stone* is not allowed in), room shakedowns, uniform haircuts, practiced sameness. . . .

"My woman is waiting outside for me. I miss her. I miss the freedom. I had my music, the peace and brotherhood of my friends, but this must come first. I wouldn't

115

feel the same if I had split. I'm no martyr, but this is something that had to be done, apparently."

* * *

Alan Sconzert is doing time in Seagoville. "I was brought up in a military atmosphere for 19 years. As a junior in high school I was even an alternate appointment to the Naval Academy, but was disqualified because of poor eyesight. Then in my senior year I began to question the morality of the Vietnam war. That summer one of my very close friends burned his draft card. This was a turning point for me. Finally two years later I also severed relations by burning my draft card. . . .

"I was arrested in May 1971 for failure to report for induction. From this point on, the entire experience was shrouded in an air of unreality. My court-appointed lawyer had formerly been a consultant for my local draft board. His partner was a former prosecuting attorney for the US who specialized in selective service violations. Both of them had a very difficult time trying to understand the rationale behind my action. Throughout their entire counseling, even during the trial, they attempted to persuade me to seek a conscientious objector's status. Even the presiding judge said the charges would be dropped were I to return to my draft board and initiate applications for CO. The judge refused to accept my plea of *nolo contendre*. My friends were not allowed inside the courtroom because they were not 'suitably attired.' I pled guilty and was sentenced to two years."

* * *

A draft board in Minneapolis turned down Seth Peterson's CO application and a judge sentenced him to probation. The probation officer noted with disapproval that Seth was living with a woman without being married to her, and so sent him to work in another state. After a short time Seth gave it up, returned to Minneapolis and wrote a long letter to his probation officer explaining that he wanted to stay home and find a job there. His probation was revoked; he is now serving time in the Federal Correctional Institution in Sandstone, Minnesota.

"I waited months for a personal appearance before the

draft board and heard nothing. Then I received a letter telling me that the board had decided not to reopen my file because there was no new evidence to warrant a re-opening, and also that my order had been postponed until a later date, at which time I was to report for induction.

"I have a friend who was present at the meeting during which the board voted whether or not to reopen my file. He said that the clerk called me crafty, cocky and belligerent and said that they should really get me this time.

". . . The trial began. My attorney started with the idea that the draft board had shirked its duty by not considering my CO form. His point was that since they had chosen not to consider the form, they had denied me all my rights of appeal under Selective Service System regulations. He presented the facts so well that the judge was on the verge of dismissing the case, but the district attorney jumped up and said, 'Your honor, the defendant is 26 years old, and if we don't convict him we can't get him again. . . .' "

* * *

A Quaker, Wayne Lauser was classified a Conscientious Objector and assigned to alternate service in a Cleveland Hospital.

"Several months later, after much personal searching, I was unable to continue cooperation with the draft. In July 1969 I began a 500-mile walk from Cleveland to Washington, D.C. Along the way I visited Quaker meetings, speaking of my action. In Media, Pa., my home town, I returned my draft classification card and on August 11, 1969, Steve Burns (another draft resister) and I walked into Melvin Laird's office and placed our draft registration cards on his desk, along with letters and minutes of support from friends."

A federal judge in Philadelphia sentenced Lauser to two years in federal prison at Lewisburg. At the sentencing, one witness quoted in Lauser's behalf a declaration the Quakers made to King Charles II in 1660:

"We utterly deny all outward wars and strife, and fightings with outward weapons, for any end, or under any

pretense whatsoever; this is our testimony to the whole world. The Spirit of Christ, by which we are guided, is not changeable, so as once to command us from a thing as evil, and again to move unto it; and we certainly know, and testify to the world, that the spirit of Christ, which leads into all truth, will never move us to fight and war against any man with outward weapons, neither for the Kingdom of Christ nor for the kingdoms of the world. . . ."

* * *

Dave Rensberger was classified a conscientious objector by his draft board, but when called for alternate service he returned his draft card instead. He was recently sentenced to three years in Federal Prison at Ashland, Kentucky.

"I believed, and still believe, that the draft violates a man's relationship with God, in which the course of his life should be determined. Government oversteps its proper authority when it *compels* a man's service, whether in the military or in an 'alternate' form of service. I suppose you could say I 'resisted' the draft; I simply ignored it, actually. Politics had little or nothing to do with the decision. I would ignore the draft in a socialist, Marxist, or Maoist country too.

". . . The few really bad experiences through which I have passed have served mainly to bring home to me the desperate need for a re-thinking of means of dealing with people given to theft and violence. Prison is not the answer, in any society. Vicious or materialistic men get more vicious and materialistic here, and everyone gets a little crazy—some more than a little."

* * *

At midnight July 10th, 1970, eight men broke into draft boards in three Minnesota towns. All eight were arrested on the spot by FBI agents who apparently had been tipped off by an informer, but the same night in a fourth community—Wabasha, Minnesota—all the local draft board's I-A records disappeared without a trace.

Two of the "Minnesota Eight"—Frank Kronke and Mike Therriault—are now out on appeal. Cliff Ulen is awaiting sentencing. All the others are locked in federal

*prisons, widely scattered to prevent them from conspiring
again: Chuck Terchick at El Reno, Kansas; Brad Beneke
at Ashland, Kentucky, Pete Simmons at Englewood,
Colorado, Don Olson at Springfield, Mo., and Bill Tilton
at Milan, Michigan. Brad Beneke and Pete Simmons,
as minors, were given indeterminate sentences which
could run as long as six years. The others all got five
years, the maximum penalty for "attempted interference
with the selective service system." This letter is from
Bill Tilton, previously vice president of the student body
at the University of Minnesota at Minneapolis-St. Paul,
now doing five years in the federal prison at Milan.*

"In vernacular terms, we tried to rip off a few draft
boards. . . . for all sorts of reasons, political and
personal. We wanted to find an impressive and educational
way to protest the war and the draft. We wanted to
physically injure the war and draft effort. We wanted to
help the Vietnamese. We wanted to give the draft-eligible
young men in these areas a chance to ignore government
pleas that they assist in the reconstruction of their own
slaughter machine. We were fulfilling a personal need
to act on our beliefs. And last but certainly not least, it
was *fun*. (Up until we were busted, of course.)

"Although I fully knew the risk I was taking, I didn't
expect to get caught. I wasn't into the 'standby' type
action that characterized the more famous draft-board
ripoffs. I'm into injuring and ultimately destroying the
American war machine. That will finally be accomplished
only by mass actions.

"The cadre action we took was an extremely small
part of the struggle that must be actively participated
in by millions of Americans before it will ever be
successful. My going to jail is far less effective a role
than the role I would have been able to play had I
stayed on the streets and continued large-scale public
organizing, but that is not to say that our situation had
no positive effect. On the contrary, I think our arrest
and trials raised the political consciousness of a great
number of Twin Citians. I just think we could have done
more had we not gotten caught.

". . . The people I see around me are not society's
excrement, as Tricky Dicky would have us believe. They

are an excellent display of our society's shortcomings and omissions. Why is it that at least half of these people are black? And a much greater percentage poor?

". . . This is not an Attica or a Tombs. Far from it. We have clean, if crowded facilities. There are four vocational training programs and high school classes for those who qualify. And we see a movie almost every weekend. But that's just the frosting on the cake, and the cake is made of shit."

* * *

The nation's two most conservative draft resisters must be Mr. and Mrs. Robert Muncaster, who live in a big house in Montgomery, Alabama next door to Governor Wallace.

Muncaster, a 49-year-old management consultant, is a rigorous believer in the Constitution. When his son Charles turned 18, he forbade him to register for the draft because the war in Vietnam had never been declared by Congress. The was was being "perpetuated by the United Nations," he said.

Muncaster is now in federal prison for interfering with the draft. His son, convicted of refusing to register, is out awaiting appeal. Mrs. Muncaster, not a woman to stand idle, has been indicted for attacking the two federal officers who arrested her husband. (Allegedly she kicked them in the shins.) She is preparing her own defense, assisted by family friend and retired rear admiral John G. Crommelin, a perpetual office-seeker and prominent Alabama anti-Semite.

* * *

Patrick Salaver is doing three years at Safford for resisting the draft.

"By birth I am Filipino, a native of southeast Asia and all too aware of the imperialistic and racist nature of the war.

"I am also aware as a human being of the nature of oppression that kills people and their culture—babies, women, old men and all. It is the same oppression that keeps third world people in the ghettos of the cities. . . . My crime was not a violent act. It had no victims, other

120

than myself perhaps. My crime was confronting a brutal system that denied me and others around the world the right of self-determination.` . . .

"This is the tenth year of our participation in the war in Southeast Asia, and it has been clear for some time to many that it was wrong. This being an election year, many politicians will at least say it was wrong. Yet I suspect that many of us will still be in jail this Christmas. . . . Set us free."

Felonious Heritage

1. Any Negro, Puerto Rican, Chicano, Indian or other member of a racial or ethnic minority who conducts, comports, represents or beholds himself to be equal to his betters and who acts or encourages others to act in a fashion consistent with that belief, is guilty of Felonious Heritage. **2.** Penalty. Members of minorities are entitled to the same sentences as their betters, if not more so.

* * *

When rioting swept through the black ghettos of Buffalo in the summer of 1967, the cops looked hard for somebody to blame. They found Martin Sostre, bookseller.

Sostre was an ex-convict who had served time at Attica on a dope charge, worked a year for Bethlehem Steel and saved his money, then opened a black liberation bookstore in Buffalo's Cold Spring black ghetto. The store offered the works of Fidel and Mao, and it attracted attention immediately; within days, FBI agents showed up and questioned Sostre about the nature of his books and why he was selling them. Later some local narcs appeared and asked Sostre point-blank what grim plot the store might be fronting for. Sostre said he was selling books.

When the riots broke out in June 1967, Sostre harbored black people in his store while police tear gas billowed through the streets outside. The store had become something of a center in the black community; black radicals and intellectuals liked to hang out there, browsing and talking. Relations between Sostre and the white cops deteriorated, if that was possible.

On July 14th, Sostre heard loud noises and emerged

from the back of the store to find a squad of plainclothesmen and uniformed cops punching aside his assistant, a woman named Geraldine Robinson. One cop produced a package full of heroin and exclaimed, "Aha, here it is! See what we found, Marty."

A group of black children in the store witnessed the bust. They said the narc pulled the package from his coat pocket.

Sostre was held on $50,000 bail, later reduced to $12,500. When he protested, his white judge suggested that perhaps Mao or Ho would go his bail.

In Washington, a representative of the Buffalo police department testified that a man he identified as "Martin X," the owner of a bookstore at Sostre's address, was responsible for the June riots. This evil bookseller, swore the cop, had taken young children into the back of his store and taught them how to make Molotov cocktails.

In this atmosphere Sostre went on trial. He represented himself, but was not permitted to visit a law library or seek out witnesses. He asked the sheriff's office to locate the black children who had been in his store when he was arrested; the sheriff said they couldn't be found. Vincent Copeland examined the case, and in his book, The Crime of Martin Sostre, presented evidence that the sheriff's office had made no effort to locate the children.

The prosecution's non-police witness was a junkie named Arto Williams. Williams had been locked up in the Erie County Jail until the morning Sostre was arrested. Hours before the bust, he had been released without bail.

Sostre was convicted and sentenced to serve 30-40 years. Handcuffed and gagged before an all-white jury, he underwent a second trial to verify his previous prison record. On March 1968 he was taken to Attica and immediately placed in solitary for refusing to answer questions about whether he intended to recruit other prisoners into an organization "suspected to be insurrectionary."

Later, Greenhaven State Prison took over Sostre. There for 372 days he was held in solitary in a 6' by 8' cell, allowed no personal belongings, no newspapers, no soap. Every half hour, day and night, for over a year, he was awakened by a guard shining a flashlight in his face from the door.

Eventually the ACLU got Sostre released from solitary and transferred to a medium-security prison at Wallkill, N.Y. He filed a $1.2 million damage suit against the state, and in a surprising decision was awarded $13,020 damages and 124 days good conduct time denied him while in solitary. Some of the damages were rescinded on appeal, but a ruling stood that prison inmates could not be punished merely for expressing their opinions and if they were, they could sue officials. But Sostre, 48 years old, is still in prison.

* * *

At age 15, Marie Hill was sentenced to die. The charge was the murder of a white grocery store clerk in Rocky Mountain, North Carolina. Marie, who is black, was seized by police in South Carolina and quickly extradited. During a week in which she was permitted neither to reach an attorney nor even to speak with her parents, Marie waived her right to a preliminary hearing and signed a confession.

She was tried within two months, on December 17th, 1968. The prosecution failed to prove even that she had been at the scene of the crime, but based its case on her confession. Marie repudiated the confession— "I had no choice"—but was found guilty of murder in the first degree.

Appeals were argued for over two years while Marie waited on death row. Finally the US Supreme Court struck down the portion of North Carolina's murder statue which prescribed a maximum sentence of life imprisonment for defendants who pled guilty, but death for those who pled innocent. The state, rather than conduct a new trial, simply commuted Marie's sentence to life.

A new appeal was launched asking for a new trial, but Marie, now 18 years old and a three-year veteran of prison, has instructed her lawyer to give up. She points out that in a couple of years, she will be eligible for parole. She has become, according to her attorney, a model prisoner.

*   *   *

Early one warm August morning in 1969, an army of New York City police blockaded the 125th Street exit of the West Side Highway and stopped a sedan in which were riding four black men—Ricardo de Leon, Jerome West, Alfred Cain and Wilbert Thomas. De Leon, West and Cain were members of the Black Panther Party in Brooklyn, and so far as they knew, their friend Wilbert Thomas was a Panther too.

Instead, Thomas was a police agent, and the car he was driving was owned by the police. The cops pulled a shotgun from a paper bag under the seat of his (their) car and arrested the three Panthers for possession of weapons and more elaborate crimes: The Panthers were said to have been on their way to knock off a Harlem hotel and shoot anybody who gave them trouble. Charges of conspiracy to commit robbery and murder were added.

As a study in how undercover agents work, the case is almost without par. Here is De Leon's account of how Thomas, the secret cop, witnessed the genesis of the Panther "conspiracy":

"A couple of days before the bust, Wilbert Thomas went to Harlem with me. We spent most of the time at the State Office Building site, which at the time was a center of controversy between elements of the community and officialdom, having been occupied by people who were opposed to building the S.O.B. We walked through the community, stopped at a bookstore, ate at a restaurant, had a couple of beers at a bar, sipped some 'bitter dog,' and rapped with people I knew casually.

"In these wanderings through Harlem, I happened to pass a building where a girl I used to be tight with lived. I checked the crib to see if she was home, and since my shadow was with me, he entered the ramshackle tenement with me. I couldn't find the girl, so I split.

"The police fabrication took my presence at that place, my knowledge of the neighborhood—I used to live two blocks away—plus a superficial conversation analyzing the role of the slumlords in the deterioration of the area, as a hook on which to string a plot to rob the landlord of rent money and 'shoot anyone who made a funny move . . .'

"In the course of ordinary conversation [Thomas] found out that brothers Al Cain, Jerome West and myself had some business to transact in Harlem that Saturday morning. Being one of the few people in the Brooklyn Party with access to a car at the time, he offered to take us there. Then by a series of lies and manipulations he pushed the time of our departure ahead from 9 AM to 6 AM to make it more convenient for the armed goons of the Safe, Loft and Burglary Squad to be waiting for us.

"As we came off the West Side Highway, Thomas by prearranged orders slowed down the car and about 40 policemen and detectives converged on us with pistols, automatic rifles, shotguns and machine guns. Shielded by bulletproof vests, police came jumping out the side of the road, out of trucks that had blocked the road, taxis and unmarked cars that had been following us all the way from the time we had crossed the bridge from Brooklyn. . . . An awesome thought sped through my mind: 'This is it, these fucking pigs are going to kill us and I ain't even got a piece.' "

Despite the passionate arguments of assistant D.A. John Fine, the trial jury wouldn't buy most of the police story and the three were acquitted of the conspiracy charges. But the sandbagging apparently worked, and the jury hung on the weapons charges when a middle-aged woman juror, according to a fellow juror, exclaimed at the end of two days and nights of deliberation: "Well, they must be guilty of something!"

A second jury convicted the Panthers of illegal possession of firearms. Cain received probation, West got three years, and De Leon, with an old string of assault and robbery charges, drew a maximum sentence of seven years in prison. He has since been indicted in connection with the 1970 rebellion in the Manhattan House of Detention for Men, also known as The Tombs, and is awaiting trial while serving the weapons sentence. He does not seem exactly penitent:

"I am imprisoned, not because I have committed any act that can even remotely be considered 'criminal.' My comrades and I were jailed for being revolutionaries. . . .

"Imprisonment for almost two and a half years has been an invaluable experience, a cram course on the nature of race and class oppression, and the Amerikan system of 'criminal justice,' its dual standards and outright corruptions, where the real criminals judge their victims. . . . Going through these hells and having a totalitarian system wage war on me and my kind has made me more determined in the pursuit of the goal that made me an 'enemy of the state'—revolutionary change in all spheres of Babylonian society."

* * *

New York Assistant DA John Fine—the same man who came up with the Ricardo de Leon Black Panther "conspiracy"—has produced a new show starring Carlos Feliciano, a 41-year-old carpenter and father of six children, in the role of a sort of Puerto Rican Mad Bomber.

It is an odd bit of casting. When arrested, Feliciano had been working for the same furniture company for 14 years. He was superintendent of the East Harlem tenement in which he lived with his wife and family. In a description of himself written from jail, he said:

"I like to behave responsibly toward my job, my wife and my children. I lived in this place for twelve years. I have no vices: I don't smoke and I drink Puerto Rican alcohol only when I must treat friends who are visiting me. My greatest pleasure, on the few days when I was not working, was to take my dear wife and children in my automobile—after having filled the trunk with food, preferably Creole such as pasteles, rice with gandules, and so on—always looking for the mountains and lakes far from the city which would remind me of my homeland."

As a young man in Puerto Rico more than 20 years ago, Feliciano was active in the Nationalist Party and served on the Revolutionary General Staff in the Nationalist uprising of 1950. When the revolt failed he was sentenced to life, and served four years before the supreme court set him free. He went back to his old furniture shop in Mayaguez, but found FBI harassment intense, and

126

when his sister sent him plane fare to New York, he took it.

In the city, Feliciano found the FBI had not forgotten him. Two weeks after he went to work for a furniture shop called London Interiors, the feds visited his employer, warned him that Feliciano was one dangerous Puerto Rican, and gave him the option of firing Feliciano or working for the FBI by reporting Feliciano's activities twice a month. To his credit, the employer told them to go to hell. Feliciano stayed there 14 years.

"One afternoon when it was already quite dark with below-zero temperature, I was leaving work with another of the employees and upon opening the door I noticed these two agents, six feet in stature, all covered with snow and almost frozen. They followed us to the next block. One of the agents approached me and, after identifying himself, told me he wanted to ask me some questions. Motioning me to one side of the sidewalk, he stated that it was his mission to learn what I was thinking now that I lived in New York. I replied: 'I think like a Puerto Rican, my home and my rights are sacred and must be respected.' After shaking hands with me, they left.

"One night when I came home from work I noticed that the door had been opened. All my old letters which I had received from Puerto Rico had been taken out of their envelopes and spread open on one of the tables. It looked like a cyclone had come through the door. That day I had left behind rings, a watch, a portable radio and other valuables, all small and easy to carry, but nothing had been taken. This was not the work of narcotics addicts. . . . Later, I learned it had been the work of the police."

When Feliciano became superintendent in his building, FBI agents visited the real estate agent and suggested he be fired. (The real estate agent, a Cuban, refused.)

· Late one night in 1963 someone fired eight pistol shots into Feliciano's bedroom, wounding him in the arm. His telephone mysteriously went dead at the time of the shooting, then came back on a few hours later. Feliciano found eight empty shells outside and turned them over to the police, but no significant police action resulted.

Finally the arrest came, on May 16th, 1970, outside

a sporting goods shop in the Bronx, and John Fine went into his act.

Fine told the courts and the press that Feliciano was, in effect, one of the most heinous criminals ever to darken the streets of Manhattan. He was responsible for bombing 35 public buildings in the city, including the public library. When arrested he had been carrying "explosive devices" in his car. He had admitted to membership in Movimento Isquierda Revolutionaria Armada, an armed underground group blamed by police for the bombings. Moreover, Feliciano was affiliated with "an alien government outside the limits of the United States," which Fine could not identify because "It would prejudice the case."

Impressed, the judges raised bail to $150,000 in Manhattan and $125,000 in the Bronx (one court for each of the two jurisdictions in which bombs had gone off). Feliciano was locked up, to remain in jail for 16 months.

Fine's story began to disintegrate at a startling rate. The indictment itself cited only one bombing and one attempted bombing: no mention was made of the other 34. A transcript of the police interrogation turned out to contain no admissions about belonging to terrorist groups —Feliciano had said only that he belonged to the perfectly legal Nationalist Party of Puerto Rico.

But Fine kept busy. Feliciano, he said, was "involved with the Cuban government" and "was formerly affiliated as an agent for a foreign government. . . . whose political philosophy is at variance with that of this government." At a bail hearing, Fine denied he had ever said anything about all the bombings not in the indictment; moments later he blurted that Feliciano was guilty of them anyway and in fact was so agonized that he was probably going to plead guilty at any moment. "My client has never wanted to plead guilty," replied Feliciano's lawyer.

After 16 months Feliciano's bail was reduced and he was released until his trial, which is about to begin.

"I wish to thank all the organizations and persons who so spontaneously and disinterestedly have come to my defense in this chapter of my life. . . . At present I do not belong to any particular political philosophy. It is my greatest pride to be a Puerto Rican. . . ."

*   *   *

For nearly 22 years Joseph Romero has been locked up for a robbery and murder committed when he was 19 years old. From his cell in the California Men's Colony at San Luis Obispo he writes that although he has completed 14,000 hours of training in lithography (the equivalent of seven years on a full-time job) and received high marks in other training courses, has never been apprehended for possession of liquor, narcotics or other contraband in prison, and generally has long proven himself ready to return to society, his parole board annually refuses to release him on the basis of "unsubstantiated accusations that I am a 'dope smuggler' or that I am a 'chieftain' in the 'Mexican Mafia' within the prison social structure." Romero says he will not be released until he admits these charges to be true.

Romero has been eligible for parole for 15 years. In 1959 he killed another inmate at San Quentin in an incident which a Marin County Grand Jury judged justifiable homicide; he says that despite his acquittal the parole board has used that killing as "a lever" to keep him in. Romero writes that a co-defendant convicted along with him was paroled after serving 13 years, arrested nine months later for possession of narcotics, drew two to ten years plus the old life sentence, and yet was paroled again last June. Apparently he was not a member of the "Mexican Mafia."

"Court action and public pressure are the only things that will help me to secure my release. I have five sisters, a brother and a son. My son returned from a tour of duty in Vietnam six months ago. Without reservations, I want my freedom and I want to be with my family. . . ."

Apparently public pressure had some effect. After writing numerous letters to legislators and newspapers, Romero in January was granted a parole date of April 17th, and in fact is now out on a kind of "temporary" parole under the prison's Release Upon Approved Parole Plan (RUAPP) program. Prison superintendent Dan McCarthy agreed that Romero had an excellent training record but said it's nearly impossible to know the reasons behind past parole board actions. "After all he had to

129

go before a different parole board each year," explained McCarthy, "a different board of 16 people each year."

* * *

The summer of 1970 marked the waning months of a nation-wide police offensive against the Black Panther Party. The previous December 4th, 300 police had raided a Panther headquarters in Los Angeles, and two days later, Fred Hampton was killed in his bed by Chicago cops. The "New York 21" were arrested in March (charged with a plot to blow up city landmarks, including a botanical garden) and by April police had assaulted Panther offices in New Haven, Detroit, Milwaukee, Dallas, Oakland and San Francisco.

So Curtiss Johnson, Richard Dowell and Fred Clark, Panthers and students at Cuyahoga Community College, could not have been completely surprised when on the afternoon of June 29th, 40 Cleveland cops armed with rifles, shotguns and submachine guns surrounded them in the Panther office at 79th and Rawlings Streets. Bullets smashed the window glass, tore apart a poster of Huey Newton, and chopped chunks of plaster from the walls. When it was over one cop had been wounded in the jaw and one Panther—Fred Clark—had been shot in the stomach and the back of the head.

The ostensible purpose of the raid was to serve Clark (and one other Panther who wasn't there) with a peace bond, the first such warrant issued in Cuyahoga County in more than 25 years. It had been sworn out on behalf of Thomas Avery, a neighborhood druggist who stood out at the trial as the only prosecution witness not on a police payroll. Avery had gone to the police with a story that the Panthers threatened his life when he refused to contribute toward playground equipment for three empty lots the Panthers had cleared. The police, more than anxious to help, got him the peace bond.

At the trial, Avery admitted that though the bond listed his children as menaced by the Panthers, he in fact had no children. An ACLU attorney present at the time of the alleged threat said it never took place.

The rest of the prosecution was given over to police. The cops testified that they had knocked politely on the

Panther's door, heard "shuffling" inside, and kicked the door down. Inside, they spied a rifle barrel poking ominously out the bedroom door, so they opened fire.

Officer Harry Leisman, who commanded the action, said that when the shooting started he stood outside and pumped submachine bullets in through the windows. The Panthers responded with blazing fire, but in the end the cops were victorious.

The evidence in support of this story proved less than adequate. Four weapons were found in the office—two rifles, a magnum pistol and an M1—but all were still fully loaded. A thorough police search turned up no spent shells; there was some speculation that Clark had swallowed them. No tests were conducted to determine whether the weapons had been fired or whether any of the defendants had fired them. Fingerprint examinations were made; they failed to link the guns with the defendants.

The cop who claimed to have shot Clark said he blew him down with a shotgun when Clark, clutching a smoking rifle, refused to surrender. Clark said that actually the police ordered him out of the bedroom, then shot him in the belly when he opened the door, unarmed. The doctor who treated Clark said a .32 or .38 bullet, not a shotgun slug, had done the job.

A predominantly white, middle-class jury weighed this evidence and sentenced Johnson, Dowell and Clark to three years in the Ohio State Reformatory. All three defendants were in college at the time; none had any prior record.

Officer Leisman, the chief raider, continued in his city's service until last Christmas Eve, when a woman and a young boy were murdered outside his house. Leisman's story to reporters was that he had been sitting quietly at home enjoying the holiday when he heard a commotion outside. He ran out to the street. A generous stranger handed him a loaded M14 (which later proved to have been stolen from the military). A man appeared menacingly in the doorway of a bar across the street. Leisman allegedly opened fire, wounding him and killing a ten-year-old boy in an apartment down the block. Then

131

Leisman is said to have walked into the bar and sprayed it with bullets. One woman fell dead.

Leisman is being held without bail, awaiting trial on charges of second-degree murder. Johnson, Dowell and Clark, convicted on the testimony of Leisman and his men, are still in prison.

* * *

One of the nation's more oblique political slogans has turned up on bumper stickers in Houston. It reads, "frijoles," and it dates back a couple of years, to when Texas' governor Preston Smith was running for re-election and got booed off the stage at the University of Texas by a crowd chanting, "Free Otis Johnson." Governor Smith expressed confusion over the scene. "What do they have against frijoles?" he asked. "I thought they were just beans."

The story may have brought a smile to the face of Lee Otis Johnson, the most famous political prisoner in the South, but it has done little else for him. He remains locked up in prison, doing 30 years for allegedly handing a cop one joint.

A student at Texas Southern University and field secretary for the Student Nonviolent Coordinating Committee, Johnson was arrested March 8th, 1968—six weeks after he was said to have handed over the incriminating reefer. Houston police said the delay was necessary to preserve the anonymity of their undercover agent, but a speech Johnson gave at a Martin Luther King memorial meeting two days before he was busted—a speech in which he was highly critical of the mayor and police chief—may have had more to do with it.

Houston DA Carol Vance prosecuted Johnson personally. "If in the future we have another white, yellow, red, green or black person who has promoted violence and destruction in this city and he gets caught selling marijuana, I may well choose to try that case," he explained.

The case attracted widespread attention. The US Commission on Civil Rights referred the matter to the Justice Department for investigation. Inquiry was made by Amnesty International, an organization in Dusseldorf, Ger-

many interested in political prisoners. Locally, a Free Lee Otis Johnson Defense Committee was formed.

All this activity offended Lt. M. L. Singleton, head of police intelligence in Houston. "He [Johnson] doesn't tell you that he and his friends were smoking marijuana, drinking Robitussin and stealing food, that they were trying to get dynamite to blow up major overpasses, power stations, telephone facilities and public buildings," he said. He failed to explain why he hadn't booked Johnson and his cough-syrup swigging cronies for all those other crimes.

Recently a federal district judge ruled that Johnson should have been granted a change of venue. He gave the district attorney 90 days to appeal the decision, retry Johnson, or release him. Indications are that Vance will decide on a new trial, in which case Johnson, even if he wins acquittal, might well be in prison for another year.

Johnson was interviewed in prison by Michael Adams for the Texas Observer:

"We blacks have built up America. We're the hardest-working people in the world. From King Cotton through every war to the present we've been the backbone of America. But in return, we've just had a bite to eat and a cup of coffee. And we've had to live in racist towns and work in racist businesses, or buy from white merchants in the black community. Whites have used the income tax, the installment plan, overhead, excise taxes, slum lords and everything else to keep us down. . . .

"In Houston we tried the system. We went to Mayor Welch and tried to talk sense. He was so busy telling us we were communist-inspired and irresponsible that we never did get to talk about real Third World problems. Then they put the police department's intelligence squad on me. They said all kinds of things, like our agitation was a front for a dope center—that I was going to blow up Houston, with my bare hands, I guess. It was just a lot of talk to inflame the police department against us. They called me a 'hard core incendiary, a wino, the leader of a hate gang.' You can't work within that kind of system. . . .

"I'm going to get out of here eventually, even if it takes the full 30 years. I've kept up with events pretty well, and I'll be ready to go back to work. I'm encouraged."

Conspicuous Youth

1. Any child who behaves in an improper fashion and whose parents do not want to take care of him is guilty of Conspicuous Youth. **2.** The definition of "improper fashion" shall be determined by adults. **3.** The relationship between such a child and the courts should be that of child to parent. Children who fail to recognize this are guilty of being Rebellious. **4.** Children have no right to due process, trial by jury, or equal treatment under the law. **5.** Penalty. Sentences need not be limited to the maximum allowed for adults. For details, judges may consult the cases below, drawn from an investigation by journalist Lester Velie and from lawsuits filed by the Chicago Legal Aid Bureau.

* * *

Carman Tate has been locked up for most of the past four years, since he was 13 years old. That was the time of the riots following the assassination of Martin Luther King, and Carman was arrested and held in a detention center for 28 days on charges of setting fire to some curtains. When he finally got to court, the charges were dismissed for lack of evidence.

A court investigation revealed that Carman's stepfather, a moonlighting Chicago cop, compelled the boy to work late hours in his store and beat him when he objected. Carman frequently was absent from school; when he did attend he sometimes fell asleep in class.

A psychiatrist recommended that both Carman and his parents receive professional counseling. Instead, the judge put him on a year's probation which required him to observe curfew and go to school regularly. The curfew was broken within four months, and Carman was locked up again. Officials at a juvenile detention center urged that his confinement be continued "because of his possible arsonist tendencies," though of course he had never been convicted of arson or anything else. He was sent to a high-security state "training school" at St. Charles, Illinois.

Paroled after eight months, Carman went home, got into a fight and was thrown out by his stepfather, the manly cop. "If I can't be with you," Carman yelled to his mother, "I might as well be locked up!" He was, first in the detention center and then at the so-called Industrial School for Boys at Sheridan, Illinois.

Sheridan is a maximum-security prison perimetered by guard towers and fences topped with barbed wire. It houses murderers as well as youths convicted of such non-crimes as truancy and running away. Eighty percent of the inmates are black; eighty percent of the guards are white. To maintain order, the guards are fond of administering shots of Thorazine, a powerful tranquilizer the side effects of which include liver and kidney deterioration, impairment of breathing and jaundice.

During the more than two years that Carman Tate has been imprisoned at Sheridan, he has been administered as many as six shots of tranquilizers, a day. He has been placed in solitary confinement for up to 30 days at a time, as much as six months in a row. The Department of Corrections has refused to release him despite recommendations of two psychiatrists that he should be let go. He is 17 years old, and by law he can be kept in prison until his 21st birthday.

* * *

At the age of ten Terry Wilson pled guilty to petty theft. His parole was revoked and he served nine months in the State Training School for Boys at St. Charles, Illinois, was paroled again for 11 months, broke parole and was sent to Sheridan. He has received the customary Sheridan treatment: solitary confinement for up to 51 straight days, shots of Thorazine, a half dozen visits from an untrained counselor, only a single visit from a psychiatrist. Had Terry Wilson been an adult accused of the same crime, he could have been sentenced to no more than one year in jail. To date, he has been imprisoned in Sheridan for three years.

* * *

Alton Stewart, 15 years old, has a measured IQ of about 75. A psychologist who examined him at age nine

135

reported that his "anti-social behavior related to his borderline intelligence, his weak reality testing, immature perceptual development, and his serious lack of emotional depths."

Turned over to the Chicago police at age 11 as an habitual runaway, Alton was judged to be a Minor in Need of Supervision and was sent to the Training School for Boys at St. Charles, Illinois. Three times he escaped the school and ran back to his mother. Finally he was transferred to Sheridan.

He has remained at Sheridan for two years, nearly half the time confined to his cell. The institution psychiatrist visited him and recommended that he receive intensive counseling, but in fact his status has been determined by the corrections department on the basis of his "academic progress," "exercise of self-control," and "good attitudes toward authority and program." It is under these rules that Alton Stewart, recognized to be of "retarded to dull normal" intelligence since the age of five, can legally be forced to remain for six more years.

* * *

Julius Addison, 17 years old and now entering his third year in Sheridan, originally was convicted of being a "Minor in Need of Supervision." This is an Illinois non-crime which applies to anyone under 18 years of age who is judged to be "beyond the control of his parents, guardian or other custodian," is "habitually truant from school," or is a drug addict. The law was enacted with the intention of protecting youngsters from being labeled "delinquent."

At Sheridan, corrections men have protected Julius by beating him and choking him with a towel, "having his ass pumped" with tranquilizers, and confining him to his cell roughly half the time, on one occasion for six consecutive months.

The state law under which this has been accomplished reads in part: "The purpose of this act is . . . when the minor is removed from his own family, to secure for him custody, care and discipline as nearly as possible equivalent to that which should be given by his own parents. . . ."

Getting Caught

Whoever uses dope in such fashion as to enable the police to detect it is guilty of Getting Caught. **1.** Anyone found with dope who lacks the financial resources for a successful defense is guilty of First Degree Getting Caught. **2.** Anyone who has made a nuisance of himself in the community and who is found to be in the immediate vicinity of a police officer at such time as the officer drops dope to the floor, sticks it in the offender's pocket or otherwise disposes of it, is guilty of Second Degree Getting Caught, or a violation of the Red-Handed Act. **3.** Penalty. Sentencing is variable, depending upon the offender's attitude, age, color, intelligence, solvency and luck.

* * *

William Jackson, 25 years old, pulled an indeterminate to seven year sentence for allegedly selling marijuana to a 19-year-old college co-ed. The sale allegedly took place in Jamestown, N.Y., December 3rd, 1968, when the girl took three envelopes of grass from the glove box of Jackson's car. He was not arrested until more than six months later, on June 14th, 1969. Convicted on the girl's testimony alone, he has served two years at Attica.

"To this day I can't remember where I was on December 3rd, 1968, and I am totally unable to refute her charges. What were you doing seven months ago at 10 AM? . . .

"I refused to consider pleading guilty, and retained a local attorney. He did nothing to help me—no motions, preliminary hearing, etc. I queried him about the trial but he assured me that I'd be acquitted. Not knowing the vagaries of criminal law I went along with him. . . . I was sentenced to an indeterminate to seven year term. The judge gave me a 'break'—I could have gotten 25 years.

"The real reason for my conviction is that a vindictive narcotics squad officer thought I had turned his daughter into a junkie, which she was, and told me he'd get me one way or another, which he certainly did.

"Since my incarceration one of the jurors has contacted my wife and said he was 'forced into a guilty verdict.' A lot of fucking good that does me—he won't make a sworn statement. . . .

"It is unlikely I'll get parole, as I went to federal court October 4th, 1971, and testified as to the brutality and stealing on the part of correction officers and state troopers here at Attica. I wasn't involved in the rebellion, but viewed it from my window and while on clean-up work. . . .

"The major bitches here are the arbitrary parole system —they don't have to tell you why you got 'hit' or what you can do to get their approval so you can be released— and good time. For every 30 days an inmate earns ten days good time. The hitch is that after you've earned this time, you must successfully complete the entire period before it's really given you. If you violate parole—say, stay out past 11 PM—they can bring you back and make you do the whole time again. The parole board also deducts parole days from men as a discipline measure and there is no redress. Few men finish their sentences when they're supposed to. I know of one man who got a seven and a half to 15 sentence in 1948 and recently went out on parole, still owing four years. . . ."

* * *

Wayne Ladd has been in and out of California penal institutions for more than 15 years, as the result of once having smoked grass with two friends. He doesn't know if he will ever be free.

"In 1956 I was arrested for smoking some marijuana with two other juveniles, with one marijuana cigarette in my pocket. Even though we were all teenagers I was charged with furnishing narcotics to other minors and possession of narcotics. I was sentenced to five years to life for the furnishing charge and one to ten years for possession.

"Here it is, almost 16 years later, and I am still trying to pay my debt for those offenses, which consisted of a total of three marijuana cigarettes. I have been paroled a couple of times and returned again as a parole violator. You can come back and forth from prison this way for the rest of your life; you can't complete a five year to life sentence and they just keep you on a string like a yo yo. They let you out on parole, and for some little trivial incident, not even a crime, you are brought back to serve X number of years until they are ready to let you out again and put you through the same thing. This can be perpetual; five years to life never terminates. . . ."

* * *

Last November, Jay Van Russell was sentenced to 15 years' imprisonment after one of the more curious trials in the history of Peoria, Illinois, or anywhere else.

The conviction was for attempting to sell heroin, although no heroin was produced as evidence and the indictment didn't claim that Russell actually had any. What happened was that two federal undercover agents telephoned Russell at his home and allegedly made a deal to buy some smack. They taped the conversation, and on the strength of the tape got Russell convicted.

The trial brought other strangeness too. Despite defense objections about hearsay evidence, a doctor who supervises a local clinic was allowed to testify that he overheard a patient say, "Here comes the dope man," when Russell appeared. A federal agent was permitted to tell the jury that Russell sold dope to an undercover man, though that alleged sale played no part in the relevant indictment or in any other.

The District Attorney claimed Russell was "at the heart of the heroin traffic" in Peoria. The jury found him guilty, and federal judge Robert Morgan gave him 15 years plus five years' probation. He is now in county jail, awaiting the result of a mental test before the sentence becomes final.

Russell, 25 years old and black, has been in trouble with the police since he was 14. In late 1970 he was indicted for alleged possession of marijuana and heroin; the charges were later dismissed at the request of the prosecutor. Recently he was fined $20 for being present in a gambling house. Prosecutors present Russell's record as evidence that he is a dope dealer; Russell says it shows police harassment.

When busted on the heroin charge, Russell was in the process of suing the city police for ripping up the interior of his car in an unsuccessful search for narcotics.

"You see, gentlemen, I sued the city. I have become a victim of prejudice by individuals using the law as an implement of persecution. I have been set up for constitutional protest against authority which has violated the law. I assure you, gentlemen, victims of circumstance can be struck down by biased officials who blatantly violate the civil rights of others. . . ."

* * *

In Texas, land of the big dope sentences, Gentry Powell III was caught riding in a truck full of grass and hash. He got 45 years.

The bust came one night a year ago, when police, tipped off by an informer, crouched in the sagebrush near a landing strip on a 4000-acre ranch owned by Powell's grandfather. As they watched, a light plane landed in the dark and two men loaded its contents into a truck. The cops followed the truck and pulled it over on the highway southeast of Karnes City, Texas. Inside they found David Curlee, Gentry Powell III, 50 pounds of hash and 400 pounds of grass.

Both defendants posted $25,000 bond. Curlee disappeared and remains a fugitive. Powell showed up for his trial last December 13th and was sentenced to 45 years in prison. The case is being appealed, but by Texas law those sentenced to more than 15 years cannot get out on appeal bond.

"After serving four years in the Marine Corps in Vietnam, it really brings me down to return to such a country, with so little compassion."

* * *

Lenny Parker is imprisoned at Terminal Island, San Pedro, California.

"On a hot and dry summer day in 1968 I made a mistake and got arrested at the Arizona-Mexico border with three grams of heroin, in a car. I was a passenger. The judge said 'Not less than six months and not to exceed ten years,' so here I am. I was 21 then. I'm 25 now. Three grams could fit in a sewing thimble—it ain't much, friend. Come 1978, it's over.

"No sob story here. No tears over spilt milk, 'cause I

blew it. But I know I was sent here because of my life-style. . . . The three grams was negligible in my book —it could have been two joints like John Sinclair or it could have been a frame like my ex-wife. The narc said she injected the baby with heroin—a six-month-old boy! —and they gave her 20. Change is coming."

* * *

The case of William "Wild Bill" House who is now in Utah State Prison, resembles hundreds of other busts involving dope dealers— a labyrinth of police duplicity and plea-bargaining, topped by a stiff sentence.

"I was arrested for a sales beef because this dude called my house and asked if I had any speed. I said no, but if any came around I would send it over. So I did, but I didn't take it over [myself]. I didn't get any money from the dude nor was I anywhere around when the deal took place.

"They arrested me and I bonded out for $2500 on December 19th, 1970. On January 15th, 1971, I was out to a friend's house and the p.gs kicked in the door and put us up against the wall. They stuck a shotgun to the back of my head and told me to run. I didn't so they began to beat me with it. I never knew they were pigs until about 20 minutes after they stopped beating me. Then they pulled out their badges.

"I was arrested for resisting arrest. They set my bail at $10,000, a little high for me to make, so they kept me locked up till the first of March, when I was to go to trial on the resisting charge. No pigs showed up at my first trial, so the judge knocked the bail down to $3500. I made that and was free. At my second trial on the resisting charge, no pigs showed up and so the judge threw it out. I am filing a suit in federal court on that charge; I sure hope it does some good.

"When I went back to my preliminary hearing on the sales beef they arrested me again in court for another charge to the same dude. I really don't know where they dreamed that one up, but they did. Back to jail and I made another bond.

"While I was out waiting for trial I was told not to fight the charges, because if I did they would file more until they got me in prison. I was going to fight the charges, but I had run out of money. So I copped to a lesser charge of possession for sale of a stimulating drug. I pled guilty and was sent here for two to ten years. This is my first felony. . .

"This state is a little heavy on the drug scene, real heavy. So if you ever drop out this way, be a little careful."

* * *

Mike Vernon, 27 years old, is locked up in the California Men's Colony at San Luis Obispo for escaping from the San Diego County Honor Camp, where he had been doing a year for possession of grass. This is his account of life there.

"Since most of the people in camp were there for drugs or some drug-related offense, and most of them were young, we often performed a weekly ritual. The camp area was abundant with Gypsum Weed, a plant of the mandrake root family which has quite a bit of belladonna in it. A truckload of naive newcomers would arrive on Wednesday, and by Saturday Wally, the brewmaster, would ship us a batch of this mystical potion and serve it as tea. What followed was a weird mystical bummer. Balance is the first thing to be affected. The next is vision, and the other senses follow. The trip usually lasted six to twelve hours. . . .

"There were about 85 to 100 dudes in camp, and most of us got high. Members of the three ethnic factions—white, black and chicano—would each go to The Man and inform him of racial tension in the camp. To avoid trouble the staff was quick to hand out tranquilizers and barbiturates. We all would save our issue for the weekend, then all three factions would gather together and fix [shoot up] our pills. This was a practice I acquired after arriving at camp, mostly to counteract the boredom and also because of the lack of marijuana. I never had occasion to shoot any drugs while on the street. . . ."

* * *

Los Angeles County sheriff's deputies raided James

142

Yazell's home one night in April 1970, and confiscated 13 ounces of grass and $237 in cash. At the trial the grass appeared; the cash had vanished. Yazell was found guilty of possession with intent to sell, and was sentenced to serve from two to ten years at the California Men's Colony.

"I have never been a longhair or hippie type. Prior to my arrest I had been steadily employed for a period of five years; owned my own mortgage-free home; and had no prior arrests for possession of marijuana. As a result of being sent to prison, I have subsequently lost my home and the respect of most of my family. Only my sister will write me. The rest of the family has disowned me for my so-called 'criminal' act."

* * *

Every so often a dope case fires the imagination of prosecutors with an almost religious zeal. The slightest taint of marijuana, like the infinitesimal stain of sin Christian zealots hold sufficient to cast a soul into eternal hell, becomes enough to send a man to prison.

Jim Mason is a recent casualty of one such crusade. His ten-year sentence for "possession" of one-40th of a gram of marijuana is being appealed, but folks have been quick to pitch in and help penalize him in the meantime.

"I was arrested for possession of narcotics (marijuana) after being stopped by the Missouri Highway Patrol for not having a license plate on my new car. While I was explaining to a patrolman that I was on my way to the license bureau to clear up the situation, the two people who had been in my car tried to throw away some dope; and the patrolmen immediately arrested all three of us for possession. On the way to the highway patrol headquarters, the patrolman who was driving my car turned to me and said, 'You know, I kind of admired them in the Old West. They would have taken guys like you out and hung them from the nearest tree.' At the headquarters they scraped *one-40th of a gram* of what proved to be marijuana from my jacket pocket.

"Later that afternoon I was officially charged with the crime, and bail for the three charges—driving with no plate, possession of narcotics, and possession of narcotics apparatus (a roach clip in the shape of a bullet and some matches)—was set at $15,300! I had absolutely no previous police record of any kind. At the time of my arrest I was a college student at the University of Missouri in Rolla. The town, located in south-central Missouri on Highway 66, has a population of about 12,000. Three days after my arrest two more UMR students were arrested, and their bonds were set at $32,500! On the same day that I was arrested, an habitual criminal was arrested for child molestation and his bond set at $5000. Even though his victim had to be hospitalized, the case was soon dismissed when the man's brother paid court costs. Compare this result to that of my case.

"Immediately after my bond had been set, the prosecuting attorney told me in the privacy of his office that he would forget all about the arrest if I would help him get to some of the big pushers. I told him I didn't know anything about dope pushers.

"During the third and final night I spent in the Phelps County Jail, someone placed a small pipebomb on a window ledge of the Phelps County Court House. Although this event almost assuredly had no connection with my case, the senile reactionary who dabbles as editor of the local newspaper took it upon himself to crusade against the communist dope peddling termites, who had invaded Rolla. I was slandered on the front page for several days until he left the America he loved for a much-needed vacation. . . .

"Four days before my trial was scheduled, my attorney called me and advised me that the prosecuting attorney had offered a deal: If I would join any branch of the armed forces, he would drop all charges. I answered that I was a conscientious objector and that if I could perform non-military duty as a conscientious objector, then I would make the deal. My lawer advised me that this would not be a suitable compromise.

"The day before my trial one of the guys arrested with me had his day in court. He was not a student, and he had a police record. Furthermore he was charged with possession of at least one ounce of marijuana and possession of a needle and other apparatus. His judge, who also presided at my trial, is on court record as opposing any leniency in drug cases. Yet when the defendant pleaded guilty, he was given a bench parole! The reason for this was simple: The sentence was recommended by the prosecuting attorney. In most court cases in Phelps County the judge seems to serve as a rubber stamp for sentences suggested by the prosecutor. In this case the defendant was told by the prosecutor that his only hope was to change lawyers and plead guilty. Fortunately for the defendant the prosecuting attorney knew of an available lawyer: his brother. This course of events seems to be well-traveled in Phelps County.

"But my day in court was much different. In his summation the prosecuting attorney lied and twisted the truth and then asked for the maximum penalty: 20 years. He stated that it was necessary to make an example of me in order to rid the community of dope pushers who were affecting junior high kids. Twenty minutes after they went out, the jury, whose average member was probably well over 60 years old, returned with a verdict of guilty and a sentence of ten years. Later I found out that they had first voted on 20 years, but one juror had held out. . . .

"My school grade point average for the fall semester last year was a 3.53 on the four-point scale; last spring it came out to 0.02. I was scheduled to graduate last spring, but the forthcoming trial was too depressing to be conducive to studying. Also I have accumulated a debt of $3000 in lawyers' fees alone. Because of the felony conviction I cannot get a job. I have lost my new car. And this summer I was married; we are expecting a kid next spring.

"But the height of humiliation was reached when I was called back to campus in September to a disciplinary hearing. I was placed on disciplinary probation 'until such time as I graduate from the University of Missouri.' The reason given was because it is against university standards of conduct to possess dangerous drugs. No stipulation was made as to where or when the possession occurred. . . . In just one semester I went from a candidate for Who's Who in American Colleges & Universities to a social outcast because I was caught with one-40th of a gram of grass."

145

*   *   *

At the end of a long day in Mexicali, Mexico, four years ago, Daniel Mrazek headed back across the border in a car with three friends. He was, he says, "too stoned to know what was going on," but his head begn to clear when customs agents stopped them, opened an attache case, and found some marijuana seeds. Mrazek's three friends identified him as the owner of the case. They were set free; he has been in prison all but two months since.

"I was beaten repeatedly by police in the Calexico city jail and forced to live in a tiny cell, with only one blanket and a Bible which I used as my pillow. When my mother finally received word and arrived at the jail two weeks after my arrest, she didn't recognize me and refused to admit I was her son. It was only then that I was allowed to receive X-rays for my broken ribs. The police said I received these injuries during an earthquake, as I fell off my bed. My cell didn't even have a bed.

". . . California Rehabilitation Center was a total loss for me. I have never to this day used heroin, and there I was, the only man out of several hundred that didn't use it or didn't ever care to start. Because I didn't feel that I had a problem, everyone looked down on me. I remained there for two years.

"After paroling I found a job in Los Angeles. After two months had passed I requested to visit my mother in Yuma. The federal probation department gave me permission, but the state parole department refused. I decided to let the Feds overrule the state and made the trip anyway. As fate would have it, I got stopped by the cops in Yuma for a traffic violation, and back I went. . . . I was given a sentence of one to ten years in state prison.

"I was 22 years old when I was arrested. Now I am 27 and still in prison. . . . I often find myself wondering what am I even in prison for. Looking back tells me that I've been a fool for penalties like grass seeds. But I am not going to stop myself. I've smoked grass for years, and will for years to come. People ask me why, and I let them know where my head is at by telling them it's a way of life I dig! Even the parole board gets to hear it once a year. . . .

"Take care brothers and sisters, and don't let the man put you in the same situation he put me in. Someday the laws will change. But until that day we all have to be cool."

SPLENDOR IN THE SHORT-GRASS

by Grover Lewis

Flying west, through Texas, you leave Dallas-Fort Worth behind and look out suddenly onto a rolling, bare-boned, November country that stretches away to the horizon on every side—a vast, land-locked Sargasso Sea of mesquite-dotted emptiness. There are more cattle down there ranging those hazy, distance-colored expanses than people, and in turn, more people than timber topping out at five feet, for this is cowdom's fabled domain, the short-grass country—*yipi-ti-yi-yo, little pardners*—the Land of the Chicken-Fried Steak, where, if your gravity fails you among the shit-kickers, chili-dippers, and pistoleros, negativity emphatically won't pull you through.

Below, there are few houses, fewer roads, and scarcely any towns. As the dun landscape slides past under the plane's port wing, the overwhelming sense of the vista is solitude, and if you happen to hail from that iron kill-ing floor down there, as I do, you begin to feel edgy and defenseless, moving across so much blank space and drenching memory.

The shuttle plane, an 18-seater De Haviland-Perrin,

seems infernally slow after the rush of the Delta jet from San Francisco; its engines are loud, too, and it bucks around in the brown overcast between Dallas and Wichita Falls like a sunfishing busthead-bronc. Fitfully, I'm riffling through the pages of an underground sheet called Dallas Notes—"Narc Thugs Trash Local White Panthers"—but the lonesome countryside below keeps drawing my mind and eye away from the real-enough agonies of Big D's would-be dope brotherhood. Somewhere down there slightly to the south, a pioneer Texan named William Medford Lewis—my paternal grandfather—lies buried in the Brushy Cemetery, hard by the fragrant dogwood trails of Montague County where he and I once tramped together in less fitful times. Besides him, that fierce, pussel-bellied old man I remember above all other men, lies his next-to-youngest son, Cecil —a ghostly wraith-memory of childhood, a convicted bank robber and one-time cohort of Bonnie and Clyde who was paroled from the Huntsville pen in 1944 just in time to die 56 days later in the invasion of Sicily—and beside Cecil, in turn, lies my grandmother, who once lifted an uncommonly sweet contralto in whatever Pentecostal church lay closest to hand.

Somewhere down there, too, slightly more to the west, in a decaying little ranching hamlet called Archer City, a protean-talented young Hollywood writer-director named Peter Bogdanovich is filming Larry McMurtry's novel, *The Last Picture Show,* in its true-to-life setting. McMurtry —Archer City's only illustrious son—previously wrote *Horseman, Pass By,* from which the film *Hud* was made. *Picture Show*—there'll be a title change before the film's release, to avoid confusion with Dennis Hopper's *The Last Movie*—is to star Ben Johnson, Clu Gulager, Cloris Leachman, Jeff Bridges, and a couple of promising young unknowns, Timothy Bottoms and Cybill Shepherd. And, save us all, I'm to be in it, too, playing a small supporting part.

* * *

The Ramada Inn on the Red River Expressway, where the 60-odd members of the *Picture Show* troupe are quartered, is big, seedy, and expensive, a quadrant of fake-fronted Colonial barracks overlooking a dead swimming pool and a windswept compound full of saw-grass and cockleburrs. "Hah yew today?" the desk clerk, a platinum-streaked grandmother in a miniskirt, trills cheerily as I check in at midafternoon.

My room—at least a city block from the lobby as the crow flies—is *de-rigueur* institutional ugly, distinguished only by a tiny graffito penciled beneath the bathroom mirror: *People who rely on the crutch of vulgarity are inarticulate motherfuckers.* In sluggish slow motion, I stretch out across the bed to doze and await instructions from somebody in Archer City, 40 miles to the southwest, where the day's shooting has been under way since early morning. When the phone jangles a few minutes later, I snap alert, sweating, disoriented. Waking up in Whiskey-taw Falls storms my mind; less than 24 hours ago, I was bombed-and strafed in the no name bar in Sausalito.

Through a crackling connection and a babble of background din, the film's production manager is shouting to ask what my clothing sizes are. "Peter wants you out here on the set as soon as possible," he commands, barking out staccato directions on how I'm to connect with a driver who'll fetch me to the location site.

Feeling wary and depressed, I wander downstairs and wait in the lobby. Christ, I haven't done any acting I'd admit to since college, when I was typecast as the psycho killer in *Detective Story*. Now, I'm supposed to play "Mr. Crawford"—the village junkie-geek of Archer City circa the Korean War era, a character maybe 20 years my senior. More type-casting, I figure sourly.

The driver, a large, loose-limbed black man named James, lifts my spirits on sight. "Fuck them long cuts, ain't I right, Grovah? I'ma take a short cut and git you to the church *on time*," he announces, pumping my hand like a handle and grinning through dazzling silver teeth. On the way out of town in a Hertz station wagon, we pass the M-B Corral, a notorious hillbilly dive where, 14 or 15 years ago, Larry McMurtry and I stood among a circle of spectators in the parking lot one drizzly winter night and watched a nameless oilfield roughneck batter and kick Elvis Presley half to death in what was delicately alluded to afterwards as a difference of opinion about the availability of the roughneck's girl friend. McMurtry and I were wildheaded young runners-and-seekers back then, looking, I think, for a country of men; what we found, though, together and apart, were wraith-like city women in blowing taffeta dresses. And the shards and traceries of our forebears, of course, trapped in the stop-time aspic of old hillbilly records.

Out on the open highway, James stomps down hard on the accelerator and free-associates about his Army days to pass the time and the miles: "Twenty-two years in all I served in the arm service . . . I ony been back in Wichita, lessee, oh, about goin' on three years now . . . Yeah, I seen action in World War II, in Korea, and in Veet-nam. Never kilt nobody, though, far's I know, and never got kilt my own self, neither. Hah! . . . If it's anything I despise to be in, it's a conflick . . . I swear, this ol' State 79 here, it's the lonesomest stretch of miles I've ever drove, you know it? Sheeit."

With a practiced snick, James spits out the window and falls silent. Beyond the weed-choked bar ditches paralleling the road, the stringy mottes of mesquite trees and stagnant stock tanks and the Christmas-tree oil rigs flash past at 80 mph under an unutterable immensity of hard blue sky. It is bluer even than I remember it, the sky, and I remember it as being blue to the point of arrogance, a galling reminder that it is harder to live in this hard-scrabble country than tap-dancing on a sofa in a driving rain. Up ahead, a rusty water tank towers over what looks like an untended automobile graveyard, and the .22-pocked city limits sign appears to identify the harsh tableau: *ARCHER CITY—Population 1924.*

* * *

The Spur Hotel, a rattletrap cattlemen's hostel commandeered by the film troupe as production headquarters, hasn't seen as much elbow-to-ass commotion since the great trail drives to Kansas in the Eighties. Throngs of stand-ins, crew technicians, bit players, and certified Grade A stupor-stars course in and out of the makeshift office like flocks of unhinged cockatoos. Phones ring incessantly; nobody moves to answer them. The location manager mutters into a walkie-talkie, and the agile-fingered mens wardrobe master deals out seedy-looking western outfits to a queue of leathery-faced extras like soiled cards from the bottom of the deck.

Making faces into the mouthpiece, the location manager does a fast fade on the field phone, pours a couple of cups of coffee, and broken-fields across the crowded room to say hello: "You play 'Mr. Crawford,' right? Far out, good to meet you . . . Don't let this spooky dump spook you, hear? Looks like a rummage sale in a toilet, don't it? Well, that's show biz. . . . As of this minute, Anno Domini, the production is—well, we're behind schedule. Which means that Bert Schneider, the producer—you won't meet him, he only feels safe back in Lotus Land—Bert's begun to act very producer-like and chop out scenes. Peter just had to red-pencil the episode where the gang of town boys screws the heifer, and I hated like hell to see it go. That sort of material is disgusting to a lot of people, but, shitfire, man, it's true-to-life. These hot-peckered kids around here still do that kind of thing as a daily routine. You've read McMurtry's book, haven't you? Why, Christ, to me, that's what it's all about—fertility rites among the unwashed." Grinning amiably, he lifts his cup in a sardonic toasting gesture: "Well, here's to darkness and utter chaos, ol' buddy."

Polly Platt materializes out of the crush, her hands in her jean pockets, Bette Davis-style. A poised, fine-boned blonde with sometimes complicated hazel eyes, she is the production designer, as well as Bogdanovich's wife. After an intense discussion with the wardrobe master about what constitutes a village geek, she coordinates my spiffy "Crawford" ensemble—baggy, faded dungarees, a shirt of a gray mucus color, and a tattered old purple sweater that hangs halfway to my knees.

Humming off-key, Polly waits while I change into my new splendor between the costume racks, and then the two of us stroll across the deserted courthouse square toward the American Legion Hall. She laughs with girlish delight as we pass the long-shuttered Royal Theater—the Last Picture Show in both fact and fantasy—and chats fondly about Ben Johnson, who's already completed his part in the film and departed:

"He's the real thing, Ben is—an old-fashioned country gentleman from his hat to his boots. Why, he didn't even want to say 'clap' when it came up in dialogue. Peter and I were both flabbergasted. Later, I asked Ben about the nude bathing scene in *The Wild Bunch*. It turns out Sam Peckinpah had to get him and Warren Oates both knee-walking drunk to get the shot, which wasn't in the original script. . . . But Ben and Peter ended up working beautifully together. Wait'll you see his rushes—" she gives a low whistle of admiration—"Academy stuff all the way, as they oom-pah in the trades."

Inside the ramshackle Legion Hall—a confusion of packed bodies, snarled cables, huge Panavision cameras, and tangled mike booms and lighting baffles—Polly leads the way to a quiet corner and begins tinting my hair gray with a makeup solvent recommended to Bogdanovich by Orson Welles. In the crowd milling around the center of the hall, I single out Cloris Leachman, whom I've just seen in *WUSA;* Bogdanovich, head bent in intent conversation with cinematographer Bob Surtees, whom I recognize from a press book promoting *The Graduate;* Clu Gulager, foppish-perfect-pretty in Nudie's finest ranch drag and manly footwear, and several teasingly familiar faces I can't quite fit names to. Glancing our way, Bogdanovich smiles and waves to indicate that he'll drop over to chat when he's free.

"Orson may turn up down here, you know," Polly muses as she dabs at my temples wth a cotton swab. "The old rogue's making a picture about a Hollywood director—*Jake Hanniford*—and as usual he wants to steal scenes from somebody else's setup, if he can. Orson thinks Peter's some kind of nutty intellectual, so he's written him into the script in that sort of burlesque part. Peter says *Hanniford's* going to be the dirtiest movie ever made. . . . Whew, you sure get to know people fast, having to fool with their hair. Let's see what you look like. Oh, fantastic, great! I like your face—it's so *ravaged*. With the hair jobbie and those grungy old clothes, you look lunchier than Dennis Weaver in *Touch of Evil*." Type-casting, I mumble under my breath.

153

Bogdanovich, a slight, grave-faced young man wearing horn-rims and rust-colored leather bell bottoms, shakes hands in greeting, eyes my scruffy get-up narrowly, and nods agreement; yes, he likes my ravaged face, too. "Just don't wander out on the streets without a keeper," he murmurs, deadpan, "I don't want you getting arrested." Motioning for me to follow, he strides briskly across the dense-packed room toward the camera setup, stopping along the way to introduce me to Cloris, Gulager, Surtees, Cybill Shepherd, and because she's standing nearby, a pale, pretty young bit player from Dallas named Pam Keller. Finally, I make my shy hellos with Tim Bottoms, the tousle-haired, James Dean-ish actor who's to play my estranged teen-aged son in the upcoming scene: "Hi, son." "Lo, dad."

Oblivious to the racketing noise and movement around him, Bogdanovich blocks out our paces and patiently coaches Tim and me on our lines. It's a muted confrontation scene the two of us are involved in, a long, Wellesian dolly shot set against the backdrop of a country-and-western dance. Tim and I rehearse our moves until Surtees signals Bogdanovich that he's ready to roll; Peter, in turn, motions for Leon Miller's string band, arrayed on a platform at the head of the dance floor, to strike up "Over the Waves." The cameras whir; we go through the motions of the complicated shot twice. The second time around, it feels good. *"Cut,"* Bogdanovich calls. "Print both takes. Good work, everyone. *Stel-lar!"*

"Academy," a disembodied voice bawls from behind a bank of glaring Klieg lights.

Feeling washed-out and blank, I settle in a folding chair on the sidelines next to Pam Keller, who is "almost 20" and who plays the part of "Jackie Lee French"— "Clu's dancing partner," she explains with a wry laugh, "which makes her a kind of semi-pro floozy, I guess." As if on cue, Gulager wanders by with chat-up on his mind; playfully, he makes a feint at Pam's ribs and bottom. "Oh, don't be such a wimp," she protests, frowning. Gulager, who speaks in a deep glottal rattle like Jimmy Stewart, gives her a pained look: "What was that you said, little lady?" "I don't stutter, buster," Pam snaps icily.

Dismissing him with a stare, Pam turns to ask what I do besides playing village junkie-geeks. Polly, who's stood by watching the exchange, grins and flashes Pam the V-sign as Gulager stalks disgustedly away: "Way to go, sweetheart. He's a real Hollywood showboat, that yo-yo."

The interminable delays between takes stretch into hours that glide past like greased dreams. Late in the evening, Pam is saying, between polite yawns, that she absolutely adores books, particularly Kahlil Gibran's *The Prophet,* and have I, by any chance, met Eric Hoffer, who she's heard somewhere also lives in San Francisco?

Around midnight, the tedium shades off into stuporous exhaustion, and abruptly seven or eight of us are headed back to the Ramada Inn in an over-stuffed Buick sedan. Pam falls asleep instantly, looking frail and vulnerable enough to resemble somebody's sister, maybe my own. To pass the time and the miles, Cloris and Gulager harmonize on old Baptist hymns, then trail off to silence. In the darkness beyond the swath of the headlights, the stringy mottes of mesquite trees and stagnant stock tanks and the Christmas-tree oil rigs flash past at 80 mph. Startled by the sight, I glimpse my bone-white hair and ravaged face in a window as I light a cigarette.

The conversation rises and falls desultorily. "Do we work tomorrow?" Gulager asks Cloris edgily. "Maybe we don't work, huh? That'd be nice. I'd like to spend the day limbering up at the Y." Cloris doesn't know, shrugs fatalistically. "God, I've just been thinking about that gross asshole who plays my husband . . . This is the saddest picture," she reflects with a wilting sigh.

* * *

The next day begins and ends with the ritual viewing of the dailies in the hotel's cavernous banquet room. Sitting with Bogdanovich, who seems tense and distracted, and Bob Surtees, who is always medium cool, I watch enough footage to confirm Polly's estimate of Ben Johnson's performance as "Sam the Lion," the dying proprietor of the last picture show—he's magnificent. Academy all the way. Then I hurry off to board the charter bus headed for Archer City.

155

On the hour-long ride to the set, I share a seat with Bill Thurman, who plays "Coach Popper," Cloris Leachman's husband in the film. Thurman, whose meaty, middle-aged face is a perfect relief map of burnt-out lust and last night's booze, is kibbitzing across the aisle with Mike Hosford, Buddy Wood, and Loyd Catlett —*Picture Show's* resident *vitelloni*. The term springs automatically to mind to describe the three randy studs because, in essence, they're playing themselves; on screen and off, they're the high-strutting young calves of this short-grass country, always on the prod for excitement, and maybe a little strange to boot. Loyd, who is 17 and something of a self-winding motor mouth, is plunking dolefully on a guitar and munching a jawful of Brown Mule. "Terbacker puts fuel in mah airplane," he explains expansively. "Say, look-a-here, Thurman, you seen our scene the other night—you thank we was any good?"

Thurman puts on a mock scowl and snarls: "Shit naw, kid, I thought yall sucked—buncha little piss-aint punks." "Hmph," Loyd snorts, "that's what that dollar whiskey'll do to your brains, Ah guess." Under his breath, he hisses: "Kiss mah root, you boogerin' ol' fart." Without preamble, he breaks into the Beatles' song about doing it in the road, and the other boys join in the singing with gusto, if no clear command of harmony.

"Me and Cloris are gettin' along real good together in our scenes," Thurman remarks, looking as if he'd give a princely sum to believe it. "I guess the production's been a little bit disorganized up to now, but all things considered, I b'lieve we got a real grabber on our hands here, don't you agree?" The *vitelloni* strike up "A Boy Named Sue," and Thurman starts reminiscing about the various "stars and gentlemen" he's had the privilege of working with. "Les Tremayne," he says. The boys segue into "Don't Bogart That Joint." "Bob Middleton . . . Paul Ford . . ." Thurman intones reverentially. *"They're - gonna - put - me - in - the - movies,"* Loyd is yowling as the bus pulls up at the Spur Hotel.

After changing into our costumes, Loyd and I walk over to the Legion Hall together. He says he wants to be an actor or maybe a stunt man—"for the money and the thrills." "There's flat nothin' to do around these parts but 'fist-fight and fuck, and Ah ain't even got a girl friend," he laments. "Sometimes Ah feel lower than whaleshit, good buddeh, and that's on the bottom of the ocean . . . Drama in high school—that's the only thang Ah was ever any good at. That and rodeoin', but mah folks made me give up ridin' bulls 'cause it's dangerous and they didn't like the company Ah was keepin' . . . Now, though, Ah've got mah foot in the door to the movies—shit, son, Ah'm gonna make $1600 on this picture just by itself—and all Ah gotta do is take the ball and run, don't you thank?"

* * *

On the set, which is being busily readied for another take in the dance sequence, the wardrobe master sits slumped on a camp stool, firmly clutching the prop purse that Cloris Leachman will need in the upcoming scene. Striding past him, the first assistant director fakes an ogling double-take: "Somehow, Mick, I don't think it's the real you—but would you be my *bubeleh* tonight?" The wardrobe master grins and lazily flashes him the bird.

"We need a huge container of water, Lou," Bogdanovich calls out to the second propman. "Waterloo!" the first assistant director crows. "That's what this whole deal is about, right?" "We hired Rube for his wit, not his talent," Bogdanovich murmurs as he peers through a view-finder.

The hall is chill and drafty; the first raw gusts of a blue norther are rattling the windowpanes and doors. I find a chair near a gas heater and sit down to scribble some notes. Nearby, Bill Thurman, Clu Gulager, and several extras are seated around a card table, playing Forty-two. "Pass, fade, or die, you mis'able sonsabitches!" Thurman keeps bawling. Pointedly ignoring him, Gulager asks his partner, a barrel-gutted oil rigger from Olney: "Are you fellows deep-bleed drilling? Are you draining off all the oil over there?" "Sheeit," the rigger drawls, "I ain't been dreenin' off nothin' lately, what with this recession got me by the short hairs."

The second assistant director stops to survey the domino game for a minute. "Sweet baby Jesus," he mutters, "if I

157

ran into this bunch in Tarzana, I'd turn out the lights and call the law."

Speaking of which, there's Joe Heathcock, the lanky apparition who plays the county sheriff in the film, proudly displaying his prop .38 police special to John Hellerman, who portrays "Mr. Cecil," a high school English teacher unjustly stigmatized as a homosexual. "My, oh, my," Hellerman, a dainty-featured little man, keeps murmuring as Heathcock waves the pistol around airily, explaining that Texas lawmen don't carry .45s much anymore— "That's just what you might call a lingerin' myth. They mostly tote these leetle ol' boogers like this here now . . . Did I tell you? I just missed gettin' hijacked to Cuba with ol' Tex Ritter oncet. He tole me later they treated him like royalty down there—fed him a steak thick as a horseblanket." "My, oh, my," Hellerman repeats uneasily, his eyes keeping track of the gun.

Heathcock, I'm not surprised to find out, was famous long ago as "Jody" in Bob Wills' Texas Playboys ("*A-ha! Come on in, Jody!*"), and nowadays gigs around Hollywood, Vegas, and Nashville for an enterprising $2500 a week. As he talks, his movements and gestures aren't so much direct thrusts as sidelong indirections— furtive, elliptical—as if he's swimming through syrup toward some improbable lover. I mark him down on sight as an all-around *rava avis,* this homely, likeable old bird, and move in closer to listen as he launches into a scarifying yarn about getting tossed in jail in Bowie, a shirttail burg not far to the south of Archer City.

"Wellser, I was a drankin' man back in them days," he recalls, sucking fire into his pipe and cackling now and then with the force of an exploding boiler. "As I recollect it, I was drivin' up from San Antone to Tulsa to meet Bob and the boys in the band, and I was about half-drunk—the last half, that is—*hah!*—so I pulled off the road and was gonna catch a leetle nap of shut-eye. Now, understand, I wasn't nothin' but a hahrd hand back then, but I had six-seven hunnerd dollars stuffed in my boot, so when somebody started shakin' my laig in the middle of the night, why, I just natcherly kicked whoever it was flush in the face. Wellser, be damned if whoever it was didn't turn out to be a Bowie con-

158

stable, and he done the same thing right back to me—I left the better half of my teeth strung out along that highway when he brang me in to the lock-up. Still and all, it was kiley a Mexican stand-off—I shinered both of his eyes and bust his nose, too, before I realized he was a po-lice. Wellser, as it happens, that leetle set-to turned out to be a turnin' point for me—I ain't had a drank since, and that was right at 20 years ago. I figgered I'd been down so long it looked like it was all up to me at that point, so I—"

"But what happened?" Hellerman asks, jaw ajar.

"Happened?" Jody blinks. "Why, I awready told you. I quit drankin'."

"I mean at the *jail*," Hellerman persists.

"Oh, *that*." Jody relights his pipe with the timing of a paid assassin. "Well, I got out with a leetle hep from some friends."

* * *

Taking a few minutes' breather, I sit down on the sidelines, idly thumbing through the pages of a paperback copy of the novel version of *Picture Show* (Dell, 75c, out of print). Set in a grim, mythical backwater called Thalia in 1951-52 (and "lovingly dedicated" to Larry McMurtry's hometown), the story focuses on a loose-knit clique of teenagers who have ultimately nowhere to go except to bed with each other, and to war in Korea.

The adults who alternately guide and misguide their young—even Sam the Lion, the salty old patriarch who rules over the town's lone movie theater—are no less disaffected by the numbing *mise en scene* of Thalia; in Dorothy Parker's phrase, they are all trapped like a trap in a trap.

The tenor of life in Thalia is described this way by a wayward mother to her soon-to-be-wayward daughter:

"The only really important thing I [wanted] to tell you was that life here is very monotonous. Things happen the same way over and over again. I think it's more monotonous in this part of the country than it is in other places, but I don't really know that—it may be monotonous everywhere. I'm sick of it, myself."

As far removed from grace or salvation as the Deity

is reputed to be distant from sin, the town boys haunt the picture show, where they're permitted a few hours of "above the waist" passion with their girls on Saturday nights. Inexorably, boys and girls together careen into out-of-control adulthood in the Age of the Cold Warrior. But as they do, the symbols and landmarks of their childhood become lost to them, and in the end, even the picture show is gone.

Weighing the book in my hand, I try to weigh it in my mind as well—objectively, if possible. The narrative is sometimes crude, more often tasteless, and always bitter as distilled gall. But it is true—true to the bone-and-gristle life in this stricken, sepia-colored tag-end of nowhere. So it goes in the short-grass country. It's hardly a thought to warm your hands over, but it occurs to me that I've been in Archer City only a scant few hours, and like that daughter's mother in Thalia, I'm already a little sick of it, my own self.

* * *

"What previous movie work have you done, little lady?" Gulager asks Pam as they idle at their toe-marks for the still-stalled dance sequence. Pam darts him a quizzical glance, decides his tone is neutral if not exactly friendly, and says that she was Charlotte Rampling's nude stand-in in an unreleased picture shot in Dallas called *Going All Out*. "Charlotte who? Never heard of her," Gulager shoots back, not neutral after all as he bends over to dust off his hand-tooled boots with a handkerchief. "Oh, you know—that girl in *The Damned*," Pam stammers, looking flushed. You saw *The Damned*, didn't you? . . . I remember seeing you in *The Killers* with Lee Marvin. I thought you were—really quite good in it."

Gulager smiles crookedly and tucks the handkerchief back in his pocket: "Everybody thought I was good in that one, including me, honey. It was made for TV, and I expected to win an Emmy nomination for it. Turned out, the picture was too violent for family viewing and none of the networks would touch it . . ." Gulager pauses, then spits out coldly: "I hate acting, anyway—despise it. *San Francisco International* on NBC this season—you seen it yet? Don't bother. It's a piece of fuckin' trash. I'm only working on that series and this picture for the money. My main drive from now on is to become a filmmaker. Control—that's the only thing worth having in this business."

Unsure what to reply, Pam clears her throat and delicately observes that Gulager sounds a lot like Jimmy Stewart at certain odd moments. Gulager laughs shortly: "I wish I had Stewart's money." "Oh, money's not everything—" she starts to scold. Gulager cuts her off: "I can't think of anything I want to do that money can't buy. Money buys talent. Talent makes movies. I want to make movies. It's that simple."

Up on the rostrum, Leon Miller's string band—two guitars, a bass, and a fiddle—saws away wearily on "Put Your Little Foot" as the two assistant directors supervise endless dance rehearsals. A grip threads his way across the dance floor, bawling, *"Hot stuff—comin' through."* The box he's carrying is marked: DON'T TOUCH—PROOFS TO TUESDAY'S SHOOTING. As they advance *one-two* and return *three-four*, Gulager and Pam continue their muted bickering until finally he flares up and calls her a "know-it-all little shit." Eyes snapping, Pam tartly informs him that you have to be a little shit before you can be a big one—"Ness pah, Big Shit?" Out on the floor, one of the extras faints, and there's another long delay. Pam wanders over to the sidelines, looking flustered. Jody, strumming Jeff Bridges' gleaming D-28 Martin, serenades her, Jimmie Rodgers-style:

> *If I can't be yo' shotgun, mama.*
> *I sho ain't gonna be yo' shell.*

Pam blushes pleased pink and mercurially changes moods. Maneuvering around to catch a glimpse of my notes, she puts on an impish smile and cajoles in an orphan-of-the-storm falsetto; "Oh, make me famous, will you, please? Are you famous by any chance? Clu Gulager is famous, you bet. He's famous-er than anybody, in fact. Just ask the rat bastard."

Near one of the too-few heaters scattered around the hall, Bob Glenn, who plays a nouveau-dumb oil baron in the film, is remarking that he appreciates the un-structured makeup of the location company—"No snotty star types, all the lead actors mingling with everybody else." Fred Jackson bobs his head in agreement: one of the stand-ins, he's a tall drink of water from over Throckmorton way who looks uncannily like Buck Owens. "Hail yes, Bawb," he says. "So far, ever'body high and low's just acted like we'us all in this thang together. You know what I mean? Dju meet ol' Ben Johnson while he'us down here? Shit, he's just *folks*, that ol' boy. He's sposed to came back one a these times and go huntin' with me. You ever do any huntin'?"

Looking sulky and bored, Loyd Catlett saunters past and overhears Jackson's question. "You damn betchy Ah go huntin'," he grumps, "but that don't mean Ah never ketch nothin'. Same thang with this picture— Ah missed out on all the good parts. Ah never git no pussy, and Ah don't git in no fights. Ah'm just a kind of sidekick for Jeff and Tim, Ah guess." "Well, I reckon you just got to keep on keepin' on, boy," Jackson says affably. Loyd can't maintain his pout for long. Soon, he's grinning toothily despite himself: "Aw, slap hands with me, you sorry hillbilly dip-shit. *Rat-on!*"

Over an electric bullhorn, the first assistant director booms out: "All right, everybody be of good cheer. All together now, let's have some *SMILES!*" "Let's have some liquor," somebody groans in reply. Scowling distractedly, Bogdanovich kicks at a thick hummock of recording cable. "Let's have some lunch," he sighs quietly.

* * *

With manic zest, Gulager titillates the townspeople dining at the Golden Rooster, Archer City's lone indoor eatery, by pasting pats of butter on his cheeks and forehead. "It wouldn't melt in your mouth, honey," Cloris observes acidly. Cybill Shepherd, who plays "Jacy," the film's teen-aged sexpot, looks pained at the buzzing commotion Gulager is causing among the diners; wordlessly, she picks up her book—Thomas Mann's *The Magic Mountain*—and leaves before the meal is served. It's an interesting choice of reading and an interesting reaction; I determine to try to talk to her if a chance arises.

A local filling station owner approaches the table and shyly asks Gulager for his autograph; the big, sunburned man pretends not to notice the trickle of butter oozing down the actor's jaw. Not to be overlooked in the crowd, Cloris launches into a rambling singsong recitative about George Hamilton taking a sleeping-pill suppository during a cab ride in Paris. She projects the maybe-apochryphal story just like an actress, but she breaks just like a little girl when nobody but Jeff Bridges laughs at the punchline. Gratefully, she tousles his hair: "Give my love to your daddy, Jeff-boy. Is he still all water-puckered from *Sea Hunt!*" Jeff grins bashfully and mumbles something into his plate.

Gulager, milking the butter *schtick* to the last drip, scrapes the runny yellow goo off his face and spreads it on a slice of bread, then wolfs it down with extravagant gusto. To a man, the diners across the crowded room crane around to watch his every move, but nobody quite applauds.

Pam, who's sat rigid with distaste throughout the meal, looks pensive during the two-block walk back to the Legion Hall. "Clu Gulager," she announces at last in a tiny, constricted voice, "is just another pretty face. All smeary with butter, at that. *Blechh!*" She reminds me of someone, Pam does. Like Loyd, in his way, and Jody, too, she reminds me of everybody decent I ever knew in this empty, perishing, hard-scrabble country.

* * *

Back on the set, the crew members are beginning to trundle the monstro Panavision equipment out into the parking lot where the night's shooting is to take place. By this time, it's 6:30, dark as the grave, and biting cold. Jody is warming his hands over a feebly-flickering heater. "You awder this bad weather, darlin'?" he teases Pam. The prop master wanders among the clusters of actors and extras huddled around the stoves, asking, "Has anybody seen a can of snow?" General laughter trails him around the room. The chief camera operator is telling a spectacular-breasted teen queen from the neighboring town of Electra about working on *Drive, He Said*. "Well, it was a weird experience, I tell you that, sugar. Jack Nicholson's what they call far out, you know? Dope and rebellion, all that shit. Me, I'm more or less a law-and-order person myself, so I told him after we saw the rough cut: 'Jack, it's a cute picture, but it's not anything I'd want to take my wife and kids to see.' Listen, uh . . . Dottie . . . I'll probably have to work here until pretty late, but, uh . . . what're you going to be up to around midnight?"

Loyd Catlett rushes in with the news that the generator truck has caught on fire. "The *lost* picture show," Mae Woods, Bogdanovich's secretary, groans, dashing outside to take a look. Fred Jackson grasps Loyd's elbow and probes for his funnybone: "You hear about that ol' hippie kid, he got the first asshole transplant?" Loyd shakes his head: "Naw—*ouch,* you sombitch!" "It rejected him," Fred guffaws. On a rump-sprung sofa near a fireplace that doesn't work, Jody strums patient accompaniment while Cybill Shepherd and Jeff Bridges try to remember the words to "Back in the Saddle." A rash of new domino games breaks out around the fires.

Outside, towering floodlights illumine the '52-vintage cars ringing the entrance to the hall. The minor generator blaze has already been dispatched by the Archer City Volunteer Fire Department, some of whose members remain behind, striking stalwart poses. As usual, the shot Bogdanovich plans is diabolically complicated:

(1) Cybill, as "Jacy," is to park her '48 Ford convertible near the hall's entrance, get out of the car, and be greeted by Randy Quaid, who plays "Lester," a goofy-looking idle-rich suitor. They're to exchange a page or so of dialogue before (2) Jeff and Tim Bottoms, as "Duane" and "Sonny," respectively, barrel into the parking lot in a battered Dodge pickup against a moving frieze of extras shown in deep focus getting out of cars, walking across the lot toward the hall's side entrance, etc. Tim exits from the truck toward that rear door while Jeff advances to embrace Cybill. During the clinch and subsequent dialogue, the camera pans around to show (3) Clu Gulager, as "Abilene," escorting Pam Keller—"Jackie Lee French"—through the front door.

"All of that in one so-called fluid take," the dolly operator groans piteously. "Hell, Peter, it's not only difficult, it's impossible." "With patience and saliva," an electrician pronounces sagely, "the elephant balleth the ant."

"Peter, can we shoot this shit?" the boomman screams out from overhead. "Or not?" "Strictly speaking, Dean," Bogdanovich mumbles, squinting at the setup, "possibly." He motions toward the first assistant director: "Meester Rubin! I theenk it iss time ve vill take a live vun." "Damn, Peter," the second assistant director snorts, "you're getting to sound just like Otto. That prick." "Ready when you are, C.B.," shouts the first assistant director.

In a sudden hush, the cameras begin to roll, but Cybill blows the take by missing her mark parking the convertible. When she stammers out an apology, the sound mixer stage-whispers gruffly: "Sympathy can be found in the dictionary between shit and syphilis, sister."

After the eighth consecutive take has gone down the tube— this time because Jeff has rammed the pickup into the side of the building—Bogdanovich murmurs through blue lips, "Well, back to the old drawing board." "We're as shit out of luck tonight as a barber in Berkeley," the key grip grumbles. Polly Platt wanders around looking worried-in-general; Fred Jackson pats her on the shoulder in paternal commiseration. "Ain't a horse that can't be rode," he philosophizes solemnly, "and ain't a cowboy that can't be throwed." "Our 1-left foot doesn't seem to know what our other left f-foot is d-doing tonight," Polly complains through chattering teeth.

Down on the shoulder of the highway, where despite the cold a sizeable crowd has gathered to watch the filming, a bandy-legged cowboy and his woman—both drunk —are quarreling bitterly about money. "Aw, hush up about it, honey," she snaps, reaching for his arm. "C'mon —less you and me *vamanos a casa*. Piss on a buncha movie stars, anyhow." *"Naw, goddamnit!"* he cries in a strangled fury, bristling away from her and fishing feverishly through his pockets. "I ain't about to haul-ass home till we get this thang settled, oncet and for all! Here, goddamn your bitchin' eyes—here's 99 cents in change. Put a fuckin' penny with that and you can buy a dollar anywheres!" Starting to sob, the woman slaps the change out of his hand and stumbles off into the darkness. After a minute, the cowboy spits toward the coins scattered in the gravel and sways off after her, howling: "Hey Trudy! Wait up a goddamn minute! I'm comin', darlin'!"

It's a wrap at last on what must be the 11th or 12th take. The actors and crew look numb and gray-faced with exhaustion; Pam looks distressed, as well. Her face is wind-chapped, she has a big red bump swelling on her forehead, and she's worried sick that she may lose her receptionist's day-job at the Royal Coach Inn in Dallas because Bogdanovich says he needs her for an additional day's shooting. "I didn't count on this movie changing my *whole darn life!*"

* * *

The troupe works till the midnight hour, then falls apart like some hydra-headed beast sawed off at the knees. In a station wagon speeding back to Wichita Falls, Gulager asks Jody how he happened to get involved with *Picture Show.*

"Wellser, ol' Reba Hancock, Johnny Cash's baby sister, she recommended me for the part," Jody answers, tamping his pipe. "She's a darlin' woman, Reba is. You know her by any chancet?"

Gulager leans forward, interested: "No, but I've met John. Worked on a benefit with him once. Has he cleaned up his act, like they say? Is he walkin' the line these days?"

Jody grins broadly: "Aw, you bet yore sweet ass he is. Ol' John's livin' real good now, real straight. I recollect he tole me oncet that he used to take up to a hunnerd pills a day—you know, what they call them uppers? But that's all spilt milk under the bridge now ... Yep, John's just bought hisself a nice home over at Nashville from Roy Osborne—and, a course, he's got June, too, which that leetle ol' girl has just done wonders for his health and his life."

"Is that where you make your home—Nashville?" Gulager asks.

"Yesser," Jody nods, "and mah own self, I couldn't be happier noplace else in the world. Shoot, I got more work comin' in anymore than I can get around to, seems like. I'm a reg'lar member of the *Grand Ole Opry,* I work on *Gunsmoke* three-four times a year. The Mills Brothers just recorded a leetle ol' song that I wrote—'It Ain't No Big Thang'—and I seen just the other day in Cashbox, I b'lieve it was, where that sucker's awready in the Top One-Hunnerd.

"Hell's bells, I had to flat up and quit *Hee-Haw*—it'us too corny for my sights, you know what I mean? Buncha sorry, white-trash mow-rons settin' around on the floor cuttin' up like fools. Then, too, Junior Samples, he's got a terrible drankin' problem, and not much sense to start with, and I got sick and tahrd of readin' his idiot cards for him . . . But, y'know, that egg-suckin' show shot up to 15 in the Nielsens last week, and John Cash's fell off to 65. Somebody's givin' John some bum goudge on per-duction, seems like to me . . .

"Yesser, I lead an awful full and happy life these days. Play goff every chancet I get. I shot a few rounds with Dean Martin not long back. You know Dino, by and chancet? Well, lemme tell you, he's a fine ol' boy —he wants to record in Nashville sometime soon. And Frank, y'know, he's awready got studio time booked over there."

Gulager coughs delicately: "That's . . . uh, Sinatra you mean?"

"Yesser," Jody nods, sucking serenely on his pipe, "that's the one."

* * *

During the post-midnight screening of some late-arriving rushes in the hotel's banquet room, Bogdanovich, Polly, Bob Surtees, and six or seven other production aides drowse through some routine interior establishing shots, then snap alert at a brace of electrifying takes showing Gulager, as "Abilene," seducing "Jacy"—Cybill Shepherd —in a deserted pool hall. Even in its unedited form, the scene has a raw and awesome power; at one point, Gulager's right eye, slightly cocked, gleams out of the eerily-lit frame like a malevolent laser beam. *"Academy,"* the first assistant director murmurs reverently in Surtees' direction. "Wow—Clu looks positively *ogreish,"* the second assistant director crows in delight. A brittle female voice pipes out of the dark at the back of the room:

"Nothing that mental and spiritual plastic surgery couldn't cure, honey."

* * *

I spend the better part of an hour the next morning reviewing the reactions of some of the local gentry to the filming of *Picture Show* on their home turf, as expressed in letters to the editor of the weekly *Archer County News*. These are heartfelt communications, I'm given to understand by a hard-drinking production secretary, from "Baptists and worse."

From the paper's October 22nd, 1970, edition:

". . . I understand that (Larry McMurtry's) book, if it can be called that, is to be translated into a movie and that portions are to be filmed in Archer City with the support and approval of the Citizenry. No doubt, a certain glamor and glitter is to be anticipated from having a few Hollywood types in the city during the filming, and perhaps some economic benefit may ensue, but if the City Dads and the School Board Members have taken the precaution to read the book, then no question can prevail as to the type of movie that will result. I, for one, feel that Archer City will come out of this with a sickness in its stomach and a certain misgiving about the support the City is lending to the further degradation and decay of the morals and attitudes we foist upon our youth in this Country. . .

"Where are the voices that should be raised in opposition to this travesty? . . . Wake up, Small Town America. You are all that is left of decency and dignity in this country . . .

Yours truly,
Noel W. Petre"

In the November 5 edition, the publisher, Joe Stults, mills about smartly over the issue in a signed column called "Joe's Jots":

"Let me be fast to point out that I do not endorse or purchase dirty or obscene books, nor do I attend or endorse dirty movies. Neither do I consider myself a literary or movie critic. I must admit I have read only a few excerpts from the book and from what I

168

read the book 'stinks.' However, on the other hand, a Wichita Falls school teacher (woman) told me that she has read all of McMurtry's books and thought they were tops . . .

"I definitely cannot see where Archer City will suffer a 'black eye' for permitting the movie to be filmed here. It has already proved to be an educational experience for many and if our morals are affected by this book or movie then maybe we need to cultivate a little deeper."

* * *

Later in the morning on the set in Archer City, the cast assembles and waits fretfully for the final hours of shooting on the dance sequence to begin. Polly Platt, renewing the tint job on my hair, is saying from behind her enormous blue oval shades: "I was a Boston deb —can you believe it?—so I had a different notion about dances when I first got here . . . Now, I'm miserable and deliriously happy at the same time. I miss my baby girls to the point of pain—they're with Peter's family out in Phoenix—but I'm elated about the way the movie's coming along . . . Of course, part of the agony is that Peter is no longer my friend or lover or companion; Peter is making a movie . . . He has a terrific nostalgia for his teen-age years in the Fifties—Holden Caulfield ice-skating at Rockefeller Plaza with wholesome young girls in knee socks, like that . . . Somehow, he's managed to transfer those feelings about his own adolescence to the totally different experience of the kids in the film . . . Have you noticed? He's very—tender with the young actors . . . So, I ended up 'doing' Cybill—her overall appearance as 'Jacy'—to lock into those longing fantasies of Peter's. In reality, I created a rival for myself, I guess . . . Well, anything for art, huh? There, now —you look properly geekish again. Get out there and wow 'em, kid. Win this one for the Gipper."

"Who's the Gipper, coach?" Cloris inquires brightly, making room for me in the shivering circle massed around a heater. Nearby, one of the never-ending Forty-two games is in progress, generating more heat than the stove. John Hellerman is dourly predicting that Mae Woods, Bogdanovich's secretary, will turn pro and start hustling in the L.A. domino parlors when she gets back home. "Forty-two again!" Mae squeals, flashing Hellerman a deep-dish grin. Chording Jeff's guitar from his perch on a prop crate, Jody serenades Ellen Burstyn, who plays "Lois," a cynical, bed-hopping socialite in the film:

> Sick, sober and sorry,
> Broke, disgusted, and blue.
> When I jumped on that ol' Greyhound,
> How come I set down by you?

By the fake fireplace, Bob Glenn is recalling the years he spent working in a repertory group in a remote area of Canada: "Only the National Geographic reviewed us," he concludes ruefully. When I laugh, he sidles nearer and asks out of the lower half of his mouth if I'm holding anything "interesting to smoke from Frisco." I give him a puzzled look; he looks at me as if I'm peculiar, too, then turns away to listen to Bill Thurman, who's describing his lady agent in Dallas: "Gawddamn, boy, her fuckin' laigs look like a sackful of doorknobs, and they run clear up to right under her tits. Shit, I can't figger out a-tall how her ol' man ever gets any." Later in the day, I do a double-take when Bogdanovich, who's been standing within earshot, incorporates the remarks almost verbatim in a colloquy between the character "Coach Popper" and his beer-guzzling cronies.

"Domino contingent," the first assistant director rasps over a bullhorn, "please hold it down to a roar. We're having a rehearsal." Warmed up by now, I stroll around for a while among the extras. Most of the men are unsmiling, stiff-starched, gleaming with brilliantine. The women, as a hard rule, are pinch-faced, mean-spirited cunts who make me wonder how I managed to couple with their spitting images so long without turning raving queer. Near the coffee urn, Gulager, his concho-studded hat tilted forward rakishly, is chousing a couple of the younger, prettier ones: "You got a boy friend, do you, sugar? And you, too, hon? Back in Alvarado? Wahl, what do those two lucky ol' boys think about you pretty little things bein' way up here all by your lonesome makin' a moom pitcher? Wahl, wahl, wahl . . ."

Over by the bandstand, where Leon Miller and his boys sit slumped like zombies after having played "Put

Your Little Foot" for approximately the 527th time, Loyd is dogging the heels of the casting director. "Ah heard they gonna aw-dition three nekkid girls from Dallas today," he whispers to me with a wink, "so Ah'm ona see if ol' Chason'll let me sneak a little peek."

It's a moment of truth for Pam, too, who's just had a long, nerve-rattling talk on the phone with her boss in Dallas. While Bogdanovich blocks out the paces of her final scene with Gulager, Thurman moseys by, notices her woebegone expression, and asks, not unkindly: "Whatsa matter, sugar? You look like somebody cut yore piggen strang." Pam makes a fetchingly grotesque face at him, but doesn't answer. "Yeah, Pam, what's up?" Bogdanovich prods with fond amusement. "You gonna get fired or what?" "I don't *know!*" she bursts out, an oyster's tear away from real tears. "A fat lot you care, anyway, Mr. Bigtime Director—you're making a *movie,* right? The show must go on, right?" "Right," Bogdanovich says evenly, turning away. Polly, who's been following the conversation, bites her lip but says nothing.

"Hell, Pam, you think *you* got problems," Thurman interjects gloomily. "Today's mah birthday—I'm 50 years old. Syrup just went up to a goddamn dollar a goddamn sop." "That so?" Gulager asks, flicking imaginary specks of dust off his glove-tight trousers. "I'll be 42 this month myself. But that's all right, I guess—Antonioni was 38 before he directed his first feature." Polly makes a deep, gagging sound in her throat that Gulager pretends not to notice.

Out on the dance floor, Bogdanovich has a setup at last. When the actors are all in position, he sings out: "This is a take, folks. Movies are better than ever! Roll 'em!"

"Mark it," the sound mixer growls.

"Five-nine-charlie-apple—take one," a grip intones, clapping a slap-stick.

"And . . . *dancing!*" the first assistant director booms out.

It's a wrap in one so-called fluid take, and the crew lustily yodels its approval: "Way to go, Pam baby!" *"Academy!"* "Nice work, Clu."

Over on the sidelines, where Pam goes to fretfully

await transportation to the airport in Wichita Falls, a spry old lady from Vernon in a bird-nest hat is reminiscing about her honeymoon on the Goodnight Ranch in 1923; wearing a new fur coat, she tells Pam with a wan smile, she lost her footing crossing a fence stile and sank neck-deep in a snowdrift. "My swan," she marvels in remembrance, "it took four big drovers to pull me a-loose. Of course, it got much colder in those days than it does now—"

Straight-arming her way up close, a blue-haired matron of 50-odd in a psychedelic-splotched pantsuit interrupts to ask Pam: "Hah yew today?" "Just fine, thank you." "Listen, can I git your autograph, dumplin'? You do play 'Jacy,' don't you?" "No, ma'am, I play 'Jackie Lee French' —" "Aw, well," the woman sniffs, "that's about as good, I gay-ess." Looking stricken, Pam signs a paper napkin, then quickly scratches off her home phone number on a sliver of envelope and hands it to me. "If you happen to see the rushes I'm in," she blurts, "call and let me know what you think, would you? I'm not sure I ever want to be in any more movies, but I'd like to know if I did good or not in this one." Hugging Polly goodbye she hurries off after a driver who'll take her the first leg of the way back to Dallas.

Loyd watches Pam leave, then turns to Polly: "She say she don't wanna be in no more movies? Is that what she said? Sheeit, boy, Ah do! Ah'd lahk to be in about a million of 'em—"

"Hush, Loyd," Polly says in an absent tone.

* * *

Feeling twitchy and fogged-out, I cash in my costume early and hitch a ride back to the Ramada Inn in Bill Thurman's blue Lincoln. Bob Glenn takes the wheel next to Gulager, while Thurman stretches out over most of the back seat, drinking what he calls "toddy for the body" —Old Taylor out of the bottle. Between jolts, Thurman is gossiping about a Dallas-based sci-fi film impresario for whom he's worked in a total of 13 Grade Z pictures: "Ol' Larry's a good ol' boy, you understand, but he cain't keep his pecker out of his pocketbook." Pause for a deep swallow. " 'Course now, Mr. Bogdanovich . . .

you know, Peter . . . he's somethin' else altogether, cain't you agree, Clu?" Every time Thurman addresses Gulager, he calls him "Clu," sometimes at both ends of the sentence.

Gulager, slumped in the front passenger's seat, doesn't deign to answer at once. Thurman goes on: "I mean, to me, I thank he's got the makin's of, uh, well . . . a great artist, maybe." "Mebbe," Gulager concedes, sounding unconvinced. "Personally, I don't like the script cuts he's making, but I guess he doesn't have much choice about it. I'm gonna fight for that scene of yours in the gym, Bill—you know, where you tell the boys they're too ugly to be girls and too short-peckered to be men—"

"Clu, would you do that, Clu?" Thurman entreats softly. "Gawddamnit, ol' buddy, I shore would appreciate it, Clu—"

"Well, I don't have any real power to do anything," Gulager snaps irritably. "I'm just another Okie from Muskogee, myself—just another hired hand working for day wages—"

Bob Glenn cuts his eyes off the road an instant: "You really from Muskogee?"

"Tahlequah," Gulager says, "29 miles outside . . . But shit, look, Thurman, that's the only reason I took my role—which is a fat zero of a nothing part—because there was a lot of other good stuff in the script. It read good to me, it read *honest*. As to whether Mr. Bogdanovich makes it or not, that pretty much depends on how this picture comes out. Both of you guys work mainly out of Dallas, right? Well, I make my living in Hollywood, and they write you off quick if you fail in my city." The cutting-edge of finality in his voice is chilling. Glenn suddenly brakes the car up short; a herd of high-stepping whiteface cattle stream across the highway. Thurman tips up his bottle for a long instant. Abruptly, it is spectral dark, and the night's chill is on us all.

* * *

San Francisco International is on TV that night. I watch part of it in my room, then drift off to the hotel bar to belt back a few healing brandies. Gulager was square on the money in his estimate of the show; with lines like "A killer in an airport full of emotional people is a bad situation," it's a disaster area looking for a landing site. Half-tight, I vow soberly never to broach the topic to him. Later, on my way to bed, there's a phone message for me at the desk from the Yankee Lady out in California: *Sleep warm.* After a bit, I do just that, dreaming at some surreal point that I'm Dennis Weaver in *Touch of Evil,* only *Touch of Evil* has somehow become a Saturday-afternoon western playing at the Last Picture Show in Archer City—the old shuttered Royal Theater—and my grandfather and I are sitting in the hushed dark alongside—who're those two ol' boys in the seats next to us?—Larry McMurtry and Elvis? —yes—and suddenly my own ravaged face swims into focus on the silvery screen, bigger than life, and the camera pulls back to show me tap-dancing on a sofa in a driving rain while Bill Thurman, Bob Glenn, and Clu Gulager ping away at my feet with six-shooters. My grandfather leans forward as the scene unreels, lifts one liver-speckled old man's hand as if to greet his own surprise, and says with an expiring sigh: *"Academy, boy. Academy all the way."*

* * *

The next day's call sheet lists the setting to be used as EXT GRAVEYARD, and summons all the principals of the cast and crew, plus "20 atmos. mourners," a location van, the generator truck, a bus, two station wagons, the director's car, and one (1) Ritter wind machine, to the Spur Hotel at 9:30 sharp. From there, the assembled caravan will converge on the Archer City Community Cemetery, where the funeral of "Sam the Lion" is to be shot.

The Archer City cemetery, a barren but neatly tended tract with a few knobby trees jutting up here and there, forms a strong, stark tableau, so devoid of ornament that each stone and plant and ruptured fissure of the land plays an intense part in the composition, subtly forcing the eye out to the horizon and up to the sky. The weather, fortunately for Bogdanovich and us all, has turned mild, almost balmy, and the wind from the sea of mesquites to the west soughs along the yellow, grassy swells that ascend in all due homage to the burial ground's only imposing structure—the Widow Taylor's marble-columned crypt, with twin potted cactus plants flanking the door like spikey tribunes. As the actors file off the bus and mill curiously about a freshly dug grave to be used in the scene, the first assistant director unslings his ever-present bullhorn and intones solemnly: "Let us now praise famous men, ladies and gents. Welcome to Lenny Bruce's cafeteria."

Bogdanovich sets up the master shot of the funeral scene with uncommon speed, but closeups and dialogue fakes last well into the morning. In off minutes, the *vitelloni* caper among the gravestones. *"It's Boot Hill, son,"* Kenny Wood squalls in the distance, *"the last roundup, motherfuckers."*

Jeff, who's by now as hooked on dominoes as Bogdanovich's secretary, starts up a game a few paces away from Larry McMurtry's family burial plot. The markers for McMurtry's paternal grantparents read:

Louisa F.   William J.

and

1859-1946   1858-1940

The sight of the stones sets up an aching urge in me to be away from the place; I've been to too many of these country boneyards for real, listening to shiny-suited shamans with faces like sprung mousetraps gibber piously over old men and women who were, somehow, in their lifetimes, a little better than they ought to have been anyway, given the time and place.

Over by the wind machine, Bill Thurman is sounding off to Bob Glenn about how loaded he'd gotten the night before: "I was so pissed outa mah mind, boy, I couldn't have drove mah dick in a can of lard. You orta been there." Glenn surveys the empty horizon and spits: "Everybody from here to the damn Atlantic Ocean is three drinks and two fucks behind, you ask me." Nearby, Clu Gulager is chatting up a pretty young hot dog from Anson: "You got a boy friend up there, do you? What's he think about you comin' down here to make a moom pitcher? Wahl, wahl, wahl . . ."

A grizzled old extra in a string tie and Mexican-tooled

175

boots squints disapprovingly at Tim Bottoms, who's lying face down on a grassy slope beyond the last row of gravestones. "Wouldn't know a gol-danged rattler if one taken a gol-danged bite out of him," he sneers, pouring together the makings out of a Prince Albert can.

Downwind from the action, Jody strums quietly on a guitar. "Oh, I had a friend named Ramblin' Bob," he sings, then looks up and notices Barc Doyle, who plays a Baptist preacher's son in the film. "Yore daddy shore dresses you tacky, boy," he cackles. Unlucky at dominoes, Jeff sprawls out in the grass to drowse in the sun, his head cushioned on a pile of jackets. John Hellerman stumbles through the maze of film equipment strewn about on the ground, looking viscerally shaken by the barrenness of the land. "Texas is almost all depleted now," Gulager tells him with a brooding scowl. "It's 20 million square acres of fucked-up land, that's it."

After awhile, when the cameras move elsewhere, I go look into the open grave wherein Ben Johnson—"Sam the Lion"—is supposed to be laid. The brand name on the casket-lowering device says *FRIGID*, and you'd better believe it, little pardners.

*　*　*

Everything about him is gigantic, this 60-odd-year-old cowboy spook who braces me later that day outside the Spur—his immense hands dangling out of the kind of gangrene-colored western tent-suit you can buy at Leddy Bros. in Fort Worth for around $400, his watermelon-sized skull bulging out of a spotless XXXXX Stetson beaver, even his blinding-white dentures glistening like a wholesaler's display of cue balls out of a massive, rutted face that looks to have been marinated a winter or two in creosote and brine. He's M. B. Garrett, as it turns out, from over in Prairie Grove—lived over there all his life, he says, has a little spread over there, in fact, just a few thousand acres, the place mostly takes care of itself these days, even though his boys have up and moved off to Dallas on him, so he's chancing a one-day flyer in this crackerjack movie-extra game . . . —and say, look-a-here, do I mind some company over to the commissary for a leetle snack to eat? He's heard the food

176

over there is right tolerable today—steak, fresh greens, and biscuits—and, anyway, he's curious about that little spiral notebook he's noticed me scratching in all day.

Sure, be glad to have you, I say, shaking hands and moving off in the direction of the dining hall. But he detains me with a polite thumb and forefinger encircling my upper arm: "You don't wanna *walk* over there, do you?" he asks anxiously. Why not? I shrug, it's only a block or two—"Because my *whiskey* is under the seat in the *truck,*" he explains patiently, pointing to a dusty Ford pickup at the curb with a bumper sticker that reads: *When guns are outlawed, only outlaws will have guns.* Oh, I hear myself saying in a faraway voice.

This M. B. Garrett from over there in Prairie Grove turns out to be a self-cooled, rapid-firing, semi-automatic sagebrush *yenta* as he fishes a fifth-sized bottle in a brown paper bag from the accumulated detritus on the floorboard and guides the Ford at a creep across the square and into a mire of unpaved streets. Between bowel-stinging jolts from the bottle, which we pass gingerly back and forth like the hot stuff it is, he geysers out jocular gossip about the McMurtry clan, past and present, and says as we pass a local doctor's pretty daughter: "Married twicet, divorced twicet. She's been warmed-over for the next feller in line twicet-over, you might say." He brakes to peer up a side road: "Might as well take the long way around. Give us another excuse to take a leetle snort."

When we pull up at the dining hall several excuses later, Garrett puts on a long, sorrowing face and announces that he has a "confession" to make—"That toddy you been drankin'? Well, I'm obliged to tell ye it was half vodka and half Old Crow. I didn't have no full dram of neither when I set out this mornin', so I just taken and mixed 'em both up in the same bottle. Hah! Bet you never knowed it, am I right? That's a good one on ye, ain't it?" Garrett is still guffawing when we unload our lunch trays at a table where the location manager is poking apprehensively at his greens and reading a paperback copy of *One Flew Over the Cuckoo's Nest.*

At the sight of the book's title, Garrett imitates a little boy reciting a nursery rhyme for the P-TA:

Wire, briar, limber-lock,
Three geese in a flock.
One flew east, one flew west,
One flew over the cuckoo's nest . . .

"And shit a big gob," he concludes in the little-boy falsetto, clicking his dentures to underscore his wickedness. Wolfing his food so he can get home and hay his stock before nightfall, Garrett slyly intimates that he himself has been interested in books for quite a spell now —for years, in fact. Yesser, why, he himself even buys a book now and again from what they call—what is it now?—aunty-quarian book dealers? Up there in New Yowrk and so on? Yesser, he himself, in matter of active fact, concentrates mainly on collecting rare editions of Texana. In matter of goddamn active fact, he owns one of the only complete collections of J. Frank Dobie in existence, and he reckons it's worth a right smart of money—at least, that's what those aunty-quarian whoosits up there in New Yowrk claim, if you can take such people at their word, sight unseen and all. Sight unseen, because he doesn't get up to New Yowrk much anymore—his wife's health ain't all that it might be now, and she never did cotton much to missing Sunday services over there in Prairie Grove, anyhow. But if my friend there and me are interested in such truck—J. Frank Dobie and all such as that— and we ever happen to get over there to Prairie Grove, why, you know, just look him up, everybody knows where his place is at . . .

After the old man takes his leave, the location manager shakes his head in wonderment. "What in the name of God's body," he whispers, "was *that?*" Somebody who's been trying to kill me all my life, I tell him as a joke. Only, judging from the way he cranes around to peer at me, it doesn't quite come out that way.

* * *

Getting dressed to go back to Wichita Falls that night, Loyd Catlett calls out to Jeff Bridges with studied nonchalance: "Whyn't you'n me run over by the high school tonight, Jeff—you know, fool around some?" Jeff explains that he isn't feeling well; when he gets back to the hotel, he says, he's going to bed and stay there for the evening. "Aw, sheeit," Loyd grumbles, crestfallen.

* * *

My part in the picture is finished by now—*Academy all the way, William Medford Lewis*—so I'm essentially hanging out the next day when the shooting commences with a brief picnic sequence in Hamilton Park—the Beverly Hills of Wichita Falls, kind of—then shifts to the Cactus Motel on Old Iowa Park Road for the exteriors of a tryst scene involving Cybill and Tim.

Every hole-in-the-road town in the short-grass country has its version of the Cactus, a sagging row of plaster-and-lathe cabins beneath an eternally winking "Vacancy" sign. Next door is a franchise tamale joint, and beyond that lies a solid mile of truck stop cafes, liquor stores, used car lots, filling stations that solicit all known varieties of credit cards, and about a hundred or so of the baddest beer bars in the Western world.

As the troupe disgorges from the bus, the sun beats down, fleets of semi trucks roar by on the highway, and a gaggle of townspeople gather to gawk and shyly shake hands with the actors they recognize. *"It's so inneresting,"* a rabbit-toothed woman in pedal pushers exclaims. "Look," somebody hisses softly, pointing at Jeff, who's hunkering down alongside Loyd on a plot of dead grass beside the generator truck, "there's Beau Bridges." "Who?" "Lloyd Bridges'es kid." "Oh."

While the prop men are dressing the scene, Bogdanovich lounges against the hood of a car, doing a fair-to-middling imitation of Peter Lorre. As all good secretaries do on such occasions, Mae Woods registers 100 on the laugh-meter. Cybill sits off to one side, intently squinting into the pica-choked pages of *Crime and Punishment*. Nearby, one of the grips is trying to shmarm over a tushy piece of the local Freez-Kreem talent: "What we're doing, see, is making a Jap-style horror flick—*It Came to Eat the Freeways,* you dig. Stars 8000 Datsuns and a beat-up old VW bus. They're still a few bit parts open, though.

Sa-ay, do you think you could play a topless sheriff at a Mississippi kill-in? I'll speak to the director about it myself. Like, gimmie your phone number and I'll get on the horn to you first thing tonight . . ." Slack-jawled but firm-butted the girl dutifully pokes through her bag for something to write on. There isn't even the faintest quiver of comprehension in her face.

Meanwhile, on their tiny plot of dead grass, Jeff and Loyd are embarked on an extraordinary exchange of their own. Jeff is saying in a casual, offhand way that he knows Loyd doesn't do much reading, but anyway, he's got this spare copy of a book called *Steppenwolf* in his room at the hotel, and he wants to lay it on him . . . you know, whatever . . .just in case Loyd ever gets the urge to read something in an off minute.

"Steppenwolf. Is that that rock group?" Loyd asks. "Shit, boy, Ah lahk rock—it puts fuel in mah airplane."

No, Jess explains—still ever so offhandedly, casually —the rock group in all likelihood took its name from the book, which is about—well, about this dude named Steppenwolf. Loyd'll just have to read about it for himself to understand . . . But if there's an overall *message* to the book . . . you know . . . well, maybe it's something like—*keep moving* . . . Or, whatever . . . It's only a book after all, but still and all, Loyd might get something out of it that might . . . you know . . . change his way of thinking, his values, stuff like that—

"Ah ain't good at books—Ah don't have to tell you that —but Ah lahk that message, whatever you call it," Loyd says, worrying at his teeth with a stem of grass. " *'Keep movin' '*"—shit, that's mah meat, awright. Listen, Jeff—you reckon Ah'd make a fair western star? Ah'm savin' mah money so's Ah can go out to California when this outfit's done shootin' here, but what happens then? How do Ah go about gettin' in the union, do you know? The Screen Actors Guild? Mr. Surtees said he wants to do some stills of me if Ah ever make it out to Holly-wood. And John Hellerman—you know, he's an awful fahn little man—he gimme a mixed drank last night up in his room at the ho-tel and tole me Ah could bunk at his place when Ah git out there. Well, shit fahr and save matches, maybe ever'thang's gonna turn out awright, you thank so?"

Jeff, no longer offhand or casual, hunches his shoulders forward intensely and gestures in an agitated circle: "I don't *know,* Loyd. Nobody knows anything for sure, so nobody can tell you anything for sure. If some dude says he can, then he's bullshitting you. That's why it's important to *keep moving*—keep tryin' to understand yourself better in the world, the *real* world of true recognitions.

"OK, so Surtees and Hellerman say they'll try to help you. We'll, I'll try, too—I'll give you my L.A. address to start with. But I don't want you to get your hopes pumped up too high, because you might not make it. Probably won't, in fact. Hell, you might even find out you don't *want* to be a movie star, blah-blah-blah. Follow me? You might find you want to be something altogether different, you know? The thing everybody has got to learn is—*channel that energy.* I mean, like in your case, don't fight with your fists anymore, all that jiveass shit you've told me about. Fuck, or eat, or climb a mountain, or do something useful instead."

Unused to such talk, Loyd passes a troubled hand across his face, then blurts impassionedly: "Gawddamn it to hell, Jeff, it's hard for me to keep thoughts lahk that in mah head, but Ah'll try, and you got mah word on it, buddeh! Hell, Ah wanna know about all that stuff you mean—values and thankin' and all that shit. You just way out ahead a me, is all, and it's hard as hell to catch up. Ah guess just bein' in this movie, gettin' to know a guy like you and all—that's changin' mah lahf, ain't it? . . .

"Ah was thankin' the other night at the house—you know, just settin' around thankin', lahk a guy'll do— and all of a sudden, Ah was on the subject of God. *Jesus Christ,* Ah says to mahself, what's goin' on here? Ah never did figger it all out to suit me, but anyways, what Ah was thankin' was—you limit yourself to God, but He don't limit Hisself to you, does He? Ah mean God can be whatever he takes a notion to be—a tree or a rock or whatever the fuck . . . But a guy cain't be nothin' but a human man, see what Ah'm gittin' at? And you know what? Alla that made me feel—lonesome, somehow.

181

Ah don't know how to explain it, but Ah guess you cain't hep but feel lonesome sometimes, can ye?"

Later, leaving to go back to the hotel, I draw Loyd to one side and thank him for being in my movie. He looks surprised for a minute, then gives me a gentle poke on the arm. "You're kiddin' me, ain't ye, doctor," he says pleasantly.

* * *

The next afternoon, under a lowering sky, Cybill puts aside her books and sets out with a male companion for a meandering stroll to the Wichita Cattle Company auction barn, located about a mile from the hotel across the kind of middle-class black ghetto that would have been unthinkable anywhere in Texas a decade ago. Along the way, she languidly waves at children playing in the scrupulously clipped yards and ticks off the key events of her *vita brevis* with the heatless detachment of a NASA lifer selecting trinkets for inclusion in a time capsule:

A wealthy "philistine" upbringing in Memphis . . . growing up absurd, all that . . . winning a "Model of the Year" contest . . . moving to Barrow Street in the Village . . . meeting an "older man," a Manhattan restaurateur, who introduced her to the Truly Important Things—music, the theater, abstract expressionism, the European literary heavies . . . "I never learned how to make friends," she reflects moodily, peering down into the dung-pungent shadows of the deserted auction arena. "But . . . I learned early how to fill needs."

Prowling around the barn's maze of tunnels and chutes, she wanders out on a raised plank walkway overlooking pens of cattle being fattened for sale. "What do cows do mostly?" she asks abruptly. The usual things animals do, she is told. "Eat, you mean? Sleep? Make love? I think I might like to be a cow."

On the way back to the Ramada, she chews on a piece of straw and confides that the illusionary business of making a movie is troubling her. "It's like living in a hall of mirrors," she says, smiling a fragile, very private smile. "It's like being dumb but reading Kafka, anyway."

* * *

The *Picture Show* cast begins to scatter in all directions like M. B. Garrett's limber-lock geese; by now, Bob Glenn has returned to the sci-fi mother ship in Dallas, Cloris Leachman and Clu Gulager have departed on separate flights back to L.A., and I'm scheduled on a San Francisco flight out early the next morning. While I'm packing, it occurs to me that I've missed seeing Pam Keller's rushes. Debating whether or not to call her, anyway, and try to bluff it through—*Terrific, Pam baby. Academy all the way*—I head down to the hotel restaurant and join Jody Heathcock and Eileen Brennan for coffee.

Eileen, who plays a salty-tongued barmaid in the film, has just boosted a pair of 89¢ sewing scissors from a five-and-dime store, and she crows about her petty thievery elatedly as she knits and purls on something gruesome and fuzzy spilling out of her lap. Jody is shyly jiving the waitresses, Carole and Winnie, as he's done with their sisters-in-aprons a thousand times before, playing one-night stands from Yazoo City to Weed. The two girls are loving it; they can't, in fact, get enough of that cool, adenoidal *a-ha,* because this guy is *Jody Heathcock,* after all, who used to be a famous bigshot with *Bob Wills,* that famous old-timey bandleader their folks used to rave about after drunken Saturday night stomps at the M-B Corral. Besides, Jody *knows—is friends with—plays goff with—* all the famous bigshots in the world—Faron Young, Roy Acuff, Dean Martin, Marvin Rainwater, Sonny James, Frank Sinatra, Stringbean, Lefty Frizzell, Ray Price, Merle Haggard, Waylon Jennings, Glen Campbell, Jim Nabors, Engelbert Humperdink, Cowboy Copas, Johnny Cash—the list is endless . . . *Hot damn!*

Winnie, arms akimbo on the counter, initiates the flirty ritual as Carole serves Jody an open-faced sandwich: "Well, hah yew today, Mr. Heachacallit?"

"Ah, I'm sick in the bed, honey. Say, look-a-here, when're you'n me goin' down the road for a leetle piece, you sweet thang?"

"Don't you take me for granite, Jody," she sniffs. "Besides, you'll have to ast my ol' man about *that.*"

Jody winks at her and turns to Carole: "What kinda sangwich is this you brang me, anyways, dear heart?"

"Freench dip. What you awdered, ain't it?"

"Well, bless mah heart, Ah must have. Listen, set down here beside me and Freench mah dip agin, darlin.' "

Carole cracks her gum and pretends not to know what he means: "Naw. I've awready eat."

"Anybody Ah know?"

"Oh, *you*. You're the filthiest-mouthed thang I've ever saw!"

"*Me?* Why, you're shore one to talk. Least Ah don't let mah meat loaf, lahk you do. What's a sorry, mattress-assed ol' gal lahk you doin' in a nice place lahk this, anyways?"

"Hmnph—*you're* gonna be the sorry one, you ol' letch. You'll never know what sweet lovin' you missed, neither."

Jody looks her up and down for a minute, from bouffant topknot to rubber soles: "Bah damn, Ah bet if you ever got to sunfishin', you'd break a man's back. What time you git off tonight? I'll be Don Ameche in a taxi, honey—all you got to do is bend over and Ah'll drive you home."

"Well . . . I don't know about *that*. I'm not even sure I lahk you anymore."

Jody drowns a final hunk of bread in his gravy boat, then rises and hitches up his trousers: "Well, that's purely up to you, dumplin'. 'Cause Ah'm *likable*."

* * *

Late that night, there's a small birthday gathering for me in Jeff's room; from Mae Woods or somebody, word has gotten around that my ravaged face is a year older. Cybill Shepherd shows up, and so do Eileen Brennan and Jody, Loyd, Tim Bottoms, and the location manager. Soon, some imported Mexican *hors d' oeuvres* are making the rounds, and Jagger is bleating "Sympathy for the Devil" on a tinny cassette machine. Jody, sucking contentedly on a pipeful of something pungently contraband-smelling, buttonholes me to ask "Say, look-a-here, Grober, you got anythang sharp and shiny to carry in yore pocket?" As a present, he gives me his bone-handle whittling knife. As my last sober act of the evening, I hand him back a penny, because when a man gives you a knife in the short-grass country, you can't accept it without giving a gift in return for fear of severing your friendship.

Loyd, his hat shoved back at an angle on his dark hair, is sitting in the middle of the floor, taking the first toke of his life in the real world of true recognitions. He sputters and coughs and grins lopsidedly: "Sheeit, that stuff makes ye feel boneless, don't it?" Before the Stones have given way to Elton John, he's sprawled out full-length, asleep. The music and the Mexican imports burn on. Sure, you can go home again, I hear myself telling someone much later, if you're making a movie.

Naked Lunch Box
The David Cassidy Story

by Robin Green

There'll be a time when this whole thing will be over. I won't do concerts anymore, I won't wake up in the morning feeling drained, and I won't be working a punch card schedule. I've had to sing when I was hoarse. I've had them with a gun at my head, almost, saying "Record, 'cause we've gotta get the album out by Christmas!" I'll feel really good when it's over. I have an image of myself in five years. I'm living on an island. The sky is blue, the sun is shining. And I'm smiling, I'm healthy, I'm a family man. I see my skin very brown and leathery, with a bit of growth on my face. My hair is really long, with a lot of grey. I have some grey hair already.

—DAVID CASSIDY

"Drive over to the Hippopotamus," Henry instructed.

"Aw, Henry, let's go back to the hotel," pleaded David Cassidy, who sat slumped down in the back seat.

"Heeey," chided Henry. "We're in the Big Apple. Let's just see what's happening."

David slumped further in the joyless back seat, muttering his consent. He was exhausted, stoned and drunk, and dizzy from the antibiotics he was taking to drive away a flu. It had been a busy day—two hour-long interviews in the morning; a press conference at New York City College; a rehearsal all afternoon; a session with gossip columnist Earl Wilson; and pictures for the Cancer Society. Then an impromptu tap dancing lesson in his hotel room with a lady he'd met at rehearsal that afternoon. Then dinner, dope, wine, and now this climbing in and out of the back seat of a car looking for what? New York action?

Well, he had his action and he wanted to go to sleep. But that wasn't what the others were into, except for Jill, who sat close to him. The Lincoln limousine pulled in front of the third discotheque they'd been to that evening. They hadn't stayed at the others because Henry didn't think they were quite right.

"We'll just go in and check it out," said Henry. "Just one more. If we don't dig it, we'll leave."

David mustered a small protest.

"Try it," laughed Henry. "You'll *like* it."

So David was herded into the Hippopotamus.

"Wait here," said Ron, David's valet. "I'll go take a look."

Ron climbed the steps to a room which poured out music and cigarette smoke, lit purple and pink.

"Where do you think you're going?" demanded the doorman, who barred Ron's entrance to the room.

"You don't understand," Ron said. His voice had a bitchy edge on it now. "I'm here with Mr. Cassidy, my employer. I have to see if the place is all right. You see, there he is right there, standing with those people just inside the door. David Cassidy."

"Where?"

"Right there," Ron was almost screaming. "In the blue coat."

The doorman squinted at the slight figure in the dark hallway, then looked back at Ron.

"That's David Cassidy!" Ron said.

The doorman looked at David again. He shrugged. "Who's David Cassidy?"

Only three weeks earlier that same David Cassidy had

set an attendance record at the Houston Astrodome, selling 56,723 tickets to two matinees on the same day.

* * *

1. Baboom, Baboom, Boys and Girls, Zing!

Madison Square Garden was filled five balconies full an hour before the matinee with 20,650 excited females—the same girls who more than 20 years ago would have wept for Sinatra and 10 years ago for Elvis. Average teen age girls who keep diaries, go steady and chew gum. And many younger ones, eight- and nine-year-olds, some with their mothers. David Cassidy's audience—who never miss a Partridge Family episode, who devote scrap books to him and wallpaper their bedrooms with his face and body.

Now they held up banners reading "David Spells Luv."

"I hope I brought enough Kleenex," worried a 16-year-old wearing a tight sweater and hot pants. "I'll probably cry. I cried when I got my ticket."

"Ooooh!" cried one small voice inside the hood of a pink and red snow suit. Eight-year-old wide-eyed Amanda Lewis clutched a $2.00 David Cassidy program to her undeveloped bosom. "He's so sexy."

One fan didn't know if David was sexy. "I'm a boy," explained Elliot Fain, age 11, from Forest Hills. "I think he's a very interesting person though."

The girls were there to scream. They screamed whenever so much as an equipment man mounted the stage. One news photographer approached a cluster of ladies. "Scream!" he directed. They screamed. He took a picture. picture.

Aproned vendors coursed through with screams of their own: Posters! Programs! Hot dogs! Popcorn!

When the lights dimmed, the show's MC—a fave DJ on WABC radio—strutted onto the stage, long-legged and agile as a circus barker. "I just saw David backstage!" he announced.

"EEEAAHHH!" went the crowd.

"Now, when I count to three I want you to say 'Hi, David!' One, two, three!"

"HI, DA-VID!" The auditorium shook.

"And now I want you kids to show the world that children your age can behave and not go crazy. Yell and scream, but stay in your seats. Let me hear you say 'I will.' One, two, three!"

* * *

In a windowless cinderblock dressing room, all David's people were assembled. Wes Farrell, record producer; Ruth Aarons, manager; Jim Flood, PR man; Steve Wax, PR man; Sam Hymen, David's roommate, Ron the valet, Henry Diltz, pop photographer, Steve Alsberg, road-manager. No Jack Cassidy, David's father, but Shirley Jones, his stepmother, with two of her three sons, and his mother Evelyn Ward with David's grandfather, 84 years old, in a grey three-piece suit.

In a corner, a pile of gifts from fans four feet high: stuffed animals, plastic flowers, incense and scented candles, shirts and hand-printed messages of undying love.

David signed autographs for promoters' and policemen's daughters, and chatted with well wishers. It was a high moment for him; a triumph, he called it. "Here I am," he said. "I've arrived."

"Think about it," said Henry Diltz. "The karma is fantastic. David was an actor, looking for a break, and then this Partridge Family TV show comes along. He wasn't a singer, but he evolved really nicely into one. Take the Stones, or Cream. After being into folk music, the blues, and rock and roll for ten, 12 years, they fill Madison Square Garden. Well, David's filling it, too, and *he's only been singing in front of people for a year!*"

Minutes before showtime, Ron helped David into his costume, a $500 white crepe jump suit slit to the navel and decorated with fringe, beads, bells and sequins around the waist.

"I wish," said David, "that anyone who has ever put down someone in my situation—the Beatles, or Presley or anyone—I wish that they could be where I am, could jump into my white suit for just one day. It's such a rush, they'd never come down to think about it.

"It's a high going out on that stage. You look around

189

and it's all there for you, people loving you like that. My friends are there with me. I'm doing what I love to do most, singing and I'm singing for people who would rather have me sing than anybody else in the world.

"There's one song I do, 'I Woke Up in Love This Morning,' and I find a little place where I can sort of point to them. And they each think I mean *them,* and I do. Whew, I can't wait. Let me get out there. Let me do it!"

David sang into the mirror as he applied pancake make-up to his face, chest and arms. He said he didn't think of anything before a concert. "I'm in a state of, 'Well, here I go,' like a runner before a race, an athlete before he takes the big dive. The roll of the drums, baboom, baboom, and then, 'Ladies and Gentlemen, boys and girls!' And I take the baton and zing . . .!"

Flanked by his valet and his road manager, David was off and running. He leapt onto the stage, welcomed by a blood curdling screech. The continuous blinking of flash bulbs gave the place a strobelit effect.

"I love you, I love you," David screamed back at them. "I love *everybody.*"

On stage this mild, quiet guy was transformed into a glistening white superstar. He gave it everything his 5'7", 125 lb. body had. Like a young and healthy animal of no particular gender he moved as he sang, in a graceful, almost choreographed way.

"I never get tired of watching David's act," said his roommate Sam Hymen, looking on from the sidelines. "And I've seen it 50, 100 times. Something's happening out there. The white costume, the big band behind him." The band played perfectly, wearing sedate matching maroon blazers. "I like to watch the audience, too, they're so turned on and happy."

In the first row, Shirley Jones sat with David's family. "It's like a revival meeting," she said, "the way he excites the audience, then calms them down."

Fans tossed stuffed animals and dolls onto the stage, and one girl managed somehow to elude guards and climb up there herself. Once there, she froze. David jumped when he noticed her, a plump girl in a blue

190

chemise. Gracefully, he took her hand and kissed her cheek.

Though no one fainted, as 24 had in Detroit, the energy was high. The girls went wild in place. The young ones grew restless when David crooned the slower ballads in a small, but soothing voice. Many older girls wept.

If David was emanating heavy vibes, they escaped one 24-year-old observer. Jill watched the show on a backstage TV screen. "It's so weird," she said. "Last night, he was really nice. He was a really good fuck." Jill shook her head. "But seeing him doing his act, I can't believe it's the same person. This act is so Las Vegas. He's like a male Ann-Margret."

Twenty thousand girls were satisfied, though, transfixed by their idol. When the hour set was over, they sat in darkness and groaned in disappointment. But not for long.

When the lights went up, they recovered and set to furious but business-like pursuit of their fantasy. Guards blocked off the backstage area, but some fans were small enough to race under their arms and between their legs, overturning one cop.

Finally, they swarmed through, searching for David, who had made good his frantic escape covered with a blanket on the back seat floor of a Japanese sedan. One vendor sold programs along the escape route, getting in a few last minute sales.

* * *

II. Twitchy Thighs and Sticky Seats

In two years, David Cassidy has swept hurricane-like into the pre-pubescent lives of millions of American girls. Leaving: six and a half million long-playing albums and singles; 44 television programs; David Cassidy lunch boxes; David Cassidy bubble gum; David Cassidy coloring books and David Cassidy pens; not to mention several millions of teen magazines, wall stickers, love beads, posters and photo albums. Among many things, including those wet theater seats.

As David himself puts it, "This is very filthy, but when

the hall empties out after one of my concerts, those girls leave behind them thousands of *sticky seats*."

Virtually unknown in the older world of rock audiences, David is an idol to television multitudes and teenage millions. The rise to fame began more than two years ago when he appeared in television programs like *Ironside, Bonanza* and *Marcus Welby MD*. And when he landed the role of a dying boy on *Medical Center*, he unmistakably began to capture viewers' hearts. Then came Keith Partridge, a weekly situation comedy role in *The Partridge Family*.

When *The Partridge Family* started, David was 20 years old. But with his exceptionally pretty face and tiny voice, he passed as the bouncy 16-year-old son in a family of four children who lived in the suburbs and made their living as a rock and roll band.

Only two years before, the show's producers had created the Monkees. With *The Partridge Family* they planned to dub the singing when the band performed, but they soon discovered—to the delight and surprise of everyone—that David himself could sing.

Soon, the television company began putting out Partridge Family records, which sold well. Soon enough, David emerged as a solo performer, cutting his own records, on tour with his own band.

"For many of the girls it's the first time their little thighs get twitchy," opined Steve Alsberg, David's road manager, as he hit down his fourth bloody mary of the flight from New York to Bangor, Maine. Steve, a 28-year-old aging surfer and an L.A. native, had been a road manager for eight years, shepherding Three Dog Night, the Turtles, the Flying Burrito Brothers and Les McCann on concert tours. Working for Cassidy, he said, was the least hassled, because the tours were more businesslike. "These people are professionals," he said of David's 15-member band, who now sat in the coach section. "They're studio musicians, men in their 30s, mostly [except for David's friend Cookie, 21, who plays guitar]. This is an easy gig for them. They don't have to do shit. They get off the plane, on a bus, do the gig, and then back again. And they're not prima donnas. All they want is to put on a satisfying show."

Tucked into the first class section—looking much smaller than his television image, David Cassidy himself ordered a glass of milk.

"I've been sick all week with the flu," David explained, "and I think it's turning into a cold." Illness notwithstanding, he had played Madison Square Garden the day before. And it had been sold out for his concert only three days after tickets had gone on sale three weeks earlier.

"Two years ago, I was getting food stamps," he marveled, this 22-year-old man set in a boy's body with a face so pretty that men do doubletakes on his posters.

He fidgeted in his seat and regarded his new companion. "You know, when I first was told about this article, I wanted to smile and say, 'I really don't care to talk to you.' I expected it would be a put-down. I mean, your readers are not going to come and see me, they're not going to buy my records. Even an article that says David Cassidy isn't so lame, or maybe he can really sing, it's not going to affect them really. They're still going to think I'm an asshole.

"I read in *Rolling Stone* once an article about the Jackson Five. It said they were the black answer to teenybopper idols, but that they had soul—unlike those white sucaryl teen throbs like Bobby Sherman and David Cassidy. I read that over five times, and I still could not believe it.

"I had some hostility towards you, and I still do probably. The magazine is very anti-me and anything I have going for me—like commercialism and all that stuff.

"I'm afraid of it 'cause it attacked me. It put a knife into me," he stabbed at his chest with a fist. "And I bled. I went omph, that hurt. So I take the knife out and I bandage myself up and I say, OK, now I'm afraid of that, right? That stuck me once and shivved me once and it wasn't really even about *me*.

"So I'm very defensive about *Rolling Stone*. I guess that's kind of a fucked way to be." He sat back and sighed. "But I would really dig reading something about me that wasn't, you know, the same old bullshit."

* * *

III. A Fig Leaf Falls: David Stands Naked

Ruth Aarons, who manages David, has been in business 20 years, and in show business all her life. Her father, Alfred E. Aarons, was one of Broadway's biggest producers in the early 1900s. Her oldest brother, Alex, with his partner, Vinton Freedley, produced all of George Gershwin's shows on Broadway, among them *Funny Face, Lady Be Good* and *Girl Crazy*. Alex and Vinton owned the Alvin Theater, a bastion of New York legitimate stage, which has since been sold. "I'm going to buy it back," said Ruth, a small, boyish woman in a trim dutch boy hairdo, "when I get crazy enough."

Before starting Aarons Management with her other brother Lisle in 1951, Miss Aarons spent five years playing ping pong. As a world tennis table champion she gave exhibition games at the Roxy Theater, the Rainbow Room, and London's Wembley Stadium.

When she tired of that, Ruth wrote song lyrics, and from that got into managing one of her clients, Celeste "Then I told David, 'Look, you've got two ways to go: New York and Los Angeles, taking on Shirley Jones, Jack Cassidy, George Chakiris, and now David.

She moved to Los Angeles in 1967, where she lives on an estate in Beverly Hills large enough to house two dogs, two horses, and a pony, as well as herself and the offices of Aarons Management.

"The only things that really interest me in the world are Tinkerbell and Captain Hook," said this shrewd, professional woman, referring to the tiny Yorkshire Terrier in her arms and a fat black dog playing near the stables.

"I've known David since he was eight," she began, settling into a plaid couch in the livingroom of her country English style house while Clide the black butler served cool drinks and lunch. "I used to watch him play baseball in the Little League here in Los Angeles.

"It wasn't until David was 18, I think it was, that I became aware that he wanted to act. His father, Jack Cassidy, came to me—we were in New York at the time —and said, 'Ruth, David doesn't want to go to college.

He wants to go into the business. As long as he's going in, you better keep an eye on him.'

"So David took some coaching lessons—how to project, that sort of thing—and a course in elocution with Philip Burton, Richard's father. Then he got a small part in a Broadway play called *Fig Leaves Are Falling*." Miss Aarons rose suddenly, circled around in place, and sat down again, tucking one leg under her. Her dog Tink echoed this action.

"Well, *Fig Leaves* folded like a tent," she recalled. "Then I told David. 'Look, you've got two ways to go: you can stay here in New York for seven years and learn to act. Or,' I told him, 'you can come back to Los Angeles and be a star.'"

* * *

"I was an actor," David explained later, thinking back to his decision to forget Broadway and return to Hollywood. "I was out to earn the bucks. I wanted to be a working actor—one who works all the time, who other actors look at and say, 'Well, he's pretty good.' Honestly, my goal was not to be a star."

Five weeks after his return to Hollywood he went from earning $150 a day to television guest-star roles. And then came the script for *The Partridge Family*.

"When I first read the script, I thought it was terrible," David recalled. "I was thinking about saying these dumb lines, like 'Gee, Mom, can I borrow the keys to the car.' I just couldn't bring myself to do it after doing all those heavy things I'd done.

"I called Ruth and said, 'You gotta be kidding with this.' And she said, 'Read it over again and call me back.' Well, I'm so soft. I read it over—twice—and then I called her back and I said, 'I guess it's not so bad.' Only because I'd gotten used to it."

And he had the same reaction to the music he was being ask to perform, first as part of the Partridge Family and later on his own. "When I first got in the studio, I said to the producer, Wes Farrell, 'I don't want to cut bubble gum records.' And he said, 'No, man, we're not going to cut bubble gum records.' Me and my friend

195

Cookie were jamming at the time, the blues, and all of a sudden I'm gonna sing, 'I Think I Love You!'"

At first, radio stations hadn't liked the song either. But it has now sold over five million copies. "When that record came out it was only Wes and Larry Uttal, head of Bell Records, who thought it was going to be a smash.

"What happened with that record was we got secondary air play on it, small towns. The primary stations didn't want it. They said, 'Let the TV show break it,' which I can understand."

Finally one town, Cedar Rapids, Iowa, played the record, and it went from 40 to one in two days.

"Now everybody cuts it. Percy Faith, the Boston Pops. And it was written for *me*. I've got good writers writing for me.

"I want people to know that I like to sing that song. I stand naked—that's the best word I can think of—and say 'This is how I am.'"

* * *

IV. Soul on Ice Cream

From the window of the Old World Restaurant on Sunset Strip, 29-year-old pop photographer Henry Diltz could see four billboards with photographs he'd taken. Most prominent in the view was the billboard of David Cassidy in a lacy white shirt. It advertised his first solo album, *Cherish*.

"I'd been sent down to *The Partridge Family* set to take pictures of David for a fan magazine," Henry recalled. "There are millions of photographers there to get David Cassidy shots, right? The best thing to get is shirt changes, because if you get four or five different shirt changes, that'll go for four or five different issues. After I'd been around for a while and got to know him, I got reluctant to ask him to do this bullshit. So one day I was on the phone with Don Berrigan, my editor. I was telling him, 'Listen, David doesn't feel like trying on the shirts you sent over.' And he said, 'Well, tell him we'll give him something. What does he want? A camera?' So I told David that and he said, 'Great, sold, you got it.'

196

"And that's nice. It's a little tip. That's saying, 'Hey, if you'll consent to this bullshit, I'll make it worth your while by giving you this Nikon.' So every shirt change we gave him another lens. It's the same as anything, just buying and selling."

Henry paused and glanced up at his artwork across the street. "Donny Osmond of the Osmond Brothers is the new idol now. They just bought Donny a Super Eight Camera. This year David won't be getting any more equipment because he's on his way out."

* * *

"Is that Star?" David asked Henry across the aisle of the airplane. "Let me see it." David leafed through the teen magazine. "Aw, look at this, Henry, this is disgusting. 'A Bubble Bath with Butch.' And this one, 'Pets of the Past.'" He held up a page filled with the face of a young star and an Irish Setter.

"I wonder where this guy's head is at," said David, shaking his head in outrage.

"He's a rascal," Henry replied. "He's a magazine publisher!"

"This time they've gone too far!" He had come across a contest to find his face in his junior high class picture. "They could at least have asked me! That's digging too deep!"

"Oh, he doesn't mean any harm," consoled Henry. "He won't do anything if you don't want. If you say to him, 'Hey, man, I don't like that,' he won't do it. But if you say, 'Don't bother that!' he'll say, 'Ah hah!'"

"Well that really bothers me. I don't need all this. I've got my cake. This is just the icing now."

"You're beautiful when you're mad," laughed Henry.

"I had never read a fan magazine before all this," David was saying, "I didn't know what a fan magazine was until they called me up and said, 'This is gonna be real good for your career, kid.' It was just after I had done my first TV things. Three shows, and they're on me like vultures.

"At first, I said, 'too much.' I bought a few of them and took them home. I saw Bobby Sherman had a thing selling love beads. I said this is a weird trip. I mean, I gotta look at myself in the mirror in the morning and it was like, I can't do it when they're writing 'David's dream wife,' and 'Kiss David.' I had a bad taste in my mouth from it. I didn't want to be that.

"So I went to them and I said, 'Listen, do me a favor. Don't put me on the cover. Could you just not do that.' Honest, I said this. This was the only major thing I ever did that slowed down the momentum." He laughed a bitter sort of laugh.

"But it was foolish, because you have no control of these things at all. I'm sure they ended up laughing at me, snickering to themselves, saying 'how ridiculous this fellow is.'

"Now I don't read them. It's a side effect that just eats away at me. I don't read them, and I don't see them. Don't tell me about them, 'cause I don' wanna know. I'm on too much of a good trip to bring myself down about stuff that's not real."

But the David Cassidy love beads, the David Cassidy bubble gum, and other merchandise now for sale? Had he found a way to adjust to that, too?

"Listen, if they're going to buy lunch boxes, they might as well buy David Cassidy lunch boxes."

* * *

Being mobbed was another occupational hazard that David was unable to adjust to. His fear sometimes caused him to behave in strange ways. Henry Diltz recalled a vacation he and David had gone on, to Hawaii.

"We got off the plane and he hiked his jacket up over his ears and stuck his head down. I said, 'David, there's nobody who knows you're coming here!' He was calling more attention by walking that way. People were saying, 'Look at that weird guy in the little hat and sunglasses, hiding his head!' But he wouldn't listen. He said he wasn't taking any chances. That if one person saw him, that would lead to three and then 15 and then 100, and he's afraid of that."

"I've been hurt a couple of times," David explained. "I've been scratched on my arms and chest, and face. Once I was hit in the face with an Instamatic camera."

The worst incident had been in Cleveland after a concert.

"Security wasn't good enough and they said, 'Listen, you may not make it.' And I didn't. It happened really fast. They crowded around and came down on top of me.

"I got down on my hands and knees and started crawling. Someone who worked for the Monkees told me to do that. And it worked. They didn't know how to deal with me in that position.

"See, what they want is your hair. They want to grab your hair. And my scalp is so sensitive, I get crazy when anybody grabs my hair. I can just cry. I can cry very easily."

* * *

"You have to pay dues for everything, whatever you do," David sighed, after giving autographs to the flight crew and various passengers. "I must have signed 80 thousand. In the beginning I'd do two thousand at once at some publicity thing at a supermarket.

"Every time I get asked I think I'm going to scream. Please, don't ask me again! My hand is falling off! The thing that irritates me is that they never want it for themselves. It's never, 'I really like you. I'd really like your autograph.' It's always, 'My daughter would never forgive me,'" David mimicked a New York accent. "'Also, my friend Joe needs two for his kids or they won't let him in the house.' I'd dig it if someone would come up and just say 'sign.'"

"I always do it, though. I mean, I can't say, 'You motherfucker, you're 8000th today!' To him it's a big thing, obviously I bring him some joy!"

On the question of politics, David said that he hadn't any. "I don't listen to the news or read newspapers. I don't know what's going on in this world, or why I should vote for George McGovern or Richard Nixon. I don't have enough time.

"I read in one fan magazine that I was very self-centered. And I *am.* I work for *me,* 18 hours a day. It's my gig. So I don't have time to get a point of view.

199

"But I've become accustomed now to handling whatever comes at me," continued the voice in the young body. "Like that press conference at the airport? I thought to myself, 'How long do I have to sit here and handle this?' It's always the same thing."

He held his fist up to his face like a microphone. "'How do you feel about the war in Vietnam?' I'm so tired of answering that question. Or, 'Being as you have an influence on young folks today, what advice do you have for them about drugs?' Ah, shit, man, take drugs."

At the press conference, David had sat with television cameras trained on him, answering questions from a television reporter, who with microphone in hand, knelt at David's feet.

"What advice do you have for the youth today?"

"What's right for me," David had said, "is not necessarily right for them."

* * *

Interlude: A Fig Leaf Doesn't Fall

Both teenaged girls wore hot pants, silver stars pasted on their red-polka-dot cheeks under heavily painted eyes. The two had camped out in front of the elevator door on the sixth floor of the Plaza Hotel all evening, waiting for David to return to his suite. When he appeared with his entourage, the girls rose. They didn't rush to David, but ran instead into each others' arms where, according to some apparent plan, they arranged themselves in a provocative pose. They smiled.

"Hi," David smiled. "What're you girls up to?"

"You!" they squealed, and kissed each other passionately. Arms around each other, the shorter girl moved one leg between the other's thigh, and with her free hand began to caress her friend's bosom.

David took Jill's arm and led her past them down the hall. The two girls stared after him, disappointed. They pleaded with Henry to intercede for them.

"David," Henry ran down the hall. "Where are you *going?*"

"Aw, Henry," David said, "chicks like that don't turn me on."

Henry talked to him in earnest tones, gesturing occasionally towards the two girls who smiled hopefully at David each time Henry pointed their way.

"But Henry, I mean, after I got done making love to that, I'd feel shitty. I couldn't look at them. I couldn't wait to get them out of my bed so I wouldn't have to see them there, and face them, and myself, too."

When David emerged from his hotel room the next morning he saw that the two bizarre would-be groupies still stood draped around each other leaning against a wall outside the sixth floor elevator door.

"You think they were there all night?" David asked Henry in the limousine en route to Madison Square Garden.

"Naw," said Henry. "I let them camp out in my room on the floor. They were strange little girls. I had to drag it out of them, but they're from New Jersey. Just two ordinary girls during the week. The big one with the moustache is a telephone operator, and the little feminine one works in a store."

"Oh, no!" groaned David, "there they are in that cab behind us." From the yellow cab following them they could see two excited females waving and smiling.

"Get rid of them Caesar. See if you can lose them." David's voice was urgent. "I don't want them around me. I don't want them near the dressing room. My *family* is going to be there."

* * *

V. Prime Times

David Bruce Cassidy was born on April 12th, 1950 in Englewood, New Jersey. He moved to Hollywood with his mother after his parents, Broadway actors Evelyn Ward and Jack Cassidy, were divorced when he was five. "I had a lot of rejection from my father when I was young," recalls David. "I never saw him after he divorced me and my mother. I wouldn't hear from him for a year. I don't feel any hostility towards him. I'm a friend of his now. But a little boy shouldn't have been shunned like that."

201

He had a normal, baseball playing childhood in Los Angeles, until he was 14 and became a bicycle thief. "I had a bike shop in my garage. I'd be walking home from school and I'd see a bike sitting there, and I'd rip it off and drive it home. I'd paint it or do something neat to it. I ended up returning a lot of them, but I sure must have caused those people a lot of grief."

It was around that time that David started seeing a psychiatrist. He's been seeing one off and on since. Also, he started experimenting with drugs. "I didn't know who I was, and I did a lot of fucking around, experimenting—not smack, but grass and speed and psychedelics. I had some bad trips—tripping for kicks in the worst, most paranoid places." He was among those 16-year-olds who in 1967 went up to Haight-Ashbury to see what was going on.

"But I wasn't taking drugs seriously. I didn't want to be a junkie. A few of my friends died, committed suicide actually.

"Then I came down with mononucleosis and spent three months in the house. No socializing, no getting high —thinking. And I found out I cared a lot about myself. I wanted to achieve something, to do something with my life."

He went back to school. "I didn't let myself get into a rut after graduation. I gave myself a two-week vacation, and then went to New York." He got his first job, working part time in the mail room of a textile firm in New York's West Side garment district, and took acting lessons at night.

And he's worked every since, except for an occasional vacation, and a three-week spell last summer when his exhausting schedule caught up with him. "I look at that scar on my stomach," he said, "and I think, if I didn't have it I'd be dead. It happened after a concert at Wildwood, New Jersey. I came back to L.A. on Sunday night to get a few hours of sleep. I had to be at the Partridge Family set at 6 AM. Well, I woke up at three in the morning, screaming in pain, holding my stomach, banging my head against the wall trying to make something else hurt until the doctor got there.

"It was gravel and stuff, from a bad diet or something,

in my gall bladder. Rather than take out the stones, they removed the whole thing."

David lives in a huge house in Encino, California, on two acres with fruit trees. It is a retreat from a hard schedule of filming five days a week, recording at night, and concert tours on weekends.

"Whenever I go over to see him, he opens the door and he's alone," observed Henry Diltz. "He leads a bachelor sort of existence. I've watched him eat dinner —a can of peaches, a piece of bread. I mean, like at Steven Stills' house there were always four or five ladies living there, hanging out in the kitchen, always making some groovy organic feast. Girls drop over and make themselves useful so that they can get to stay. They drop by and say, 'Where's the vacuum cleaner.' They start to vacuum and people say, 'Hey, she's together. She's groovy. Keep her around, She knows how to *vacuum.*'

"There's nothing like that at David's house. He prefers to be alone. I'm sure he could have his house full of girls if he'd rather, but he's a quiet sort of guy.

"Like the trip to Europe last winter. He wanted to go totally alone. Every magazine offered to pay his way and mine, and buy him a VW camper. We talked about it and David said no, because then he'd have to worry about whether he got a little zit or something. I mean, I could go hang out with David Crosby on his boat and he'd run around naked. He wouldn't care. But David's serious about his career, and his image—partly because of the family thing, Ruth and Shirley and being Jack Cassidy's boy. And he has that image of Keith Partridge to uphold.

"And he's not as old as David Crosby. He hasn't been into the rock and roll world. It's different on the road, too. It's not motels and groupies. It's very fast-paced and business-like. That other thing will come later for David. Remember his audience is still 11 years old."

Next to David's white Corvette in the driveway of his Spanish-style house is Sam Hymen's VW Bug. Sam is David's friend of ten years and now lives in a small cottage in the backyard. Sam lays naked, long and slender, dark-haired and dark-eyed, sunning himself next to the swimming pool, recalling the early days of his friendship with David.

At University High School in Hollywood, before David was expelled for cutting 102 of one semester's classes, he and Sam had belonged to the same "social club." "Those clubs were either football clubs or fighting clubs. We were both wimps, so we belonged to the fighting club for security. We would have been killed playing football.

"At the end of the ninth grade we started tripping with drugs. David was never really sold on LSD, he didn't have that many good trips. He was more into hash. He always had more hash than anyone else I knew."

After David returned from New York he lived with his mother again. Then he and Sam moved out of their parents' homes and into a house in the Hollywood Hills. "I was working as a film editor," Sam recalled, "and David was just starting to happen as an actor. He never talked about it much, but he'd stay up a night alone, thinking it all out. He kept a lot to himself. and still does."

David doesn't have many hobbies, though he skis and goes scuba diving when he can. He spends most of his time off playing the guitar, sitting on his amp, at his new house in Encino listening to Steven Stills, Neil Young and David Crosby, imitating the songs. And writing songs of his own. To date, David has recorded only one of them: "Ricky's Tune," a song about his recently deceased dog.

"I think David's a little frustrated with what he's doing now on *The Partridge Family*. He can't demonstrate much acting ability doing that. He knows he has talent; he wants to develop it and direct it to his peers and be accepted by them. That's what he's trying for now."

"He doesn't have an old lady at the moment," Sam continued. "He doesn't have time, really. We were just talking about where we'd like to be in a year or two: get some land, eat fruit, make music, go scuba diving. We'd still produce artistically. But we both agreed that it would all be worthless if you didn't have a lady. Good friends as we are, we can only fill so much of each other's needs. Some people can be complete with someone in their own sex, but I can't and neither can David."

Sam turned over to sun his other side. "I think what's made it a nice relationship with David is that I've never relied on him. I've stayed strictly independent. I have to work for everything I get. David's respected that." Last April, Sam quit his film editor job to merchandise posters and programs at David's concerts.

Sam paused, thoughtful for a minute. "The merchandising trip is my reality now," he went on. "It may seem totally lame and fucked up to someone else, but it's my life. I know I'll always be in business," he chuckled " 'cause I love money, and in this business you've got to make it when you can."

* * *

VI. "An unhappy artist never works out, longevity-wise."

According to David Cassidy's biography sheet, put out by his public relations firm: "Most artists, overwhelmed by their swift elevation to love object status, fail to provide for that inevitable rainy day when fans regroup around next year's superstar. And the artist finds himself a has-been at 21. Not so, David Cassidy."

At least, that's what his management is hoping. "People say we have to hang on to his youth audience," said Ruth Aarons. "But that's like Peter Pan, and David is maturing. Of course, the long haul is hardest to sustain. But with a good proper structure behind him, David will continue to grow. I depend on his instinct and his following to tell me where to place him in this market."

His management was looking into movies and TV specials "with meaning" which would appeal to older audiences. And David would continue recording.

"To me," Ruth went on, "David is the inherent consummate entertainer. He has an instinctive command of audiences. The way he leaps out and bounces around on the stage, his little yellings of 'I love you'—it's exciting, and theatrically effective. He projects a joyful, affirmative sexual appeal. He does not infer destruction. Like Sinatra in the Forties he has that touchable, vulnerable, clean attraction.

"He is *not,* as some critics say, a *hoax* that's being foisted on the public—a figment of someone's imaginings, a put-on. He's *not* a make believe performer.

"And no matter what happens, he still has done something few have achieved."

Jim Flood, the man in charge of David's publicity, is among those interested in helping David grow. To take the job handling David, Flood had dropped his other clients: Jerry Lewis, Mary Tyler Moore, to name a few.

"This whole thing with David is for me, personally, a calculated risk," said Flood. "With all the time I've invested in David this last year, I'll still make half the money I used to. It's a gamble. It could not work out. But it will. And there's no way David will wind up a broke rock star."

Besides Ruth and Jim to look out for him, David also has a financial advisor, Lee Bush. At first, Bush refused to divulge how much the teen idol business brought David last year, or to predict what he would make in the next year.

"People think in terms of gross," said the white-haired, cigar-chewing Bush. "Like at Madison Square Garden, they grossed $130,000. But there were huge expenses." Profits from the concerts go, not to David, but to Daru Incorporated, a corporation whose name combines David's with Ruth Aarons'!

"Besides expenses," Bush continued—expenses such as David's weekly allowance of $150—"don't forget the government is one of his partners." Anyone who makes over $100,000 a year is taxed 50 percent on the first $100,000 and 70 percent on every $100,000 after that by the federal government. And then there's a California tax of 11 percent. "But it's a way of life you learn to live with," he sighed.

To help him live with this way of life, Bush invests David's money in municipal bonds, which yield only 4½ percent interest annually, but are tax-free investments. Also, David owns oil stock, and is looking into buying land in Hawaii.

"I will say, in effect," Bush finally said, "that last year David made a quarter million dollars, and should he keep his health, and keep working, we look forward to another good year."

* * *

Smoking a joint and drinking wine ordered from room service at the Plaza Hotel, David watched the March 10th episode of *The Partridge Family*.

Keith and his family were driving to the country for a week's vacation from their busy schedules as rock and roll stars. En route, their psychedelic painted bus breaks down. They seek help from a country couple, who recognize them and plot to keep them there so that they'll perform at a benefit for a neighboring Indian reservation.

"Watch," David predicted. "Here's where I do my pouting schtick. I always have to do one of these things."

On the screen, Keith is annoyed at the delay, and puts up a fuss when his mother suggests he take his younger brother Danny fishing. While cleaning the fish in their captor's garage, Keith finds a case of the stuff needed to repair their bus. He realizes that the couple is lying to them. Holding one of the fish he has caught in his hand, he says to Danny, "There's something fishy here." Laughter, on the television and from David's corner.

Keith stalks into the couple's house to confront them. But the two still hide their intentions, and Keith is chastised by his mother for being suspicious.

The next day, the couple takes the Partridge Family to the Indian reservation, where they see the plight of the Indians.

"Someone should do something," says Keith's mother.

"That's what everybody says," moralizes the country woman.

Keith's mother apologizes and asks what she can do to help.

"Well," replies the woman, "there is going to be a fair for the Indians this afternoon. Perhaps you could entertain."

Just then, the younger son, Danny, finds a leaflet announcing that his family was scheduled to perform that afternoon. Everyone laughs, realizing that there has indeed been a plot all along.

The plot thickens when the Partridge Family manager finds one of the leaflets, which has reached him somehow, in Las Vegas. He drives out to prevent the concert which is against the terms of the family's contract. Discovering this, the couple send the manager on a wild goose chase.

"Watch this," David laughed. "This is really funny."

In full color the manager is scared foolish by a band of Indians pretending to be on the warpath. Meanwhile, the Partridge Family performs on a stage atop their bus, and everything works out for the best.

* * *

"Well," said Bob Claver, executive producer of *The Partridge Family,* "let's face it. No TV program is going in any time capsule. But we try to make them as good as we can, under the circumstances.

"The show's not meant to be realistic. It's entertainment. Viewers would like to be in that family. The characters are good looking, they're in show business, and they seem not to have the problems that plague most people. We deal in fantasy, and I can't see where it's all so ruinous." Especially since, he explained, they try to instill a moral message in every program.

Claver puffed thoughtfully on a Pall Mall, relaxed on the couch of his plush office at Screen Gems in Hollywood. Behind him, the wall was decorated with full color TV Guide portraits of faces unrecognizable to anybody but a TV buff. Claver explained they were the stars of *Bewitched, I Dream of Jeannie, The Flying Nun, The Bobby Sherman Show,* and *The Partridge Family.*

Claver said he likes working with David. "He's willing to play a fool. Every once in a while Shirley Jones, who plays the mother, will object to something in a script. She'll say, 'A mother would not do this.' But David, he never objects."

When the idea for a show based on the real-life Cowsills came up, the producers, Claver said, planned to put out records and merchandise as they had for the Monkees, the Flying Nun and other properties.

According to Steve Wax, public relations man for Bell Records, the records provide the greatest revenue for Columbia, which owns Bell as well as Screen Gems.

Wes Farrell was assigned as producer to create a sound for the show. Steve Wax put a record on his office stereo, "So you can get an idea soundwise what I'm talking about."

Through a speaker in the ceiling came David's wispy voice.

> I am a clown, I am a clown,
> You'll always see me smile,
> You'll never see me frown,
> Sometimes my scenes are good,
> Sometimes they're bad,
> Not funny ha ha; funny sad.
>
> I am a clown, look at the clown,
> Always a laughing face,
> Whenever you're around,
> Always the same routine,
> I never change,
> Not funny ho, ho; funny strange.

"That song is too heavy for ten and twelve-year-olds," said Wax. "But at FM stations, the David Cassidy name is not accepted. They're really concerned with images, not sound. I think it's hypocrisy."

"Bubble gum music?" said Wax. "You've got to remember that good and bad is a relative term. People say to me, how can you promote that stuff? But I'm paid to do a job, so what do my personal likes have to do with it? If that's what the people want, how can I deny it to them?"

Wax said Bell had invested a lot of time and money on David because they expect him to be a big act for them. Now, he said, they want him to develop as an artist. "Not too fast, though. If you change your image too fast, like Bobby Darin tried to do when he went off to Big Sur to write his own material, your following will rebel.

"And," he added, "if we try to make him into something he's not, we'll have an unhappy artist, and an unhappy artist never works out, longevity-wise."

* * *

VII. A Fern Unfolds

"David's passed his peak already," calculated Gloria Stavers as she sat behind the grey metal desk from which she edits *16 Magazine,* the premier teen publication with a monthly readership estimated at 6,500,000. "But his effect will last until the end of the year."

Gloria's hair is pulled severely into a high ponytail. She is wearing black slacks, sneakers, and a camel-hair sweater. "I don't always look this way," she explained in a hard voice bearing traces of her North Carolina upbringing. "I can actually be very charming and well-groomed when I need to be."

Gloria Stavers won't reveal her age. She doesn't want her readers to know. She has been in the teen mag business for 15 years now . . . her's, 16, is the undisputed leader in the field, possibly because of her enthusiasm. She reads every one of the fan letters that come to her office each week, to be stored by the thousands in shopping bags stacked in rows in the drab reception room of her stale-smelling office at 745 Fifth Avenue in New York.

The average age of her readers is 13½ years, 99 percent between age 11 to 15. "It's an oral age for the girls. Their idea of sex is malts and hamburgers, a kiss. It's a romantic thing, not physical nor orgiastic. They think of their idol as a teddy bear, a blanket, a cuddly thing.

"16 is a fantasy escape for them. When you're 12 years old and you hate your mom and dad and you can't do anything right, and if you're lucky you have a best girlfriend, you turn to 16. And we give them something to fantasize about.

"We also turn them on to subtler stuff. We offer gospel and jazz and we plug *Siddhartha* and Blake, which Dylan suggested. He also suggested *Naked Lunch,* but we censored that. As Dylan said to me, we're sort of like a candy store." Her voice softens as she speaks of Dylan.

"But he said, 'The truth is where the truth is, and it's sometimes in the candy store.'"

She returned to her chair. She leaned back, eyes narrowed, and considered the full-color, shirtless, hairless chest of the David Cassidy poster on the wall opposite her. 16 never retouched his pictures, she said, pimples notwithstanding.

"It was two, two and a half years ago when I first met David. I'd heard of him before that. It was earlier in 1970, six months before Screen Gems showed the pilot for *The Partridge Family*. It was the kids, in their letters, that first brought him to my attention. He had done a bit on *Medical Center* as a hemophiliac—I remember what it was because all their letters had it spelled wrong."

At that time, explained Gloria, there was a *lull* in the teen idol field. Long ago there had been Elvis, Ricky Nelson, Fabian, Bobby Rydell and Frankie Avalon. Then there had been a "blond period": Richard Chamberlain and David McCallum of *The Man From UNCLE*, followed by the Beatles, The Dave Clark Five and the Stones. And then, the Monkees.

"The Monkees were the biggest," she says. "They got 14,000 letters a day. David only got 3000 at his peak."

Just then an office assistant entered, a pale young man with unnaturally yellow hair. He handed her a letter.

"What the hell is this?" she yelled, waving the letter at the fellow. "Where the hell did they get this 16 stationery?" The boy accepted her rage impassively. "No teenagers in the office, you hear? They end up wrecking the place. Just wait until summer when they ain't got nothing to do. They come in here . . ."

The fans are always trying to get to Gloria, which was why her office was hidden behind an unmarked door on a different floor then listed in the office building's directory.

She was calm again. "Where was I? Oh, the Monkees. Did you know they are suing Screen Gems? I can't remember the exact details. Wait, I've got the clipping around here somewhere." She rose again and flew around the office, leafing through stacks of letters, old magazines, and xeroxes of news items. "Ahah, here it is."

"David Jones and Mickey Dolenz," she quoted, "are

suing Screen Gems for $20,000,000. The plaintiffs charge breach of contract, fraud, deceit, misrepresentation, conspiracy to deny them royalties for discs, merchandising, song writing and producer royalties, and also personal appearance coin."

Gloria explained that Screen Gems, (owned by Columbia Pictures), makes most of its money from merchandising. She stated that income from merchandising the Monkees and other Screen Gems properties—what with records, posters, and various other items—had once saved Columbia Pictures from going under. But the Monkees saw none of that money. They were paid a weekly salary, and ended up with nothing at all, which is why they were suing.

Screen Gems also holds the rights, Gloria said, to David Cassidy. "David is on strings with Screen Gems," she said, "but that's the game. David was complaining about that one day, and I said, 'David, nobody twisted your arm and made you sign the fucking contract. You wanted this. If the chain fits, rattle it,' I told him. I remember he laughed sheepishly and said, 'rattle, rattle.' There's no crap with David."

She paused for a moment. "Where was I? Oh, yes. The TV pilot. Well, when I saw *The Partridge Family* pilot, this was in 1970, I said here we go again. I'd been waiting for him for one and a half years. So I got all my guns ready—you know, we have certain standard material—a master questionnaire. I can't show it to you, though. I've got enough of those creeps from other magazines copying my stuff already. But all I need is to see David twice a year. I can get so much stuff out of him.

"David is very well-managed, and that's important. These idols don't last long unless they are. The fans grow up, their crushes don't last. Coloner Parker made Elvis last 15 years. Ricky Nelson was the same thing, that TV show sustained for five years. The Nelson family was very strict. I had to meet the parents, and you know, I did my number. *16 Magazine* was the *only* one that got to him.

"Well, David's manager, Ruth Aarons, decided to go full speed ahead with David and not drag it out. I

212

remember the first time I saw him: Ruth had told him to bring a present with him. We have these giveaway contests of stuff we collect from stars; David brought me a green-and-white high school basketball T-shirt with Number 13 on it, and some pictures. He said, 'What do you want me to do?'

"It was a great beginning. I said to him, 'you'll learn fast.'

"I liked him right away. He was shy and polite. He was like a young, beautiful green fern unfurling," which she described with long, graceful fingers. "I felt motherly towards him. I wanted to help him grow. I told him he had a duty now to do it right. 'Give it the mostest and enjoy every minute of it.' I taught him a few tricks on how to pose for the camera. I wanted to shield that tender plant from too much burning sun."

At first, she recounted, David had balked when he read some of 16's stories about him. "He came to me and said, 'Don't write all that stuff like you write, gooey stuff.' He cared too much about what his friends would think. So I said to him 'Listen, you're not Bob Dylan.' But that was just at first. Now he's on top of it. He's able to take the long view of things. He's grown into a pliable, firm plant."

* * *

The airplane taxied to the terminal in Bangor, Maine, where David was due to give another matinee for 5000 girls before his return to Los Angeles. "You cannot make a teenage idol." David was saying, "What you can do is, you can find a pretty face on the screen, like those teen magazine editors do. They'll take a kid off the street, put him in a magazine and write a lot of baloney on him, make him seem like he's busy and working and hot.

"And he'll get mail, just from kids seeing his face. They'll write fan letters. But they won't invest all their bread into, um, David Cassidy buttons, rings, posters and so on, just from seeing a picture of a guy who's cute. They're not that stupid. You can only hype them to a certain degree.

"There has to be something there. They've got to see

213

him on television, or hear him on records, and *there's gotta be something there.* They *can't* just manufacture someone and expect him to be big and successful."

David was angry, now, at some invisible antagonist. "I think those teen magazine editors think they're a lot more heavy and powerful than they really are." He looked out the window. "Oh, no! What a bummer!"

Outside, hundreds of fans stood in snow, waving banners expectantly. "Look at all those fans," David moaned. "Standing out there in the cold, waiting for me. I feel rotten, I look terrible. After a weekend of killing myself, I have to show up and smile. I can't handle it. I ain't going. I'm staying right here."

David sat with his arms folded across his chest, staring out the window. The men in the band filed past him, out to a waiting bus. Ron, Henry and Steve were ready to go. "Well," said David, softening, "I suppose I should put on my coat."

THE WORLD'S GREATEST HEARTBREAKER
Tales of Ike and Tina Turner, God Knows How Many Ikettes, and the Closed Circuit TV System

by Ben Fong-Torres

Walk into what, from the outside, looks to be another well-paid, well-kept home in suburban Inglewood, California, and you're hit: a huge, imperial oil painting of Ike and Tina Turner, dressed as if for a simple, private wedding, cicra 1960, modest pompadour and formal mink. *A thriller? The killer, honey* . . . Also in the foyer, under the portrait, a small white bust of John F. Kennedy. Next to him, the Bible, opened to Isaiah 42 —A New Song to the Lord. The smell is eucalyptus leaves and wet rocks; the sound is water, bubbling in one of several fish tanks and, over in the family room, splashing, programmed, is a waterfall.

Two trim young housekeepers stir around the kitchen; dinner is cooking at 4 PM. Ike is asleep upstairs, and Tina is out with a son at football practice. But you cannot just plop down somewhere, adjust yourself, and be comfortable. Next to the waterfall there's a red velvet sofa, designed around a coffee table in the shape of a bass guitar. Or, in the blue room, the blue couch, whose back turns into an arm that turns into a tentacle. Above that, on the ceiling, is a large mirror in the shape of a jig-saw puzzle piece, and against one wall is a Zenith color TV, encased in an imitation ivory, whale-shaped cabinet.

(Tina, later, will say: "Ike did the house. It was Ike's idea to have the TV in the whale shape. I thought, *'Oh wow!'* I felt it was gonna look like the typical entertainer's house, with the stuff not looking professional. But everything turned out great. I'm very proud of it.")

It *is* very personal, but there are all these *mail order* touches. The neo-wood vertical frame with four bubbles to hold color pictures of the Turners' four sons. The JFK bust. On the wall, over a mantel, a large metallic Zodiac sunburst, with no clock in the middle. Also, a Zodiac ash tray atop the guitar-shaped table. (Ike showed his refurnishing job off to Bob Krasnow of Blue Thumb Records one day last year, and Krasnow remarked: "You mean you actually can spend $70,000 at Woolworth's?")

Atop a white upright piano complete with gooseneck mike, there's the gold record—not "A Fool in Love," or "It's Gonna Work Out Fine," or "I Idolize You," but, rather, "Come Together," the single on Liberty, their seventh or eighth label in ten years. And next to that, some trophies—a couple that the kids have earned, and a couple that Tina has earned. TO THE SWEETEST WIFE AND MOTHER, TINA TURNER. LOVE'S YEA. IKE TURNER AND YOUR FOUR SONS. Another, larger one, Olympiad, with a small gold-plated angel holding a torch above her, hara-kiri: TO TINA TURNER. THE WORLD'S GREATEST HEART-BREAKER 1966. LOVE IKE TURNER.

Tina's not back—half an hour late—and now I'm down to the sunlit bookshelf in the corner. A neat junior edition of encyclopedias. A couple of novels—Crichton's *Andromeda Strain;* Cheever's *Bullet Park.* But the main line appears to be how-to's, from Kahlil Gibran and astrology to a series of sharkskin suit-pocket hardbounds: *How to Make a Killing in Real Estate, How to Legally Avoid Paying Taxes,* and *How to Scheme Your Way to Fortune.* Atop the pile, a one-volume senior encyclopedia: *The Sex Book.*

Someone once called Tina "The female Mick Jagger." In fact, to be more accurate, one should call Mick "The male Tina Turner." After all, in 1960, Ike and Tina and the first of God knows how many Ikettes began doing their revue, and, as Tina tells it, "Ike used to move on stage. He was bow-legged and bow-hipped and when he moved from side to side, he had an effect he used to do with the guitar, and I used to do that, 'cause I idolized him so. Before I fell in love with him I'd *loved* him. We were very close friends. I thought there was nobody like Ike, so I wanted to be like Ike. I wore tight dresses and high heels, and I still moved, and that's where the side-step came from."

Philip Agee, who was 17 when he first saw them in 1960 in St. Louis, became such a fan that he has put out a book on them—for a seminar course in printing at Yale. *Tina Pie* is a collection of the colorations of Ike and Tina's romance and career, tawny browns and flashy reds and moanful yellows and hurtful blues. Silkscreening the act through the dark years and into the fast ones, with even remembrances from Tina's mother, or various of Phil Agee's friends and fellow-worshippers.

"Tina came out and up on the stage. Nobody screamed or fainted. We were just real glad to see her. She always wore sparkling dresses and very high-heeled shoes with no backs and holes in the toes. Sometimes she was pregnant, singing with her stomach stuck out, stomping her high-heeled shoes with stiff legs. They would sing special songs when you asked them. Everybody liked 'A Fool in Love.' 'Staggerlee' was my favorite. When Ike started slow, 'When the night was clear and the moon was yellow, and the leaves came tumbling down . . .' by the time 'ba-da-, ba-da, ba-doo' ended, everybody was out on the floor. During their breaks the juke box played again. Tina disappeared and the men sat at card tables near the stage drinking with their blond girlfriends. When the men started playing again, Tina appeared for the second show. By 11:00 it was over. Pat's dad picked us up and drove me home. We went every Tuesday while they were in St. Louis.

217

"Tina Turner's part Cherokee and so's my Mom, so so am I."

—KATHY KLEIN

By 1966, there was more practiced flash. You learn what *works*. The Ikettes came storming out of the wings in a train formation, in mini-skirted sequins, haughty foxes thrusting their butts at you and then waving you off with a toss of their long whippy hair. Tina came out, eyes flashing until she became a fire on the stage. And across Broadway, there's your Motown act, the Marvellettes in their matching long evening gowns or the Tops in pink velvet, doing soul-hula, singing through choreographed smiles. Tina *spits* sex out to you. And Mick Jagger:

Before that breakthrough tour with the Rolling Stones in 1969, Ike and Tina had worked with them in England in 1966. "Mick was a friend of Phil Spector," says Tina. "And the time we cut 'River Deep Mountain High,' Mick was around. [This is at Gold Star, Phil's favorite studio in Los Angeles] I remembered him but I never talked to him. He's not the type to make you feel you could just come up and talk to him. Mick, I guess, thought the record was great, and he caught our act a couple of times. Mick wasn't dancing at the time . . . he always said he liked to see girls dance. So he was excited about our show, and he thought it'd be different for the people in England.

"I remember I wasn't mingling too much—Ike and I were having problems at the time, and we stayed mad at each other—but I'd always see Mick in the wings. I thought, 'Wow, he must really be a fan.' I'd come out and watch him occassionally; they'd play music, and Mick'd beat the tambourine. He wasn't dancing. And lo and behold, when he came to America, he was doing *everything!* So then I knew what he was doing in the wings. He learned a lot of steps and I tried to teach him like the Popcorn and other steps we were doing, but he can't do 'em like that. He has to do it *his* way."

"River Deep Mountain High." To hear that song for the first time, in 1967, in the first year of acid-rock

218

and Memphis soul, to hear that wall falling toward you, with Tina teasing it along, was to understand all the power of rock and roll. It had been released in England in 1966 and made Number Two. In America, nothing. "It was just like my farewell," Phil Spector says. "I was just sayin' goodbye, and I just wanted to go crazy for a few minutes—four minutes on wax."

Bob Krasnow, president of Blue Thumb, knew Ike and Tina from their association with Warner Brothers' R&B label, Loma, in 1964. He was an A&R man there. "Spector had just lost the Righteous Brothers," he recalls, "and at the same time, Ike was unhappy," having switched to Kent Records.

"Spector's attorney Joey Cooper called and said Phil wanted to produce Tina—and that he was willing to pay $20,000 in front to do it! So Mike Maitland [then president at Warners] gave them their release, and they signed with Philles.

"Watching Phil work was one of my greatest experiences," says Krasnow. It was indeed a special occasion. Only "River Deep" was cut at Gold Star; the other three Spector productions were at United. (There was only one Philles LP ever made with Ike and Tina, which was finally re-released last year by A&M.) And Ike didn't attend.

"Dennis Hopper did the cover on that LP. He was broke on his ass in Hollywood and trying photography. He said he'd like to do the cover. He took us to this sign company, where there was this 70-foot high sign for a movie, with one of those sex stars—*Boccaccio '70* or something. And he shot them in front of that big teardrop. Then the gas company had a big sign, and Hopper took them there and shot them in front of a big burner."

On stage, there may be reason to compare Tina Turner to Mick Jagger; Tina, in fact, is more aggressive, more animalistic. But it is, indeed, a stage:

"I don't sound pretty, or good. I sound, *arreghh!* Naggy. I can sound pretty, but nobody likes it. Like I read some article in the paper that Tina Turner had never been captured on records. She purrs like a kitten on record, but she's wild on stage. And they don't like a record like

'Working Together.' I *love* that record. I love that *River Deep Mountain High* album, but nobody likes me like that. They want me sounding all raspy, so . . . I have to do what Ike says.

"My whole thing," she once said, "is the fact that I am to Ike—I'm going to use the term 'doll'—that you sort of mold . . . In other words, he put me through a lot of changes. My whole thing is Ike's ideas. I'll come up with a few of them, but I'm not half as creative as Ike."

* * *

The world's greatest heartbreaker drives up in her Mercedes sedan and strides in, all fresh and breezy in a red knit hotpants outfit, third button unbuttoned, supple legs still very trim at age 32 charging onto 33. ("Everyone thinks I'm in my forties, but I was only around 20 when I started. Born November 26, 1939," she says, very certain.)

Tina's hair is in ponytails, tied in brown ribbons; she is wearing brown nail polish and red ballet-type slippers. Here in the living room of her $100,000 house, she is trying to paint a portrait of the offstage, in-home Tina Turner. There are four bedrooms, she says, four baths, and, let's see now . . . 13 telephones. Additional phone cables are employed in the closed-circuit TV system, a system like the one in Ike's studios less than a mile away. There, Ike can sit in his office and push-button his way around the various studios, the writers' room, the entrances, the hallways. Just recently, he was laughing about the time he punched up the camera scanning the bedroom in the private apartment he keeps there, and what did he and the people around him (Tina was at home) see but some heavy fucking going on, one of his musicians and a groupie. And everyone's lapping it up, and finally, when the sideman is caressing one of his nightstand's firm-nippled breasts, Ike's bodyguard springs out of the office, and the next you see him, he is piling into the bed, over most of that same station . . .

But later. Tina Turner is trying to paint a picture here. "I just got rid of the housekeeper. I get housekeepers and they sort of do just things like vacuuming and dusting, and nothing else is done—like the mirrors—and I'm a perfectionist, and that would never be. People think I'm probably one of those that lounge around, but I'm always on my knees—I do my own floors 'cause no one can please me. When I was in the eighth grade I started working for a lady in Tennessee keeping her house; she more or less taught me what I know about housework."

Tina also tries to do most of the cooking, even if she usually does report to the studios around 4 P.M. to do vocals. She also likes to do gardening. "Every now and then I get out and turn the dirt . . . but now I've started writing, and Ike, every time I turn around, he says, 'Write me this song.' So I went out and bought some plants and when I was in the hospital I got a lot of plants that I really love, and I sort of take care of them like babies."

"Ike is a very hard worker," a friend is saying. "He's such a driver. Last winter Tina was sick with bronchial pneumonia, 104 temperature, in the hospital with her body icepacked to bring the temperature down. And Ike was visiting, and he was going, 'You get out and SING, or you get out of the house!'"

Tina doesn't discuss such things, even if her talk is often punctuated by references to Ike as the manager, the brains, the last word; despite his back-to-the-audience stance on stage. But in *Tina Pie*, Phil Agee's book, there's a piece of conversation backstage between Tina and one of Phil's friends:

Pete: I thought maybe you wouldn't be here tonight.

Tina: No, I never miss a performance. The doctor came to the hotel today, brought a vaporizer and that helped it a lot. I haven't coughed anything up today—so I was kind of worrying if it was okay. I always go on. Whatever's bothering me—I don't care how bad it is—I drop it when I go on stage. I hadn't coughed up anything today. You know that kind of hypnosis—I don't know what it's called—where you induce yourself into a trance?

(Tina's friend): Self-hypnosis.

Tina: Yeah, that's it. I hypnotize myself, and I forget the cold and stuff.

221

"Dope?"

Bob Krasnow repeats the question, only in a softer voice. "Let me close the door a minute." (A few weeks before, I asked an ex-Ikette about Ike Turner and sex. "Sex? Oh, my god, that's another volume," she'd said. "I'll have to get a *cigarette* on that one!")

Krasnow: "Tina is so anti-dope I can't tell you. She's the greatest woman I've ever known, outside of my wife. She has more love inside her body than 100 chicks wrapped up together. And she's so straight, it's ridiculous.

"As for Ike . . . Ike was not into dope at all until three, four years ago. One night in Vegas we were sitting around and got started talking about coke. He didn't care about it, and I said—and Ike, you know, is like 40 or so—and I said, 'One thing that's great about coke is you can stay hard—you can fuck for years behind that stuff.' That's the first time Ike did coke."

Krasnow can't help but continue. "That night he made his first deal—bought $3000 of cocaine from King Curtis, and he bought it and showed me, and I laughed and said, 'That's no coke; that's fucking *Drano!*' Since then, he's learned." What—to lighten up on drugs? "No—to tell what good coke is and what bad coke is."

Krasnow worked with James Brown at King for years before he joined Warners and signed Ike and Tina to Loma. His evaluation: "Ike is ten times a bigger character than James Brown. And they're both fucking animals. How can I put this? Say, whatever you can do . . . they can do ten times as much. And Ike—he's always putting you to the test.

"What I like best about Ike is also what I hate: He's always on top of you."

"I find him one of the most fascinating people I've met," says Jeff Trager, who did promotion work at Blue Thumb. "If he knows you he can be real warm, and do whatever he can for you. There's just no limit to Ike Turner. He'd carry around $25,000 in cash in a cigar box—with a gun. He'd drive around town, man, sometimes to Watts, sometimes Laurel Canyon, in his new Rolls Royce to pick up coke. And he is real sinister-looking."

"In Las Vegas," says Krasnow, "I brought some friends

into the dressing room, and Ike pulled out his big .45 —just putting them on. Another time he came into the front room at Blue Thumb and threw $70,000 on the floor, in cash, and dared anyone to touch it. Just to blow everybody's mind."

"Krasnow and Ike are *both* crazy," says Trager. "Ike would storm into the office with a troop of people, six-foot chicks, a bag of cocaine. Really, really crazy. He always came in. He loved Blue Thumb, and he was always saying he'd come back. Krasnow says he couldn't afford him now."

Krasnow produced both their Blue Thumb albums and brought "I've Been Loving You Too Long" to Turner. "He hated Otis Redding," Krasnow says. "He just didn't think Otis had it." The Ike and Tina version sold some half million copies. Blue Thumb was also a good showcase of Ike Turner's fluidity as a blues guitarist, and of the flexibility of the Ike and Tina sound—from "Dust My Broom" and "I Am a Motherless Child" to the stark raving "Bold Soul Sister." Ike Turner, who places "River Deep" up next to "Good Vibrations" as his two favorite records, says the Spector production didn't get airplay because the soul stations said "too pop" and the white stations said "too R&B."

"See, what's wrong with America," he told Pete Senoff, "is that rather than accept something for its value . . . America mixes race in it. Like, you can take Tina and cut a pop record on her—like 'River Deep, Mountain High.' You can't call that record R&B. But because it's Tina . . . But I can play you stuff like Dinah Washington on Tina. I can play you jazz on Tina. I can play you pop on Tina. I can play you gutbucket R&B on Tina like we have on our Blue Thumb record . . . really blues. I can play you that stuff, then I could play you the Motown stuff."

Ike and Tina had a showcase at Blue Thumb, but no cross-market success. "Bold Soul Sister" went to number one at KGFJ, the black station in L.A., but Jeff Trager remembers, the program director at light, white KRLA refused to play it. "No matter what. I asked him, 'What if it went to number one?' and he said 'I don't care; I'll never play it.'" Whether too R&B or what, the program director at KFRC, the Bill Drake station in San Francisco, wouldn't play "I've Been Loving You Too Long," which Krasnow, its producer, called a "pop record." KFRC had to be forced—by its sales—to put the song on the playlist.

What finally carried Ike and Tina through was the 1969 Rolling Stones tour, where the revue broke out with "Come Together," in its own raw style, Tina snake-snapping across the stage, punching out the John Lennon lyric. Raves everywhere, and the mass magazines were stung to attention. *Playboy* and *Look* ended up using the same phrase to characterize Tina's entrance: "like a lioness in heat." *Vogue* did a photo spread. And Ike and Tina got booked into Vegas and both Fillmores. Liberty Records began taking big money, so big that even Krasnow encouraged Turner to go to them as an exclusive artist. "We didn't have a contract, anyway," says Krasnow. "It was just on a piecemeal basis." That's when Ike refurnished his $100,000 home and began building his lavish studios.

Tina is sitting in the "game room" of the studios. The move to interpreting white rock and roll, she says, was quite natural.

"We went to a record shop in Seattle, Washington, and someone was buying 'Come Together,' and I said, 'Oh, Ike, I gotta do it on stage, I love that record.' That's the thing I think of—the stage—because it's action, you know. And 'Honky Tonk Woman,' that's me. And then people came to us and said, 'You gotta record that song, it's so great.' And we said 'What's so great about it; we're doing it just like the Beatles or the Rolling Stones', and they said 'No, you have your own thing about it.' So when we cut the album, we were lacking a few tunes, so we said 'Well, let's just put in a few things that we're doing on stage. And that's how 'Proud Mary' came about. I had loved it when it first came out. We auditioned a girl and she had sung 'Proud Mary.' This is like eight months later, and Ike said, 'You know, I forgot all about that tune.' And I said let's do it, but let's change it. So in the car Ike plays the guitar, we just sort of jam. And we just sort of broke into the black version of it. It was never planned to say, 'Well, let's go to the record

shop, and I'd like to record this tune by Aretha Franklin'
. . . it's just that we get it for stage, because we give
the people a little bit of us and a little bit of what they
hear on the radio every day.

"My mother—her radio was usually blues, B. B. King
and all. But rock and roll was more me, and when that
sort of music came on, I never could sit down. I've always
wanted to move."

Tina gave a slightly—shall we say—different account to
Changes magazine:

Tina: I guess 'way before the Stones asked us to tour
with them, Ike started to get into the hard rock thing,
dragging me out of bed to listen to this or that, and at
4 o'clock in the morning.

Ike: She didn't like rock.

Tina: Finally, he said 'You going to have to sing it,
so you may as well like it.' So I started to listen to rock.

* * *

"They are really making it now," says Krasnow. "Really.
Everytime he plays a place—like last week, Carnegie
Hall—it's sold out a week before. And everybody's
raving about the show." But there was a time . . .

"I got pissed at him 'cause we worked our asses off
to get him on the Andy Williams *Love* show. We had
dinner afterwards, and I said, 'This is it! You've made
it, man!' He was back playing the bowling alley the next
night. I kept saying, 'Why play for $1000 a night when
you can get $20,000 now?' I mean, he was just touring
himself out." Ike himself says, "It doesn't matter to me;
we've got a living to make." Recently, he has relaxed
the road pace, from six nights a week all year to two
or three nights a week.

Ike and Tina are now regularly on TV—on variety
shows, talk shows, and specials; they were in Milos For-
man's *Taking Off* and *Gimme Shelter,* and they helped
celebrate Independence Day this year in Ghana. *Soul to
Soul.* And what is now apparent is that in Africa or in
Hollywood, in bowling alleys or in the Casino Lounge of
the Hotel International, the Ike and Tina Turner Revue,
with the Ikettes and the King of Rhythm (nine pieces
plus Ike) is pretty much the same show:

The band member doing the introductions and shameless album plugs; the Kings warming up with a couple of Motown-type power tunes, followed by the Ikettes singing "Piece of My Heart" or "Sweet Inspiration," then Tina running on, churning through "Shake Your Tail Feather," then saying a heartly hello and promising "soul music with the grease." Tina's recitations and spoken paeans—and Ike's wise-ass, not-quite-inaudible cracks, are all pregreased . . . *Mama don't cook no dinner tonight, 'cause Daddy's comin' home with the crabs* . . . When Tina sings, "I been lovin' you . . . too long . . . and I can't stop now," bossman Ike invariably croons, " 'Cause you ain't ready to die . . ."

The Otis Redding song is the show-stopper. Back in '67, Tina was simply breathing heavily over the instrumental passage; by '69, she was touching the tip of the microphone with both sets of fingers oh, so gently. Now, of course, it's a programmed gross-out, with Ike slurping and slushing and Tina rigid over the mike doing an unimpressive impression of an orgasm while Ike slams the song to a close, saying "Well, I got mine, I hope you got yours." In 1969 it was a solid salute to sex as a base for communication. Now, the subtleties gone, it's just another request number to keep the crowd happy.

"We cut the song," says Tina, "and Ike kept playing the tune over and over and I had to ad lib, so I just did that—just what comes into your head. So we started doing it on stage. How could I stand on stage, I felt, and say 'Oh baby, oh baby, *uhh*'—I'm just going to stand there, like an actress reading the script without any emotion? So I had to act.

"What I did on the Rolling Stones tour was only what had matured from the beginning. I don't think it can go any further, because it's, as they say in New York, it's getting pornographic. I agree, because like now Ike has changed words which makes it obvious what that meant when we first started doing it. I was thinking it meant sensually but not sexually. Sometimes he shocks me, but I have to be cool. Sometimes I want to go, 'Ike please.' I start caressing the mike and he goes, 'Wait 'til I get you home,' and I feel like going, 'Oh, I wish you wouldn't say that.' Everything else I feel like I can put up with, but

226

not that. But like I can't question Ike because every-thing that Ike has ever gotten me to do that I didn't like, was successful.

"I think in the early Sixties it would have really been out of bounds—like, I probably would have been thrown off the stage. But today, it's what's happening. That's why I can get by with it."

From *Tina Pie,* this strange crossfire: ". . . It could be nice but it would probably turn out awful—especially with that dirty ol' Ike hounding me. I sat through the first half of the second show with him and he kept telling me he want to give me a fit and just 'cause he had Tina didn't mean he couldn't want me, too. He's got the greatest skin going but that's about it.

—MELINDA
New York City

Melinda Who?

—IKE TURNER
New York City

Tina is giving me a tour of Ike's new main studios—the master control room with the $90,000 board featuring the IBM mix-memorizer (a computer card gives an electronic readout on the mix at whichever point the tape is stopped), a second studio marked STUDIO A (Ike Turner's, can you guess, is STUDIO AA), a writers' room, business offices for his various managers and aides, a playroom furnished with a pool table, Ike's own office, and, inevitably, Ike's private apartment suite. Again, it is disgusting, flowers chasing each other up the wall, a cinerama mural of a couple in embrace next to the breakfast table and refrigerator. Again, sofas, of Ike's own design, with hard-on arms. White early American drapings and chairs, and a draped, canopied bed so garish that Tina turns to Ike and says, "Can I tell 'em what we call this room? We call it 'the Whorehouse.' "

There's a double-door air closet at the entrance to Ike's private quarters, where he spends so many nights, "be-cause of all the work to be done." This is the Trap. You bust into Bolic Sound, and all the doors are automatically locked, leading you down the hall, into the stairwell in front of the apartment. The only way to open the door there is by dialing a secret telephone number. And the only word that can get to you will come from above you. Ike's got a TV camera there, too.

Ike Turner has moved around from label to label for ten years. Ike and Tina began with "A Fool in Love," which Ike cut with Tina when the original singer for his composition didn't show up at a date. That record hit in 1960 and was on a midwest R&B label, Sue. It was followed by "It's Gonna Work Out Fine," but the head of Sue delayed its release so long—he sent the master back three times, said Ike—that he split in 1964, going to Warner Bros.' fledgling R&B label, Loma, for a pair of live LPs recorded in Ft. Worth and Dallas by "Bumps" Blackwell, now manager of Little Richard. 1963 to 1966 was a dark period for the Revue—they made what they could on the road, and they had no hit records—and Loma records were hard to find.

Ike then took his act to Kent, a label he'd worked for in earlier days when he traveled the South scouting and recording, on a cheap Ampex tape recorder, bluesmen like B.B. King and Howlin' Wolf. This time around, he managed a hit for the Ikettes, "Peaches and Cream." But, he said, "They tried to steal the Ikettes. They sneaked around and tried to buy the girls from under me." Then it was Spector, won over by Ike and Tina's work as a substitute act in the rock and roll film, *T'N'T Show*. But after "River Deep" bombed, said Ike, "he got discouraged and went down in Mexico making movies." Phil recommended Bob Crewe as a producer, a single didn't hit, and they moved to an Atlantic subsidiary, Pompeii Records. "We were lost among all of Atlantic's own R&B stuff," Ike said, and that's when he ran into Krasnow. With no contract ever signed with Blue Thumb, Ike actually made a deal with United Artists/Liberty in mid-1969, before the Stones tour, through their New York-based R&B label, Minit.

"Spector gave Ike an absolute guarantee of hits forever," says Bud Dain, then general manager at Liberty. What Minit promised was a $50,000 a year guarantee "plus certain clauses—a trade ad on every release, sensitive timing of releases . . . but Minit was a mistake. They defaulted on the contract, and Ike was free to break the contract."

Then Ike and Tina toured with the Stones, and the next time Ike talked with Liberty, Liberty was talking about $150,000 a year guarantee, for 2 albums a year. Ike signed in Jaunary, 1970.

"The first LP was *Come Together*, in May," said Dain. "Now Ike wanted to build his own studios. The option came up again in January, 1971. The album sold well, but we couldn't exercise the option unless he'd sold 300,000. And he only had one album out that year. But he needed $150,000, and Al Bennett [president at Liberty] believed in him. We gave him the money." With the second advance, Ike's studios were well underway, and he got another hit record, the single on "Proud Mary."

"Then he came in—he needed another $150,000. He got that in June. So there's a total of $450,000 in advances." And that's why United Artists may yet be Ike and Tina's final home. Ike Turner must produce those two albums a year, and UA has no choice but to promote its ass off.

* * *

Ike's head is on one's woman's lap; his knee-socked feet on another's. His thin frame is blanketed by a trench coat, a sleeping bridge across the sofa in the dressing room. Tina has her back to them. She's working her hair into shape for the second show this Friday night, and Ike's getting the only rest he's gotten all day. And after the second show, he'll jump off the revolving stage of the Circle Star Theater in San Carlos, then back to the nearby San Francisco Airport to return to his studios to cut instrumental tracks the rest of the night and into the day, then back up to San Francisco and to the Circle Star mid-Saturday evening.

In the hallway, after the second show Friday, he stops long enough to give you a solid shoulder grab—a football coach's kind of friendly gesture—and a warm hello. He turns to the zoftig lady photographer nearby, glancing right through her tangle of cameras and giving her the onceover. He asks if maybe she wouldn't fly down with him. "What? You got a boyfriend?"

"This is the critical point of our career; I can't lighten up now," he says, and is off to the airport. At 2:30 in the morning, Tina—who doesn't return to L.A. with him—shows up at a banquet room in her hotel for a photo session. The photographer's assistant asks, "What's your advice for people getting into the business?" Tina, at 3 AM, is serious: "Have some kind of business knowledge."

In the dressing room between shows, she had said, "I'm glad I got Ike, 'cause I would've quit years ago. I probably would've worked for promoters and not get paid. Our policy is to have our money before we go on stage. Even if it's for the President."

Just before the Stones tour, Ike and Tina were booked for the Ed Sullivan Show, in September, 1969. "And he got his money in front," says Jeff Trager. Most promoters say 50 percent deposit, the rest after the show. "So Sullivan comes up to Ike before the show, and Ike hasn't got his guitar with him, and it's showtime. Sullivan asks where his guitar is, and Ike tells Ed he needs 'the key to the guitar,' the key being the money." Sullivan paid.

"You have to protect yourself," Tina is saying to the two women on the sofa with Ike. Road manager Rhonda Graham, a stern, curt white woman, is seated nearby, in front of a rack full of Tina's costumes and shoes. "In the early Sixties we went through that . . . if you don't know these people, some of them just take the gate and leave."

"Three, four years ago, they were playing a club," Trager recalls, "and Rhonda had a cigar box at the door. And one dollar would go into the box, one dollar to the club. At Basin Street West he got cash all the time."

But if you are black and in the music business, you get burned until you either quit or learn. Turner learned, through all the different labels and beginning in the late Forties. In Junior high, he says, he'd decided to devote himself to "giving people music sounds that they could really dig . . . and put their feet to. I'm not a very good speaker, so I try to express myself when I play."

Turner told Pete Senoff: "I started professionally when I was 11. The first group I played with was Robert Nighthawk, then Sonny Boy Williams. This was like back in 1948-1949. I went to Memphis in about 1952. That's where I met Junior Parker, Willy Nix, Howlin' Wolf. I was just playing with different groups all around . . . playing piano. From Junior Parker, I left Memphis and went to Mississippi, where I met the people from Kent and Modern Record Company. That's when I started scouting for talent for them. That's when I started recording B.B. King, Roscoe Gordon, Johnny Ace, Howlin' Wolf. We were just going through the South and giving people there $5 to $10 or a fifth of whiskey while we recorded over a piano in their living rooms.

"I wrote 32 hits for that firm, but I didn't know what a songwriter's royalties were. I didn't know nothing, man. They were sending me $150 a week, which was enough to keep me very happy in Mississippi, but not enough for me to get away to find out what was really going on."

Right after high school, Ike had formed the first Kings of Rhythm; their first job was in Lulu, Mississippi, and each King got 18 cents for the night's work. One time, they went to Memphis and recorded "Rocket 88" at B.B. King's label. It was a local hit. "But some dude at the record company beat me," Ike said, "and I only got $40 for writing, producing, and recording it. And the lead singer took the band from me and went on his own." Ike went back to Memphis, gigging around. After the record company job, he went back to his hometown, Clarksdale, reformed the Kings of Rhythm, and ended up in St. Louis. From 1954 to '57 he played all around the city.

One night, 17-year-old Annie Mae Bullock went to see Ike's show. She had moved to St. Louis two years before to join her sister. "She'd been telling me about Ike Turner, who was like a legend in St. Louis—you know, his picture and name spread about the newspapers. I went to this club to see what it was all about. I remember Ike was on top of the piano like Jerry Lee Lewis and the band was walking, and everybody was moving. Well, I've always sung and one night I asked Ike if I could sing and he said OK, but he never called me."

Annie Mae went out again, another night in 1957, to the Club Manhattan. On a B.B. King tune, with Ike on organ, the drummer went to the audience and set the mike in front of her sister—"teasing, I guess. She said 'No,' so I grabbed the mike and started singing. Ike looked up all surprised, like, 'Oh wow, she can really sing.'" She became a regular, singing on weekends, until she cut "A Fool in Love" in 1960, and the demo became a hit. By that time, they'd been married—"in 1958," says Tina, "one of those house things, little preacher things, sort of quiet, saying, 'OK, let's do it.'"—and Ike changed Annie Mae's name to Tina.

"He's always looking for something different in a name," she said. Bolic Sound, the name of the studios, is taken from her maiden name.

Tina was born in Brownsville, Tennessee, and grew up in Knoxville. They way she stretches her limbs on stage, she looks tall, and her high cheekbones give her a proud Indian appearance. But she's only 5'4", and as for Indian blood: "It's in the family, but I don't know where or from what tribe. My grandmother really looked like an Indian, though. She was maybe one-fourth Cherokee."

Tina never studied music. Of course, she learned some from church—in Knoxville, she went to Baptist church and sang in the choir and, in high school, she sang some opera. But mostly she remembers a baby-sitter taking her to "sanctified church, a religion, they call it holiness—it's where they play tambourines and dance, but not just dancing—dancing like *godly* to the fast music, sort of like today. I remembered the excitement of the music; it inspired you to dance."

*   *   *

"Before Ike," says Tina, gingerly feeling the cuff of her hotpants, "I didn't—I never owned a record player. I listened to songs on the radio, but I never knew the artists went out and performed. I never connected the two. It's like you're dumb, you don't know how they make movies. I never knew . . . I just thought I'd be singing in a church the rest of my life and marry."

232

The dumb kid travels the world and meets royalty, and her innate sensibility shows through. In Ghana: "I went to see where they kept the slaves before they brought them to America—and it was very interesting and touching. They kept the women on one side in a room this big [about 20 by 30 feet]. The only light was three holes at the top, and only the sea light came in. A lot of them got diseases from the dampness of the sea; it formed a sort of crust on the wall. They had to live in all that filth; there was no bathrooms, no nothing. Like just women over here and men over there—the men in a much larger room—and they'd open the door so they could 'multiply,' as they called it—in all that filth. It was really something to see where you came from—where it all began.

"I knew nothing about NY-kruma . . . is that how you say . . . Nkruma—none of that. I never did much reading. Everything I could have learned in America in two years, I learned in a week's time. But I went out and toured, going like 100 miles out of the main town. I got a chance to see how the real people live. Huts, no electric lights, no windows. They lived down in the fields.

"But I never go out a lot. Never saw the Statue of Liberty, which I'd really want to—especially since I've seen the Eiffel Tower. But I never feel like it; you get in the habit of sleeping all day. But there isn't a whole lot to see in America. We tore all our historical things down. Like there's no Indians, no real Indians for you to go out and see.

"Every now and then I read. Like for instance I took time to read what I wanted to about astrology, and I took time to read up on the health food thing." Tina is trying to move away from meat, and her kids "are doing vitamin pills, wheat germs, and sunflower seed flour. But I like a good steak now and then . . .

"I read the Jacqueline Kennedy, the Ethel Kennedy book. From the very beginning I never paid any attention to the political end of America. So then when President Kennedy became president, I became interested, because for some reason I liked him. Every time they said the

233

President's going to speak, I watched. Something about that family—they're real people. I don't know what it is—lively, life-like."

Ike and Tina played Hyannisport once—"a very small, really cute town for a married couple that's not interested in the city life and wants to live an old-fashioned sort of clean-cut life"—and got an invitation from Ethel to visit the Kennedy estate.

"You could feel there was a real family. Like my family, it's too late now. Sure, it's my family, and they know, but I'd like to have been able to teach them things before they reached the age of 13 where . . . you know how kids question things, why say it this way or . . . that's what they do, automatically know that this is the right way and why, not just because I say it is . . . But you start from the root. Because my oldest son, he's really prejudiced, and I don't know why, because we've always mixed, being entertainers. And Greg's got this thing, 'Ahh, wow, mother, she's white . . .' None of the other kids are like that, but he's really . . ."

* * *

Ike is playing his new sides in his office, and everybody's moving, just so, head nodding, lower lip out a little, legs maybe churning a bit, and this photographer is sitting there, tapping both feet lightly on the floor, and Ike strikes an accusatory pose: "See? *See?* You white people—You have to move from *inside!* Man, white people put black people off beat clapping so long . . ."

Which is not the way the Turners usually talk about their audiences. "OK," says Tina. "In the beginning we worked the chitlin' circuit, and now we go back, and it's really terrible. They really don't listen now, because they feel like, 'Well, we knew you first.' Black people seem to be like 'We know what Ike and Tina can do' . . . like at one of our gigs, a guy right down front kept passing a cigarette the whole time, anything to distract from what's going on stage. Instead, with a white audience, they sit and listen, and you have their attention. Or they leave. But they never start walking around or start a fight.

"Like I'm not shameful of my people or anything, and I've had a lot of people come and say, 'Mama, when you gonna grow out the hair?' 'Where's the natural?' I told them, 'I'm black, you can see it.' I don't have to wear a big wooly head of hair. I like straight hair, I wear it, I feel myself, you don't see me walking around trying to be white . . .

"Ike could do this better than myself, but have you ever noticed that when black people go to a dance, they dress the complete thing, the high-heeled shoes, the purse. But the whites, they just wear something they'll be comfortable in. All right, so I think that the black person a lot of times doesn't go to see what is there, he goes to be seen. And like you find in the middle of a number where you're really trying to climax your show, someone gets up and walks straight across right in front of you— a woman most likely, or a man dressed with a hat that's tilted and all the colors, and the flaps on his shoes, and you know, they don't think a lot about being entertained. They want to do the entertaining."

* * *

"I knew there had to be a time for us. I'd go and catch shows that people said were great that did nothing for me. And I felt our show was much better. And I knew we had to get some records out, but I didn't feel that it was going to be the records. I felt it was going to be a timing. I didn't know that the timing would be a change in the world, but I thought it would be a certain time, like maybe the 70's, But all of a sudden, remember when they used to call longhairs beatniks? OK. Now they call them hippies. The hippies came and more of them came and more and more. They took over San Francisco, they took over the highways, they just took over. That was the beginning of the change.

"They changed minds; they said, 'Well, why?' and everybody else said, 'Yeah, why?' And that's who accepted us. They felt like 'why dress up, for the acts.' 'Why is it that a woman can't wear short dresses or whatever?' You understand what I'm saying? And here I was that they could say, 'Here is Tina Turner, here is the Supremes.

Why is it that Tina Turner isn't as good as the Supremes? Because you're of this—would it be—'culture'? No—you would say that the Supremes could play for a more *sophisticated* audience, but Tina Turner couldn't. And the hippies would say 'Why?' So everybody got into the 'why' bag and I sit right down in the middle . . . And sayin' that this girl and their act is just as good as these other people; it's class. Really, they just got polished down, and for the other set of people.

"I never did like James Brown. I always did like Ray Charles. He was my only influence, because I always liked to sing more or less like men sing, and sound like they sound. Like he and Sam Cooke were my influences."

What Tina likes, and what she aims for when she choreographs the Ikettes—is *action*. "I let an Ikette wear an Afro once," she says—"Esther, the little short one, because it fit her personality and she wanted to. But I've found that long hair adds to the action of our show. Esther was on television with a natural, and she said, 'Why is this, I don't look like I'm doing anything.' The difference was the difference in the action. We went on stage once, and I wore a fur dress and the Ikettes wore leopard furry dresses—but you gotta work harder, because there's no swing. Every time I wear a chiffon dress, everyone says 'What's wrong with you tonight, Tina? You weren't moving.' The chiffon hides the action."

Before any given date, Tina will run the Ikettes through rehearsal, "all day and all night and they eat at the house. If I'm training a new girl, we rehearse every day from 2 to 6 for two weeks, like a constant grind, because there's a lot for her to learn and she's still going to forget when she gets on stage, because once the music hits you and the audience and the stage and the lights, a different thing comes over you. But now with an old set of girls, I don't have to call a rehearsal, I'll say in the dressing room, 'Hey, let's put this step in or change this routine.' It's a matter of like driving somewhere, someone gives you directions—you go so many blocks and turn left—that's how I get it over to them."

Friday night at the Circle Star, the Ikettes were by themselves, each packaged in silver micro-minis, combing out their hair and laughing insults at each other, like dormitory girls.

The Kings of Rhythm were into the first of the usual two-number set, and the Ikettes, right on time, were adjusting their sequin chokers and ready to put on their medium-heels. As one, they laughed about the bad old days.

* * *

Various ex-Ikettes had said how difficult Ike and Tina were, how selfish they were, how stingy (one ex said Ikettes got $30 a night if they were within 50 miles of L.A.; an extra $5 outside—this in '68 and '69—"and we paid our own rent; they just paid transportation"). Another girl spoke about a fine system—$10 for a run in an Ikettes' stockings; $25 for "laughing too loud"— even if it happened off-stage, in a hotel room. She also spoke of Ike putting down their singing and hiring local session singers for his albums. When they were called in for a session, she said, they weren't paid—except for "Bold Soul Sister." The Ikettes, she said, wrote the song, but didn't get credit—"only $15 each for that session."

And the turnover. "They give excuses like, 'Lots of girls have to get married.' But most of them just can't take their baloney. Of course when you leave you have a bad attitude. I was so naive—Ike'd holler on stage, and it was hard to concentrate on what you were doing." But, she admitted, it was good training—not unlike boot camp. And there've been plenty who've served—including Bonnie Bramlett, in 1965—and another soulful white singer, Kathy MacDonald. Ike found her at the Fillmore West and wanted to sign her as a solo artist, and she sang on "Come Together," but she stayed with her job in the chorus behind Joe Cocker.

"It was very common to get approached by Ike," said one former Ikette. "He'll just approach anything in a skirt. He'd be shrewd about it, buy you things and make you think twice about it. Tina may know all this, but she tries to act like she doesn't. They're not as happy as they put out front."

* * *

The current Ikettes, a minute before curtain call, put on happy faces. "The last time there was a fine was almost two years ago," says Edna, and she proceeds to knock on wood. Esther "Bills" Jones and Jean Brown Burks ("Brown is my *maiden* name," she emphasizes) join her, slamming their knuckles on their vanity table in unison and laughing. "Tell the girls you talked to that things have changed," said Esther, who's been an Ikette for three years. Edna dropped out for a year—she had TB —and rejoined, a year ago. Jean dropped out for two years after working two years. She's been back six months.

Driving from her house to the studios, Tina talks about interviews. Her least favorite question is about the different Ikettes. "Lord knows how many there've been," she says, evading another question by adding, "They leave for one reason or another." Bonnie Bramlett, she says, "would have lasted, but we went to the South, and we had trouble down in Louisiana, guess she looked too white. We put a scarf on her and we felt she'd pass as 'a yellow nigger,' but they just sort of knew, and they blocked us and everything . . . But whenever I run into anyone like with a good voice that could be an asset to the group—if they can dance—I hire. I don't worry about color.

"Yeah, I work with the Ikettes on their records because a lot of times they can't always do Ike's ideas—control the voice and all. Sometimes we have to use other outside voices for certain sounds . . ."

As for Ike and Tina and whether they're a woosome twosome—it's difficult to tell. Ike makes himself unavailable—by his pace—and lets Tina do the talking. When they do an interview together, invariably they disagree and chide each other. Posing for a photo, Ike is asked to embrace Tina; he does, and warns: "Better catch this quick; I don't do this often." In the dressing room, while Tina talked, Ike slept. In the hallway, while Ike chatted, Tina was in seclusion.

Ike Turner spends most nights in his private apartment —"the Whorehouse,"—a mile away at his new studio, Bolic Sound, but Tina says she stays there whenever she can. And yet she's upset now because Ike was talking to the telephone man the other day about buying cable lines, so he can hook up another remote camera from his office and watch what's going on at home.

CHARLIE SIMPSON'S APOCALYPSE

by Joe Eszterhas

RIGHT AFTER the sun comes up, first thing folks do around Harrisonville, Missouri, is go up to the barn and see if the mare is still there. Horse-thieves drive around the gravel roads and brushy hills in tractor-trailers looking to rustle lazyboned nags. Then they grind them up into bags of meat jelly for the dogfood people. It's getting so that a man can't live in peace anywhere, not even on his own plot of land.

Harrisonville is 40 miles southeast of Kansas City along Interstate 71, just down the blacktop from the red-brick farmhouse where Harry S. Truman, haberdasher and President, was born. The little town is filled with weeping willows, alfalfa, Longhorn steer, and Black Whiteface cows. Life should be staid and bucolic, a slumbering leftover of what everyone who buys the $3.00 Wednesday-night Catfish Dinner at Scott's Bar B-Q calls Them Good Old Days. But it isn't like that anymore. There's always some botheration to afflict a man these days and if it isn't the horse-thieves or the velvetleaf that plagued the soybeans last year, then it's them vagrant tornadoes.

240

They call this lush area Twister Alley. Of all the woebegone acreage in America, Harrisonville and the fast-blink single-gas-station towns clustered about it—Peculiar, Lone Jack, Gunn City—attract more funnel clouds and 90 mph whirlwinds each hardluck year than anyplace else. The whirlwinds sweep down across greenbacked rows of wheat and corn, tottering power lines and flame onto dried haystacks—raising hell two or three times a season with the insurance rates and the little money a farming man has left after Uncle Sam takes his share. For some reason the land provokes these killer-storms and, out around a bonfire on a warm spring night, a man can sit around with his Mail Pouch and wait for jagged strips of angry lightning to neon the wisteria and the hollyhock.

Except for the twisters, the horsethieves and the velvet-leaf, it is like any other tacky, jaundiced Southern town. It carries a weighty but atrophied Dixie tradition, having once been a proud link of the Confederacy, although it is not very far from the Kansas border-town where John Brown, saintly revolutionary murderer, launched his bloodbath a century ago. Its most famous citizen is a machinist named Jerry Binder, who won a ballyhooed $5000 suggestion award from Trans World Airlines for improving the turbine of the JT3D jet engine. Billy Quantrill's Civil War raiders once raped and ravaged here to historical acclaim and Harry "Harricula" Truman, or just plain "Harry S." (as they say at Scott's Bar B-Q) visited here one Appreciation Day not long after he dropped the Aye-Tomic Bomb. Harry S. chewed saucy chicken wings on the courthouse steps and told the folks the White House was nothin' but a big white jail.

Harrisonville serves as Cass County's seat—population 4700—and by 1980 will be only a few miles south of the exact demographic center of America. It will be at the very heart of the calcified Heartland, a patriotic foot-note which pleases the town's flaccid watery-eyed mayor and dentist, Dr. M. O. Raine, to no end.

This spring the last snowfall was shoveled away on April Fool's Day and folks started getting ready for the summer: The Harrisonville Fire Department tested its six Civil Defense Air Raid-Tornado Warning sirens and

even the 89-year-old Harrisonville Hotel, the oldest building in town, its roof damaged by generations of funnel-
clouds, got a homey facelift. Its eroded brick was
scraped and washed down. The Missouri Turkey Shoot
Season was opening; the American Legion Building at
303 Pearl Street, a mausoleum of cigar butts, housed
a nightly clap-happy gospel meeting—"Do You Want
To Be Saved?"—and the Peculiar Panthers knocked off the
favored Harrisonville Wildcat basketball team 66-65.
The Chamber of Commerce announced "real-big, real-
good" news—the long-delayed acquisition of a shiny new
cherry-topped 1972 ambulance.

Less than a month later on a muggy thunderheaded
warm day, Friday, April 21st, at 5:55 PM, the Civil
Defense sirens let out a high-pitched scream that cut
across the wheatfields for miles around. Folks hurried to
their citizens' band radios to await emergency instructions.

They thought it was another goddamn tornado.

They couldn't understand the breathless disjointed
words which G. M. Allen, town banker and fire chief,
garbled at his white-helmeted Civil Defense volunteers
in the hamlets and hollows around town.

What in tarnation was G. M. talking about? "Hippies
. . . Killed two policemen . . . Dead . . . M-1 carbine
. . . Blood all over the place . . . the Simpson boy . . .
Come on into town . . . Bring your guns . . . There's
more of 'em . . . Yo, a revolution."

I. Charlie Simpson's Mad-Dog Dance

ON FRIDAY, APRIL, 21ST:

Astronaut John W. Young leaped up off the moondust
and exuberantly saluted the American flag. At North
Carolina State University, a thousand kids danced around
a handpainted sign that said: NIXON'S MACHINE IS FALL-
ING. In Lawrence, Kansas, 600 persons met in front of
Strong Hall to plan an anti-war march.

At 5:55 PM on the town square in Harrisonville, Missouri, Charles Simpson, 24 years old, 6'3", 180 pounds,
flowing shoulder-length gunmetal black hair, known to
his friends as "Ootney," leaped out of a red Volkswagen.
He was an asthmatic who liked Henry David Thoreau

242

and had eyes like razor-slits. The car was driven by a friend, John Risner, 26, a pallid Navy veteran, the son of a former deputy sheriff, beer-bellied, wire-bearded, blue-jeaned, wearing a picaresque black felt English derby hat. The car had a peace symbol in its windshield.

Charles Simpson jumped out of the car on Independence Avenue, less than a thousand feet across the street from the Allen Bank and Trust Company, a modernized plate-glass structure facing the courthouse. It was minutes away from closing. Simpson was a farmboy who grew up in the apple-knocker village of Holden 24 miles away, the son of a totally disabled World War II combat veteran. He started walking south on Independence Avenue. He was wearing knee-popped bellbottoms, a waist-length Army fatigue jacket, and yellowed dry-goods boots caked with mud and cowflop. He had high jutting cheekbones, a hooked and fist-kissed nose, a swarthy complexion, and uneven calcimine-white teeth. His eyes were coal-black and slanted. There was whipcord in his muscles but he looked a little funny when he suddenly crossed the street and started running.

As he loped across Independence onto Pearl Street, he reached under his patched Army jacket and took out an M-1 semi-automatic carbine with clip and over 140 rounds of ammunition. It was the same weapon which National Guardsmen used at Kent State University in 1970, killing four students and wounding nine. He had used the combat-regulation weapon in the fields around town with his friend Rise Risner, target-shooting overfed squirrels, moonlighting packrats, and non-returnable bottles of Budweiser beer.

On this Friday afternoon, as Charles Simpson reached for the M-1 under his fatigue jacket, he saw two brown-uniformed members of the Harrisonville Police Department—Donald Marler, 26, and Francis Wirt, 24, a Vietnam veteran, back from the war only four months and a policeman less than a month. They were part of the department's foot-patrol, recently pressured by the town's businessmen to keep an ever-alert eye on the square. Both men were armed with holstered police-regulation .38s. Both men knew Simpson.

As Friday afternoon traffic backed up around the

243

square—the shops were closing and each of the town square's four corners is red-lighted—Charles Simpson leaned into a crouch and aimed his semi-automatic carbine waist-high at the two policemen. They were less than 100 feet away. He fired a quick burst of bullets. The two policemen went down poleaxed. A lady 20 feet from the gunfire fainted and her car rammed into the Happiness-Is-Tastee-Freeze delivery truck in front of her.

Simpson ran toward the two policemen sprawled on the concrete. Both were moaning, bleeding badly, unable to return fire. He stood rigidly over both men, pointing the muzzle down over first one and then the other, and fired two more staccato bursts into their bodies at point-blank range. The bullets, made for warzones, ripped into and through the bodies. Patrolman Marler was hit twice in the chest, twice in the abdomen, and once in each hand. Wirt was shot twice in the abdomen and three times in the right arm. His elbow looked as if it had been fragged.

Simpson spinned, turning to the Allen Bank and Trust Company, and ran inside. He didn't say anything. He didn't aim the carbine at anyone. He pointed it willy-nilly toward a rear wall covered with advertising slogans —INVEST IN AMERICA, BUY U.S. SAVINGS BONDS— and fired again. Bullets ricocheted around the floor and walls, wounding two cashiers. Simpson turned again, ran outside, waving the rifle in front of him, and ran west on Pearl, heading toward the town's water tower—HI THERE! CLASS OF '69—and the Cass County Sheriff's office. He was a death-dealing whirligig. He had a shit-fire grin on his face.

The sheriff's office is about a thousand feet west on Pearl Street from the Allen Bank. Across the street from it is the Capitol Cleaners, which holds a monopoly on the town's laundry trade, offers STARCH BARGAINS.

As Charles Simpson dashed from the bank to the sheriff's office down the narrow street, a 58-year-old man with boils on his neck named Orville T. Allen was getting out of his battered pick-up truck in front of the cleaners. He had operated a dry-cleaning store in nearby Garden City for 27 years and was there to pick up some part-time weekend laundry.

Charles Simpson saw Orville Allen across the street, a man in faded khaki pants he had never seen before, and aimed his carbine. The burst caught Allen in the chest. He dropped to the pavement, twisted on the ground, turned his bleeding chest to the sky, and clasped his hands in prayer. "God," he moaned. A trail of blood trickled across the street toward the sheriff's office.

Sheriff Bill Gough, 46, a hulking and slow-footed man, had just taken off his holstered .38 revolver and was sitting down reading that week's issue of the *Democrat-Missourian*. The paper had come out that noon and carried a frontpage story about an 18-year-old Kansas kid the sheriff's deputies had arrested for possession of marijuana. Gough heard something rat-tat-tat outside his office as he scanned the paper, but he didn't think it was gunfire. He thought it was some fool beating a piece of tin with a stick. He went outside, unarmed, to see what all the commotion was about.

As he got outside, he saw Simpson coming toward him, the M-1 aimed headhigh. He tried to duck but wasn't quite fast enough (although the savage reflex-like twist of his big body probably saved his life). He was hit in the right shoulder and the left leg but staggered inside his office. His wife, sitting at a desk, screamed. He knocked her to the floor, grabbed his revolver, and flung himself behind a desk with such force that his elbows were purple for weeks. Covered with his own blood, Sheriff Gough aimed the revolver at the door and waited for Simpson to open it. His hands shook. He was afraid he'd lose control and wildly pull the trigger before Simpson stuck his head inside.

But when he hit Gough in the street, Simpson spun around and, waving the gun wildly in the air, started trotting back toward the square. Allen's body lay a few feet away from him. Suddenly, in front of the Harrisonville Retirement Home, a dim gray-slab matchbox of a building across the street from Allen's bleeding body, he stopped. He bent down, put the carbine inside his mouth, sucking the barrel. He fired his last burst. He blew the top of his head off. His mad-dog dance was over.

He had fired more than 40 rounds. Four people were dead, three wounded. The town's shiny new Chamber of Commerce ambulance drove around the square and collected bodies. As the Civil Defense sirens screamed and G. M. Allen's volunteer firemen hosed down the bloodstains, gun-wielding deputies and policemen grabbed all the longhairs around the square and took them to Bill Gough's jail.

II. The Hippies, and G. M. Allen

ALL ROADS LEAD TO THE SQUARE, an editorial in J. W. Brown's shopping-news weekly, the Cass County *Democrat-Missourian,* once said with prophetic innocence. "At least that's what it seems like to outsiders. The Square seems to us to be a big chunk out of the past, sitting in the middle of the present. The cobblestone streets, the old hotel and courthouse, are probably taken for granted by the townspeople." Charles "Ootney" Simpson's fierce assault on the town square was the final escalation of a guerrilla war of raw nerves and icy glares. It was fought for control of a seemingly insignificant logistical area: courthouse steps, shrubbery encircling it, and sidewalks facing its entrances on Wall and Pearl Streets. To understand the fated intensity of this cornpone guerrilla war, one must understand the uniquely claustrophobic architecture of the square itself and its place in Harrisonville's rustic-schizoid tradition.

The courthouse anchors the square, surrounded on four sides by contrasting clapboard and imitation brick shops. It is the epicenter of a tight and walled-in rectangle decorated by butterflies and honey-bees. The cobblestoned pavement on the four streets surrounding it— Wall to the south, Lexington to the east, Pearl to the north, Independence to the west—is chokingly narrow. It is less than 30 feet from the courthouse curb to any of the businesses on its sides. The streets were designed for horses and buggies, not delivery trucks. All the streets are one-way in a looping arc; you have to drive through Lexington and Pearl to get to Independence. Since the streets are so narrow, the shops on all sides—like South Side Prescriptions, Felix Hacker's Paint Supplies, Ballon's Dry Goods and Wright's Shoe Palace—are literally but steps away from whatever is happening around the courthouse. If someone sitting on the courthouse steps shouts

246

an epithet—"Off the pigs," for example—the shout will echo dramatically, reverberating through the little stores where, in years past, only the cash registers made noise.

The courthouse was built in the first decade of the 20th century. It is red-brick, three stories tall, topped by a cupolaed belltower and a flagpole. The bells ring once a year—on the Fourth of July. The flagpole is bare; a new one splits the grass in front of the War Veterans statue and flies the flag 24 hours a day. The building sits atop a mound-like elevation exactly 16 steps above the neatly-swept sidewalk. A black iron railing leads to the south side doors, which are flanked by four columnar graystone pillars. The elevation transforms the courthouse steps into a stage. If Old Lloyd Foster, for example, who ebulliently runs South Side Prescriptions, glances out his store window at the courthouse, he is looking up. The building is at the tip of his nose.

On the Wall Street side of the courthouse there is a fixed metal sign that says: LEARN TO LEAD! ARMY NCO CANDIDATE SCHOOL. The same kind of sign on the Independence Street side in blue and red says: THE MARINE CORPS BUILDS MEN—2735 B TROOP. Six feet of manicured grass and shrubbery surround the building on all sides. The clock atop the belltower is dead. It's been stuck for more than a decade. For some bizarre reason, the clock's hand paralyzed at different times—it is 2:20 to the south, 6:25 to the east, 1:20 to the west. The northern clock face has been removed—pigeons flutter there. A deeply-carved inscription above the southern doors says: A PUBLIC OFFICE IS A PUBLIC TRUST.

The courthouse steps and the town square have served for generations as a place of public lolling. Saturday-night hoedowns were celebrated there; its four streets were barricaded and strung with multi-colored lightbulbs. Three times a year there was a carnival. And gradually the town fathers—meaning the bankers, aldermen, and Chamber of Commerce officials (the mayor was always a yo-yo)—accepted too that the courthouse steps and shrubbery served as a haven for grizzled lushes to gulp their pints of Missouri corn whiskey. Every small town has its drunks, but they always become harmless and somewhat valuable characters, walking examples to contrast with Godfearing lives. The old bullshit artists are happy enough just to be left alone. They exude alcohol and sour courtesy, never fuss anyone, and the judges and deputies avert their eyes and walk smugly past them to wood-paneled chambers where decanters of aged bourbon are kept out of sight.

In the late summer of 1971, the town drunks abandoned the courthouse steps and claimed they were being spooked out. The figures now lazing in the shade and dangling their legs were a bewildering new phenomenon and no one knew quite what to make of them. They were townie kids who had grown up around Cass County and played for the Harrisonville Wildcats, getting their first fifths of sourmash from tight-mouthed Old Lloyd Foster. But when Old Lloyd looked across at these homegrown kids now, they gave him a fright. They were different. They had changed. They were their own kids but . . . somehow they weren't their own kids anymore. They wore their hair long and untrimmed and grew chinbound moustaches and billowing beards. They wore all manners of beegum strawhats and cropduster clothes—always bluejeans and a lot of Army jackets, engineer's boots, and $2 teeny-shoes which Old Lloyd's son, Don, sold them at the Sears Country Catalog Store. They played riotous Frisbee in the middle of the street and collected wilted flowers in back of Vann's Florist Shop and decked themselves out with dead roses and carnations. They wore "love crosses" around their necks from which Jesus' body had been blasphemously ripped away.

Some of the women who came in once a week to Connie's Beauty Salon said they called them filthy names and scratched their privates. Some of the policemen said they called them "Pigs" face to face and were always talking about their godalmighty "Civil Liberties." Some of the businessmen claimed the one word they heard echoing around the square from morning 'til closing was a four-letter word they couldn't even repeat out loud what with women and children in town. "There was no doubt about it," said 60-year-old J. W. Brown, editor and publisher of the *Democrat-Missourian,* a flatulent pipe-smoking country gentleman. "What we had here were our own hippies, settin' up there, raisin' hell, callin' our women names, drinkin' wine and smokin' some of that marijuana. I even heard tell they was right up there in the bushes havin' sexual intercourse. Yes sir, Sex-You-All intercourse. Now those old drunks who used to set up there, those old boys never did any of that."

Sex-You-All debauchery 16 steps above ground level right at the nosetips of righteous town merchants is not what the new courthouse squatters had in mind. Not at all. They were there in the beginning because there was no other place to go. Where could you go in Harrisonville?—this small time place haunted by homilies, platitudes, and bushwah. Into Guido's Pizza Parlor? Well, maybe, but couldn't stay there too long. As time went by Win Allen, the kingpin, Rise Risner, Ootney Simpson, George Russell, Harry Miller, and the Thompson Brothers hung around the square because it got to be an entertaining mock-serious game. They were liberating Harrisonville, Missouri, showing the Sho-Me State some puffed-up balls. They were fighting their revolution against people they had cowedly called "Sir" all their teenage lives.

Beer-bellied Rise Risner and Gary Hale, a reedy and subdued James Taylor look-alike, went off to the Navy as cowlicked country boys and came back dazedly turned-on, rejecting everything around them. They were home but home sure as hell didn't feel like home.

Liberating Harrisonville meant a lot of mind-blowing. They soon found themselves romantic figures, idolized by some of the high school kids. They conducted hoohawing teach-ins in front of the War-Vets statue as Legionnaires stood around on the sidewalk in their peaked caps and called it "jackrollin' the blind." They'd read selections from Abbie Hoffman, Timothy Leary, and Bobby Seale in stentorian tones, lifting their voices to phrases like "Off the pigs!" and "Up against the wall, motherfucker!"

They had Dylan and Jimi Hendrix tapes in their cars and boomed "Stone Free" and "Lay Lady Lay" in the night. They smoked as much dope as was available and there was always more than enough. The Army had planted crops of hemp during World War II and five-foot high marijuana plants shadowed the wheatfields.

Snake-charmed, the high school kids started imitating them, of course, using words like "motherfucker" and acting heavylidded in civics class just for the aggravation of it. The principal, an ex-Marine, freaked, naturally, and zeroed-in on the new villains at council meetings when the school budget was discussed and the vandalism dollar-damage was counted. Only the year before, the principal fired a matronly English teacher who made *Stranger in a Strange Land* required reading. The townspeople picked up the taboo: the lady was once seen going into a liquor store and the town's elders were soon saying she was fucking and sucking all the seniors in her classes.

So these plowboy hippies—who were convinced, perhaps from experience, that their elders still cornholed cows when they got horny—came to dominate the town's consciousness and its square. And of all the revolutionaries and sugartits cavorting around the square, two seemed the most frightening—the Simpson boy, who'd always rub his pecker when a woman went by, and The Nigger, one of the town's six blacks. Win Allen, 24, frail and bird-like, with bloodshot eyes and a habit of slurring his words, made no secret of the fact he was shanghaied into Uncle Sam's Army, went AWOL, and managed to con himself a dishonorable discharge. He was a Bad Nigger as opposed to his younger brother, Butch, 17, a walking bowling ball who played forward for the Harrisonville Wildcats scoring an average 15 points a game. Butch was a Good Nigger. But Win (short for Edwin) had an Afro popout hairdo and was always up there on the steps, holding hands with a white girl, talking about Love, and waving books like *The Fire Next Time* and *Do It!*

Every time one of Bill Davis' policemen or Bill Gough's deputies passed the square, Win Allen would cheerfully yell: "Hey, here comes The Pigs." He even spoke his special blackevil language, and pretty soon half the kids in the high school were using this garbled childrenese, not just ordinary hippie words the townspeople heard in television commercials but words they'd never heard before. Words like "bro" and "gritting down" (eating) and "Crib" and "P-ing down" (sexual intercourse) and "bogosity" (anything he disagreed with). But the single phrase which all the kids were using was just gibberish for anything that Win liked. When Win liked something as much as he liked P-ing down, he said: "Most ricky-tick." "Most ricky-tick" was being heard all over town. A high school senior even used it in an essay on "The Prospect of Marriage." The townspeople would go home at night, after having to endure the raucous courthouse shenanigans all day, and their own kids would say bogosity and gritting down and most ricky-tick.

Some action clearly had to be taken. G. M. Allen, fire-chief, got up at a special Chamber of Commerce meeting and said with hawkshaw eloquence: "I'm an American, damn it, and I'm proud to be an American and I don't go for all this hangin' the flag upside-down stuff."

G. M. Allen had another reason for urging civic action, a pocketbook reason. Rise Risner and Charles Simpson and Win Allen and the rest of that pestiferous crew had become an economic menace. Business was off all over town, from the Capot Department Store to alderman Luke Scavuzzo's grocery. Some of the people who shuffled in to make their monthly mortgage payments to G. M. Allen's bank told him they were afraid to come into town. The hippies. The hippies were scaring business away. Harrisonville just couldn't sit around and let itself get overrun, G. M. Allen said.

The aldermen agreed that action had become a matter of local survival, although one of them, sucking his teeth, pointed out alternatives—"Don't stretch the blanket, now, G. M."—explaining the financial setback. There was a nationwide economic crisis and wage-price freeze and 11 miles down Interstate 71 one of those deluxe glass and chromium shopping centers, calling itself Truman Corners, had just opened up. Maybe folks were shopping there.

"Maybe so," G. M. Allen told the tooth-sucker, "but they'd be leavin' their money here if it weren't for them hippies," and the Chamber of Commerce spring offensive, to recapture the town square for the old drunks, was under way.

III. The Battle of the Town Square

ACTUALLY, THE ALDERMEN had two offensives to mount at the same time, and they were both G. M.

Allen's hardnosed command: Operation Hippie and Operation Tornado.

To facilitate the war against tornadoes, G. M. Allen thought it would be a civic coup if the Fire-Fighters Association of Missouri—tornado-watchers of the entire state—held their annual convention in Harrisonville. The aldermen, perhaps contemplating the weekend revenue from 500 firefighters and their wives gratefully applauded G. M.'s boosterism. G. M. lined the convention up for Friday, April 21st. There would be a tornado committee meeting Saturday morning and a brass-band parade Saturday afternoon. Doris' House of Charm announced it would offer a "Fireladies' Shampoo Special" for its beehive-headed lady tourists. As a further step, G. M. ran off hundreds of emergency doomsday leaflets and distributed them in the stores around the square. His directive began: "When a tornado is spotted in the Harrisonville area, six sirens around the *city* will sound a long *blast* for three minutes. Our air-raid emergency *bombing warning* differs from a storm warning by sounding an up-and-down warbling *blast* rather than a long continuing *blast*. BE ALERT, G. M. ALLEN, FIRE CHIEF."

To facilitate the offensive against hippies, G. M. figured it was necessary that everyone in town understand the critical nature of the crisis. He arranged with the Kiwanis Club to import a "drug addict expert." The "drug addict expert" was Robert Williams, the police chief from Grandview. Chief Williams, a man of profound second-hand insight heard about drugs and hippies all the time from his police friends in Kansas City.

"It's approaching a crisis stage," he told the Kiwanians. "Police can't even eliminate the problem. We've got to wake up and take a hard stand. What we've got to do is stand up and inject some old-fashioned moral values before all our young fall victim to those older marauders who prey on them." The Harrisonville Community Betterment Council appointed a Drug-Abuse Committee.

Late at night on March 23rd, G. M. Allen, a delegation of town businessmen, and members of the city council met with police officials at G. M.'s Citizen's National Bank on Wall Street. A list of crimes the hippies were suspected of was compiled. Someone broke into the courthouse one night by forcing open a window and crept up three flights to the belltower. Nothing was damaged, or stolen, but three marijuana cigarette butts were found on the floor. Several merchants claimed to have received anonymous threatening phone calls. The caller always used the word "motherfucker" and threatened "torching." In nearby Archie, a carload of the hippies—Risner, Simpson, Win Allen—were seen driving through and that same day bomb threats were reported at the Archie State Bank and the Archie Elementary School. And they all knew, G. M. Allen scowlingly said, about the obstruction of traffic in the square.

The mobilization meeting agreed on some immediate measures: The shrubbery around the courthouse would be trimmed so there couldn't be anymore sexual intercourse going on up there. Superwatted bright lights, the kind used in urban high-crime areas, would be erected around the square. Chief Davis promised a new foot patrol, two of his nine men acting as roving beatmen, walking in circles around the square 12 hours a day. A list of city ordinances—"Ordnances, man," Win Allen would say, "dig?"—was drawn up for city council approval.

"Vulgar, profane, or indecent" language in public was punishable by a $500 fine or 60 days in the county jail or both. Picketing and parades were illegal unless authorized by the city attorney or Chief Davis. And the topper, a declaration of virtual martial law: Any assembly of three or more persons in the town square was declared an illegal assembly punishable by a $1000 fine.

G. M. Allen, the little man with bifocals and the Alfred E. Newman haircut that stopped a full inch above his red-veined ears, was happy as a clam. He had a responsibility as fire chief and Civil Defense coordinator and he intended to live up to it. "You listen to TV, it used to be cowboys and indians, now it's 'Kill the Cops,' " he'd say. He was a World War II combat veteran who'd raised four decent law-abiding kids and, even though his youngest daughter had gone to school with Risner and Win Allen and had liked them, even though she was "a little bit oversold on Civil Rights," G. M. Allen was convinced that what they'd decided in his bank that night was for the betterment not only of Harrisonville but of America too. "If they don't believe in America," he told the meeting, "they should get the hell out."

Hours after the anti-hippie-frisbee-promiscuity meeting ended, a 30-pound-slab of concrete was tossed through the $495 plate-glass window fronting G. M. Allen's bank. He sputtered down half a block to see J. W. Brown at the *Democrat-Missourian* and ordered a boldset black-bordered ad. He was petrified with emotion. The Citizens National Bank was offering a $500 reward for "information leading to the arrest and conviction of the person or persons who maliciously broke our window."

For Rise Risner, Gary Hale, Win Allen, and Ootney Simpson, the "shit coming down from the black sky" was a routine part of "life in the Hick City."

During the second week of April, as the footpatrols made ten minute reconnaisance sorties around the square, Win Allen came up with what he told Charles Simpson was "Dee-Vine Inspiration." Saturday, the 22nd, would be a national day of protest against the War in Vietnam. Win Allen decided he was going to organize Harrisonville's own anti-war march, a ragamuffin parade of cowdunged kinds screaming anti-imperialist slogans right under the Harrisonville brownshirts' noses. On Wednesday, April 19th, Win Allen and Ootney Simpson, friendly, grinning, and wary, marched to the office of the city attorney and asked for a parade permit. They were told they didn't need one. "We want somethin' in writin', not jive," Win said. "Go ahead and march," the ferret-faced attorney smiled. But he'd give them no paper.

Charles Simpson, who trusted his instincts, was sure it was a boobytrap. "The fuckers'll just bust us," he said.

But Win's dreams escalated: The march would protest not only the war but the new town ordinances. Win would carry a sign that said DOWN WITH NIXON'S WAR and Ootney would carry a sign that said DOWN WITH G. M. ALLEN'S WAR.

"It's gonna be most ricky-tick," Allen said.

"Crazy fuckin' niggers," Simpson laughed.

G. M. Allen heard about the anti-war march The Nigger and the hippies were planning and went to see

Chief Davis about it. He wasn't going to have his big weekend spoiled. The Fire-Fighters Association of Missouri would be in town and each of the forty departments was going to bring its fire engine. At two o'clock Saturday afternoon, after they finished caucasing over the tornadoes, all those beautiful firetrucks, their sirens blasting, would be driven around the square.

All the firefighters would be in their starched parade outfits and the sidewalks would be filled with farmers who'd come into town to see the firetrucks and would spend a few dollars while they were there. It would be the biggest thing on the square since the horseshoe-pitching contests they used to hold. G. M. Allen was damned if he was going to let those spitshined firetrucks be set upon by an army of crablice—hometown purvoids spewing filth, contumely, and treason.

* * *

THE DAY AFTER the haggling session with the city attorney was spent coordinating Saturday's anti-war march. Win Allen and Ootney Simpson discussed logistics with Rise, Gary Hale and the others—and just about everyone agreed that it was a trap, the march certain to end inside Sheriff Gough's roach-crawling jail. But no one cared. They were high on their own daydreams. They'd march anyway. Fuck it: The theatrical aspects were simply too tempting, too ricky-tick to worry about the whip and thud of the brownshirts' new Japanese billyclubs. They would march up Wall Street, gathering at Guido's Pizza Place minutes before the firefighters' cortege was to assemble near the Missouri Farm Association silo. The square would be decked with bunting and the farmers would be tip-toeing around the sidewalks waiting for the sirens when, led by Win Allen, led by a nigger, the outlaws would shamble into that red-white-blue arena, blowing minds, ruining everything, filling the square with clenched fists and that eyeteeth-rattling cry: "ONE TWO THREE FOUR WE DON'T WANT YOUR FUCKIN' WAR."

Word went out Thursday to the timid and sheepish "Teeny Bros" at the high school that all those interested in going to jail for the war should come down to the square after school and Win or Rise or Ootney would give them the lowdown. A lot of kids showed up because the Teeny Bros themselves were in the process of launching a guerrilla action of their own, a pep-rally protest against Bar B-Q Ham on Cheese Bun, Chicken Fried Steak-w-cream-gravy, and Cheeseburger Noodle Loaf. The Teeny Bros were actually threatening to take to the streets carrying 'big signs that said, No More Bar B-Q Ham and waving the signs in front of the struck-dumb principal's office.

The Teeny Bros drifted into town that afternoon, keeping a paranoid eye out for the footpatrols, and organized themselves into action groups. The freshmen and sophomores—"The Snots"—would all paint signs. The Snots were more than anxious to paint words like No More War and demonstrate their militance. As the day wore on and the footpatrols told Chief Davis there seemed to be a pow-wow of outlaws in town, some of the outlaws got bored and went home while other part-time badmen slouched by, having heard about Win's Dee-Vine Inspiration from some squiggly excited Teeny Bro. Charles Simpson went home around 4 o'clock to his Holden farmhouse, reluctantly, going along with Win's fantasy, noting the ironies offered by the prospect of the two parades. The firefighters would be cheered because they drove shiny engines; the outlaws would go to jail because they dreamed of a warless world. "Fuck it, they'll just bust us," Ootney told Win Allen again, "the whole shit just turns my teeth sour." Ootney was tired. He was going home and he was going to mow-down some squirrels with his itty-bitty machine gun.

Harry Miller was one of the hangers-on who slouched by—about an hour after Ootney left to do battle with his doomed squirrels. Harry Miller drove into the square, nodding respectfully at the brownshirts, and then cat-footed over to Rise and Win and some of the others. Everything looked cool: Win was chasing dragonflies.

Harry Miller is 24 years old and his jeans are too tight because there is a gut bulging at his belt. His face is puffy and there is a Brando-like sluggishness, a hovering petulance, about him. He doesn't rattle very easily and he looks like he can take care of himself—a veteran of bicep-building Army infantry training. He looks like a young Bill Haley. His hair is parted in the middle and shoved to the sides but his hair isn't long enough and sometimes a few hairs dangle onto the forehead forming perfect curleycues.

It was near 5:30. The air was stuffed with heat and they were thirsty. Win and Rise and Gary Hale and Harry Miller and George Russell and John Thompson, their smart-cracking court-jester, walked across the street to Lloyd Foster's drugstore. One of the Teeny Bros whose mother had given him allowance money that day was sent inside to spend it on a carton of Pepsi-Cola.

"Here we are," Harry Miller says, "standin' not exactly under the drugstore's roof but out in front, near the Sears store, which Old Lloyd's boy, Don, runs. So we're waitin' for this kid to bring us some bellywash. We are standin' right beside a mailbox which is public property. OK, out of nowhere, Don Foster drives up. Man, I seen that car comin', you could tell he was gonna do somethin', it was in his eyes, like he already knew he was gonna do this. OK, when he comes over there, there were already police parked on the other side of the square so we couldn't see 'em. Don Foster pulls up and he immediately jumps out and storms up. He's a big guy, wears nice cowboy boots, got sideburns, carries a pencil behind his ear, walks around wantin' everybody to cut down trees.

"So he storms up and he starts sayin', 'Get away from my store.' He says to Win, 'Get your black ass out of here.' So he starts violently throwin' shit and John Thompson says, 'Listen, man, we pay taxes, I'm not gettin' out of here.' So the Foster dude says, 'Oh, you wanna fight, I'll fight you.' So he pushes John with both hands, just pushes John and knocks him back. John weighs about 40 pounds less than the dude and most of his weight is stuck up on top of his head in his hair. Well, right then I caught a sense, I knew exactly what was gonna happen. OK, so then the old man, Old Lloyd, comes runnin' out and starts throwin' some bogus shit. I don't know what he was sayin,' just yellin' and screamin.' Somehow Don Foster got a hold of John again and pushed him again.

257

"So I got in between them. I says to Foster, 'Man, leave us alone, you're tryin' to fight us, you wanna get us throwed in jail, just leave our asses alone, we're not goin' to jail for you.' And he says: 'You get out of the way or I'll smack your ass, buddy.' So I got out of the way and they got off by theirselves again and started pilin' at it. So his father, Old Lloyd, says: 'By Gawd, I'm gonna call the police.' So he walks back to his store, takes about four steps, doesn't even get to the phone, turns back out again watchin' them hassle, and here comes the police already turnin' the corner of the courthouse, boogeyin' from the courthouse. OK, after they turn the courthouse, it is like 50 feet before the first one gets to the fight—here's John and this Don Foster on the ground.

"The Foster dude is on top smackin' John beside the head. John's on the bottom gettin' ahold of him by the neck and the ear. So here's Sgt. Jim Harris, the police officer, the other two pigs are behind him. OK, so Harris, 500 feet away, his club in the air, runnin' right at him. Here's John on the bottom with Foster on top of him. So Harris twists around and leans down so he can hit John even with Foster on top of him. He hits John in the shoulder and across the side of the face. Foster jumped off and the other two policemen picked up Foster's jacket for him. Foster got his jacket and walked up beside his old man and Old Lloyd starts pointin' at us, sayin' 'Him and him and him' and points to Win and says: 'The Nigger, The Nigger, The Nigger,' over and over again. So the pigs put us all under arrest for disturbin' the peace and start walkin' us over to the jail in the sheriff's office. Eight of us: Rise and Win and Gary Hale and John Thompson and George Russell and some of the others.

"On the way over there, one of the pigs decides he's gonna have a little fun with Win so he sticks Win in the spine with his nightstick as hard as he can. When Win turns around the pig yells, 'The Nigger's resistin' arrest.' When we get to the jail we says, 'We wanna file a complaint against the Foster dude for pushin' John,' 'cause I mean, if they're gonna play the game on you, you might as well play it back on them. Chief Davis is there and the sheriff is there and Sgt. Jim Harris is there and they all said they didn't have the authority for us to file a complaint.

"So we had to just scream, say, *'Goddamnit, I want a damn report! I wanna file a complaint!'* I mean we had to scream for 15, 20 minutes. Finally they brought the city attorney down and he gives us two sheets of paper with nothin' on it except the top says 'Municipal Court' and some bogus printed stuff. But all they had us do was sign our names on it and that couldn't—man, when you file a complaint there's somethin' wrote down there and you read it, so that couldn't have been any real complaint form. OK, so that was just to get us to shut up. They throw us in jail and we knew it was bogus, we just took it as it was, $110 apiece. Then our Nigger, he was about the last one to come in. We hollered across the monkeybars over to his cell and we say—'Hey, Win, how we gonna get out?' And he says: 'You know, I don't know, my bail's $1100.'

"That jail is like the inside of a toilet bowl in a place where everybody's got the backdoor trots, know what I mean? We had to take a shit, well, we had to get a *Look* Magazine and tear the pages and put it on the seat it was so grubby. The shitter didn't really have a seat on it. They had some drunks over in the bullpen but they didn't say nothin' to us, nobody said nothin'.

"There were cops crawlin' out of the ratholes, we must have scared the pricks off of 'em. Here's eight guys in jail, right? They had six Highway Patrolmen there, they had five guys from the city police department, they had five guys from the sheriff's department, about seven policemen from the surrounding towns in the county."

"The chief of the fire department," Harry Miller says, "yes siree, G. M. Allen comes in all aflutter. Had this little red firehat on, Number 4. He says, 'Did you get 'em all? Anybody hurt?' G. M. walks up and down real slow, lookin' at us, lookin' us over, lookin' us in the hair, and then he says: 'Where's The Nigger? I got somethin' to say to The Nigger.' "

Win Allen says: "Dig, here I am, under arrest, in the clink. And this dude comes up to me in his little cute firehat and I expect him to say somethin' to me about what happened. So he comes up to me, gets real friendly allasudden and whispers, 'Win, I want you to come see me tomorrow about that bill you owe me.' He has the fuckin' audacity to come to me in the clink and talk to me about a loan my family owes him."

A 16-year-old dimple-cheeked high school dropout named Robin Armstrong, a strangely vague and muted farmgirl whose father blew his brains out two years ago—"I'm fed up with everything; people are just so fuckin' ignorant anymore"—was standing in front of the firetruck. All of her friends were in jail and she was screaming, "You fuckin' pigs!" and the firemen were clutching their gleaming hatchets.

Her mother drove up then and Robin Armstrong, trembling with fear and fury, started running like a panicked jackrabbit down an alley.

"I saw it from the window," Harry Miller says. "Robin starts boogeyin' in-between the jail and the rest home, she's gonna run down this old road because she don't want her mother to capture her ass. So the firetruck has a tank with 200 pounds of pressure in it and you know that big hose they have—well, they open that big hose up and hit Robin in the back with it and knock her on the ground. They skidded her face across the gravel."

Mrs. Armstrong, 40ish and sagging but dressed as if she still knew how to please, went up to her sobbing daughter whose mouth was bleeding, and slapped her hard. She called her daughter a "little hoor" and then she sashayed back to the fireman who was still holding the hose. And then she thanked him.

The outlaws spent their night in the crabseat wiping their asses with *Look* Magazine and organizing their Saturday parade, wondering all the time how they'd make bail. One of their bros was up all night, making phone calls and asking the parents to bail their kids out and getting nowhere. They didn't want to spend their money.

As the sun came up, red-eyed Ootney Simpson had figured out only one way to get his friends out of jail. At 11 o'clock Friday morning, Ootney Simpson, smiling like a dimwit fool, worn down to the edge, showed up at the sheriff's office. The outlaw looked the sheriff in the eye and put $1500 in cash on the counter. It was his life's savings, the bankroll for the plot of land he dreamed about. His dream was dead. A sweat of fatigue caked his face.

"Simpson's the name," the dreamer said, "revolution's my game. Free The People!"

* * *

IV. Ootney Simpson's Dream

THEY CALLED HIM "OOTNEY" because of a shriveled old geezer named Jimbob Jones who runs a carry-out grocery on Number Seven Highway about four miles from town. Jimbob Jones took a weird shine to Charles Simpson and whenever he and his friends would wander in for their quarts of strawberry wine and sixpacks of beer, Jimbob Jones would cackle: "Well, looky here, Rootin' Tootin' Mr. Simpson." So Rise and Win called him "Rootin' Tootin'" at first, and then "Tootney" and gradually bastardized it into Ootney.

When Ootney showed up at the jail that Friday morning with his packet of liberating $100 bills, Rise and Win weren't surprised. It was just like Ootney—whenever something had to be done, Ootney was there to do it. As his father says, "All his life he'd go out there in the hayfield and keep up with the best of 'em."

He was of the hayfield and the barn, grew to manhood there and loved it. He lived in Holden, a town smaller and even more backwoods than Harrisonville, a place where the cemetery is still called "the boneyard," a police station is a "booby hutch," and the mentally retarded are "cabbageheads."

Ootney's father, Charles B. Simpson, is 53 years old and looks 75. He looks like a man who is going to die and has looked that way for years. He stands 5'9", weighs 102 pounds, sports a Hitler moustache, a red baseball cap, and a cardigan sweater which the moths have savored for years. He walks with face-twisted pain and a briar walking stick with a vulcanized rubber tip, his leg having been broken into pieces by shrapnel on the African front in WWII. He raised three kids and supported a wife, did as much work as he could, pinched pennies, lived on hot dogs and beans, and waited for the disability checks. Four years ago his wife left him and, except for Charles, the kids got married and left him too.

The corpse-faced veteran and his boy were never too close and it was only in the past year or so that they did much talking. It was hard for the old man to move and he spent long hours sitting in his rocking chair in the room with the calico rug and the big calendar filled with bone-chilling winter scenes. He sat in the rocking chair with his baseball cap pulled over his grey eyes, the cane draped over a thigh, staring at the walls and the dates on the calendar. The boy would come into the room, his long hippie hair in his face, squat down on the rug, and they would talk. They talked about the land and the crops and the war, about policemen and guns and steer, about Henry David Thoreau and Abbie Hoffman and General of the Army Douglas MacArthur. "The boy expressed his feelings too plain," the old man says, "you can't do that."

He was always telling the old man about Thoreau and although the old man didn't know too much about him, he listened. Thoreau lived by a pond and his friends were plants and animals. He didn't pay taxes because he wouldn't support a government which practiced slavery.

The old man didn't have too much to say about Henry David Thoreau but a man talking to his son has to have something to say, so he told the boy stories about General Douglas MacArthur. The old man admired General Douglas MacArthur as much as the boy admired Henry David Thoreau. So he told his stories. How General MacArthur won the Philippines from the Japs. How he could have beat the Chinese across the Yalu River if Harry S. Truman hadn't had stopped him. How Harry S. Truman once wanted to be a piano player in a whorehouse and that's where he belonged. How General Douglas MacArthur should have been President and the country wouldn't be in the fix that it's in.

The old man didn't know exactly what the boy did all the time in Harrisonville. One time Al Wakeman, the Holden police chief, came over and told the old man to keep his damn boy the hell out of trouble. Charles was always roaring up and down the streets on his motor-cycle. "Disturbing the peace," the chief said.

Ever since he was a kid, Ootney had a bad case of asthma. He'd have an attack and his nose and throat would swell up, shutting most of his breathing off. That kept him out of the Army. "One shot-to-hell veteran's enough in the family," the old man says. "He went to high school but he didn't graduate—he had mumps real bad his senior year," Rise Risner adds: "He just farted school off. He said, 'Man, you fuckers are just teachin' me a bunch of lies, you're not teachin' me anything I wanna learn.' He finally got into a big hassle with a teacher one day, just never did go back. He was real intelligent, he could see through shit. He'd always tell you the truth, even if it hurt. He'd say, 'Look you mother-fucker, you've been layin' down some phony shit.' "

When he dropped out of high school, Ootney Simpson went to work at a foundry in Kingsville. He was bored with the job but worked at it for more than a year. He said he wanted to save enough money to build himself the world's most souped-up drag racer. "He saved up a bunch of money," Rise says, "and he got fired 'cause he took off one weekend. He told his supervisor, 'Well, I'm not gonna be at work a few days.' So he came back and they said, 'Well, you know, since you didn't notify any-body that you were gonna be haulin' ass for these few days, you're fired.' So he started thinkin'. He went back raisin' hell. He went right into the personnel department and said, 'Look you motherfuckers, I did notify you. I want this changed. I still wanna be fired but I want this to read that I notified you and you let me go,' and so after that he started collectin' unemployment."

Ootney was spending a lot of time in those days with his younger brother, Elywn, 23. "Bubber" looked like a chunkier Ootney—the same coal-black eyes, hair as long and parted the same way down the middle. Bubber also worked at the foundry and, together, they were building their dream drag racer, blowing most of their money on new manifolds and sparkling chrome treasures.

Win Allen says, "Like the cat and Bubber, they used to race their drags in Kansas City, makin' cars and doin' some racin' and then one day Bubber, says, 'We're just gettin' screwed, people are just takin' our money,' and so they stopped racin'." Rise adds: "They put $10,000 into their dream car, Ootney was just floatin' along, searchin', he broke his back on that car. And they put ten grand into it and that's when Bubber got married and Bubber's wife said, 'All right, you gotta get rid of that race car.' Well, Ootney and Bubber were in a partnership, you know, he says to his wife, "OK, honey, I'll get rid of that racin' machine for you.' And they sold the major part of it for $1000. So they took a $9000 beatin' right there.

"Bubber and Ootney broke bad after that, like Bubber's wife was always hasslin' Charles even. Bubber picked up all this pseudo-shit—shit like trailers and pickup trucks. Like he was working 16 hours a day in two different foundries. He worked at one in Harrisonville and he got off work there at 3:30 and he had to haul ass to punch in on time to get to the other foundry by 4. Just to feed his wife. Well, that's about when Ootney's head started to spin. He didn't give a fuck about the money, but he just knew that whatever he was searchin' for he couldn't find at a drag strip. That's when he started showin' up around the square with us and gettin' into readin'.

"After a while he started talkin' to us about Thoreau," Rise says, "and he said the only thing he and Thoreau differed on was women. Like Ootney man, he dug on women. I mean he didn't fall in love with 'em or get stuck on 'em he just dug to fuck, just P-down, man. He just loved it. He could fuck all night and he still couldn't have enough. He was crazy about it. But he said he had to have women around him all the time and that's the only thing he and Thoreau differed on because Thoreau says in one of his books, he goes, 'A Woman would be a foe to my career,' and Ootney goes, 'Old Henry David, he must not have liked to fuck.'

"If Ootney felt like takin' off his clothes, he didn't give a fuck who was there, no, he'd take his clothes off and jump in a river and take a bath or somethin'. Nothin' embarrassed him, nothin' natural. And he was crazy-good with women. Any woman you ever seen in your life, Ootney Simpson could scheme her into the fuckin'

264

bedroom. It was like he was above women, they owed it to him to fuck him. He was a peach, true beautifulness. He had this long black hair and he had this big beard for a while that was like right under his eyes, hair all over him, skinny. His eyes had a sparkle, the whites were real big, this hooked nose, a real freak, a freak all the way. When he let his beard grow, the only thing you could see was the eyes—just the whites of 'em, 'cause the rest of him was dark. Sometimes he wore great big baggy Army pants. He was a real killer, man.

"He was real weird in a lot of healthy ways. Like he hated telephones. He'd fuckin' drive 40 miles to tell a dude some little-ass thing rather than call him on the phone. He hated phones. He said, 'If you can't look a man in the eyes when you're talkin' to him to tell him somethin', it ain't worth nothin'." He said, 'Anything that you lay on somebody that you feel is a part of you, you gotta look them in the eyes, feel their soul right there.'"

Harry Miller says, "He was full of feelings, just look at him and you could tell. Just look at his face and you'd say, 'Man, that guy there, he'll give me a dollar to get somethin' to eat.' It seems like anytime somebody was depressed, he was around to help them out. His feelings were so sensitive, like you couldn't gross him out, but he had such feeling for his friends. He could stand 50 feet away and somebody would jump up on you and the vibes from Ootney would knock him down. If we were havin' a hassle in town, fuckin' Ootney would pick up the vibes 30 miles away.

"Some of his fuckin' acts you could never forget," says Harry. "One time an ex-Marine from out of Vietnam, been home three months, comes up to Pat and Ernie's Bar and drinks 15 beers and an old guy that we used to know in high school brings him over to Rise's house, we called it the Hippie House, and Ootney is there. So they come in and the Marine starts throwin' down shit about—'Gawddamn, you don't faaght for your country, ya oughtta be shawt.' I was in bed but Ootney heard it. This guy was gonna fire on Rise's ass. Ootney gets up stark nekid, walks in there, and comes down into shit like Rubin jumpin' a Chicago pig's ass or somethin'.

265

And jumps all over the Marine. He looks the dude back about three steps and he grabs his prick and shakes it at the Marine and turns around and just shoots him the moon and then he gives him the finger. Man that Marine, he ran away."

Rise says, "But he was always gettin' into some shit. Like there was a cloud over him and it rained pigs everytime Ootney made a move. Like even when he wanted to do nothin' but listen to a rock and roll concert. He dug Black Sabbath. Black Sabbath cost him $150. He went up to Kansas City to see 'em and, first, he lost his ticket so he had to buy another ticket when he got up there and there was another dude there, a friend of ours who didn't have any money and didn't have a ticket either. So Ootney bought him a ticket. Plus all the other shit, miscellaneous money bullshit from that day. Then after the concert he was takin' a piss outside, you know, in the street, and he got busted for his piss and it cost him $100.

"Another time he was with a dude and the dude was drivin' through Kingsville, the town where the foundry is, and the pigs busted this guy for a faulty exhaust or somethin'. And so they were sittin' in the pig's cruiser and they had to wait for the county pigs to get there and give them the ticket because those pigs were just flunkies or somethin'. So Ootney says to the pig, 'Am I under arrest?' And the pig goes, 'No, you're not under arrest.' So Ootney gets the keys from the dude who drove the car and he just jumps in and speeds away at like 100 mph, makin' a U-turn and givin' the pigs the finger and everythin'. He keeps racin' on at 100 mph and the pigs put out a roadblock for him 'cause he's tearin' up the countryside. He stops off at his place in Holden and puts his brother Bubber's motorcycle helmet on and some gloves and comes roarin' back to Kingsville 'cause he knows the pigs must be after him. Well, he roars right around that roadblock at 100 mph and drives right back up to where his friend is sittin' in the pig's car. One of the pigs pulls out his gun and he was pointin' the gun and shakin' and sayin', 'Get your ass over here, Simpson.' And Ootney has on this helmet and gloves and he just

266

freaked them out. 'Course he spent that night in jail too."

Win Allen says, "Like the time we were over in Holden and I was found guilty of contempt of court, that was an outtasight scene right there. Like Rise and Ootney and I and his brother Bubber were there and Bubber had a traffic violation that he was found guilty of and he didn't do nothin' wrong. So when the judge tells him that he's guilty, seeing that I dig on freedom of speech, I say, 'Bullshit' and the judge fined me. After a while the judge calls me up there and he says, 'Do you know the prior defendant?' And I say, 'Yeah, I know him, he's a citizen of America.' So after a while one of the pigs says, 'Boy, come along with me.' 'Boy,' dig? And I was gonna slide with him you know. So Ootney says, 'Stop the music, I'll pay the nigger's fine.' They freaked out. They didn't know how to react. They smiled. And Ootney says, 'We'll teach the nigger a lesson once we got him into his cage.' Sheeit, we laughed all the way out of town. The judge musta thought Ootney was gonna cut my dick off and put it down my throat or somethin'."

Over and over again, in the past few months, Charles Simpson told his friends about the plot of land that he was going to buy. "I'm gonna live just like Thoreau," he told them, "just like old Henry David." He'd laugh. "Fuck all you longhaired hippie dudes."

"He was gonna buy these 12 acres," Rise says, "aww, fuck, that's all he did for a couple months—just dream about and plan his land. That's all he wanted and the fuckin' redneck farmer told him, 'Yeah, I'll sell it to you.' It is a shitty piece of land but Ootney liked it, just rocks and all barren, real freak's land. The redneck tells him, 'All we gotta do now is send off to the capital and get a few papers, make out the forms and everything' and so Charles, he had the money, he made all the arrangements, all he had to do is give the redneck the money and take over. It would be his land. He used to take us out there and we'd sit around on the rocks and smoke a few joints and Ootney would say, 'Welcome to my land, this is my land.' Well, somethin' happens and the redneck goes, 'Aw, hell, I don't wanna sell it, there's too much red tape and I don't wanna sell it to no hippie anyway.' That broke Ootney's back."

On Wednesday, April 19th, Charles Simpson found out he couldn't have his barren rock-filled dreamworld. On Friday, the 21st, he withdrew his dream money to bail out his outlaw friends.

He went home and told his father he'd gotten the money from the bank and the shot-apart, ashen-faced old man sitting in the rocking chair said:

"What about the land?"

"It don't matter now."

He reached into a closet and took out the M-1 semi-automatic carbine he had bought from a friend and said he was leaving for Harrisonville to get his friends out of jail.

"What you takin' the gun for?" the old man asked.

"Gonna shoot me some targets," his boy said.

V. The Shit Comes Down from the Sky

SIMPSON'S MY NAME, revolution's my game" didn't go over very well with Sheriff Bill Gough, but he didn't say anything about it. Those longhairs were making noise all morning and driving him batty. It would be a real pleasure to get them out of his jail. He'd take those friendly old juiceheads any day. It looked like a long weekend was cropping, what with the fire-fighters coming in that night and those crazy longhairs still talking—right in jail—about holding their protest march tomorrow.

So he didn't give the Simpson boy any trouble when he said, "Free The People!" in a shade louder voice than the sheriff liked to hear in his office. He counted the stacks of bills and looked up just how much the bond was and told his deputy to start getting the longhairs out of their cells. Simpson had a big grin on his face, but he looked like he hadn't slept for weeks. The whites of his eyes were more red than white and his hands were skittery. When the Anderson boy came in, Simpson looked at him as if he were going to kill him and before the sheriff could do anything, Simpson had the Anderson boy by the lapels. "Now listen here," the sheriff said, "you fight in here, both of you are gonna go to jail, I don't care how much money you got."

268

Rise Risner had just been brought out of his cell and was standing next to the counter when John Anderson walked through the door. "Anderson works at TWA with some computers, but he always made out that he was a friend of ours, rappin' to us and stuff. Anderson was there the night before, Thursday, when we were being taken to jail. Well, he had enough money on him to get some of us out and he didn't do it. He didn't want to spend his damn money. Ootney found out about it and when he saw Anderson he said, "Look you fucker, you're supposed to be a friend of ours. I don't want you to ever fuck me over like that."

Ootney looked strungout to everyone. "He was tired, yeah," Win Allen says, "but it was more. He was pissed off bad. I think the money had a lot to do with it— like, this was the money he was gonna buy his land with, dig, and it had turned into jail money. And he was pissed off about me, too. Like Charles really dug me. So when he found out my bond was so high, a thousand dollars more than the others, that really pissed him off bad. He told me after he got us out, he said, 'Nigger, if your face was as white as my ass, you wouldn't be havin' all this shit.' He goes, 'These fuckin' crackers, they gonna lynch you up against a tree one night.' Then he laughed. Ootney was like that. He was jolly and jivin' but the vibes were like off center, it was like there was a bomb inside his head."

Standing around the watchtower outside the jail, they decided it was more important than ever to stage their anti-war march. They went to George Russell's house, where Ootney "leaned up against a wall and looked like he was gonna fall asleep."

"You fuckin' jailbirds kept me up all night," he said.

"Ootney lost his beauty sleep," they hooted.

Rise says, "We were real determined we had to be in that square the next day marchin' with those signs and screamin'. The bust was the best example of the kind of shit we had all felt. Old Lloyd just had to point his finger and say 'Him and Him' and it was enough to send us all to the crabseat."

Win Allen decided they'd hand pamphlets out Saturday as they marched around the square "so the Truth can be put up on the walls." Hasty essays had to be written about war, repression, racism, and the new town ordinances.

"Come on, Ootney," Win said. "Help us write some of this shit."

"OK," Simpson said. "I'll write how much I like fuckin'."

They raspberried him and thew him lip-smacking mock farts, figuring, as Rise says, "We better leave old Ootney alone 'cause he looked pretty tired." But Simpson brightened after a while and, before the meeting ended, offered to help after all. A friend of his in Holden had a mimeo-machine and he would take the essays over there and have them run off.

"Ootney's the production manager," Rise yelled, and, as the others laughed, Simpson came alive, dancing around, his fists flying, shadowboxing Rise's belly.

"Come on, come on," he yelled, "Charles Simpson's gonna take on all you creepo fuckers."

Rise says, "After a while we split up and Ootney took the stuff we wrote up and he was gonna take it over to Holden to the friend of his that had the machine. He asked me if I wanted to go over there with him and I said sure. We piled on into his 1952 Chevy. That was Ootney's batmobile. It was an old, fallin' apart car that made a lot of noise. He loved the car, said it was a real Hippie car. So we drove on out and we got outside a place called Strasburg and the goddamn car blows up. So we sat there not believin' it, you know, here we are and I just got out of jail and Ootney didn't get any sleep and now the goddamn car blows. Well, we couldn't believe it. We were so pissed off we couldn't do nothin' but stand there and mumble and say fuck it and laugh.

"So we decided we were gonna hitchhike into Holden and then hitchhike back to Harrisonville. Ootney had his sleeping bag in the back and the M-1 but I didn't think nothin' of it 'cause he and I were always goin' target shootin' with the thing. So he puts the rifle into his sleepin' bag and we're standin' there hitchhikin' and the car's still smokin'. Then this dude from Harrisonville that we know comes along and picks us up. He's goin' back to Harrisonville so he drives us back there and we get my car. We drive into Holden and drop the shit off with the mimeo guy and then we had nothin' to do. So Ootney says. 'Let's just take the gun and shoot some target practice.' We were gonna spend the night out in the woods."

As Charles Simpson and Rise Risner drove from Holden to Harrisonville late Friday afternoon, they talked. The radio was thumping and Rise only half-listened. The conversation was like a hundred others they had had. "Nothing much," Rise says. "Just a lot of shit, rap talk. Maybe he was trying to tell me somethin', but if he did, maybe I wasn't listenin' that close."

They talked about astrology. Ootney was a Pisces and as they speeded past the wheatfields and around the greening countryside, he talked to Rise about being a Pisces, about how he'd read a book that said he'd be nothing but a dreamer all his life and he'd never make any money. He said that this book said a Pisces was "self-destructive."

"So what does that mean?" Rise asked.

"I don't know," Ootney laughed. "Maybe it means I'm fucked up."

"Yeah, it means you'll fuck yourself to death," Rise said.

They talked, too, about dope. Ootney said he hadn't done any dope for some time and didn't want to do any dope, "because everytime I smoke a joint I think about how everybody's fuckin' us over and I get all depressed and down."

As Rise drove into town, he heard Charles Simpson say a few quiet sentences that would forever stick in his mind.

"Everytime I turn around, I'm gettin' fucked up somehow. My old man's dyin' and my old lady leaves and the pigs are always hasslin' me. Shit, I can't buy a piece of land even when I got the money. I can't drive around without my car blowin' up on me. It's always the same shit. Ain't it ever gonna stop?"

"When we got into town," Rise says, "we were stopped at the red light and the radio was playin' the new Stones song. I was beatin' on the dash and sayin' 'Tumblin'-tumblin',' and all of a sudden Charles jumps out of the car and runs up the street. He was out of the car and halfway up the street before I even knew what happened. And I freaked right there. What the fuck was he doin'? He had the fuckin' gun. What the fuck was he runnin' up the street for with that fuckin' gun in his jacket?"

Rise panicked. He made a U-turn, stepped on the gas, and "started boogeyin' out of Harrisonville, goin' the other direction."

When Simpson jumped out of the car, Charles Hale, Gary's younger brother, saw him and ran up to him. He asked Simpson if he had seen Gary.

"He just shook his head," Charles Hale says, "the only thing I noticed was, he had this great big beautiful smile on his face."

Gary Hale was on the other side of the square with Win Allen and some of the others. "So all of a sudden," Win says, "we heard this *rat-tat-tat-tat-tat* like. And I said, 'Hey Gary, that sounds like some caps, man, like somebody bustin' some caps,' and he said, 'That's what it sounds like to me.' We looked at one another and we got vibes instantly, we said, 'Wait a minute, man, who's all here?' So then we see people startin' to run and we started boogeyin' and we heard these two pigs were shot. And then we heard, 'There's a dirty hippie down there, dead,' and we all—like we saw Charles' body—and like we couldn't identify with that blood."

Rise drove around for a while, scared, and then, finally, drove back to the square. "By the time I got there the two dead pigs had been taken off the street but Charles was still layin' in the street where he had shot himself, all covered up. All I could see was his boots stickin' out from under the plastic bag. My knees just kind of buckled and I was leaned up against this building and I just kind of went down. I just passed out on the sidewalk and I lay there a few seconds. There's this woman who runs the cleaners and I've known her all my life and she goes:

" 'Well, he tried to shoot me, Johnny' and I didn't say anything.

" 'Why did he try to shoot me, Johnny? I didn't do

anythin' to him,' and I just screamed, 'Shut up, goddamn you, just shut up.' "

G. M. Allen was about to leave the bank for the day when he saw people running and heard the police sirens. He ran over to the other side of the square, saw the people in front of the Allen Bank and Trust Company, and heard about two policemen killed and the Simpson boy in the alley with his head blown off. He wasn't surprised. He expected something like this all along. He felt it in his bones. He turned and headed back to his office as fast as he could. He had to activate the Civil Defense sirens and get on the CB band and tell his volunteers to get into town. Gary Hale saw him rushing across the square and went up to him.

"You satisfied now?" Gary Hale said. "You see what you've done?"

"Get out of my way, you little bastard," G. M. Allen said.

He got to his office and as he pushed the button and the sirens started screaming, G. M. Allen had a comforting thought.

It was 6 o'clock and the firefighters coming for their convention would be checking into their motels. They'd have more than enough manpower in Harrisonville that night to handle whatever would happen. 500 firefighters from all across the State of Missouri would be there.

And right then G. M. Allen said a prayer. He thanked the Lord for giving him the wisdom to plan the convention for the right time—"when the hippies started doing their killing."

* * *

VI. Life Among the Razorbacks

FIREFIGHTERS watchdogged the street corners that night with hatchets and shotguns in their hands. The square was barricaded and police cruisers shadowed all the streets leading into town. A rifleman armed with a carbine very much like Charles Simpson's perched in the courthouse belltower, which commands an overview and a clear shot to every cranny of the square. Around 11 o'clock a thunderstorm rolled in with its gnarled bolts of field-lightning and the rain sent the gunmen scurrying to their cars.

About an hour after the shooting, Win Allen was walking across the square and a policeman went up to him and said, "You got two of ours, now it's time we get some of you." When a curfew was announced that night, Win and Rise and the others got out of town fast and decided to stay out.

"There was blood in those people's eyes," Rise says. "It was like we'd all pulled that trigger, not just Ootney. They couldn't do anything to Ootney because he was smart and blew his brains out, but we were still there. I was really scared. Those people were crazy. The pigs were lookin' at us like they could hardly wait to tickle their triggers. We knew that if any of us like made the smallest wrong move, one of us would be dead and they'd just make up some bogosity and get away with callin' it justifiable murder."

G. M. Allen says, "I was just happy we had all those men in town. Besides that, we had policemen come from as far as 50 miles away. We didn't know what to expect, but we were ready. We thought some of the hippies might wanna shoot some more policemen or some innocent people. It didn't make sense, not any of it, unless you figure the whole thing was planned and Simpson was just talked into killin' those policemen for the sake of their revolution."

On Saturday, the 22nd, the national day of protest to end the Vietnam War, the curfew was lifted—but only during the day, until six o'clock that night. Some of the firefighters and policemen got some rest, but gunmen still patrolled all sides of the square and a rifleman still stood guard in the belltower, using binoculars to scan the alleys and the rooftops. Harrisonville's first anti-war protest was, naturally, cancelled, and after only brief debate, the firefighters decided to cancel their parade.

"You mean we drove those trucks all the way out here for nothin'?" a firefighter asked G. M. Allen.

"It ain't fair, sure," G. M. Allen said, "but I figure a lot of people are gonna be too scared to come into town."

He was wrong. Except for the longhairs, everyone

within a hundred miles seemed to drive into Harrisonville that day. Traffic was backed up for half a mile, all the way to the FINA gas station, and people stood in clusters around the spots which had been pools of blood the day before.

In the course of florid descriptions, rumor fed upon rumor. The Simpson boy had eaten LSD just before he did his killing. The gun was traced to the Black Panther Party in Chicago. Simpson had belonged to a Communist hippie group in Kansas City. FBI men were coming into town. The longhairs had decided to kill the whole town, just like Charles Manson had killed those people in California. They found some dynamite hidden in the MFA silo. The courthouse would be burned that night. The hippies had a list with the names of townspeople who were going to be killed on it. The National Guard was coming in.

And the pickup trucks carrying whole families of people who hardly ever came to town kept coming in on this day. Excited little kids stood by the Retirement Home's grey walls and asked, "Is this where he killed himself, mommy?"

Saturday night, the gunman in the belltower saw something move on the roof of the Harrisonville Hotel. He yelled to the firefighters across the street and, within minutes, the hotel was surrounded by dozens of men carrying all sorts of weapons—from Colt .45s to mail-order Lee Harvey Oswald specials.

"Give yourself up," a deputy's bullhorn echoed. "You're surrounded."

There was a crash on the pavement and an old wino who'd found a comfortable place for the night yelled, "Don't shoot, don't shoot, I'm comin'," and miraculously no shots were fired. The doddering old drunk had dropped his pint of whiskey from the rooftop in pants-pissed fear and a deputy was assigned to sweep the glass off the street.

The burials were held Monday. Patrolman Donald Lee Marler's was the first. More than 50 policemen came to the funeral, some of them from Kansas City. Marler's open casket was in the church foyer but was closed minutes before his wife and family got there. The minister said, "The fact that everyone dies is proof that all have sinned. But God says it does not end there. Our friend took the short cut home." The city council held a meeting before Marler's funeral and voted to pay for both Marler's and Wirt's funerals. A reporter asked if the curfew would be extended and Mayor M. O. Raine, the dentist who'd once pulled one of Charles Simpson's teeth, said, "This is a black day and I don't like to have too many decisions made when people are so emotional so I'm not gonna make that decision now."

Charles Simpson was buried last—in Chilhowee, a tiny town not far from Holden, where his grandparents are buried. Rise Risner, who was one of the pallbearers, says, "There was a whole lot of people there, I think about half of 'em were pigs because a lot of 'em had cameras. This dude, this minister, like you could tell he wasn't too happy about havin' to bury Ootney. He was just goin' through the motions, like he was the one who got stuck with buryin' a sack of shit. That's what the vibe was, that's what his face said. The minister was talkin' about how Jesus died and all this shit and he didn't say one fuckin' thing about Charles. They didn't have anything about him even, they didn't say one fuckin' think about his life. Nothin'. He was rappin' shit about fuckin' buryin' Jesus and 'He rose' and all this shit. I thought he was talkin' about Charles for a long time until I figured out what he was talkin' about. John Thompson was singin' 'Blowin in the Wind' and we all chimed in."

After the ceremony, as they were bringing the casket out of the church, in the glare of television cameras and wire service photographers, the pallbearers clenched their fists and held them to the sky, their other hand on the wooden box that had Charles Simpson's body in it. "We gave the power fist 'cause we figured that would be a way of showin' everyone that Ootney was a brother," Rise says, "no matter what kind of shit they were sayin' about him. He was one of us. We did it 'cause we loved him."

Some of the townspeople saw and others heard about the pallbearers' clenched fists and, at first, no one knew what to make of it. But then G. M. Allen told Mayor

Raine he heard it meant someone else was going to die and Mayor Raine told some of the councilmen and by nightfall the word was out all over town: The hippies were going to kill another policeman. So the curfew was extended still another night and the rifleman still crouched in the belltower.

The curfew was lifted, finally, the next day, but Win Allen and Rise Risner and Gary Hale and the others still didn't feel safe going into town. They drove out to the City Park about a mile from town and were surrounded by guns within minutes.

"You gonna get your asses outta here," a policeman told Rise Risner, "or we gonna get even."

Win and Rise collected all of their friends and left town, camping out in an open and nearly inaccessible field about six miles away. "I was afraid they'd come to one of our houses like one of those lynching parties on TV and just take us," Rise says. "It was cold out there and it rained and we were wet as hell, but we were alive."

By Friday, feelings ran so ugly that the Rev. W. T. Niermeier, who had sermonized at Patrolman Marler's funeral, wrote a column for the *Democrat-Missourian* that said:

"A word of God for our community at this time. Recompense to no man evil for evil. Live peaceably with all men. Dearly beloved, avenge not yourselves. Thou shalt not follow a multitude to do evil."

That day's *Democrat-Missourian* carried a news story about the shooting but nothing about the circumstances. "Well, I didn't want to write too much about Simpson," said J. W. Brown, the editor, "not after all the trouble he caused us. I figure folks just wouldn't want to read about him and if folks don't want to read about somethin', I don't print it." That same day, the newspaper was awarded its 16th Blue Ribbon Weekly Newspaper citation by the Missouri Press Association—for "outstanding performance in the field of journalism."

The next issue of the paper carried a new two-column ad. The ad was the result of all the funerals J. W. Brown had to attend that week. He talked to some of the directors and they determinded that the funeral homes didn't do much advertising in the *Democrat-Missourian* and the next week, the bold black-bordered ad, which in a perverse way Charles Simpson had solicited, said:

Friday afternoon, a week after the shooting, G. M. Allen was talking to one of his friends about the list the hippies were supposed to have with the names of the people they were going to kill on it. G. M. Allen said he heard that he was Number One on that list. "I don't hold too much by it," G. M. Allen said, "maybe there isn't even any list—but, my God, they try somethin'—well, I was in the Infantry during the War, they better think about that."

A few days after that, Luke Scavuzzo, who runs Scavuzzo's Grocery and is an alderman, was doing a radio talk show in Kansas City and he said: "Maybe some people in town pushed those kids too much." Now, Luke Scavuzzo said, "Some people have learned they better *ease up*." By nightfall, town scuttlebutt held that Luke Scavuzzo was saying they were going to *"give up."* The next day about 20 people came in to tell Luke Scavuzzo they weren't going to buy his groceries anymore because of what he said.

"Luke had to go around for a whole week tellin' everybody he never said that," G. M. Allen says. "He should have known better. Nobody's gonna give up or ease up. Are we supposed to wait around till someone else gets killed?"

A few weeks after Ootney Simpson fired his M-1 on the town square, the Civil Defense sirens screamed again and people ran to their citizens' band radios expecting to hear the worst of their fears confirmed. More trouble. Another killing. The voice of G. M. Allen was as breath-

less and garbled as the last time. But this time there was
little to worry about. It came out of the east and over-
turned a mobile home and knocked down some outhouses
and then it was gone.

Just another goddamn tornado.

I GOT INTO HARRISONVILLE about two weeks after the
shooting. The first person I saw was Win Allen. He was
lying on the courthouse steps, pressed flat with his face
to the cement. He didn't move and he stayed that way, as
still as the pennies on a dead man's eyes. Win and Rise
and the others had decided it was safe enough to go back
into town. The old mock-heroic game for the town square
would go on. Four dead men weren't going to get in the
way.

I got out of the car and walked into the drug store
for a pack of Luckies and an old man behind the counter
was staring out the window at Win Allen. He watched
me get out of the car and his eyes must have picked out
the Missouri plates on it because when I walked in his
tone was conspiratorial and trusting. "See that nigger boy
up there," Lloyd Foster said, "he's been climbin' those
steps every day for four days now and just layin' down
up there. He goes up there and he looks around and he
puts his fist up in the air and then he lays down on top
of his face. He pretends he's dead. They say it's a way of
rememberin' the crazy hippie that killed our policemen."

I was wearing a tie and a blue blazer and the next few
days I wore the same get-up, exaggerating the effect,
walking around with a fat Special Corona 77 cigar sticking out of my mouth. I sought out townspeople in the most
razorbacked bars in town, buying them beer and malt
liquor and getting them to talk. I slicked my hair back
above my ears and bought a bottle of gooey hair-oil and
—with cigar and coat and tie—I must have looked re-
spectable enough to them because pretty soon they were
buying me beers. I told them I was from a magazine in
San Francisco and forgot to say which one. I think the
cigar and the slick hair got through. When I got back
to the motel at night and looked in the mirror I saw some
guy I remembered from somewhere but I couldn't place
him.

When I was finished talking to the townspeople I drove back to my motel and washed my hair and changed. I put my jeans on and let my hair fall down over my ears and put on my leather jacket and drove back into town. I was getting pretty tired of cigars anyway. I found Win Allen and told him I was from *Rolling Stone* and wanted to talk about Charles Simpson, and Win Allen almost cried he was so happy. "Man," Win said, "we been watchin' you watchin' us and we figured you was FBI. With that cee-gar." We laughed.

That night we gathered near the square—one of the cops I'd talked to spotted me and gave me a fixed hard glare—and drove about ten miles out of town into the middle of a wheatfield. We found a clearing that suited us and built a bonfire. It was a cloudy spring night, about 70 degrees, and the lightning was already playing patterns off to the east. There were about a dozen of us and we had eight or nine bottles of red wine and a dozen six-packs of beer. We also had a bagful of tongue-burning Missouri weed.

The fire was roaring and Rise Risner's red Volkswagen, which had been pulled as close as possible, played Dylan, Hendrix, and, what the hell, Jose Feliciano. The people here were Charles Simpson's best friends. We were talking about a man who had killed three innocent people in cold blood. They were calling him a brother and telling me how much he loved people and how he believed in the The Cause.

"Sometimes Ootney said he thought violence was the only kind of revolution there was," Rise said. "But dig," Win said, "as far as a violent revolution—anytime someone infringes on me and fucks me, it makes me mad, that's the way Charles was thinkin' too."

"A lot of freaks you meet in places," Rise said, "somebody will rip them off or something and they'll haul ass. But we're not that way. We're country boys. We're willin' to fight the motherfuckers if they wanna fight us."

"Ootney was smart," Rise said, "he killed himself to keep the pigs from havin' the satisfaction of killin' him or lockin' him up in some honky jail. He was into so much cosmic shit, man. He was so heavy with that, it was a religion to him. Like some religions say self-destruction is the best thing you can do for your God, that's why they burn themselves. I know Ootney had to feel the same thing."

"One time Ootney was in a black neighborhood," Win said, "and somebody said somethin' about Jesus to him and Ootney said, 'The only way that Jesus and I differ is that he was willin' to die for the people around him and I'm not ready for that yet.'"

"I think he was Jesus," Rise said, "as far as I'm concerned he was Jesus."

"Because that cat just laid down the truth, man," Win said. "Everything that came out of his mouth was truth and supposedly like Jesus laid down the same thing. And when he got up the stuff to die for The Cause, Charles became of the same instance. He was groovy, outtasight, he had so much compassion for people, sentimental about a lot of things, sensitive."

It had been a long few days and I had scrutinized too many vivid details of four vicious killings and something in my mind flailed out now—Jesus Simpson, murderer, cold-blooded killer, compassionate, sensitive, sentimental. It could have been the fatigue or the Missouri weed or the beer mixed with wine, but I saw too many grotesqueries leaping about in that blazing bonfire.

"As far as I'm concerned," Rise said, "Charles isn't dead. It is just somethin' Charles wanted to do and if Charles wanted to do it, I can't say anything about it."

"Yeah," I said, "but what about the people killed and their wives and kids? Don't you care about that?"

"Well, you know," Rise said, "how can I criticize it. It's Charles' thing. Like it was a far-out thing to do."

We were gathered around this bonfire on a spring night in Missouri and the date was the fourth of May, 1972. I'd never had much luck with the fourth of May. On this day in 1971, I was standing around a green field at Kent State University listening to requiems and eulogies. And on this day in 1970 I was running dazedly around those same lush fields looking at pools of blood and asking National Guardsmen why they had killed four innocent kids.

And now I was talking to some kids asking them why one of their best friends killed three innocent people with the same kind of gun the Guardsmen used and all they could say to me was:

"Like it was a far-out thing to do."

I told them the story of my May 4ths and Win Allen said:

"Well, dig, man, now it's four to three."

"Right on," Rise said.

"Old Ootney," Win said, "Old Ootney. That gun was outtasight, man. Like the first time I went to his crib I saw it and I said, 'Ootney, is that yours?' and he said, 'Yeah, a friend of mine gave it to me,' and I said: 'Wow, man, sometime when you and I go fishin' and out in the woods, maybe I can dig on it.' Like Charles had this big Buck knife with a holster on it and this most beautiful fishin' pole and he said—he said whenever he went home, he just fondled the stuff all the time, felt it up and dug it."

"Yeah," Rise said, "Ootney loved nature."

SHOWDOWN IN REYKJAVIK
Bobby Fischer Prepares for His Most Important Match

by Thomas Powers

WHEN MASTERS play chess it is very, very rare for a game to end in checkmate. It probably does not happen once in a thousand games. Long before that moment the loser will resign, usually with a gesture. He may stand up or reach across the board to shake his opponent's hand or simply snort in disgust and lean back in his chair. He may resign when he is only a pawn down, or when he loses a maneuver for position. He may resign so early in the game that inexperienced players can't understand what he was worried about.

The reason for resignation is always the same: if the game continues, he will lose. Losing is so painful to a serious player it must be masked and disguised. By resigning the loser ritually indicates that he accepts the outcome, thereby retaining a measure of dignity. Nevertheless, he is a beaten man, if only until the next game.

When Bobby Fischer appeared on the Dick Cavett show last winter he was asked what part of the game he liked best. Sweetest, he said, was the moment when it became clear his opponent would lose, "and I feel I can crush his ego." This has been the theme of his life. In 1958, after winning the US championship when he was only 14, he said the same thing another way: "I like to see 'em squirm."

Losing players do squirm and after the game will blame anything for the loss: a cold, a bad night's sleep, an opponent's cigarette smoke or heavy breathing. Fischer himself, perhaps the world's greatest player, also has a reputation as the world's worst loser. He used to complain about the lighting, the temperature, the audience. Losers' excuses are shameless because losing is so bitter.

Back in the Fifties, when Fischer was first beginning to play chess seriously at the Manhattan Chess Club, his reaction to losing was almost epic. "He took it very seriously," said one strong player who beat him at rapid chess during that period.

How seriously?

"Very seriously."

But what did he do?

"Well . . . once he cried for half an hour."

This was not an exaggeration; he meant 30 minutes of uncontrolled weeping. At times half the club gathered around and tried to convince Fischer there was more to life than chess, it was only a game, nobody can win all the time. It had no effect whatever.

If Fischer is the world's greatest player, it is precisely this quality which makes him so. Emmanuel Lasker (1868–1941), a world champion known for still playing strong chess when he was in his 60s, once called chess "a bloodless combat." His point was that in chess everything is at stake; it is far from just a game. A decisive loss can break a man. Fischer's bitter shame when he lost as a kid is equalled now by a fierce, absolutely single-minded will to win.

When Fischer sits down to play he is out to destroy his opponent, whether it's a grandmaster or just an acquaintance. "The only time I ever played with Bobby we were on a plane together," said a man who handled Fischer's business affairs at one time. "I'm not a good player. I play.

"The change was immediate. Suddenly this diffident kid becomes strong and masterful. There is a seriousness, an intensity." The man set up a board to show what happened. "I played a Queen's pawn opening. Bobby responded with a knight, I protected with a pawn, then he brought out his Queen's pawn and I started to think. First I thought maybe the knight [here he touched his knight as if about to move it], changed my mind and brought out my bishop to King's Bishop four.

"Bobby said, 'Wait.' He reached over and put my bishop back. He tapped my knight. He was *not* smiling. 'You touched the knight,' he said.

"Touch move! You touch it, you move it! This is like a little friendly sparring with Sonny Liston and suddenly he takes off the gloves and says, 'OK, from here on it's bare knuckles.'

"When Bobby sits down across the table you feel the hostility. He compresses himself like a bullet. You sense this man is dangerous. This man can really hurt you. He can destroy you."

Last year Fischer decisively defeated two Russians and a Dane for the right to challenge the current world champion, a 34-year-old Russian named Boris Spassky. Fischer, 29, had seemed close to the championship twice before, once when he was only 18, but each time something went wrong. In 1962, he said, the Russians cheated. Five years later he walked out of the Interzonals in Tunisia over a procedural point. Last year, however, Fischer seemed to have his temper under rigid control, his game had never seemed stronger, he even seemed ready to compromise on the site and circumstances of the match.

Early this year the Federation Internationale des Echecs (FIDE) scheduled the 24-game match to begin on June 22nd in Belgrade, Yugoslavia, Fischer's first choice. After 12 games it would move to Reykjavik, Iceland, a condition Fischer had resisted and then, surprising friends who know his capacity for stubborn inflexibility, finally accepted.

"One of the reasons Bobby didn't want to play in Reykjavik," said a man who helped arrange the match, "was he wanted a big hall and a big crowd to watch the expression on Spassky's face when he crushed him." Fischer had also protested that television facilities in Iceland were inadequate; Americans wouldn't be able to watch him win. FIDE insisted, however, and Fischer gave in. He had been preparing for this moment all his life, after all. For ten years he had claimed he was the world's greatest player and now he was about to prove it. It would be an exhausting ordeal of three games a week for at least a month, perhaps two. In such a match no excuses are possible. If Fischer did not win he would be the lesser man.

It is difficult to describe the excitement this match aroused in world chess circles. Americans are generally indifferent to chess. The recent US championships were held in the cafeteria of the old Herald Tribune building in New York City, and even in that small, low-ceilinged room the 14 players often outnumbered the spectators. Outside the United States, however, the Fischer-Spassky match was considered perhaps the most important ever played. The Russians have dominated world chess since its reorganization in 1948; no American has ever been champion. Fischer claims to be, and is widely regarded as, the world's greatest player and yet always, inexplicably, he lost or refused to play when the critical moment arrived.

With everything seemingly settled Fischer went into seclusion at Grossinger's in upstate New York, a 1000-acre resort where fighters have often trained but never before a chess champion. Fischer, tall and broad-shouldered, with a long face and powerful jaw muscles, was an unobtrusive presence. He slept until noon, ate alone at a well-lighted table in the dining room and studied Spassky's games, which he carried around in a red loose-leaf notebook. He played occasional tennis, sometimes swam in the pool and every night at ten past ten he listened to *Church of the Air,* a religious program vague on theology and precise on questions of right and wrong. When newsmen came to see him he refused to open the door. "Shove off," he told one reporter from the *New York Times.* "I've got a right to my privacy." When this reporter called him for the *n*th time, he picked up the phone, said, "Yes?" listened a moment and hung up.

The first hint that things were about to fall apart came early in March when old friends couldn't get him, either. Then word spread that Fischer had broken with Col.

Edmund B. Edmundson, president of the US Chess Federation, a longtime friend and advisor who had probably done more to arrange the Fischer-Spassky match than any other individual. "Edmundson had carried Fischer along like a premature baby," said one man who knew both.

Fischer was said to be unhappy with arrangements for the match. Who was going to own rights to all the film? Who was going to get television rights? "You sold me out to the Russians," he yelled at Edmundson and then refused to see or even speak to him. Finally, late in March, Fischer sent a telegram to FIDE demanding more money. FIDE responded with an insulting ultimatum and the dispute quickly began to slip out of control.

"The match is off," said one old friend of Fischer's when Belgrade withdrew its offer to sponsor the first half of the match. "They'll never play. Fischer's been right in the past but this time he's gone too far. Maybe he's chicken, I don't know. There are a lot of people around here getting damned tired of that sonuvabitchin' kid."

The Bobby Fischer Chess Wallets

Fischer is about as easy to reach as Richard Nixon. In the summer of 1961, Fischer, then 17, gave a long, candid interview to Ralph Ginzburg, who used it. Fischer was perhaps *the* most callow kid to come out of Brooklyn in this century. Ginzburg's article in the January, 1962, issue of *Harper's* revealed Fischer, accurately but not fairly, as a vulgar, boastful kid with pathetic pretensions to being a sharp dresser and nifty guy. He dismissed the Russians as "patzers" (the ultimate insult in chess circles), said he could give knight odds to any woman in the world and win, ridiculed his high school teachers and talked a good deal about what he was going to do with all the money he was going to make. Since then Fischer has been decidedly hard to reach.

A preliminary attempt last August got nowhere. "Send him a letter," said Fran Goldfarb, who works at the Manhattan Chess Club. "He'll come by eventually and get it, but . . ."

Yes?

"There's generally a question of, ah, money."

287

Requests for an interview never got far enough for the question of money to come up. Letters were sent and messages were left but none of them provoked an answer. Last fall Fischer was in Argentina for his match with Tigran Petrosian and then he spent a number of weeks in Brazil giving exhibition matches. When he got back to New York he moved into the Park Sheraton Hotel (a room without a view) and finally answered his phone late one night in January. "If I get some time I'll call you, OK? I'm very busy right now, you know? Lot to do. Busy, busy."

He did not get any time. He flew to Iceland with Edmundson, then went out to the West Coast, played some exhibition matches and finally retreated to Grossinger's where he became even harder to reach as the match with Spassky approached. Eventually he stopped answering his phone altogether.

Fischer used to be secretive about his theories of chess, fearing a rival might steal his ideas, and he is still secretive about his personal life. This tends to obscure the fact that, in the usual sense, he has almost no personal life. His parents were divorced when Fischer was two and he has never met his father, who is said to live in Germany. His mother was an adolescent's nightmare who once tried to sell "Bobby Fischer Chess Wallets," would rise with shrill questions at meetings of the US Chess Federation and in the summer of 1960 chained herself to the White House gate to protest the government's refusal to send a chess team to a tournament in East Germany.

The government ignored her, but Ammon Hennacy of the Catholic Worker Movement recruited her for a San Francisco-to-Moscow peace march held that fall. She left Fischer, then 17, alone in Brooklyn, married a man she met on the march and now lives in England. Fischer has not seen her since.

"Playing chess is all I want to do, ever," Fischer once said. His only other interests are passing enthusiasms for custom-made clothes, pure food, and portable radios, which fascinate him because they go on *instantly*. When he was still in his early teens he went through a period of intense religious preoccupation. He carried a Bible wherever he went, studied it obsessively and eventually joined

Try the crisp, clean taste of Kent Menthol.

The only Menthol with the famous Micronite filter.

Micronite filter.
Mild, smooth taste.
America's quality
cigarette.
Kent.

King Size or Deluxe 100's.

the fundamentalist Church of God, which observes Jewish holidays. He used to refuse to answer his phone between sunset Friday and sunset Saturday and still won't compete on the Sabbath.

Fischer worries constantly about money but is often careless in spending it. He has few friends and all of them are chess players. When he is in New York he often kills a long evening analyzing games with Bernard Zuckerman, who makes a meager living as a chess professional but has a solid reputation for his knowledge of the openings. Fischer's two closest friends are said to be Jim Gore, a once-strong player who abruptly stopped competing years ago and now works as a bank teller, and Jackie Beers, a mediocre player who has been banned from most New York clubs because of his foul temper when losing.

The thing for which Fischer's friends most value him is an elusive purity of spirit, an integrity of purpose which springs from his respect for chess not just as a game or an intellectual discipline, but something eternal, beautiful and true. This unbending dedication does not make him easy to be with, however.

"I do not exactly look forward to an evening with Bobby," said one world-chess player who has known him for years. "I get tired of talking about those fabulous shoes some Argentine makes, or how television will make you sterile, or all the things they put in food. You can't discuss politics with him because this is the greatest country in the world, and I'm not interested in radios.

"It's just as bad when you go somewhere with him. I remember one time a few years ago when I was going to the gym for a workout and Bobby said, 'Can I come?' I said sure. My God what a production! First he had to do this and then he had to wait for that and then he couldn't find something else.

"If you want to have dinner with him you eat at midnight, and if you go for a walk that long loping stride wears you out. When you're playing chess or analyzing games he's fantastic, but otherwise he's a very difficult companion. He tries to be friendly but it just doesn't work."

The central fact in Fischer's life is isolation. For a

while he had an apartment in Brooklyn and later one in Los Angeles, but since 1969 he has lived in hotel rooms. When he was younger he was an enthusiastic collector of chess books, but several years ago he sold his collection to Walter Goldwater, president of the Marshall Chess Club, for $500, a bargain. (One dealer had offered him $650 but Fischer said no, and having said no, refused to go back to him when he found no one willing to pay more.) Fischer carries most of what he owns with him and leaves the rest with friends. He rarely sees his sister; his friendships are all professional and he is awkward with girls. One who dated him on a single occasion reported succinctly, "Never again." If Fischer did not have chess he would be utterly alone.

A Sacrificial Queen

Chess is an ancient game played on a board of 64 alternating black and white spaces. Two players each have 16 pieces of six different types. Each type can move in a certain way: one unobstructed space forward, any number of unobstructed spaces in a straight line, any number of unobstructed spaces in a diagonal line, and so on. The object is to capture the enemy's king. The number of possible moves is, of course, huge. Luck is not involved, except in the sense you can't play well with a fever of 102. In any given game it is not mortal men who compete, Fischer and Spassky, say, but black and white. The strongest play (not player) wins. This gives chess an absolute, even Platonic quality. There is no attack which cannot be defeated if only it is foreseen early enough in the game, and there is no defense which cannot be overcome. The moves exist; one has only to discover them.

The open and yet absolute quality of chess gives it a fascination which can lead to obsession. Lenin once warned a friend, "Do not forget that chess, after all, is only a recreation and not an occupation." Most players come around to this point of view in time (perhaps reluctantly, like poets who teach), but for young players first immersing themselves in the game, chess is everything.

There are about 75 chess bums in New York who live by giving chess lessons, playing in the rapid chess tournament held every Friday night at the Manhattan Chess Club and winning five and ten dollar games from players with more enthusiasm than talent. The Manhattan and Marshall Chess Clubs have the best facilities but are relatively expensive. Cheaper are the Chess House on West 72nd Street, which never closes; the Chess and Checkers Club near Times Square, known as the Fleahouse, and half a dozen Village coffee houses where boards and tables are available for the price of an espresso. When the weather is good the regulars also play at the tables in the southwest corner of Washington Square park.

A *Lives of the Chess Players* would read much like Samuel Johnson's *Lives of the Poets*. Young men of passion and a certain talent emerge from obscure backgrounds. For a year or two they are seen everywhere, they are considered to have promise, they dream of beating the masters whose play they analyze with such quick confidence. A lucky few find patrons or chess sinecures. The rest live in bleak rooms, eat badly, spend all their time with men and sleep by day. For almost all, there is a bitter moment when the limits of their talent become clear. Unlike Johnson's poets they do not hang themselves or die in debtors' prisons, but rather disappear into minor lives as bank tellers, public accountants or high school teachers. It is not unusual for such failed masters never to play again.

It has been a long time since Fischer played with the passionate amateurs in Washington Square, but it was in New York that he learned to play the game. In the late Fifties he used to give knight-odds to second-rate players for a dollar a game. He never liked coffee house chess (the lighting is always bad), but he still drops in at the Chess House from time to time. "We've missed you," Charles Hidalgo says whenever he comes in. "Where've you been?" Fischer's answer is always the same "Busy, busy."

Like the other New York players Fischer has done his share of hustling. It's a question of eating. Prize money is notoriously low and no one can win all the tournaments. In July 1963, Fischer played in the Western Open in Bay City, Michigan. One night during the tournament he was challenged to a private game at high stakes by a rich Chicago amateur named Norbert Leopoldi. They played all night and Fischer won close to $1000. Leopoldi balked at paying. Fischer argued but finally settled for half. By that time it was dawn. During the tournament later in the day, while his opponent was brooding over a move, Fischer dozed off. "Hey!" said his opponent. "Bobby! We're playing a game of chess!" Fischer woke up and won.

Fischer was recognized as a prodigy of sorts from the beginning, of course, but he did not attract serious attention until the US Open championship held in 1956, when he was 13. One of his opponents was Donald Byrne, now a professor of English at the University of Pennsylvania. Byrne was (and still is) a very strong player. He had the benefit of years of experience and of the first move, with the white pieces.

Early in the game Fischer sacrificed his Queen, a surprising move under any circumstances, astonishing in these, and Byrne did not quite know what to make of it. This was back in Fischer's informal period, when he showed up everywhere in a baggy sweater and scuffed shoes, a kid with a thin, serious face and a bristling crewcut. Like all players he kept his eyes on the board, with only a quick glance at his opponent from time to time. Serious chess is played poker-faced. If Fischer appeared a little nervous, Byrne was not alone in figuring it was the panic of watching a game collapse. Byrne apparently concluded the Queen sacrifice was the desperation move of an overrated *wunderkind* out of his depth. Still, the word went out something extraordinary was taking place, and people began to drift over to watch.

After a few moves Byrne's position began to seem weak, then distinctly alarming. Move by move, following an inexorable pattern growing out of Fischer's Queen sacrifice, Byrne lost control of the game and was finally forced to resign. The game was the sensation of the tournament: a sacrificial combination which took nearly 20 moves to come to fruition! Fischer still considers it his best game, and Hans Kmoch, a respected chess annotator, called it the game of the century.

Despite this dazzling victory Fischer came in eighth overall. The next year he won the open ($750 in prize money) and that winter he took the US Championship.

In 1958 FIDE made him an international grandmaster, the youngest in history.

This was probably the period of Fischer's headiest confidence. One night after playing with friends at the Manhattan Chess Club he joined a group going over to the Stage Delicatessen for something to eat. One of the group asked Fischer if he thought he was better than the Russian player Mikhail Tal.

"Yes," said Fischer.

Paul Keres?

"Yes."

Smyslov?

Petrosian?

"Yes," shouted Fischer. "Don't ask me anymore! I'm better than anybody!"

Not everybody agreed, and in the summer of 1961 the US Chess Federation arranged a 16-game match between Fischer and Samuel Reshevsky, who had been a chess prodigy, had dominated American chess for years and was still one of the strongest American players. For Reshevsky, of course, the match was far more important than it was for Fischer. He was in his 50s, a short, straight-backed, balding man unwilling to consider his strength gone. If he lost to an 18-year-old kid his whole career would be permanently shadowed.

The match began in New York, then shifted to Los Angeles, and was to have returned to New York for the final four games. The 12th game, with Fischer and Reshevsky tied at 5½ points, was scheduled for 11 AM Sunday morning, August 13th.

Fischer, who sleeps until noon, refused to play at that hour. Irving Rivise, the referee, insisted. Fischer felt this was unfair, against the rules and unnecessary. He said no. What had begun as a procedural difficulty quickly developed into a contest of wills between Fischer, who already had a reputation as something of a *prima donna,* and the US Chess Federation, which insisted chess would be played by its rules or not at all.

Rivise made no attempt to reach a compromise (which Fischer almost certainly would have rejected anyway). If anything, he deliberately sharpened the conflict. On Saturday he called Fischer at his hotel and told him there would be no change in the hour, that Fischer's clock would be started promptly at 11 AM, that he would forfeit the game if he did not appear by noon, and that Rivise would have a car waiting at Fischer's hotel just in case he decided to give in. Surrender in the face of such an ultimatum was of course unthinkable. Fischer stayed in his room and the game was forfeited.

The result was a huge controversy which dominated chess magazines for months. Long after the aborted match Fischer and Reshevsky publicly shook hands, but the bitterness remained. Reshevsky, now in his 60s and wearing a toupee, his chess strength inevitably failing, still talks to friends of a rematch. After all, he says, he is the only player who has never lost a match to Fischer. If he won, his whole life might still be vindicated. Fischer's attitude has all the cruelty of strength; he might do it for the money, but certainly not for the sport.

The controversy over the Fischer-Reshevsky match was immediately followed by another over Fischer's failure in the candidates' tournament for the world championship held on Curacao, a Dutch island in the Caribbean, in June, 1962. Fischer had dominated the Interzonals in Stockholm the previous fall and he expected to win the candidates' tournament, too. When he only tied for fifth place behind the four Russian entrants, he was stunned and angry. That summer he wrote a bitter account of the tournament which appeared in the August 20th issue of *Sports Illustrated*. The Russians, he said, had cheated.

Cheating at chess is not like cheating at cards; it is both harder to do and harder to prove. The main form of cheating by the Russians, Fischer said, was their willingness to draw games with each other, once after only 14 moves. Chess is exhausting; a drawn game is worth half a point to the players and leaves them fresh for their next opponents. Even worse, Fischer suggested, was the possibility the Russians were actually prepared to dump games to each other, piling up points for one of their own. "I will never again play in one of these tournaments," Fischer wrote. Eventually, despite indignant Russian denials, FIDE switched from the old system of round-robins to a series of head-on matches, and Fischer began to play again. In a sense he had willed the new system into being, but in the process he had come very close to excluding himself from international competition altogether.

By that time it was clear Fischer was potentially his own worst enemy. Commentators began comparing him to Paul Morphy (1837–1884), an American player of such grace and strength he is still considered by some to have been the world's greatest. Like Fischer, Morphy had a brilliant early career. On a tour of Europe in 1858 when he was only 21, he defeated all the strongest players with one exception, the aging but arrogant English champion, Howard Staunton, who rejected Morphy's challenge with a snort of public contempt. Morphy was shattered, despite the fact he was almost universally considered the stronger player. Two years later he retired from all competition and spent the rest of his life in semi-seclusion in New Orleans, living on a tiny inheritance and sinking into an eccentricity which bordered on insanity.

In 1967 Fischer walked out of the world championship Interzonals in Tunisia over a minor dispute about playing conditions. During the following 18 months he rarely appeared and never competed, and a large section of the chess world was convinced his career was over. Fischer himself apparently feared the same thing. He later told friends he spent that year and a half trying to face and overcome the contradictions of his own character. He was only partly successful. He is far less touchy than he used to be, but he still won't bend when he thinks he is right. He refused to compete in the 1969 US Championship, for example, and was allowed to take part in the current world Championship cycle only because another American, Paul Benko, gave up his right to do so. When FIDE gave Fischer an ultimatum in late April to accept the title match as arranged or lose his chance to play Spassky, a lot of Fischer's friends figured his last chance was gone. They were almost right.

'Right Is Right, Fair Is Fair'

Paul G. Marshall is a medium-sized man, solid but not fat, with the deep, raw voice, pleasing to the ear but alarming to the mind, of a man who has been smoking four packs a day for decades. Over the phone he sounds 60; in person he looks 40. He is a lawyer who represents entertainment people, David Frost among others, and two months ago he he was asked by a friend to straighten out the Fischer-FIDE dispute.

"The president of FIDE," he said in his mahogany-paneled, high-ceilinged (the air space alone must cost $10,000 a year) office on 57th Street, "is Dr. Max Euwe, a cultured, aristocratic European of the best type. He's a beautiful man, I have the highest regard for him, but he had never negotiated anything like this before. There had never been a match like this before.

"FIDE asked for bids but they had no standards for judging them, they just accepted the ones with the most money. Edmundson suggested to Bobby that they bring in a lawyer but Bobby said, 'No, we'll do this the way we always do it,' and so Edmundson went over to Amsterdam and negotiated the contract. When Bobby found out what was in it he was furious. He hasn't spoken to Edmundson since.

"So then Bobby sent off a lot of ill-advised telegrams to FIDE saying, 'I'm not going to do this or that,' when he should have said, CONDITIONS UNCLEAR. PLEASE ADVISE. Andrew Davis is Bobby's lawyer but he couldn't handle this either and Bobby stopped talking to him, too. Andy called me up in Europe and said 'Please jump in,' and I said, 'What for?' and he said, 'For nothing.'

"Bobby is an honorable guy but he's not a nice guy. In fact he's a bit of a sadist. At first he was terribly suspicious: 'What are you getting out of this?' I said, 'Nothing.' He said, 'If you're not getting anything out of it why are you doing it?' I told him I wanted to see him beat the Russians. After he decided he could trust me he wouldn't speak to anyone else.

"At this point Dr. Euwe decided to leave on a seven-week vacation and while he was gone the secretary of FIDE, a *petit bourgeois* European who hates Bobby, was in charge of the negotiations. At first he wouldn't give me Dr. Euwe's number and then when he did I was calling him in places like Perth, Australia, and Suribayo.

"The secretary was in effect accusing Bobby of refusing to play. My attitude was, 'Of course we're going to play, but what does that mean?' The secretary said, 'It's all in the contract, read the contract.' So I said, 'I'm a lawyer. Are you a lawyer? I've read the contract and I still don't know what it means.' He said, 'It means what it means.' "

After a lot of phone calls and trips across the Atlantic, paid for by Frost, Marshall clarified the terms of the contract, but by that time FIDE had issued a new ultimatum. If Fischer didn't agree to play the entire match in Iceland beginning July 2nd he was out and Tigran Petrosian would take his place. The deadline was Saturday, May 6th. Marshall was on the phone with Fischer at Grossinger's every couple of hours and finally at 8:30 Friday night Fischer said Marshall could send a telegram accepting FIDE's arrangements.

"You've got to remember two things," Marshall said. "First, Bobby never made any money in his life. Everyone who dealt with him when he was 14, 15, used him. If there was any money to be made they took it. They'd call him up and say, 'Come on out here, we'll pay your bills, we'll give you a couple of bucks on the side.' And when it was over they'd stick him with a huge hotel bill. Here's a 15-year-old kid with no money, all alone, a huge bill, crying.

"The second thing is when Bobby hits on a point he thinks is fair, it's not fair like it was you or me, a matter of opinion, it's fair like it's from Olympus.

"After this was all over I told him I didn't like him. I didn't like the way he treated people, the way he humiliates people. Andrew had been his lawyer for five years, he refused to even talk to him. Colonel Edmundson had carried him like a baby, he wouldn't talk to Edmundson. You don't treat people who love you that way.

"I said, 'You're making the title look cheap. You're doing all this for an extra $10,000? $15,000? You worked 15 years for this?'

"And he said, 'Well right is right and fair is fair.' "

To the Iceland Station

The question inevitably arises, will Fischer beat Spassky?

A year ago Andrew Soltis, a reporter for the *New York Post* who is the Marshall Chess Club champion and author of a short book on Spassky's games, thought Spassky would win. In their five games together, after all, Spassky had won three times and drawn twice. Soltis decided he was wrong after he saw Fischer's record last year. He began by defeating Mark Taimanov of Russia and Bent Larsen of Denmark, both serious candidates for the world championship, in two 6-0 matches which were unprecedented in chess history. (Larsen was devastated by his humiliating loss—not even a single drawn game!—and only now is approaching a point where he can discuss the match easily.) Fischer's 6½–2½ victory over Tigran Petrosian in Buenos Aires last October was almost as extraordinary. Petrosian is a master of defense and it is extremely difficult to beat a master who is determined to draw. Fischer's success in doing so convinced Soltis that Fischer is in one of those half-magical moments of a great player's life when he is all but unbeatable.

When Fischer began to play competitive chess 15 years ago, championship play was characterized by technical mastery and by caution. A long romantic period had ended in the last decades of the 19th century with an improvement in analytical theory and defensive technique. Attack based on brilliant intuition was replaced by an emphasis on accuracy. Instead of responding aggressively to aggressive attack, the so-called "hyper-modernists" simply waited for a mistake. They read everything and remembered everything; one mistake was all they needed. Petrosian was a typical hyper-modernist in this sense. He played for the draw unless he saw a clear opportunity to win, and he was satisfied to carry a tournament by half a point. It takes skill to win this way, but the result is a style of play which appeals to the conservative, *burgher* element in the human soul.

Fischer changed all that. His Queen sacrifice against Donald Byrne in 1956 revealed the soaring, romantic streak in his nature. When an inexperienced player takes such chances, however, he often makes fatal technical errors. Since then Fischer has combined his early daring with a mastery of technique so deep that experts generally designate him the world's most accurate player. This means that he does not make mistakes, of course, but it also means that his moves tend to be the best possible moves in a given situation. Some championship games go on forever and wander all over the board. Fischer drives for directness and simplicity. His goal is perfection, the move which is exactly right.

Fischer's brilliance and his technical mastery are probably enough to win him the world championship. The quality which makes him possibly the greatest player in history is his will to win. The importance of will in chess is the hardest thing to comprehend for some one unfamiliar with the game. Lasker was speaking of will when he said of another player, "He lacks the passion that whips the blood." In the literature it assumes Nietzschean proportions. The greatest respect is always reserved for the players who fought the hardest, who refused to despair, who could lose an important game and still come back to win, who could overcome sickness, age and private unhappiness to play strong games. Will in chess means concentrating all the resources of one's mind and spirit on a single problem with a fierce lucidity. No chess player can explain how one exerts will, anymore than motorcycle riders can explain how you turn: you just . . . *turn.* Without will a chess player can never rise above a certain level and Fischer's will is legendary.

Inexperienced players take a will to win for granted because they don't really know how to play any other sort of game. They go after an opponent's king because they don't know how to fight for position, and they win or lose because they don't know how to draw.

Fischer has nothing but scorn for players who are quick to draw, content with half a point. Arthur Bisguier, a former US champion, once told a friend at the Manhattan Chess Club, "People don't realize what it is to sit down against Fischer in a serious game." He explained that he was afraid to ask for a draw because Fischer's answer almost invariably was a brief, humiliating "no." If Fischer loses a maneuver for position he will go on fighting long after other players would have resigned, and he will fight for a win when other players would consider themselves lucky to draw.

Bisguier has played Fischer often but the only game he ever won was the first.

"He plays every game as if it's the last thing he's going

to do on earth. Other players save themselves. Not Bobby. [Jose] Capablanca [the great Cuban champion] never won a game he didn't have to in his life. He was lazy. Fischer is never lazy.

"The second time we played he offered me a draw and I refused and then somehow I managed to lose. And thereafter I managed to lose in many strange ways. Sometimes I have been in a strong position and I will say to myself, 'Bisguier, how are you going to lose this game?' and finally I find a way to make a mistake.

"I think part of it is knowing that the game is going to continue until someone is beaten. You're going to be playing for hours. You can't help dreading the ordeal. So I try to hurry the game, bring it to a climax early, and I make mistakes. Fischer destroys the spirit."

Behind all discussion of Fischer's prospects in Iceland is the assumption that a Fischer defeat is not only unlikely but unthinkable. Fischer's entire life has been a prelude to this match. Part of his strength as a player has been his willingness to make personal sacrifices for chess no one else has been ready to equal. He dedicates himself to chess the way other men dedicate themselves to philosophy, mathematics or God. He studies the game harder, he has a deeper respect for its inner beauty, he plays for the *game* and does not flinch from the dangerous position that winning is everything.

Other players hold back some fragment of their self-respect. Faced with a defeat, they are ready to console themselves with the thought that, after all, chess is only a game. Fischer holds back nothing. For him chess is not a game but life. He risks everything—pride, identity, manhood—every time he sits down to play. If he lost to Spassky . . . Fischer's friends hesitate to go on.

Capablanca wrote in his autobiography, "There have been times in my life when I came very near thinking that I could not lose even a single game. Then I would be beaten and the lost game would bring me back from dreamland to earth."

It is a return some great players never make. William Steinitz (1836–1900), the founder of positional theory and one of the great champions, died in poverty and delirium. At the end of his life he believed he could still play the chess of his youth, that he was in communion with God, that he played chess with God, and that he could give God pawn and move, and still win.

STRANGE RUMBLINGS IN AZTLAN

The ✛ Murder ✛ and Resurrection
of Ruben Salazar by the
Los Angeles County Sheriff's Department ✛
Savage polarization & the making of a Martyr ✛
Bad news for the Mexican-American ✛ Worse
news for the pig ✛ ✛ And now the New Chi-
cano ✛ riding a grim new wave ✛ ✛ ✛ The rise
of the Batos Locos ✛ Brown Power and a fistful
of reds ✛ Rude politics in the Barrio ✛ ✛ Which
side are you on ✛ brother? ✛ There is no more
middleground ✛ No place to hide on Whittier
Boulevard ✛ ✛ No refuge from the helicopters
✛ No hope in the courts ✛ No peace with the
Man ✛ No leverage anywhere ✛ and no light at
the end of this tunnel ✛ ✛ ✛ Nada ✛

by Hunter S. Thompson

Morning comes hard to the Hotel Ashmun; this is not a place where the guests spring eagerly out of bed to greet the fresh new day. But on this particular morning everybody in the place is awake at the crack of dawn: There is a terrible pounding and shrieking in the hallway, near room No. 267. Some junkie has ripped the doorknob off the communal bathroom, and now the others can't get in—so they are trying to kick the door down. The voice of the manager wavers hysterically above the din: "Come on now, fellas—do I have to call the sheriff?" The reply comes hard and fast: "You filthy gabacho pig! You call the fuckin sheriff and I'll cut your fuckin throat." And now the sound of wood cracking, more screaming, the sound of running feet outside my door, No. 267.

The door is locked, thank Christ—but how can you say for sure in a place like the Hotel Ashmun? Especially on a morning like this with a mob of wild junkies locked out of the hall bathroom and maybe knowing that No. 267 is the only room within lunging distance that has a private bath. It is the best in the house, at $5.80 a night, and the lock on the door is brand new. The old one was ripped out about 12 hours earlier, just before I checked in.

The desk clerk had gone to a lot of trouble to get me into this room. His key wouldn't fit the new lock. "Jesus Christ!" he kept muttering. "This key *has* to fit! This is a brand new *Yale lock*." He stared balefully at the bright new key in his hand.

"Yeah," I said. "But that key is for a *Webster* lock."

"By God you're *right!*" he exclaimed. And he rushed off, leaving us standing there in the hallway with big chunks of ice in our hands. "What's wrong with that guy?" I asked. "He seems out of control—all this sweating and grappling and jabbering . . ."

Benny Luna laughed. "Man, he's nervous! You think it's *normal* for him to be lettin four nasty lookin Chicanos into his best room at three in the morning? With all of us carryin chunks of ice and funny-lookin leather bags?" He was staggering around the hall, convulsed with laughter. "Man, this guy is *freaked!* He doesn't know *what's* goin on!"

"*Three* Chicanos," said Oscar. "And one hillbilly."

"You didn't tell him I was a writer, did you?" I asked. I'd noticed Oscar talking to the man, a tall sort of defeated looking Germanic type, but I hadn't paid much attention.

"No, but he recognized *me,*" Oscar replied. "He said, 'You're the lawyer, aren't you?' So I said 'That's right, and I want your best room for this gabacho friend of mine.'" He grinned. "Yeah, he knows *something's* wrong with this scene, but he doesn't know what. These guys are scared of *everything* now. Every merchant on Whittier Boulevard is sure he's living on borrowed time, so they

303

go all to pieces at the first sign of anything strange going on. It's been this way ever since Salazar."

The room clerk/manager/keeper/etc. suddenly rounded the hallway corner with the right key, and let us into the room. It was a winner—a run-down echo of a place I stayed in a few years ago in the slums of Lima, Peru. I can't recall the name of that place, but I remember that all the room keys were attached to big wooden knobs about the size of grapefruits, too big to fit in a pocket. I thought about suggesting this to our man in the Hotel Ashmun, but he didn't wait around for tips or small-talk. He was gone in a flash, leaving us alone to deal with a quart of rum and God only knows what else. . . . We put the ice in a basin next to the bed and chopped it up with a huge rigging knife. The only music was a tape cassette of *Let It Bleed*.

What better music for a hot night on Whittier Boulevard in 1971? This has not been a peaceful street, of late. And in truth it was *never* peaceful. Whittier is to the vast Chicano *barrio* in East Los Angeles what the Sunset Strip is to Hollywood. This is where the street action lives: the bars, the hustlers, the drug market, the whores—and also the riots, the trashings, killings, gassings, the sporadic bloody clashes with the hated, common enemy: The cops, the Pigs, the Man, that blue-crusted army of fearsome gabacho troops from the East L.A. Sheriff's Department.

The Hotel Ashmun is a good place to stay if you want to get next to whatever's happening on Whitter Boulevard. The window of No. 267 is about 15 feet above the sidewalk and just a few blocks west of the Silver Dollar Cafe, a nondescript tavern that is not much different from any of the others nearby. There is a pool table in the rear, a pitcher of beer sells for a dollar, and the faded Chicano barmaid rolls dice with the patrons to keep the jukebox going. Low number pays, and nobody seems to care who selects the music.

We had been in there earlier, when not much was happening. It was my first visit in six months, since early September when the place was still rancid with the stench of CS gas and fresh varnish. But now, six months later, the Silver Dollar had aired out nicely. No blood on the floor, no ominous holes in the ceiling. The only reminder of my other visit was a thing hanging over the cash register that we all noticed immediately. It was a black gas mask, staring blindly out at the room—and below the gas mask was a stark handprinted sign that said: "In memory of August 29, 1970."

Nothing else, no explanation. But no explanation was necessary—at least not to anybody likely to be found drinking in the Silver Dollar. The customers are locals: Chicanos and barrio people—and every one of them is acutely aware of what happened in the Silver Dollar Cafe on August 29, 1970.

That was the day that Ruben Salazar, the prominent "Mexican-American" columnist for the *Los Angeles Times* and News Director for bilingual KMEX-TV, walked into the place and sat down on a stool near the doorway to order a beer he would never drink. Because just about the time the barmaid was sliding his beer across the bar a Los Angeles County sheriff's deputy named Tom Wilson fired a tear gas bomb through the front door and blew half of Ruben Salazar's head off. All the other customers escaped out the back exit to the alley, but Salazar never emerged. He died on the floor in a cloud of CS gas—and when his body was finally carried out, hours later, his name was already launched into martyrdom. Within 24 hours, the very mention of the name "Ruben Salazar" was enough to provoke tears and fist-shaking tirades not only along Whittier Boulevard but all over East L.A.

Middle-aged housewives who had never thought of themselves as anything but lame-status "Mexican-Americans" just trying to get by in a mean Gringo world they never made suddenly found themselves shouting "Viva La Raza" *in public*. And their husbands—quiet Safeway clerks and lawn-care salesmen, the lowest and most expendable cadres in the Great Gabacho economic machine—were volunteering to *testify;* yes, to stand up in court, or wherever, and calling themselves Chicanos. The term "Mexican-American" fell massively out of favor with all but the old and conservative—and the rich. It suddenly came to mean "Uncle Tom." Or, in the argot of East L.A.— "Tio Taco." The difference between a Mexican-American and a Chicano was the difference between a Negro and a Black.

All this has happened very suddenly. Too suddenly for most people. One of the basic laws of politics is that Action Moves Away from the Center. The middle of the road is only popular when nothing is happening. And nothing serious has been happening politically in East L.A. for longer than most people can remember. Until six months ago the whole place was a colorful tomb, a vast slum full of noise and cheap labor, a rifle shot away from the heart of downtown Los Angeles. The barrio, like Watts, is actually a part of the city core—while places like Hollywood and Santa Monica are separate entities. The Silver Dollar Cafe is a ten-minute drive from City Hall. The Sunset Strip is a 30-minute sprint on the Hollywood Freeway.

Whittier Boulevard is a hell of a long way from Hollywood, by any measure. There is no psychic connection at all. After a week in the bowels of East L.A. I felt vaguely guilty about walking into the bar in the Beverly Hills Hotel and ordering a drink—as if I didn't quite belong there, and the waiters all knew it. I had been there before, under different circumstances, and felt totally comfortable. Or almost. There is no way to . . . well, to hell with that. The point is that this time I felt *different*. I was oriented to a completely different world—15 miles away.

MARCHA POR LA JUSTICIA

THERE ARE NO POLICE COMMUNITY RELATIONS IN THE CHICANO COMMUNITIES. NO, EVER SINCE THE POLICE RIOT ON AUGUST 29TH IT HAS BECOME TOO OBVIOUS TO IGNORE THE FACT THAT THE LAPD, THE SHERIFFS, AND THE HIGHWAY PATROL HAVE FOR YEARS BEEN SYSTEMATICALLY TRYING TO DESTROY THE TRUE SPIRIT OF OUR PEOPLE. IN THE PAST, POLICE HAVE BROKEN UP EVERY ATTEMPT OF OUR PEOPLE TO GET JUSTICE, THEY HAVE BEATEN YOUNG STUDENTS PROTESTING POOR EDUCATION, RAIDED OFFICES, ARRESTED LEADERS, CALLED US COMMUNISTS AND GANGSTERS IN THE PRESS, AND EVERYTHING ELSE ON THE STREETS WHEN THE PRESS WAS GONE.

EVEN MORE INSIDIOUS THAN THE DIRECT POLITICAL

306

REPRESSION AGAINST LEADERS AND DEMONSTRATIONS ARE THE CONTINUOUS ATTACKS ON THE EVERYDAY LIFE OF PEOPLE IN THE BARRIOS. ALMOST EVERY MONTH EACH BARRIO HAS SUFFERED THROUGH AT LEAST ONE CASE OF SEVERE BRUTALITY OR MURDER AND THEN STRUGGLED TO DEFEND FRIENDS AND WITNESSES WHO FACE BUM RAPS. ONE WEEK IT'S SAN FERNANDO, THEN LINCOLN HEIGHTS, EAST L.A., VENICE, THE HARBOR AND POMONA ....THEY HIT ONE BARRIO AT A TIME, TRYING TO BREAK OUR UNITY AND OUR SPIRIT.

ON AUGUST 29TH, THROUGH ALL OF OUR BARRIOS WERE DEMONSTRATIONS FOR PEACE AND JUSTICE AND THE POLICE RIOTED AND ATTACKED. OUT OF FEAR, THEY INSTALLED MARTIAL LAW, ARRESTING AND ABUSING HUNDREDS OF COMMUNITY PEOPLE. THEY KILLED GILBERTO DIAZ, LYNN WARD, AND RUBEN SALAZAR, THE MAN WHO COULD TELL OUR STORY TO THE NATION AND THE WORLD.

WE MUST NOT FORGET THE LESSON OF AUGUST 29TH THAT THE MAJOR SOCIAL AND POLITICAL ISSUE WE FACE IS POLICE BRUTALITY. SINCE THE 29TH POLICE ATTACKS HAVE BEEN WORSE. EITHER THE PEOPLE CONTROL THE POLICE, OR WE ARE LIVING IN A POLICE STATE.

WE MUST NOT ALLOW THE POLICE TO BREAK OUR UNITY. WE MUST CARRY ON THE SPIRIT OF RUBEN SALAZAR AND EXPOSE THIS BRUTALITY TO THE NATION AND THE WORLD. THE CHICANO MORATORIUM COMMITTEE CALLS UPON YOU TO SUPPORT OUR NON-VIOLENT MARCH FOR JUSTICE THROUGH THE BARRIOS OF THE GREATER LOS ANGELES AREA.

CARAVANS WILL BE COMING FROM DOZENS OF CITIES AND AROUND OUR BARRIOS. WE WILL ALL MEET AT THE E.L.A. SHERIFF'S SUB-STATION ON 3RD STREET BETWEEN FETTERLY AND WOODS. AT 11:00 AM JANUARY 31, 1971. JOIN YOUR LOCAL CARAVAN. FOR FURTHER INFORMATION CALL 268-6745.

—Handbill from the National
Chicano Moratorium Committee

My first night in the Hotel Ashmun was not restful. The others had left around five, then there was the junkie eruption at seven . . . followed an hour later by a thundering, low-fidelity outburst of wailing Norteno music from the jukebox in the Boulevard Cafe across the street . . . and then, about nine-thirty, I was jerked up again by a series of loud whistles from the sidewalk right under my window, and a voice calling "Hunter! Wake-up man! Let's get moving."

Holy jesus! I thought. Only three people in the world know where I am right now, and they're all asleep. Who else could have tracked me to this place? I bent the metal slats of the venetian blind apart just enough to look down at the street and see Rudy Sanchez, Oscar's quiet little bodyguard, looking up at my window and waving urgently: "Come on out, man, it's time. Oscar and Benny are up the street at the Sweetheart. That's the bar on the corner where you see all those people in front. We'll wait for you there, OK? You awake?"

"Sure I'm awake," I said. "I've been sitting here *waiting* for you lazy criminal bastards. Why do Mexicans need so much fucking sleep?"

Rudy smiled and turned away. "We'll be *waiting* for you, man. We're gonna be drinkin a hell of a lot of bloody marys and you know the rule we have down here."

"Never mind that," I muttered. "I need a shower."

But my room had no shower. And somebody, that night, had managed to string a naked copper wire across the bathtub and plug it into a socket underneath the basin outside the bathroom door. For what reason? Demon Rum, I had no idea. Here I was in the best room in the house, looking for the shower and finding only an electrified bathtub. And no place to righteously shave—in the best hotel on the strip. Finally I scrubbed my face with a hot towel and went across the street to the Sweetheart Lounge.

Oscar Acosta, the Chicano lawyer, was there; leaning on the bar, talking idly with some of the patrons. Of the four people around him—all in their late twenties—two were ex-cons, two were part-time dynamite freaks and known fire-bombers, and three of the four were veteran acid-eaters. Yet none of this surfaced in the conversation. The talk was political, but only in terms of the courtroom. Oscar was dealing with two hyper-political trials at the same time.

In one, the trial of the "Biltmore Six," he was defending six young Chicanos who'd been arrested for trying to burn down the Biltmore Hotel one night about a year ago, while Governor Ronald Reagan was delivering a speech there in the ballroom. Their guilt or innocence was immaterial at this point, because the trial had developed into a spectacular attempt to overturn the entire Grand Jury selection system. In the preceding months, Acosta had subpoenaed every Superior Court Judge in Los Angeles County and cross-examined all 109 of them at length, under oath, on the subject of their "racism." It was a wretched affront to the whole court system, and Acosta was working overtime to make it as wretched as possible. Here were these hundred and nine old men, these *judges*, compelled to take time out from whatever they were doing and go into another courtroom to take the stand and deny charges of "racism" from an attorney they all loathed.

Oscar's contention, throughout, was that all Grand Juries are racist, since all grand jurors have to be recommended by Superior Court Judges—who naturally tend to recommend people they know personally or professionally. And that therefore no ratbastard Chicano street crazy, for instance, could possibly be indicted by "a jury of his peers." The implications of a victory in this case were so obvious, so clearly menacing to the court system, that interest in the verdict had filtered all the way down to places like the Boulevard, the Silver Dollar and the Sweetheart. The level of political consciousness is not normally high in these places—especially on Saturday mornings —but Acosta's very presence, no matter where he goes or what he seems to be doing, is so grossly political that anybody who wants to talk to him has to figure out some way to deal on a meaningful political level.

"The thing is to never talk down," he says. "We're not trying to win votes out here. Hell, that trip's been done, it's over. The idea now is to make people *think*. Force them to think. And you can't do that by walking around slapping strangers on the back and buying them beers." Then grinning. "Unless you happen to be babbling drunk or stoned. Which is certainly not my style; I want to make that one thing very clear."

But today the talk was easy, with no ulterior politics. "Say, Oscar," somebody asked. "How do we stand on that Grand Jury thing? What's our chances?"

Acosta shrugged. "We'll win. Maybe not on this level, but we'll win on appeal."

"That's good man. I hear you're really workin out on the bastards."

"Yeah, we're fuckin em over. But that one might take another year. Right now we have to think about Corky's trial. It starts Tuesday."

"Corky's in town?" The interest is obvious. Heads turn to listen. Rudy eases back a few feet so he can watch the whole bar, scanning the faces for any that might be *too* interested. Paranoia is rampant in the barrio: Informers. Narcs. Assassins—who knows? And Rudolfo "Corky" Gonzales is a definite heavy, prime target for a frame or a set-up. A scholarly, soft-spoken, ex-boxer, his Denver-based "Crusade for Justice" is one of the few *viable* Chicano political organizations in the country. Gonzales is a poet, a street-fighter, a theorist, an organizer, and the most influential "Chicano leader" in the country next to Cesar Chavez.

Whenever Corky Gonzales appears in East L.A.—if only to stand trial on a misdemeanor weapons bust—the level of political tension rises noticeably. Gonzales has a very intense following in the barrio. Most of his supporters are young: Students, dropouts, artists, poets, crazies—the people who *respect* Cesar Chavez, but who can't really *relate* to churchgoing farmworkers.

"This weekend is going to be hell," Oscar had told me the night before. "Whenever Corky's in town, my apartment turns into a fucking zoo. I have to go to a motel to get any sleep. Shit, I can't stay up all night arguing radical politics when I have to be in court the next morning. These wild-eyed fuckers show up at all hours; they bring wine, joints, acid, mescaline, guns . . . Jesus, Corky wouldn't dare take that kind of risk. He's already here, but I don't know where he's staying. He's checked into some kind of goddamn Holiday Inn or something, about five miles out on Rosemeade, but he won't tell anybody where it is—not even me, his lawyer." He smiled, "And that's pretty shrewd, because if I knew where he was I might go over there some night all twisted and crazy about calling a general strike at dawn, or some other dangerous bullshit that would freak him."

He nodded, smiling lazily down at his drink. "As a matter of fact, I *have* been thinking about calling a general strike. The movement is so goddamn splintered right now that almost anything would help. Yeah, maybe I should write Corky a speech along those lines, then call a press conference for tomorrow afternoon in the Silver Dollar." He laughed bitterly and called for another bloody mary.

Acosta has been practicing law in the barrio for three years. I met him a bit earlier than that, in another era—which hardly matters here, except that it might be a trifle less than fair to run this story all the way out to the end without saying at least once, for the record, that Oscar is an old friend and occasional antagonist. I first met him, as I recall, in a bar called "The Daisy Duck" in Aspen, when he lumbered up to me and started raving about "ripping the system apart like a pile of cheap hay," or something like that . . . and I remember thinking, "Well, here's another one of those fucked-up, guilt-crazed dropout lawyers from San Francisco—some dingbat who ate one too many tacos and decided he was really Emiliano Zapata."

Which was OK, I felt, but it was a hard act to handle in Aspen in that high white summer of 1967. That was the era of Sergeant Pepper, the Surrealistic Pillow and the original Buffalo Springfield. It was a good year for everybody—or for *most* people, anyway. There were exceptions, as always. Lyndon Johnson was one, and Oscar Acosta was another. For entirely different reasons. That was not a good summer to be either the President of the United States or any angry Mexican lawyer in Aspen.

Oscar didn't hang around long. He washed dishes for a while, did a bit of construction work, bent the County Judge out of shape a few times, then took off for Mexico to "get serious." The next thing I heard, he was working for the public defender's office in L.A. That was sometime around Christmas of 1968, which was not a good year for anybody—except Richard Nixon and perhaps Oscar Acosta. Because by that time Oscar was beginning to find his own track. He was America's only "Chicano lawyer," he explained in a letter, and he liked it. His clients were all Chicanos and most were "political criminals," he said. And if they were guilty it was only because they were "doing what had to be done."

That's fine, I said. But I couldn't really get into it. I was all *for it,* you understand, but only on the basis of a personal friendship. *Most* of my friends are into strange things I don't totally understand—and with a few shameful exceptions I wish them all well. Who am I, after all, to tell some friend he shouldn't change his name to Oliver High, get rid of his family and join a Satanism cult in Seattle? Or to argue with another friend who wants to buy a single-shot Remington Fireball so he can go out and shoot cops from a safe distance?

Whatever's right, I say. Never fuck with a friend's head by accident. And if their private trips get out of control now and then—well, you do what has to be done.

Which more or less explains how I suddenly found myself involved in the murder of Ruben Salazar. I was up in Portland, Oregon at the time, trying to cover the National American Legion Convention and the Sky River Rock Festival at the same time . . . and I came back to my secret room in the Hilton one night to find an "urgent message" to call Mr. Acosta in Los Angeles.

I wondered how he had managed to track me down in Portland. But I knew, somehow, what he was calling about. I had seen the L.A. *Times* that morning, with the story of Salazar's death, and even at a distance of 2000 miles it gave off a powerful stench. The problem was not just a gimp or a hole in the story; the whole goddamn thing was wrong. It made no sense at all.

The Salazar case had a very special hook in it: Not that he was a Mexican or a Chicano, and not even Acosta's angry insistence that the cops had killed him in cold blood and that nobody was going to do anything about it. These were all proper ingredients for an outrage, but from my own point of view the most ominous aspect of Oscar's story was his charge that the police had deliberately gone out on the streets and killed a reporter who'd been giving them trouble. If this was true, it meant the ante was being upped drastically. When the cops declare open season on journalists, when they feel free to declare any scene of "unlawful protest" a free fire zone, that will be a very ugly day—and not just for journalists.

For thirteen devastated blocks, darkened stores stood gaping, show windows smashed. Traffic signs, spent shotgun shells, chunks of brick and concrete littered the pavement. A pair of sofas, gutted by fire, smouldered at a curbside splashed with blood. In the hot blaze of police flares, three Chicano youths swaggered down the ruined street. "Hey brother," one yelled to a black reporter, "was this better than Watts?"

—Newsweek, Feb. 15, '71

Ruben Salazar is a bonafide martyr now—not only in East L.A., but in Denver and Santa Fe and San Antonio, throughout the Southwest. The length and breadth of Aztlan—the "conquered territories" that came under the yoke of Gringo occupation troops more than 100 years ago, when "vendido politicians in Mexico City sold out to the US" in order to call off the invasion that Gringo history books refer to as the "Mexican-American War." (Davy Crockett, Remember the Alamo, etc.)

As a result of this war, the US government was ceded about half of what was then the Mexican nation. This territory was eventually broken up into what is now the states of Texas, New Mexico, Arizona and the southern half of California. This is Aztlan, more a concept than a real definition. But even as a concept it has galvanized a whole generation of young Chicanos to a style of political action that literally terrifies their Mexican-American parents. Between 1968 and 1970 the "Mexican-American Movement" went through the same drastic changes and heavy trauma that had earlier afflicted the "Negro Civil Rights Movement" in the early Sixties. The split was mainly along generational lines, and the first "young radicals" were overwhelmingly the sons and daughters of middle-class Mexican-Americans who had learned to live with "their problem."

313

At this stage, the Movement was basically intellectual. The word "Chicano" was forged as a necessary identity for the people of Aztlan—neither Mexicans nor Americans, but a conquered Indian/Mestizo nation sold out like slaves by its leaders and treated like indentured servants by its conquerors. Not even their language was definable, much less their identity. The language of East L.A. is a speedy sort of *cholo* mixture of Mexican Spanish and California English. You can sit in the Boulevard Cafe on Whittier on a Saturday morning and hear a young Chicano ex-con explaining to his friends: "This goddamn gabacho parole officer tells me I have to get the sewing machine back. I talked to that goddamn vendido and the vieja tambien, and they tell me don't worry, we won't say nothing that would send you back to the joint. But the gabacho keeps pushin me. What can I do?" And then, suddenly noticing a vagrant gringo nearby, he finishes the whole story in rapid, angry Spanish.

There are a lot of ex-cons in the Movement now, along with a whole new element—the *"Batos Locos."* And the only difference, really, is that the ex-cons are old enough to have done time for the same things the *batos locos* haven't been arrested for, yet. Another difference is that the ex-cons are old enough to frequent the action bars along Whittier, while most of the *batos locos* are still teenagers. They drink heavily, but not in the Boulevard or the Silver Dollar. On Friday night you will find them sharing quarts of sweet Key Largo in the darkness of some playground in the housing project. And along with the wine, they eat seconal—which is massively available in the barrio, and also cheap: a buck or so for a rack of five reds, enough to fuck *anybody* up. Seconal is one of the few drugs on the market (legal or otherwise) that is flat guaranteed to turn you *mean*. Especially with wine on the side and a few "whites," bennies, for a chaser. This is the kind of diet that makes a man want to go out and stomp people . . . the only other people I've ever seen heavily into the red/white/wine diet were the Hell's Angels.

The results are about the same. The Angels would get loaded and then snarl around looking for somebody to chain whip. The *batos locos* get loaded and start looking

314

for their own kind of action (burning a store, rat-packing a nigger, or stealing some cars for a night of high-speed cruising on the freeways). The action is almost always illegal, usually violent—but only recently has it become "political."

Perhaps the main Movement/focus in the barrio these days is the politicalization of the *batos locos*. The term translates literally as "crazy guys," but in harsh political terms it translates as "street crazies," teenage wildmen who have nothing to lose except their hostility and a vast sense of doom and boredom with the world as they know it. "These guys aren't afraid of the pigs," a Chicano activist told me. "Hell, they *like* a fight with the pigs. They *want* it. And there's a hell of a lot of 'em, man. Maybe two hundred thousand. If we can organize these guys, man, we can move on *anybody*."

But the *batos locos* are not easily organized. For one thing, they're hopelessly ignorant about politics. They hate politicians—even Chicano politicians. They are also very young, very hostile, and when you get them excited they are likely to do almost anything—especially when they're full of wine and reds. One of the first overt attempts to bring the *batos locos* into the new Chicano politics was the mass rally against police brutality last January 31st. The organizers took great care to make sure the thing would be peaceful. The word went out all over the barrio that "this one has to be cool—no riot, no violence." A truce was arranged with the East L.A. sheriff's dept.; the cops agreed to "keep a low profile," but they nonetheless sand-bagged and barricaded the sheriff's substation right next to the site of the rally in Belvedere Park.

Writing in *The Nation*, a Chicago priest named David F. Gomez described the scene as the rally gathered steam:

Despite the tension, a fiesta atmosphere prevailed as Chicanos sat on the scarred grass of the park's soccer field and listened while barrio speakers aired grievances of police brutality and the gringo occupation of Aztlan. Oscar Acosta gave the most rousing talk of the afternoon. *"Ya es tiempo. The time is now! There's only one issue. Not police abuse. We are going to be clubbed over the head for as long as we* live because we're Chicanos! The real issue is *nuestra tierra,* our land. Some people call us rebels and revolutionaries. Don't believe it. Emiliano Zapata was a revolutionary because he fought against other Mexicans. But we are not fighting our own people but gringos! We are not trying to overturn our own government. We don't have a government! Do you think there would be police helicopters patrolling our communities day and night if anybody considered us real citizens with rights!"

The rally *was* peaceful—all the way to the end. But then, when fighting broke out between a handful of Chicanos and jittery cops, nearly a thousand young *batos locos* reacted by making a frontal assault on the cop headquarters with rocks, bottles, clubs, bricks and everything else they could find. The cops withstood the attack for about an hour, then swarmed out of the place with a stunning show of force that included firing deadly buckshot balls out of 12-gauge shotguns straight into the crowd. The attackers fled through the backstreets to Whittier Boulevard and trashed the street again. The cops pursued, firing shotguns and pistols at point blank range. After two hours of street warfare, the toll was one dead, 30 serious injuries and a little less than a half million dollars worth of damage—including 78 burned and battered police cars.

The entire L.A. power structure was outraged. And the Chicano Moratorium Committee was aghast. The rally's main organizer—24-year-old Rosalio Munoz, a former president of the UCLA student body—was so shocked by the outburst that he reluctantly agreed—with the sheriff—that any further mass rallies would be too dangerous. "We will have to find a new way of expressing grievances," said a spokesman for the more moderate Congress of Mexican-American Unity. "From now on the course will be to play a low profile."

But nobody spoke for the *batos locos*—except maybe the sheriff. "This violence was not caused by outsiders," he said, "but by members of the Chicano community! They can't say we provoked them this time." This was a definite switch from the standard-brand cop-analysis of "Mexican violence." In the past they had always blamed it on "Communists and Outside Agitators." But now, it seemed, the sheriff was finally catching on. The real enemy was the same people his men had to deal with every goddamn day of the week, in all kinds of routine situations—on street-corners, in bars, domestic brawls and car accidents. The *gente,* the street-people, the ones who *live* there. So in the end, being a sheriff's deputy in East L.A. was not much different from being a point man for the Americal Division in Vietnam. "Even the kids and old women are VC."

This is the new drift, and everybody in East L.A. who's willing to talk about it uses the term "since Salazar." In the six months since the murder and the unsettling coroner's inquest that followed it up, the Chicano community has been harshly sundered by a completely new kind of polarization, another painful amoeba-trip. But the split this time was not between the young militants and the old Tio Tacos; this time it was between student-type militants and this whole new breed of super-militant street crazies. The argument was no longer *whether* to fight—but When, and How, and with What Weapons.

Another awkward aspect of the new split was that it was no longer a simple matter of "the generation gap"—which had been painful, but essentially simple; now it was more than a conflict of lifestyles and attitudes; the division this time was more along economic, or *class* lines. And this was painfully complex. The original student activists had been militant, but also reasonable—in their own eyes, if not in the eyes of the law.

But the *batos locos* never even pretended to be reasonable. They wanted to get it on, and the sooner the better. Anytime, anywhere: Just give us a reason to work out on the pig, and we're ready.

This attitude created definite problems within the movement. The street people had right instincts, said the leadership, but they were not wise. They had no program; only violence and vengeance—which was wholly understandable, of course, but how could it *work?* How could the traditionally stable Mexican-American community gain anything, in the long run, by declaring total war on the gabacho power structure and meanwhile purging its own native *vendidos?*

317

Ruben Salazar was killed in the wake of a Watts-style riot that erupted when hundreds of cops attacked a peaceful rally in Laguna Park, where 5000 or so liberal/student/activist type Chicanos had gathered to protest the drafting of "Aztlan citizens" to fight for the US in Vietnam. The police suddenly appeared in Laguna Park, with no warning, and "dispersed the crowd" with a blanket of tear gas, followed up by a Chicago-style mop-up with billyclubs. The crowd fled in panic and anger, inflaming hundreds of young spectators who ran the few blocks to Whittier Boulevard and began trashing every store in sight. Several buildings were burned to the ground; damage was estimated at somewhere around a million dollars. Three people were killed, 60 injured—but the central incident of that August 29th, 1970 rally was the killing of Ruben Salazar.

And six months later, when the National Chicano Moratorium Committee felt it was time for another mass rally, they called it to "carry on the spirit of Ruben Salazar."

There is irony in this, because Salazar was nobody's militant. He was a professional journalist with ten years of experience on a variety of assignments for the neoliberal *Los Angeles Times*. He was a nationally known reporter, winning prizes for his work in places like Vietnam, Mexico City and the Dominican Republic. Ruben Salazar was a veteran war correspondent, but he had never shed blood under fire. He was good, and he seemed to like the work. So he must have been slightly bored when the *Times* called him back from the war zones, for a raise and a well-deserved rest covering "local affairs."

He focused on the huge barrio just east of city hall. This was a scene he had never really known, despite his Mexican-American heritage. But he locked into it almost instantly. Within months, he had narrowed his work for the *Times* down to a once-a-week column for the newspaper, and signed on as News Director for KMEX-TV—the

"Mexican-American station," which he quickly transformed into an energetic, aggressively political voice for the whole Chicano community. His coverage of police activities made the East Los Angeles sheriff's dept. so unhappy that they soon found themselves in a sort of running private argument with this man Salazar, this Spic who refused to be reasonable. When Salazar got onto a routine story like some worthless kid named Ramirez getting beaten to death in a jail-fight, he was likely to come up with almost anything—including a series of hard-hitting news commentaries strongly suggesting that the victim had been beaten to death by the jailers. In the summer of 1970 Ruben Salazar was warned three times, by the cops, to "tone down his coverage." And each time he told them to fuck off.

This was not common knowledge in the community until after he was murdered. When he went out to cover the rally that August afternoon he was still a "Mexican-American journalist." But by the time his body was carried out of the Silver Dollar, he was a stone Chicano martyr. Salazar would have smiled at this irony, but he would not have seen much humor in the way the story of his death was handled by the cops and the politicians. Nor would he have been pleased to know that almost immediately after his death his name would become a battle cry, prodding thousands of young Chicanos who had always disdained "protest" into an undeclared war with the hated gringo police.

His paper, the L.A. *Times,* carried the account of its former foreign correspondent's death on its Monday front page: "Mexican-American newsman Ruben Salazar was killed by a bullet-like tear gas shell fired by a sheriff's deputy into a bar during rioting Saturday in East Los Angeles." The details were hazy, but the new, hastily revised police version was clearly constructed to show that Salazar was the victim of a Regrettable Accident which the cops were not aware of until many hours later. Sheriff's deputies had cornered an armed man in a bar, they said, and when he refused to come out—even after "loud warnings" (with a bull horn) "to evacuate"—"the

319

tear gas shells were fired and several persons ran out the back door."

At that time, according to the sheriff's nervous mouthpiece, Lt. Norman Hamilton, a woman and two men—one carrying a 7.65 automatic pistol—were met by deputies, who questioned them. "I don't know whether the man with the gun was arrested on a weapons violation or not," Hamilton added.

Ruben Salazar was not among those persons who ran out the back door. He was lying on the floor, inside, with a huge hole in his head. But the police didn't know this, Lieutenant Hamilton explained, because, "they didn't enter the bar until approximately 8 PM, when rumors began circulating that Salazar was missing," and "an unidentified man across the street from the bar" told a deputy, "I think there's an injured man in there." "At this point," said Hamilton, "deputies knocked down the door and found the body." Two and a half hours later, at 10:40 PM, the sheriff's office admitted that "the body" was Ruben Salazar.

"Hamilton could not explain," said the *Times,* "why two accounts of the incident given to the *Times* by avowed eyewitnesses differed from the sheriff's accounts."

For about 24 hours Hamilton clung grimly to his original story—a composite, he said, of firsthand police accounts. According to this version, Ruben Salazar had been "killed by errant gunfire . . . during the height of a sweep of more than 7000 people in (Laguna) Park when police ordered everyone to disperse." Local TV and radio newscasts offered sporadic variations on this theme —citing reports "still under investigation" that Salazar had been shot accidentally by careless street-snipers. It was tragic, of course, but tragedies like this are inevitable when crowds of innocent people allow themselves to be manipulated by a handful of violent, cop-hating anarchists.

By late Sunday, however, the sheriff's story had collapsed completely—in the face of sworn testimony from four men who were standing within ten feet of Ruben Salazar when he died in the Silver Dollar Cafe at 4045 Whittier Boulevard, at least a mile from Laguna Park. But the real shocker came when these men testified that

Salazar had been killed—not by snipers or errant gunfire —but by a cop with a deadly tear gas bazooka.

Acosta had no trouble explaining the discrepancy. "They're lying," he said. "They *murdered* Salazar and now they're trying to cover it up. The sheriff already panicked. All he can say is, 'No comment.' He's ordered every cop in the county to *say nothing* to anybody—especially the press. They've turned the East L.A. sheriff's station into a fortress. Armed guards all around it." He laughed. "Shit, the place looks like a prison—but with all the cops *inside!*"

Sheriff Peter J. Pitchess refused to talk to me when I called. The rude aftermath of the Salazar killing had apparently unhinged him completely. On Monday he called off a scheduled press conference and instead issued a statement, saying: "There are just too many conflicting stories, some from our own officers, as to what happened. The sheriff wants an opportunity to digest them before meeting with newsmen."

Indeed. Sheriff Pitchess was not alone in his inability to digest the garbled swill that his office was doling out. The official version of the Salazar killing was so crude and illogical—even after revisions—that not even the sheriff seemed surprised when it began to fall apart even before Chicano partisans had a chance to attack it. Which they would, of course. The sheriff had already got wind of what was coming: many eyewitnesses, sworn statements, first-hand accounts—all of them hostile.

The history of Chicano complaints against cops in East L.A. is not a happy one. "The cops never lose," Acosta told me, "and they won't lose this one either. They just murdered the only guy in the community they were really afraid of, and I guarantee you no cop will ever stand trial for it. Not even for manslaughter."

I could accept that. But it was difficult, even for me, to believe that the cops had killed him deliberately. I knew they were capable of it, but I was not quite ready to believe they had actually done it . . . because once I believed that, I also had to accept the idea that they are prepared to kill anybody who seemed to be annoying them. Even me.

As for Acosta's charge of murder, I knew him well enough to understand how he could make that charge *publicly* . . . I also knew him well enough to be sure he wouldn't try to hang that kind of monstrous bullshit on me. So our phone talk naturally disturbed me . . . and I fell to brooding about it, hung on my own dark suspicions that Oscar had told me the truth.

On the plane to L.A. I tried to make some kind of a case—either pro or con—from my bundle of notes and newsclips relating to Salazar's death. By that time at least six reportedly reliable witnesses had made sworn statements that differed drastically, on several crucial points, with the original police version—which nobody believed anyway. There was something very disturbing about the sheriff's account of that accident; it wasn't even a good *lie*.

Within hours after the *Times* hit the streets with the news that Ruben Salazar had in fact been killed by cops—rather than street snipers—the sheriff unleashed a furious assault on "known dissidents" who had flocked into East Los Angeles that weekend, he said, to provoke a disastrous riot in the Mexican-American community. He praised his deputies for the skillful zeal they displayed in restoring order to the area within two and a half hours, "thus averting a major holocaust of much greater proportions."

Pitchess did not identify any "known dissidents," but he insisted that they had committed "hundreds of provocative acts." For some reason the sheriff failed to mention that his deputies had already jailed one of the most prominent Chicano militants in the nation. "Corky" Gonzales had been arrested during Saturday's riot on a variety of charges that the police never really explained. Gonzales, fleeing the combat zone on a flatbed truck with 28 others, was arrested first for a traffic violation, then on a concealed weapons charge and finally for "suspicion of robbery" when police found $300 in his pocket. Police Inspector John Kinsling said it was a "routine" booking. "Any time we stop a traffic case and find there is a weapon in the car and that its occupants have a sizeable

322

amount of money," he said, "we always book them for suspicion of robbery."

Gonzales ridiculed the charge, saying, "Anytime a Mexican is found with more than $100 he's charged with a felony." The police had originally claimed he was carrying a loaded pistol and more than 1000 rounds of ammunition, along with many spent cartridges—but by Wednesday all felony charges had been dropped. As for "robbery," Gonzales said, "only a lunatic or a fool could believe that 29 people would rob a place and then jump on a flatbed truck to make their getaway." He had climbed aboard the truck with his two children, he said, to get them away from the cops who were gassing the rally, to which he'd been invited as one of the main speakers. The $300, he said, was expense money for himself and his children—for meals in L.A. and three round-trip bus tickets from Denver.

That was the extent of Corky Gonzales' involvement in the Salazar incident and at a glance it seems hardly worth mentioning—except for a rumor on the Los Angeles lawyers' grapevine that the robbery charge was only a ruse, a necessary holding action, to set Gonzales up for a "Chicano Seven" conspiracy bust—charging that he came from Denver to Los Angeles with the intention of causing a riot.

Both Sheriff Pitchess and Los Angeles Police Chief Edward Davis were quick to seize on this theory. It was the perfect tool for this problem: not only would it frighten the local Chicanos and hamstring nationally known militants like Gonzales, but it could also be used to create a sort of "red menace" smoke-screen to obscure the nasty realities of the Ruben Salazar killing.

The sheriff fired the first salvo, which earned him a giant banner headline in Tuesday's L.A. *Times* and a heavy pro-police editorial in Wednesday's *Herald-Examiner*. Meanwhile, Chief Davis launched a second blast from his listening post in Portland, where he had gone to vent his wisdom at the American Legion convention. Davis blamed all the violence, that Saturday, on a "hard core group of subversives who infiltrated the anti-war rally

323

and turned it into a mob," which soon ran wild in a frenzy of burning and looting. "Ten months ago," he explained, "the Communist Party in California said it was giving up on the blacks to concentrate on the Mexican-Americans."

Nowhere in the *Herald* editorial—and nowhere in either statement by the sheriff and the police chief—was there any mention of the name of Ruben Salazar. The *Herald,* in fact, had been trying to ignore the Salazar story from the very beginning. Even in Sunday's first story on the riot—long before any "complications" developed—the classic Hearst mentality was evident in the paper's full-page headline: "East Los Angeles Peace Rally Explodes in Bloody Violence . '. . Man Shot to Death; Buildings Looted, Burned." Salazar's name appeared briefly, in a statement by a spokesman for the L.A. County sheriff's department—a calm and confident assertion that the "veteran reporter" had been shot in Laguna Park, by persons unknown, in the midst of a bloody clash between police and militants. So much for Ruben Salazar.

And so much for the Los Angeles *Herald-Examiner*— a genuinely rotten newspaper that claims the largest circulation of any afternoon daily in America. As one of the few remaining Hearst organs, it serves a perverted purpose in its role as a monument to everything cheap, corrupt and vicious in the realm of journalistic possibility. It is hard to understand, in fact, how the shriveled Hearst management can still find enough gimps, bigots and deranged Papists to staff a rotten paper like the *Herald.* But they manage, somehow . . . and they also manage to sell a lot of advertising in the monster. Which means the thing is actually being read, and perhaps taken seriously, by hundreds of thousands of people in America's second largest city. At the top of Wednesday's editorial page— right next to the Red Menace warning—was a large cartoon titled "At the Bottom of it All." It showed a flaming Molotov cocktail crashing through a window, and on the bottom (*bottom,* get it?) of the bottle is a hammer and sickle emblem. The editorial itself was a faithful echo of the Davis-Pitchess charges: "Many of the dissidents came here from other cities and states to join agitators in Los Angeles to set off a major riot, which was planned in advance . . . That the holocaust did not erupt into greater proportions is due to the bravery and tactics of the sheriff's deputies . . . Those arrested should be prosecuted to the fullest extent of the law. Precautions must be doubled to prevent a recurrence of such criminal irresponsibility." The continued existence of the Hearst *Examiner* explains a lot about the mentality of Los Angeles —and also, perhaps, about the murder of Ruben Salazar.

So the only way to go was to reconstruct the whole thing on the basis of available eyewitness testimony. The police refused to say anything at all—especially to the press. The sheriff said he was saving "the truth" for the official coroner's inquest.

Meanwhile, evidence was building up that Ruben Salazar had been murdered—either deliberately or for no reason at all. The most damaging anti-cop testimony thus far had come from Guillermo Restrepo, a 28-year-old reporter and newscaster for KMEX-TV, who was covering the "riot" with Salazar that afternoon, and who had gone with him into the Silver Dollar Cafe "to take a leak and drink a quick beer before he went back to the station to put the story together." Restrepo's testimony was solid enough on its own to cast a filthy shadow on the original police version, but when he produced two *more* eyewitnesses who told exactly the same story, the sheriff abandoned all hope and sent his scriptwriters back to the sty.

Guillermo Restrepo is well known in East L.A.—a familiar figure to every Chicano who owns a TV set. Restrepo is the out-front public face of KMEX-TV news . . . and Ruben Salazar, until August 29, 1970, was the man behind the news—the editor.

They worked well together, and on that Saturday when the Chicano "peace rally" turned into a Watts-style street riot, both Salazar and Restrepo decided that it might be wise if Restrepo—a native Columbian—brought two of his friends (also Columbians) to help out as spotters and de facto bodyguards.

Their names were Gustavo Garcia, age 30, and Hector Fabio Franco, also 30. Both men appear in a photograph (taken seconds before Salazar was killed) of a sheriff's deputy pointing a shotgun at the front door of the Silver Dollar Cafe. Garcia is the man right in front of the gun. When the picture was taken he had just asked the cop what was going on, and the cop had just told him to get back inside the bar if he didn't want to be shot.

The sheriff's office was not aware of this photo until three days after it was taken—along with a dozen others—by two *more* eyewitnesses, who also happened to be editors of *La Raza,* a militant Chicano newspaper that calls itself "the voice of the East L.A. barrio." (Actually, it is one of several: The Brown Berets publish a monthly tabloid called *La Causa.* The National La Raza Law Students' Association has its own monthly—*Justicia O!* The Socialist Workers Party covers the barrio with *The Militant* and the East L.A. Welfare Rights Organization has its own tabloid—*La Causa de los Pobres.* There is also *Con Safos*—a quarterly review of Chicano Art and Literature.)

The photographs were taken by Raul Ruiz, a 28-year-old teacher of Latin American studies at San Fernando Valley State College. Ruiz was on assignment for *La Raza* that day when the rally turned into a street war with the police. He and Joe Razo—a 33-year-old law student with an M.A. in psychology—were following the action along Whittier Boulevard when they noticed a task force of sheriff's deputies preparing to assault the Silver Dollar Cafe.

Their accounts of what happened there—along with Ruiz's photos—were published in *La Raza* three days after the sheriff's office said Salazar had been killed a mile away in Laguna Park, by snipers and/or "errant gunfire."

The *La Raza* spread was a bombshell. The photos weren't much individually, but together—along with Ruiz/Razo testimony—they showed that the cops were still lying when they came up with their second (revised) version of the Salazar killing.

It also verified the Restrepo-Garcia-Franco testimony, which had already shot down the original police version by establishing, beyond any doubt, that Ruben Salazar had been killed, by a deputy sheriff, in the Silver Dollar Cafe. They were certain of *that,* but no more. They were puzzled, they said, when the cops appeared with guns and began threatening them. But they decided to leave anyway—by the back door, since the cops wouldn't let anybody out of the front—and that was when the shooting started, less than 30·seconds after Garcia was photographed in front of that shotgun barrel on the sidewalk.

The weakness in the Restrepo-Garcia-Franco testimony was so obvious that not even the cops could miss it. They knew nothing beyond what had happened *inside* the Silver Dollar at the time of Salazar's death. There was no way they could have known what was happening *outside,* or *why* the cops started shooting.

The explanation came almost instantly from the sheriff's office—once again from Lt. Hamilton. The police had received an "anonymous report," he said, that "a man with a gun" was inside the Silver Dollar Cafe. This was the extent of their "probable cause," their reason for doing what they did. These actions, according to Hamilton, consisted of "sending several deputies" to deal with the problem . . . and they did so by stationing themselves in front of the Silver Dollar and issuing "a loud warning" with a bullhorn calling all those inside to come outside with their hands above their heads.

There was no response, Hamilton said, so a deputy then fired two tear gas projectiles into the bar through the front door. At this point two men and a woman fled out the back and one of the men was relieved by waiting deputies of a 7.65 caliber pistol. He was not arrested—not even detained—and at that point a deputy fired two more tear gas projectiles through the front door of the place.

Again there was no response, and after a 15-minute wait one of the braver deputies crept up and skillfully slammed the front door—*without entering,* Hamilton added. The only person who actually entered the bar, according to the police version, was the owner, Pete Hernandez, who showed up about half an hour after the shooting and asked if he could go inside and get his rifle.

Why not? said the cops, so Hernandez went in the *back door* and got his rifle out of the rear storeroom—about 50 feet away from where Ruben Salazar's body lay in a fog of rancid CS gas.

Then, for the next two hours, some two dozen sheriff's

deputies cordoned off the street in front of the Silver Dollar's front door. This naturally attracted a crowd of curious Chicanos, not all of them friendly—and one, an 18-year-old girl, was shot in the leg with the same kind of tear gas bazooka that had blown Ruben Salazar's head apart.

This is a fascinating tale . . . and perhaps the most interesting thing about it is that it makes no sense at all, not even to a person willing to accept it as the absolute truth. But who could possibly believe it? Here, in the middle of a terrible riot in a hostile ghetto with a Chicano population of more than a million, the Los Angeles sheriff's department had put every available man on the streets in a vain attempt to control the mass looting and arson by angry mobs . . . but somehow, with the riots still running in high gear, at least a dozen deputies from the elite Special Enforcement Bureau (read TAC Squad) are instantly available in response to an "anonymous report" that "a man with a gun" is holed up, for some reason, in an otherwise quiet cafe more than ten blocks away from the vortex of the actual rioting.

They swoop down on the place and confront several men trying to leave. They threaten to kill these men—but make no attempt to either arrest or search them—and force them all back inside. Then they use a bullhorn to warn everybody inside to come out with their hands up. And then, almost instantly after giving the warning, they fire—through the open front door of the place and from a distance of no more than 10 feet—two highpowered tear gas projectiles designed "for use against barricaded criminals" and capable of piercing a one-inch pine board at 300 feet.

Then, when a man carrying an automatic pistol tries to flee out the back door, they take his gun and tell him to get lost. Finally, after firing two more gas bombs through the front door, they seal the place up—without even entering it—and stand around outside for the next two hours, blocking a main boulevard and attracting a large crowd. After two hours of this madness, they "hear a rumor"—again from an anonymous source—that there might be an injured man inside the bar they sealed off two hours ago. So they "break down the door" and find the body of an eminent journalist—"the only Chicano in East L.A.," according to Acosta, "that the cops were really afraid of."

Incredible as it seems, the sheriff decided to stick with this story—despite a growing body of eyewitness accounts that contradict the police version of "probable cause." The police say they went to the Silver Dollar Cafe to arrest that "man with a gun." But eight days after the killing they were still trying to locate the source of this fatal tip.

Two weeks later at the coroner's inquest, the sheriff's key witness on this critical point mysteriously disappeared. He was a 50-year-old man named Manuel Lopez who claimed all credit for the tip with his tale of having seen two armed men—one with a revolver and one carrying a rifle in the port arms position—go into the Silver Dollar shortly before Salazar was killed. Lopez quickly "motioned to" the sheriff's officers stationed nearby, he said, and they responded by parking a patrol car directly across the six-lane boulevard from the Silver Dollar's front door. Then using a loud bullhorn, the deputies gave two distinct warnings for everybody in the bar to "throw out their weapons and come out with their hands over their heads."

Then, after a five or ten-minute wait, Lopez said, three rounds of tear gas were fired at the bar, with one projectile glancing off the front doorway and two whooshing through a black curtain that was hanging a couple of feet back from the open doorway. It was too dark to see what was happening inside the bar, Lopez added.

By his own admission at the inquest, Lopez' behavior on the afternoon of Saturday, August 29th, was somewhat singular. When the riot broke out and mobs began looting and burning, Mr. Lopez took off his shirt, donned a fluorescent red hunting vest and stationed himself in the middle of Whittier Boulevard as a volunteer cop. He played the role with such zeal and fanatic energy that by nightfall he found himself famous. At the height of the violence he was seen dragging a bus bench into the middle of the boulevard in order to block all traffic and divert it off to side streets. He was also seen herding bystanders away from a burning furniture store . . . and later, when the riot-action seemed over, he was observed directing a group of sheriff's deputies toward the Silver Dollar Cafe.

Indeed, there was no arguing with his claim two weeks later that he had been right in the middle of things. His testimony at the inquest sounded perfectly logical and so finely informed that it was hard to understand how such a prominent extroverted witness could possibly have escaped being quoted—or at least mentioned—by the dozens of newsmen, investigators and assorted tipsters with access to the Salazar story. Lopez' name had not even been mentioned by the sheriff's office, which could have saved itself a lot of unnecessary public grief by even *hinting* that they had a witness as valuable as Manuel Lopez. They had not been reluctant to display their other two "friendly" witnesses—neither of whom had seen any "men with guns," but they both backed the Lopez version of the actual shooting sequence. Or at least they backed it until the cops produced Lopez. Then the other two witnesses refused to testify at the Coroner's inquest and one of them admitted that his real name was David Ross Ricci, although the police had introduced him originally as "Rick Ward."

The Salazar inquest rumbled on for 16 days, attracting large crowds and live TV coverage from start to finish. (In a rare demonstration of non-profit unity, all seven local TV stations formed a combine of sorts, assigning the coverage on a rotating basis, so that each day's proceedings appeared on a different channel.) The L.A. *Times* coverage—by Paul Houston and Dave Smith—was so complete and often so rife with personal intensity that the collected Smith/Houston file reads like a finely detailed non-fiction novel. Read separately, the articles are merely good journalism. But as a document, arranged chronologically, the file is more than the sum of its parts. The main theme seems to emerge almost reluctantly, as both reporters are driven to the obvious conclusion that

330

the sheriff, along with his deputies and all his official allies, have been *lying* all along. This is never actually stated, but the evidence is overwhelming.

A coroner's inquest is not a trial. Its purpose is to determine the circumstances surrounding a person's death—not who might have killed him, or why. If the circumstances indicate foul play, the next step is up to the D.A. In California a coroner's jury can reach only two possible verdicts: That the death was "accidental," or that it was "at the hands of another." And in the Salazar case, the sheriff and his allies *needed* a verdict of "accidental." Anything else would leave the case open—not only to the possibility of a murder or manslaughter trial for the deputy, Tom Wilson, who finally admitted firing the death weapon; but also to the threat of a million-dollar negligence lawsuit against the County by Salazar's widow.

The verdict finally hinged on whether or not the jury could believe Wilson's testimony that he fired into the Silver Dollar—at the *ceiling*—in order to ricochet a tear gas shell into the rear of the bar and force the armed stranger inside to come out the front door. But somehow Ruben Salazar had managed to get his head in the way of that carefully aimed shell. Wilson had never been able to figure out, he said, what went wrong.

Nor could he figure out how Raul Ruiz had managed to "doctor" those photographs that made it look like he and at least one other deputy were aiming their weapons straight into the Silver Dollar, pointing them directly at people's heads. Ruiz had no trouble explaining it. His testimony at the inquest was no different than the story he had told me just a few days after the murder. And when the inquest was over there was nothing in the 2025 pages of testimony—from 61 witnesses and 204 exhibits—to cast any serious doubt on the "Chicano Eyewitness Report" that Ruiz wrote for *La Raza* when the sheriff was still maintaining that Salazar had been killed by "errant gunfire" during the violence at Laguna Park.

The inquest ended with a split verdict. Smith's lead paragraph in the October 6th *Times* read like an obituary: "Monday the inquest into the death of newsman Ruben

331

Salazar ended. The 16-day inquiry, by far the longest and costliest such affair in county history, concluded with a verdict that confuses many, satisfies few and means little. The coroner's jury came up with two verdicts: death was 'at the hands of another person' (four jurors) and death was by 'accident' (three jurors). Thus, inquests might appear to be a waste of time."

A week later, District Attorney Evelle Younger—a staunch Law & Order man—announced that he had reviewed the case and decided that "no criminal charge is justified," despite the unsettling fact two of the three jurors who had voted for the "death by accident" verdict were now saying they had made a mistake.

But by that time nobody really gave a damn. The Chicano community had lost faith in the inquest about midway through the second day, and all the rest of the testimony only reinforced their anger at what most considered an evil whitewash. When the D.A. announced that no charges would be filed against Wilson, several of the more moderate Chicano spokesmen called for a federal investigation. The militants called for an uprising. And the cops said nothing at all.

There was one crucial question, however, that the inquest settled beyond any reasonable doubt. Ruben Salazar couldn't possibly have been the victim of a conscious, high-level cop conspiracy to get rid of him by staging an "accidental death." The incredible tale of half-mad stupidity and dangerous incompetence on every level of the law enforcement establishment was perhaps the most valuable thing to come out of the inquest. Nobody who heard that testimony could believe that the Los Angeles County Sheriff's department is capable of pulling off a delicate job like killing a newsman *on purpose*. Their handling of the Salazar case—from the day of his death all the way to the end of the inquest—raised serious doubts about the wisdom of allowing cops to walk around loose on the street. A geek who can't hit a 20 foot wide ceiling is not what you need, these days, to pull off a nice clean first-degree murder.

But premeditation is only necessary to a charge of *first*

332

degree murder. The Salazar killing was a second-degree job. In the terms of Section 187 of the California Penal Code and in the political context of East Los Angeles in 1970, Ruben Salazar was killed "unlawfully" and "with malice aforethought." These are treacherous concepts, and no doubt there are courts in this country where it might be argued successfully that a cop has a "lawful" right to fire a deadly tear gas bazooka point-blank into a crowd of innocent people on the basis of some unfounded suspicion that one of them *might* be armed. It might also be argued that this kind of crazed and murderous assault can be accomplished without "malice aforethought."

Maybe so. Maybe Ruben Salazar's death can be legally dismissed as a "police accident," or as the result of "official negligence." Most middle-class, white-dominated juries would probably accept the idea. Why, after all, would a clean-cut young police officer deliberately kill an innocent bystander? Not even Ruben Salazar—ten seconds before his death—could believe that he was about to have his head blown off by a cop for no reason at all. When Gustavo Garcia warned him that the cops outside were about to shoot, Salazar said, "That's impossible; we're not doing anything." Then he stood up and caught a tear gas bomb in his left temple.

The malignant reality of Ruben Salazar's death is that he was murdered by angry cops for no reason at all— and that the L.A. Sheriff's department was and still is prepared to defend that murder on grounds that it was entirely justified. Salazar was killed, they say, because he happened to be in a bar where police thought there was also a "man with a gun." They gave him a chance, they say, by means of a bullhorn warning . . . and when he didn't come out with his hands up, they had no choice but to fire a tear gas bazooka into the bar . . . and his head got in the way. Tough luck. But what was he doing in that place, anyway? Lounging around a noisy Chicano bar in the middle of a communist riot?

What the cops are saying is that Salazar got what he deserved—for a lot of reasons, but mainly because he happened to be in their way when they had to do their duty. His death was unfortunate, but if they had to do it all over again they wouldn't change a note.

This is the point they want to make. It is a local variation on the standard Mitchell-Agnew theme; Don't fuck around, boy—and if you want to hang around with people who do, don't be surprised when the bill comes due—whistling in through the curtains of some darkened barroom on a sunny afternoon when the cops decide to make an example of somebody.

The night before I left town I stopped by Acosta's place with Guillermo Restrepo. I had been there earlier, but the air was extremely heavy. As always, on stories like this, some of the troops were getting nervous about The Stranger Hanging Around. I was standing in the kitchen watching Frank put some tacos together and wondering when he was going to start waving the butcher knife in my face and yelling about the time I maced him on my porch in Colorado (that had been six months earlier, at the end of a very long night during which we had all consumed a large quantity of cactus products; and when he started waving a hatchet around I'd figured Mace was the only answer . . . which turned him to jelly for about 45 minutes, and when he finally came around he said, "If I ever see you in East Los Angeles, man, you're gonna wish you never heard the word 'Mace,' because I'm gonna carve it all over your fuckin body.")

So I was not entirely at ease watching Frank chop hamburger on a meat block in the middle of East L.A. He hadn't mentioned the Mace, not yet, but I knew we would get to it sooner or later . . . and I'm sure we would have, except that suddenly out in the living room some geek was screaming: "What the hell is this goddamn gabacho pig writer doing here? Are we fuckin *crazy* to be letting him hear all this shit? Jesus, he's heard enough to put every one of us away for five years!"

Longer than that, I thought. And at that point I stopped worrying about Frank. A firestorm was brewing in the main room—between me and the door—so I decided it was about time to drift around the corner and meet Restrepo at the Carioca. Frank gave me a big smile as I left.

Several hours later we came back. Guillermo wanted
to talk to Oscar about putting pressure on the KMEX-TV
management to keep him (Restrepo) on the air. "They
want to get *rid* of me," he explained. "They started the
pressure the day after Ruben was killed—the next fuckin
day!"

We were sitting on the floor in the living room. Outside, overhead, the police helicopter was looping around
in the sky above Whittier Boulevard, sweeping the neighborhood with a giant searchlight beam that revealed nothing—and served no purpose except to drive the Chicanos
below into a seething rage. "Those sons of bitches!"
Acosta muttered. *"Look* at that goddamn thing!" We had
all gone out in the yard to stare up at the monster. There
was no way to ignore it. The noise was bad enough, but
the probing searchlight was such an obvious, outrageous
harassment that it was hard to understand how even a
cop could explain it away as anything but deliberate
mockery and provocation.

"Now *tell* me," said Acosta. *"Why* are they doing a
thing like this? Why? You think they don't *know* what
effect it has on us?"

"They know," said Restrepo. He lit a cigarette as we
went back inside. "Listen," he said, "I get about fifteen
telephone calls every day from people who want to tell
stories about what the police have done to them—*terrible*
stories. I've been hearing them for a year and a half,
every goddamn day—and the funny thing is, I never used
to believe these people. Not completely. I didn't think
they were *lying,* just exaggerating." He paused, glancing

335

around the room, but nobody spoke. Restrepo is not entirely trusted in these quarters; he is part of the establishment—like his friend, Ruben Salazar, who bridged that gap the hard way.

"But ever since Ruben," Restrepo continued, "I *believe* these stories. They're true! I realize that, now—but what can I do?" He shrugged, nervously aware that he was talking to people who had made that discovery a long time ago. "Just the other night," he said. "I got a call from a man who said the cops killed his cousin in the yail. He was a homosexual, a young Chicano, nobody political —and the police report said he hung himself in his cell. Suicide. So I checked it out. And, man, it made me sick. This guy's body was *all bruises,* black and blue marks all over him—and right across his forehead he had 16 fresh stitches.

"The police report said he tried to escape so they had to dominate him. They got him sewed up at the hospital, but when they took him to yail, the warden or yailer or whatever they call the bastard wouldn't *accept* him, because he was bleeding so bad. So they took him back to the hospital and got a doctor to sign some paper saying he was OK to be put in the yail. But they had to *carry* him. And the next day they took a picture of him hanging from the end of the top bunk with his own shirt tied around his neck.

"You *believe* that? Not me. But you tell me—what can I *do?* Where do I look for the truth? Who can I ask? The sheriff? Goddamn, I can't go on the air with a story about how the cops killed a guy in the yail unless I *know* something for proof! Jesus Christ, we all *know.* But just to know is not enough. You understand that? You see why I never made that story on TV?"

Acosta nodded. As a lawyer, he understood perfectly that evidence is *necessary*—on the air and in print, as well as in the courtroom. But Frank was not convinced. He was sipping from a quart of sweet Key Largo wine, and in fact he didn't even know who Restrepo was. "Sorry, man," he'd said earlier. "But I don't watch the news on TV."

Acosta winced. *He* watches and reads *everything.* But most of the people around him think The News—on the

TV or radio or newspapers or wherever—is just another rotten gabacho trick. Just another bad shuck, like the others. "The news," to them, is pure propaganda—paid for by the advertisers. "Who pays the bill for that bullshit?" they ask. "Who's behind it?"

Who indeed? Both sides seem convinced that the "real enemy" is a vicious conspiracy of some kind. The Anglo power structure keeps telling itself that "the Mexican problem" is really the work of a small organization of well-trained Cómmunist agitators, working 25 hours a day to transform East L.A. into a wasteland of constant violence—mobs of drug-crazed Chicanos prowling the streets at all times, terrorizing the merchants, hurling firebombs into banks, looting stores, sacking offices and massing now and then, armed with Chinese sten pistols for all-out assaults on the local sheriff's fortress.

A year ago this grim vision would have been a bad joke, the crude ravings of some paranoid hysterical Bircher. But things are different now; the mood of the barrio is changing so fast that not even the most militant of the young Chicano activists claim to know what's really happening. The only thing everybody agrees on is that the mood is getting ugly, the level of tension is still escalating. The *direction* of the drift is obvious. Even Gov. Reagan is worried about it. He recently named Danny Villanueva, onetime kicking specialist for the Los Angeles Rams and now general manager of KMEX-TV, as the Governor's personal ambassador to the whole Chicano community. But, as usual, Reagan's solution is part of the problem. Villanueva is overwhelmingly despised by the very people Reagan says he's "trying to reach." He is the classic *vendido*. "Let's face it," says a Chicano journalist not usually identified with the militants, "Danny is a goddamn pig. Ruben Salazar told me that. You know KMEX used to be a good news station for Chicanos. Ruben was the one who did that, and Danny was afraid to interfere. But within 24 hours after Ruben was murdered, Villanueva started tearing up the news department. He wouldn't even let Restrepo show films of the cops gassing people in Laguna Park, the day after Ruben died!

Now he's trying to get rid of Restrepo, cut the balls off the news and turn KMEX-TV back into a *safe* Tio Taco station. Shit! And he's getting away with it."

The total castration of KMEX-TV would be a crippling blow to the Movement. A major media voice can be an invaluable mobilizing tool, particularly in the vast urban sprawl of Los Angeles. All it takes is a sympathetic news director with enough leverage and personal integrity to deal with the news on his own terms. The man who hired Ruben Salazar, former station director Joe Rank, considered him valuable enough to out-bid the blue-chip *Los Angeles Times* for the services of one of that paper's ranking stars—so nobody argued when Salazar demanded absolute independence for his KMEX news operation. But with Salazar dead, the station's Anglo ownership moved swiftly to regain control of the leaderless news operation.

Guillermo Restrepo, Salazar's heir apparent, suddenly discovered that he had no leverage at all. He was muscled into a straight newscaster's role. He was no longer free to investigate any story that he felt was important. . . . If the Chicano Moratorium Committee called a press conference to explain why they were organizing a mass rally against "police brutality," for instance, Restrepo had to get permission to cover it. And Chicano activists soon learned that a two-minute news feature on KMEX was crucial to the success of a mass rally, because TV was the only way to reach a mass Chicano audience in a hurry. And no other TV station in L.A. was interested in any kind of Chicano news except riots.

"Losing Ruben was a goddamn disaster for the Movement," Acosta said recently. "He wasn't really *with* us, but at least he was interested. Hell, the truth is I never really liked the guy. But he was the only journalist in L.A. with real influence who would come to a press conference in the barrio. That's the truth. Hell, the only way we can get those bastards to listen to us is by renting a fancy hotel lounge over there in West Hollywood or some bullshit place like that—where *they* can feel comfortable —and hold our press conference there. With free coffee and snacks for the press. But even then, about half the shitheads won't come unless we serve free booze, too. Shit! Do you know what that *costs?*"

This was the tone of our conversation that night when Guillermo and I went over to Oscar's pad for a beer and some talk about politics. The place was unnaturally quiet. No music, no grass, no bad-mouth *bato loco* types hunkered down on the pallets in the front room. It was the first time I'd seen the place when it didn't look like a staging area for some kind of hellish confrontation that might erupt at any moment.

But tonight it was deadly quiet. The only interruption was a sudden pounding on the door and voices shouting: "Hey, man, open up. I got some *brothers* with me!" Rudy hurried to the door and peered out through the tiny eye-window. Then he stepped back and shook his head emphatically. "It's some guys from the project," he told Oscar. "I know them, but they're all fucked up."

"God *damn* it," Acosta muttered. "That's the last thing I need tonight. Get rid of them. Tell them I have to be in court tomorrow. Jesus! I *have* to get some sleep!"

Rudy and Frank went outside to deal with the brothers. Oscar and Guillermo went back to politics—while I listened, sensing a downhill drift on all fronts. *Nothing* was going right. The jury was still out on Corkey's case, and Acosta was not optimistic. He was also expecting a decision on his Grand Jury challenge in the "Biltmore Six" case. "We'll probably lose that one, too," he said. "The bastards think they have us on the run now; they think we're demoralized—so they'll keep the pressure on, keep pushing." He shrugged. "And maybe they're right. Shit. I'm tired of arguing with them. How long do they expect me to keep coming down to their goddamn courthouse and begging for justice? I'm *tired* of that shit. We're *all* tired." He shook his head slowly, then ripped the poptop out of a Budweiser that Rudy brought in from the kitchen. "This legal bullshit ain't makin it," he went on. "The way it looks now, I think we're just about finished with that game. You know at the noon recess today I had to keep a bunch of these goddamn *batos locos* from stomping the D.A. Christ! That would fuck me for good. They'll send me to the goddamn pen for hiring thugs to assault the prosecutor!" He shook his head again. "Frankly, I think the whole thing is out of control, but I know it's going to be heavy, I think maybe the real shit is about to come down."

There was no need to ask what he meant by "heavy shit." The barrio is already plagued by sporadic fire-bombings, explosions, shootings and minor violence of all kinds. But the cops see nothing "political" in these incidents. Just before I left town I talked on the phone with a lieutenant at the East L.A. sheriff's office. He was anxious to assure me that the area was totally pacified. "You have to remember," he said, "that this has always been a high-crime area. We have a lot of trouble with teen-age gangs, and it's getting worse. Now they're all running around with .22 rifles and handguns, looking for fights with each other. I guess you could say they're sort of like the Blackstone Rangers in Chicago, except that our gangs are younger."

"But they're not into politics like the black gangs in Chicago?" I asked.

"Are you kidding?" he replied. "The only political thing the Blackstone Rangers ever did was con somebody out of a federal grant for a lot of money."

I asked him about some of the stories I'd heard about bombings, etc. But he quickly dismissed them as rumors. Then, during the next half hour of random talking about things that had happened in the past few weeks, he mentioned one dynamiting and a building burned down at East Los Angeles College, and also the firebombing of a local *vendido* politician's real estate office. "But they hit the wrong guy," the Lt. said with a chuckle. "They bombed another realtor who happened to have the same name as the guy they were after."

"Que malo," I mumbled, lapsing into my own dialect. "But aside from all that, you people don't see real trouble brewing? What about these rallies that keep turning into riots?"

"It's always the same bunch of troublemakers," he

340

explained. "They take a crowd that's gathered for other reasons, and then they subvert it."

"But that last rally was called to protest *police brutality*," I said. "And then it turned into a riot. I saw the films—50 or 60 police cars lined up bumper to bumper on Whittier Boulevard, deputies firing shotguns into the crowd . . ."

"That was *necessary*," he replied. "That mob was out of control. They *attacked* us."

"I know," I said.

"And let me tell you something else," he went on. "That rally wasn't *really* about 'police brutality.' The guy who organized it, Rosalio Munoz, told me he was just using that slogan to get people out to the park."

"Well, you know how they are," I said. Then I asked him if he could give me the names of any Chicano leaders I should talk to if I decided to write an article about the scene in East L.A.

"Well, there's Congressman Roybal," he said. "And that real estate man I told you about . . ."

"The one who got fire-bombed?"

"Oh no," he replied. "The other guy—the one they *intended* to firebomb."

"OK," I said. "I'll write those names down. And I guess if I decide to look around the barrio you guys could help me out, right? Is it safe to walk around out there, with all these gangs running around shooting at each other?"

"No problem," he said. "We'll even let you ride around in a radio car with some of the officers."

I said that would be fine. What better way, after all, to get the inside story? Just spend a few days touring the barrio in a cop car. Particularly right now, with everything calm and peaceful.

"We see no evidence of any political tension," the Lt. had told me. "We have a great deal of community support." He chuckled. "And we also have a very active intelligence bureau."

"That's good," I said. "Well, I have to hang up now, or I'll miss my plane."

"Oh, then you've decided to do the story? When will you be in town?"

"I've been here for two weeks," I said. "My plane leaves in ten minutes."

"But I thought you said you were calling from San Francisco," he said.

"I did," I said. "But I was lying." (click)

It was definitely time to leave. The last loose end in the Salazar case had been knotted up that morning when the jury came back with a "guilty" verdict for Corky Gonzales. He was sentenced to "40 days and 40 nights" in the L.A. County jail for possession of a loaded revolver on the day of Salazar's death. "We'll appeal," said Acosta, "but for political purposes this case is finished. Nobody's worried about Corky surviving 40 days in jail. We wanted to confront the *gabacho* court system with a man the whole Chicano community knew was technically innocent, then let them draw their own conclusions about the verdict.

"Hell, we never denied that *somebody* had a loaded pistol in that truck. But it wasn't Corky. He wouldn't dare carry a goddamn gun around with him. He's a *leader*. He doesn't have to carry a gun for the same goddamn reason Nixon doesn't."

Acosta had not stressed that point in the courtroom, for fear of alarming the jury and inflaming the gringo press. Not to mention the cops. Why give them the same kind of flimsy excuse to shoot at Gonzales that they had already used to justify shooting Ruben Salazar?

Corky merely shrugged at the verdict. At 42, he has spent half his life gouging Justice out of The Man, and now he views the Anglo court system with a quiet sort of fatalistic humor that Acosta hasn't learned yet. But Oscar is getting there fast. The week of April Fools Day, 1971, was a colossal bummer for him; a series of bad jolts and setbacks that seemed to confirm all his worst suspicions.

Two days after Corky's conviction, Superior Court Judge Arthur Alarcon—a prominent Mexican-American jurist—rejected Acosta's carefully constructed motion to quash the "Biltmore Six" indictments because of "subconscious, institutional racism" in the Grand Jury system. This effort had taken almost a year of hard work, much of it done by Chicano law students who reacted to the verdict with a bitterness matching Acosta's.

Then, later that same week, the Los Angeles Board of Supervisors voted to use public funds to pay all legal expenses for several policemen recently indicted "for accidentally" killing two Mexican nationals—a case known in East L.A. as "the murder of the Sanchez brothers." It was a case of mistaken identity, the cops explained. They had somehow been given the wrong address of an apartment where they thought "two Mexican fugitives" were holed up, so they hammered on the door and shouted a warning to "come out of there with your hands over your head or we'll come in shooting." Nobody came out, so the cops went in shooting to kill.

But how could they have known that they'd attacked the wrong apartment? And how could they have known that neither one of the Sanchez brothers understood English? Even Mayor Sam Yorty and Police Chief Ed Davis admitted that the killings had been very unfortunate. But when the Federal D.A. brought charges against the cops, both Yorty and Davis were publicly outraged. They both called press conferences and went on the air to denounce the indictments—in language that strangely echoed the American Legion outcry when Lt. Calley was charged with murdering women and children at My Lai.

The Yorty/Davis tirades were so gross that a District Court judge finally issued a "gag order" to keep them quiet until the case comes to trial. But they had already said enough to whip the whole barrio into a rage at the idea that Chicano tax dollars might be used to defend some "mad dog cops" who frankly admitted killing two Mexican nationals. It sounded like a replay of the Salazar bullshit: same style, same excuse, same result—but this time with different names, and blood on a different floor. "They'll put me in jail if I won't pay taxes," said a young Chicano watching a soccer game at a local playground, "then they take my tax money to use it to defend some killer pig. Hell, what if they had come to my address by mistake? I'd be dead as hell right now."

There was a lot of talk in the barrio about "drawing

343

some pig blood for a change" if the Supervisors actually voted to use tax funds to defend the accused cops. A few people actually called city hall and mumbled anonymous threats in the name of the "Chicano Liberation Front." But the Supervisors hung tough. They voted on Thursday, and by noon the news was out: The city would pick up the tab.

At 5:15 PM on Thursday afternoon the Los Angeles City Hall was rocked by a dynamite blast. A bomb had been planted in one of the downstairs restrooms. Nobody was hurt, and the damage was officially described as "minor." About $5000 worth, they said—small potatoes, compared to the bomb that blew a wall out of the District Attorney's office last fall after Salazar died.

When I called the sheriff's office to ask about the explosion they said they couldn't talk about it. City Hall was out of their jurisdiction. But they were more than willing to talk when I asked if it was true that the bomb had been the work of the Chicano Liberation Front.

"Where'd you hear that?"

"From the City News Service."

"Yeah, it's true," he said. "Some woman called up and said it was done in memory of the Sanchez brothers, by the Chicano Liberation Front. We've heard about those guys. What do *you* know about them?"

"Nothing," I said. "That's why I called the sheriff. I thought your intelligence network might know something."

"Sure they do," he said quickly. "But all that information is confidential."

Mark and the Seven Wisemen: Everybody Needs Milking

Mark Spitz look-a-like contest. First prize: one sexy, petite, foxy chick, 23, intelligent, long golden hair. Enter now. Send photo and phone to . . .

> —Letter to an alternative newspaper,
> which as a matter of policy
> does not print sex ads.

by Tim Cahill

Following roughly in the footsteps of, and appealing to much the same audience as Tom Jones and Burt Reynolds; Mark Spitz—national hero—has become a symbol of the thrusting unattainable to millions of American women. The new, pelvic heartthrob, as it were.

Today he is seen on billboards, in milk commercials, and is involved in any number of deals which primarily involve the use of his name. His new coaches, upon whom he depends absolutely, are business managers and press agents who fear his widely noted tactlessness could endanger their percentage profits and who keep him from the media with the stubborn tenacity of men sitting on a gold mine. They know there is a goodly number of people who find it easy to ridicule Mark Spitz. In Hollywood, for instance, where the currently chic thing to do is to have a private screening of *Deep Throat* in your home, the hosts intersperse the reels with Spitz milk commercials in much the same way your local theater shows Porky Pig cartoons.

The majority of Americans, however, see Spitz as a

hero; a man roughly equal in patriotic stature to the astronauts. Nearly a third of a million Mark Spitz posters have been sold since September. They show a man on top of the world, smiling triumphantly. Friends from the old days remember the smile well, but they say that in the most recent photos, they detect a note of dark and puzzled brooding.

The posters, in which Mark wears a pair of brief competition trunks, sell well, both to women and to the gay community. In no other world sport is a man quite so naked, with the sole exception of Sumo wrestling. Sumo wrestlers, though, are less attractive than swimmers. They express—in the extreme—the objections some women have to athletes as a whole. They are too bulky, they are cruel, they sweat and they smell.

Swimmers, by contrast, are lean and supple. Their sport is gentle and as beautiful in its way as ballet. They are clean and they give off only the faintest odor of chlorine. To add to their appeal, they come from a desirable social caste: the WASPish upper middle class. For this reason swimming has been called a country club sport. It now costs between $800 and $1200 a year for a parent to send his child to meets where he encounters national class competition. There are entrance fees, transportation costs, and motels to pay for. Over a career spanning an average of ten years, this is a substantial investment.

There are absolutely no black swimmers of national caliber. Some coaches have actually tried to make the case that a black swimmer is less buoyant than a white, that he has an unfavorable bone-muscle density to lung capacity. Probably more to the point is the fact that there are no social and economic gains to be made in the sport. As soon as there are a thousand professional swimmers making a living in the water, this buoyant upper-middle-class sport will undoubtedly be integrated rapidly.

As it stands, a swimming career represents only financial sacrifice to an athlete's parents. It is a further and somewhat bewildering fact that swimmers, while they may be the best in the state or the country or the world, get about as much space on the sports' page as a good exciting Little League game. Reporters don't buddy up to

346

them and learn their names. At the University of Wisconsin, where I swam on an athletic grant-in-aid, we used to joke about what we considered the archetypal swimming-photo mention. It would be a dark shot of a lot of splashing water with an arm dangling out and a caption that read: "unidentified swimmer wins race."

For the athlete, with no hope of money and little chance for fame, workouts are mostly a matter of agony. In context then: It's six o'clock on a Monday morning and the first day of double workouts for the summer swim team. A hypothetical athlete is two miles through what seems like an endless four-mile grind. In this outdoor pool, in the early morning chill, steam rises from his churning body. His chest is knotted with pain—asphyxiating fatigue is the technical term—and his thighs and upper arms literally burn with exhaustion. Standing above, one can see that the blood is not carrying waste away from the overworked muscles quickly enough. The shoulder girdle and upper back are an unpleasant shade of blue.

"Hurt, pain, agony," are the words Mark Spitz' Indiana coach used to use to inspire his swimmers. (My coach would say, "Pain is the purifier" or, "There is no barrier.")

Those who concern themselves with questions of motivation have called swimming—this lonely and punishing pursuit—the sport of masochists. It may be more accurate to think of swimmers as ascetics, involved, perhaps unconsciously, in a religion of pure competition. In this faith, stopwatches become sacred objects, and they are greatly feared. Times are a measure of dedication and success. Today they are calibrated to the inarguable 1/100 of a second; and the fast ones—world records—are Goals, to be Peaked for, often over periods of ten years and more.

It is no coincidence that many athletes, having quit swimming, fall into severely disciplined religious lives. At least three people who swam with Mark Spitz have spent time in Krishna Consciousness temples.

Coaches are easily seen as priests; Zen masters of the twin demands of the sport which are technique and motivation. Mark Spitz had natural technique. George Haines, his Santa Clara coach said, "I don't think anyone taught Mark very much in terms of stroke."

347

What Spitz didn't have, and what he desperately needed, was a nebulous quality swimmers call "pysch." Out of the water he was nervous and unsure of himself. He borrowed strength of character from seven men: his father and his three coaches then; his press agents and business managers now.

The most difficult period in his life was the four years previous to and culminating in the 1968 Olympics. At 14 he was already outswimming college competitors. It was clear he had the potential to become invulnerable, and the older men began to work on his weakest point. He was made to feel stupid and socially inept, where in actuality, he was merely blunt about his own abilities and monumentally tactless.

At the Mexico City Olympics, in '68, Spitz won only two gold medals, while some national magazines had predicted he could bring home as many as eight. Mark himself announced to the world that he would win six. It is doubtful that Spitz would have quit swimming at this point, but he probably wouldn't have had the triumph in Munich had he not gone to Indiana University where coach-psychologist Doc Counsilman had assembled the finest freshman team in the history of college swimming.

Among his peers at last, Mark tried hard to win acceptance. He allowed himself to be spit on night after night in a freshman team tradition. It was much like his fraternity initiation, where he allowed himself to be covered with honey, as well as molasses and eggs. He came up smiling, and slowly found himself admitted into a small circle of friends. Accepted at last, Spitz slowly worked on rebuilding his delicate psych.

* * *

Mark Spitz, like a piece of fine clay, has been pummeled and molded and shaped literally since birth. His father, Arnold Spitz, likes to think of himself as a "forceful individual" and an "agressive businessman." Arnold Spitz always knew that with his help, Mark could be the best swimmer in the world.

World-class swimmers now begin training about the age of five. Physiological tracts for coaches remind them that in swimming, "asphyxiating fatigue precedes all others and does not harm the organism." This means that a coach can work a child to exhaustion with a clear conscience; and it is worth noting that swimming is the only sport in which this is true.

Children, however, do not naturally work themselves to the fainting point. This is where the ten-and-under mother comes in. Two-time Olympian Brian Job, Mark's teammate at Santa Clara, explains the syndrome: "There's probably some psychological name for it, but your parents, through you, are fulfilling their dreams." Brian's mother, he says, pushed him from age five on, swimming him literally until he cried. "I don't really believe I had a free choice in the matter. She would say, 'If you want to quit, you can quit.' Of course, I knew what was lurking behind all that."

When he was 14, Brian's mother enrolled him in Santa Clara High School, where George Haines, the appointed 1968 Olympic coach, coached the campus team. Brian lived in an apartment, 2800 miles from his home in Ohio.

"Mark's situation was worse than mine," Brian says. "His father was right there all the time, pushing him, whereas my mother was the drive behind me and she pushed from afar. They had an article that said Mark's father said to him, 'There's eight guys in the pool: seven of them are bums.' OK, well, my mother never went that far, but if I didn't win, I was up shit creek. I'm serious. I'd just feel like shit. Have to listen to everything I did wrong. And I'm not really sure whether it's true or not, but from everything I've seen, Mark's father was even more so than my mother.

"The article presented his father in such a way that people took it as a put-down, but to me it showed his father in a way that you could really see what was behind Mark. Some people I know picked it up and ran to me and read the quote where his father says, 'Mark is beautiful because I made him.' And the guy said, 'If my father said that about me, I'd shoot him; I'd hit him; I'd do something.' But see, that's the way Mark's father was. His father and mother—the whole situation—I sort of believe was the ten-and-under mother syndrome."

When Mark was nine, his father turned his career over to Sherm Chavoor, owner and coach of the Arden Hills

Swim Club just north of Sacramento. When he was ten, his Hebrew classes conflicted with swimming practice, and Arnold Spitz yanked his son out of the classes, reportedly telling the Rabbi: "Even God likes a winner."

Chavoor, a short, blunt-spoken man in his middle 50s, who still likes to think of himself as a crew-cut flyboy from the Second War, is a curious combination of coach and businessman. A non-swimmer himself, he has taken nine athletes to the Olympics and the Arden Hills Club has accumulated a total of 16 gold medals. He owns Arden Hills, a swimming and tennis complex with a country club-like social facility. He drives a Mercedes 280 SL and describes Arden Hills as a "very valuable club." His original investment came with money that he made as a school administrator and he continued to build on the strength of "business investments and so forth."

"I don't know of any way of working youngsters other than working them real hard," Chavoor says. "I believe in stroke mechanics and technique, but I believe that's the incidental part." Mark left Chavoor at 12, but he was to return to him at 19 for summer workouts. It was during this time that Mark began to absorb much of Chavoor's economic philosophy.

When Mark was 14, his father quit a job he had held for 18 years so that the family could move to Santa Clara where Mark could train under George Haines. The appointed Olympic coach, a serious and aloof man who is simultaneously feared and respected by his swimmers, changed Mark from a distance freestyler to a butterflyer because "the US needs butterfliers in 1968." Many people say it was Haines who gave Mark his considerable stroke technique.

It was at Santa Clara that some nationally known swimmers, Olympic heroes themselves, began a four-year program of psych that was to devastate Spitz in the 1968 Olympics. Chavoor says: "They harassed him. They said he was a cocky kid, and they don't know Mark Spitz. Mark Spitz is not cocky. He's a nice boy. He's timid."

Haines says: "He talked a little too much, but so did some of the other kids. He got a lot of his talking ability from his father. He was fairly cocky and a lot of the older boys didn't like the idea of being beaten by a young upstart. I think they were at fault, a lot of the older boys on the team, for him not swimming well in the 1968 Olympics."

One of those older boys was Don Schollander, the blond golden boy of the '64 Olympics, who came home with four gold medals. "I think Mark looked up to Schollander," Haines says, "and if you ask Mark to this day who his hero was, I think he says Don Schollander. The only thing is, Don is a little older, and no older swimmer likes to have a youngster get right next to him every day in practice and have his sights on him. And this is what Mark did. They call it dragging on each other . . . or pacing them. Pressure built up on them."

Schollander was in college when Spitz started swimming with him in the summers. He was charming and articulate and had been tapped for Yale's prestigious Skull and Bones Society. In swimming circles he was known as a psych artist, a man who could destroy an opponent's concentration before a race with a seemingly innocent comment. One All-American swimmer said, "Schollander might say something like, 'Gee, how do you swim so fast with such a poor kick?' The gun would sound and the other guy would forget everything he wanted to do. All he would be able to think about would be, 'what's wrong with my kick?' "

With Mark Spitz, this particular psych amounted to a subtle and destructive four-year campaign. As Brian Job remembers it: "The first time I ever worked out with Schollander, Mark was in the next lane over. . . . The situation was where Mark would come up with a joke, but maybe it wouldn't be appropriate at the time, but it might be sort of funny and Schollander would just jump on his head. He would say, 'Oh Mark, that's the most disgusting thing I ever heard,' or something like that. But Schollander could say something and pull it off as being really funny. If Mark would say something similar, Schollander would come down on him. I'm sure that psychologically it stemmed from the fact that here was this kid who was going to be beating Schollander and Schollander knew it.

"It was a problem for Mark. Every time he'd open his mouth, he was made to look like a fool. If it were you,

you'd probably start saying things that are really just foolish and not appropriate, and completely lose any sense of humor or sense of what to say. Mark continued doing that for a long time. And people would remark, 'Oh God, what an ass.'

"I mean, no one on the team hated Mark. He really just wanted to be one of the guys. He was set apart because he was so amazingly good. And he just wanted to be one of the guys.

"I was just a young whatever myself, but I got in my 'Oh, Mark's.' He could come up with some incredibly bad stuff. . . . He really didn't have any sense for what was appropriate to say at the right time." Job believes Spitz has matured considerably over the past four years, though he says, "he still flips every now and then. I've seen a few quotes in the paper that I think were true because it sounds like the old Mark again."

(Job could have been referring to the comment Mark made in Munich in reply to a question about how he felt as a Jew in Germany. "I always liked the country," Mark said, "even though this lampshade is probably made out of one of my aunts.")

As Spitz continued to come up with more and more "incredibly bad stuff," his teammates began to treat him like a mental defective. They said he was stupid, and Mark, the moldable, believed them. "He wasn't that quick," Brian Job remembers, "but he really didn't have any confidence in himself." Job, an A-average engineering student at Stanford, makes a meaningful qualification. "I don't believe that intrinsically he's any less intelligent than anyone else."

In an effort to gain some sympathetic attention at Santa Clara, Mark made another tactical error. He developed a severe case of prima donna hypochondria, according to a former fellow swimmer. There were causeless earaches, nonexistent strained muscles, and a host of major and minor ailments. "Oh God," he would say, having read some article about what gives you pain when you swim, "God, I feel the lactic acid building up in my body." A few days later he would come up with another pain. "Oh God, I got a heart attack. My heart hurts, my heart hurts."

"Guys jumped on him really fast about that," Brian Job remembers. "They said, 'Mark, that's ridiculous.' But he kept it up and that was when people would unconsciously lose respect for him."

In 1967, Don Schollander told *Sports Illustrated:* "I don't associate with Mark. I generally hang around with guys my own age. Mark is immature in a lot of ways, but basically he's a pretty good guy." In 1968, a few months before the Olympics, the psych was coming down a little harder. Schollander, Mark's hero to this day, told the same magazine: "Mark is not very intelligent. His inane comments used to bother me. Now, they make me laugh."

At the Olympics, Mark was "eventually shot down by everyone," according to Job—who came out of nowhere that year to take a surprise bronze medal. "We spent nearly a month and a half at training camp and guys did some really crummy things. Like: Mark didn't want to take his gamma-globulin shots, and so . . . I wasn't the first, but I picked up the same thing. We were all coming out of the thing going, 'Ahh, ohh God,' and faking like it really hurt. And that scared the hell outta Mark. He's naturally tan and I've never seen him turn this white. He went to his room and got sick. . . . The guys were making fun of him because he passed out when they took blood."

Sherm Chavoor asserts that some of the harassment in '68 was specifically anti-Semitic. Brian Job was startled, nearly sickened, when Mark's own teammates, watching the live events on closed circuit TV, actually stood and cheered when Doug Russel beat Mark in his premier event, the 100-meter butterfly.

It is true that Mark was under a doctor's care for a cold, for diarrhea, and for altitude sickness (a good many athletes fell prey to Mexico City's 7500 feet), but his poor showing, many say, was really the result of a textbook case of psych. After the races, Spitz dropped into a severe state of depression. He was used to measuring his worth in wins and losses; he knew that God likes a winner and that he was one of the seven bums in an eight-lane pool. That fall, instead of going to Long Beach State College, as he had planned, he spent six months brooding, treading water in a sea of bad psych.

"When Mark came to Indiana," one coed remembers, "he was always going like this." She pulled her face into a puzzled frown, the kind of expression you might make if you woke up one morning and found that someone had taken everything you owned out of your room. "He had all this tension in his brow."

James "Doc" Counsilman, the Indiana swimming coach, has taken his team to over 80 straight dual meet victories and five straight NCAA titles. He met Mark in Fort Lauderdale, Florida, in December of 1968.

"Mark," he said, "I understand you're all set to go to Long Beach."

Spitz had given some indeterminate reply and Doc talked him into a visit to the Indiana facilities in Bloomington. As Counsilman remembers it, "he was interested in dentistry, but Long Beach didn't have a particularly good pre-dent course. Mark didn't think he was smart enough to go into a big university and study dentistry. When I told him that he was, he was very much flattered."

Doc may have laid it on a touch thick, however. When the announcement came that Mark had decided on Indiana, Counsilman was quoted nationally as saying, "The happiest day of my life will be when I say, 'Take a look in my mouth, Dr. Spitz.'"

In his first semester, spring of 1969, Counsilman gave Mark the Cattell Personality test, which showed that he was extremely tense. "The second year I gave the test," Counsilman says, "he scored perfect on being relaxed. He'd lost his tenseness and he stayed that way."

Doc teaches sports psychology at Indiana and he had a pretty good idea about what was bothering Mark. "He becomes part of a group more slowly than the average person. And that's because, I think, he's been hurt a fair amount. The older swimmers had the social know-how and intimidation factor to shoot down a little kid and knock him flat. I think this is what happened to Mark."

Counsilman held a team meeting in which he told his swimmers, "Mark Spitz is coming to school and I know he has a reputation, but I personally like him and I want you to give him a chance. You know how I feel about guys belittling, browbeating, and picking on an individual. I'm not going to have any of that crap on this team. Not with Mark Spitz, or anybody. I don't tolerate that."

At least one Santa Clara swimmer has the impression that the Indiana men were *ordered* to like Mark. "*Time* or somesuch magazine had this article about how they loved Mark at Indiana, which was utter bullshit. We talked to the same guys in that article and some of them were close friends and they would write back and say that they hated Mark more than we did. A friend of mine went up to two guys quoted in the article and said, 'No kidding, you guys really like Mark?' And they both look at each other and say in this robot voice, 'We . . . really . . . like . . . Mark.' They made little quote marks in the air with their fingers. I mean, it was so obvious what they were doing."

Once again, it was the older swimmers who resented Mark the most. And Spitz himself was sometimes characteristically blunt about himself. Once, sitting in a room with a freshman friend, he smiled a puzzled little smile and said, "I just can't believe how good I am."

The freshmen, Mark's peers, were more forgiving. They devised a formulation to explain the all-too-frequent Spitz *faux pas*. It was as if he was born without tact and common sense, they concluded, in the same way other people are born without arms or legs. He was something of a social paraplegic, no more to be hated, in their eyes, than, say, someone with a deforming birth defect.

The more they gave Mark a chance, the more relaxed and the less obnoxious he became. Tom Warburton, a college All-American presently living in New York and writing songs, talks about some of the ways people got to know Mark Spitz. "The freshman team at IU has a tradition" he says, "and every night after supper we'd go over to the pool and we would play rag-tag. Like I have to hit you with a knotted up towel and then you're it and you have to hit someone else. Only the way we played it, it was goob-tag, which is like rag-tag, only whoever is it, you spit on them. You're right there in the water and it sounds very disgusting, but we were all into it.

"If you throw the towel and miss, then you have to go get it and they'd all let it happen all over you. If there's

355

20 guys there and I throw it and miss and it lands behind them, I have to run through all of them and they just spit on you. And then, oh man, it feels like somebody opening up an egg on your head or your back. And Spitz—he wasn't very good at rag-tag. Being the fastest swimmer didn't help because you have to be good at throwing, you have to be a good tactician, and you have to run. It was a big thing: the whole thrill of victory, agony and defeat. And Spitz was 'it' more than anybody.

"I don't know. I always wondered if people were persecuting him. But he was always 'it,' and I laid some amazing goobers on his head.

"We got to know each other through that. And Mark was very good-natured and happy and he would laugh. I would say he was pretty much one of the guys."

Counsilman made sure there were tutors and that Mark studied. "If Mark likes you," Doc says, "he'll go out of his way to please you." One way he pleased Counsilman that spring and during the next three years was to come over to the coach's house every night and study. He would sit in the den, at Doc's desk. At the end of the semester, Mark had compiled a near-A average in solid academic courses such as chemistry and zoology. His self-estimation soared.

That summer Doc said: "The kids all like him; he's actually learned to laugh and smile."

Out of the water, Mark tended to talk about material things he wanted: A camera, a stereo, clothes and cars. He and some pre-med students planned to buy a plane together when they got established in their professions. One of the would-be plane buyers, now in medical school in Dallas, remembers that Mark had no burning ambition to fix the nation's teeth. "He liked to work with his hands, and he was good at it. He felt that he could make money at it. He always said he wanted his wife to have nice things."

Some of the freshmen fixed him up with girls in that first spring. Doc remembers that some coeds tended to idolize him, particularly the Jewish girls. They would stop over to his apartment and bring him cookies, which embarrassed him. He was sometimes attracted to a girl who was cool to him, and, remembering the other girls, he'd have difficulty approaching her. One girl he eventually dated remembers his opening line that got him nowhere. "Uh, would you like to come over to my apartment and wash my dishes," he asked her shyly.

"Mark was never the aggressor in any social situation," Counsilman says. "It was the girl who would be the aggressor. When he dated a girl, he would go with her pretty steady. The thing that amazed me was at the Olympics someone asked, 'How did you train so hard?' He said, 'I picked a girl at one end of the pool and one at the other and I'd go from one to the other.' I guess the image they want is Burt Reynolds and—at least when he was in school—nothing could be further from the truth. I mean, he was just the kind of guy you'd want your daughter to go out with. And he wasn't the type of guy your daughter would *want* to go out with.

"I should add that he really tries to please those he likes, and he'll make a good husband because he likes intimate relationships and he doesn't like a mass of people."

The last home swimming meet at the end of his career was declared "Mark Spitz Day," at Indiana. Sportswriters called it the "end of an era." He had graduated in three and a half years, taken difficult courses, and compiled a 2.7 grade point average. He had been elected co-captain of the team. He had friends. The University president attended the meet and shook his hand. He was awarded two standing ovations and, when he waved his goodbye to the crowd, those sitting closest to him saw that there were tears in his eyes.

* * *

Coming off the high psych of Indiana, Mark set records at the 1972 Olympic Trials in Chicago. He had returned to businessman-swimming coach Sherm Chavoor in the summer of 1970, and Chavoor made every effort to "work with Mark upstairs," which is a way of saying that he was always there with reservoirs of encouragement and strength.

Spitz was never a verbal psych artist like Schollander, but in Munich he psyched them all. One sportswriter,

357

comparing Munich to Mexico, said that Spitz was "four years older and ten years wiser."

The fact that he wore his hair slightly longer than everyone else—and that he grew a moustache—was one of the great psych coups of Olympic history. If swimming is indeed a kind of secular religion, then shaving your head for a big meet is a sign of dedication in the same way hairlessness is a sign of dedication to Krishna or Jesus. Swimmers are full of tales about people who blew the big one by a tenth of a second; slowed down, one is given to understand, by the drag of a thatch of hair a quarter inch too long.

If anyone thought he was going to psych Mark Spitz, he must have given up all hope when he realized the boy was actually going to swim with a moustache. It was as if the fastest runner in the 100-meter dash had decided to do the race with a sixpack of beer under one arm.

*   *   *

At the training camp, just before the swimmers left for Munich, one of the coaches asked Mark Spitz if he thought he might like to act in movies.

"I don't know," Mark said. "The people I've seen make a career in Hollywood haven't turned out too happy." "For Mark," an old friend says, "that was really a profound remark."

About the same time Sherm Chavoor was saying, "Mark will never go to dental school. He's going to win so many medals, he'll be a millionaire." Just after the Olympics, Chavoor put a more specific price tag on those medals. "I said, boy, he'll make five million dollars. I almost said seven million, one for each gold medal, but I said five, and I still think he can do it."

Immediately upon his return from Munich, Chavoor received a call from Norman Brokaw, a senior executive partner of the William Morris agency, the largest talent agency in the world. After the second world record, Brokaw, watching the tube, told himself, "That boy has charisma." Chavoor turned Mark's reins over to Brokaw.

There is a "Game Plan" for Mark's new career. As outlined by Brokaw in a *Life* magazine article, it called for an association with a major blue-chip company, followed by a massive merchandising campaign, and culminating in a series of televised specials and Hollywood films.

Brokaw and his associates convinced Mark to move to Los Angeles, specifically to Marina Del Rey, a luxury singles apartment complex on the Pacific Ocean. He's purchased a new wardrobe and a Lincoln Continental, and has taken up sailing. He will marry UCLA coed and part-time model Susan Weiner late this spring. The two were introduced, a spokesman said, by their fathers.

In the past few months, there have been charges that Spitz is led around Hollywood by his new managers like a steer with a ring in its nose. "Mark has been coached by coaches and they told him what to do to guide him," Sherm Chavoor points out. "He had his own ability to think, but right now he's going into a new field and . . . other people will do his thinking for him until he gets to a certain point where he feels confident."

Not all of Mark's former coaches are happy with his Hollywood adventure. "Mark Spitz is a very impressionable person," Doc Counsilman says. "You can talk him into almost anything. It's just amazing. You give him a suggestion and he'll think about it for a while and it becomes real."

Counsilman may have been thinking about the time the Indiana team was flying to an important meet and the swimmer sitting behind Mark saw that he was breaking out in measles. He surreptitiously got up and told Doc, who told the other swimmers to act as if Mark were perfectly healthy.

"Hey," Mark said, looking at his hand, "I think I've got measles."

"Nonsense," Doc told him. "Those are freckles."

Mark swam three winning races in the meet. On the plane back to Indiana, the team told Mark, yes, you have the measles. He spent the rest of the flight lying on the floor between the seats.

"Because Mark is so easily manipulated," Doc says, "you have to be careful to let him make his own decisions. He has to be careful that he is still his own boss and that he doesn't let his managers and other people tell him what to do."

359

Doc adds a familiar line: "The people I've seen make a career in Hollywood haven't turned out too happy."

But it was Sherm Chavoor and not Doc Counsilman who was at Mark's side during the Olympics, and it was Chavoor who pointed him toward Hollywood. "I think people who resent Mark for cashing in on his medals are stupid, jealous people," Chavoor asserts strongly. "I don't care if you are a millionaire five times over. Fine. More power to you. It helps our economy. You'll spend the money. Heck, any man has that prerogative in the United States, which is a fabulous country. He should make everything he can. It'll help our economy."

* * *

There is a sickly, sad syrup of deja vu that flows through the crevasses and fills the canyons of the Mark Spitz story. It is composed of the not coincidentally similar history of perhaps the greatest swimmer of modern times, the hero of the 1924 and 1928 Olympics, Johnny Weismuller. He was the prototype of the lean limbed, awshucks American hero. The story is that the writer Cyril Hume saw him working out in a Los Angeles health club. Hume took one look at the man's physique and told him, "We want you to play Tarzan."

Weismuller clinched the job with a two-word reply. "Me? Tarzan?" he said.

MGM picked up his contract and the rumor—a fairly well substantiated one—is that the studio felt an unattached beefcake star was preferable to a married one. They gave his wife $10,000 and suggested she blow town. Which she did.

Weismuller made it a habit never to read his contracts or check his books. He hired financial managers to do that. He played in 17 Tarzan films, married four more times, once to Latin sexpot Lupe Velez—"Johnny ees my beeg guy"—who, sometime after the divorce, did herself in with seconals in the time-honored Hollywood tradition.

In 1944, Johnny's agency, William Morris, closed a deal with Columbia studios. Johnny would play Jungle Jim. At the age of 45, he found himself battling evil witchdoctors, gorillas, rampaging rhinoceroses, giants and head hunters. In one of the last of the series, he was crowned King of the Pygmy Moon Men while, on an adjacent stage, Columbia was shooting Marlon Brando in *The Wild One*.

When the Jungle Jim episodes dribbled to a halt in the early Fifties, Weismuller mysteriously found himself nearly bankrupt. A restaurant owner sent two heavies out to his house to impound his Cadillac until he paid a $200 bill. A bill Weismuller never saw because he turned it over to his trusted manager, Bo Roos of Beverly Management Company. Weismuller's biographer, Narda Onyx, said that Johnny immediately made a phone call.

"Listen, Bo," he said, "what are you doing to me? I've made millions over the years. Where did the money disappear to? I haven't lived that high. You're my business manager . . . *you're* wealthy. Tell me, Bo, why is it I don't have a quarter?"

Roos delivered the kiss-off. "What do you want from me, Johnny? I'm a sick man! And you make me nervous. I'll talk to you tomorrow."

Tomorrow never came and presently Weismuller was seen on late night TV advertising Kevo-etts vitamins. He later endorsed Bakelite-Krene swimming pools but backed out of the deal when he discovered that they fell apart when filled with water. Later he lent his name to Weismuller Steel-Porcelain Pools, a better constructed pre-fab. He worked as a publicist for Big Boy hamburger franchises. Today he helps with the publicity for the Swimming Hall of Fame in Fort Lauderdale, Florida.

In 1968, he showed up at the Olympics. Mark Spitz and the sprinter Jerry Heidenreich were coming around one side of the pool when they saw a well-preserved older man with long black hair beckoning them. They knew who he was, but there was an unholy aura of failure about him and they walked by pretending not to notice. "Mark, Mark," he called, and his voice seemed high and scratchy to the Olympians.

"Mark, it's me . . . Johnny."

* * *

Stan Rosenfield is the man you talk to if you want to talk to Mark Spitz. I first contacted him shortly after Christmas of 1972, and he promised me an interview as soon as possible. Three months later I had still not talked to Spitz nor could Rosenfield give me an approximate date.

Rosenfield works for Mark's press agency, Jay Bernstein and Associates. He is a short, neat, dark-haired man who looks younger than his 34 years. He seems a little overwhelmed by his job, which apparently consists of telling most callers they can have interviews and then stalling them until they give up. Some of the people who call Rosenfield have been waiting long enough to get hostile.

"Bear in mind," Rosenfield says, "that we have had some 450 requests and we have to take them one at a time. Also Mark has been sick [with hepatitis] for nearly two months, and we have a backlog."

How many media people had talked to Mark since, say, Christmas? Rosenfield reminded me that Spitz has a very busy schedule, hesitated for a moment and came up with five or six names. An AP reporter had talked to him for a few minutes. There was a five-minute call to *Seventeen* magazine. "And we have had press conferences where as many as 75 representatives of the press have been present, so we certainly aren't hiding him."

There had been an in-depth piece in *Life* just after the Olympics. Aside from that, the reigning Spitz experts in the print field seem to be a *Newsweek* reporter who spent 15 minutes with Mark between tapings of the Bob Hope Show, and a woman writer from the *New York Times Magazine* who spent a somewhat longer time with Spitz at Jay Bernstein's home in Los Angeles. Both stories implied that Mark had been told not to talk to the press, that the press was being kept from him, and that his managers and agents seemed to exercise an unhealthy degree of control over the young hero.

"When we have a press conference, we call all the people who have requested interviews and . . . " Rosenfield hesitated. There had been at least two press conferences since I made my original request, and we both knew he had not bothered to contact me.

"How come you didn't call me?" I asked.

Rosenfield shrugged, smiled absently, and muttered something about not having *complete* control . . .

He seemed desperately anxious that my article not say what was perfectly obvious in the face of it: that he and Jay Bernstein and Associates were keeping the media at arm's length in much the same way a nervous father might lock his virgin daughter in the cellar.

* * *

Mark Spitz has been known to take bits and pieces of his personal style from the older men he is close to. Today he is close to Jay Bernstein, a bright, 35-year-old press agent with a large Sunset Strip office and some 40 employees. Bernstein has a roster of clients ranging from Susan Hayward and Milton Berle to Isaac Hayes and Bruce Dern. He is the publicist for the Miss America contest and the Ralston Purina TV specials, among others. A chauffeur drives his car, which is equipped with a telephone and a TV. His employees are equipped with electronic buzzers which they wear on their belts. When Jay buzzes, they stop whatever they are doing and call him. All this, Bernstein explains, saves time. He presented some credible examples. "Time is all you have to sell in this business," he said.

I knew that Norman Brokaw was handling Mark's career and I wondered if the fact that Brokaw's son, David, had recently been hired at Bernstein's had any connection with Jay's landing of Spitz, which must be the account of the year. Jay said that it did not. Seventy percent of his clients were William Morris clients. He'd had a healthy relationship with Morris for ten years. David had been hired as a publicist "six or eight months ago." Whether that was shortly before or shortly after Bernstein got the Spitz account, Jay didn't know. He allowed that this all "sounded bad," and assured me that no one had asked that question before. He said that someone related to someone from the Morris agency worked with Nat Lefkowitz, Mark's business manager. Jay implied that there was no connection in either case.

Did Bernstein, I wondered—shades of Johnny Weismuller—actually suggest to Mark that he not get engaged. Yes, he had done that, but it was before Mark ever met Susan Weiner. And that was only because fans are a very special thing. . . . Jay thought it sounded bad, the way he was wording it. Fans are fickle, and Bernstein, as a "commercial being" felt it would be best if Mark didn't mention women because the press tends to exaggerate these things. Now that Mark is engaged, he is very happy for him.

"People say I tell Mark what to do and I promise you, I do not," Bernstein said. For instance, as soon as he met Susan, "he began mentioning her name" all over the place in direct contradiction to Jay's advice.

He described Mark as "very warm, very bright."

* * *

Norman Brokaw, 45, is the key man in Mark Spitz's new career. He screens offers, makes deals, tries to protect Mark in terms of residuals, re-use, and the various intricacies of legal infighting. He is a short, soft-spoken man with a fatherly smile that is barely offset by a modish, dry-look hair trim. He greeted me cordially and asked if I had seen Mark on the television the night before.

In a previous phone conversation, he had suggested I watch the show, a Bob Hope special. The format was a sort of athletic Academy Awards ceremony where seven athletes were given $5000 apiece to turn over to their favorite charity. Mark was named male amateur of the year and athlete of the year. Flanked by Bob Hope and John Wayne, he donated his $10,000 to the new Mark Spitz Swim Center at the $100 million Cedar-Sinai Medical Center, which will be the largest medical facility west of the Mississippi when it is completed. Brokaw is on the board of directors at the new facility.

Over the phone, Brokaw had said, "You watch Bob Hope and you'll see the real Mark Spitz. He's just a superb human being. What more can I say? I'm not just saying this because he is my client. I said, 'Mark, they need money for this project,' and he said 'Norman, I'm going to raise funds for it.' And he did."

In his Beverly Hills office, Brokaw explained that Mark had made a lifetime commitment to the swim center. "One of the things you might want to know about Mark, and one of the reasons that I think he is one of the finest, most outstanding young men that I've ever met, and one of the brightest and most decent men I've ever known, has to do with a very touching thing that happened here. We get thousands of letters a week for Mark Spitz, but I remember one in particular. It was from a young boy and it said, 'Mark Spitz, I love you,' or something to that effect. An adult letter was attached to it. It was from the boy's mother and it said, 'Dear Mark, the attached letter is from my son who is retarded. He has never been able to speak and has never been able to swim. But ever since the Olympics, he is now able to say, 'Mark Spitz.' He has been taking swimming lessons and is no longer afraid of the water.'

"That sat well in our minds. And when we knew we were going to go ahead with the pool, I discussed it with Mark and we immediately committed him to a lifetime association with the Center.

"I think you should know that Mark considers himself very fortunate to accomplish what he did and he told me, 'Norman, I'd like to help others now.' So in addition to Cedar-Sinai, you will see within the next 90 days two or three other major commitments which will be slanted towards helping people all over the country. Help to people of all denominations, etc. Help for the health and welfare of as many as possible."

We talked about the press and Mark Spitz. There had been a rash of recent stories that called him "self-centered," or "insensitive," and once even "snake-cold and arrogant."

"The press likes to build up heroes and then tear them down," Brokaw explained. A buzzer on his desk sounded. "No, ask them to wait," he said into the phone. I learned later that it was Mark Spitz and Susan Weiner who were waiting.

It occurred to me that the sudden move to altruism, not a part of the original Spitz Game Plan, would certainly result in better press for Mark. However, I couldn't bring myself to quit believing that it was all a cynical plot to effect a shift in public opinion, though it would surely do just that.

"Mark is one of the finest, warmest, brightest people I've ever had the pleasure of working with," Brokaw was saying. "And I'm not just saying that because he's my client."

365

Aside from the charities, the Game Plan is proceeding apace. Mark has made a "lifetime association" with Schick Electric, Inc., the blue-chip company the plan called for. Merchandising was going well. Mark has signed a contract to help promote Spartan Pools and has told a press conference that he hoped his appointment would "make younger kids go to their mothers and fathers and say, 'Let's get a pool.'" He has a contract with a firm that manufactures swim fins, goggles and masks; and another contract with a major manufacturer of water games. There was a captioned picture book in the offing as well as a deal with a manufacturer of sporting apparel.

He has appeared on *The Bill Cosby Show* and *The Sonny and Cher Hour*. Plans call for a TV special, starring Mark Spitz and produced by David Wolper, which could be aired this fall. If Brokaw and Spitz decide on a suitable script, he may make a movie as early as the winter of 1973. There are plans for an animated Mark Spitz cartoon show for Saturday morning TV.

I had been in Bloomington, Indiana in late February, a month previous to my visit with Norman Brokaw, and there Doc Counsilman's son, James, told me that Mark called Doc and talked at length about Hollywood. He seemed depressed, and talked about the possibility of returning to Bloomington and going to dental school.

Norman Brokaw quickly set the record straight. "At the present time, Mark is not going back to dental school. In fact, just recently, in order to make room for someone on the waiting list, he informed the school that business plans would prevent him from going forward at this time. My own opinion is that it is doubtful that he will return to dental school."

Asked to describe the private Mark Spitz, Brokaw said, "I consider myself a good judge of people and I'm not making this statement just because I represent Mark Spitz, but I must truly say that he is one of the finest young men I've ever met. He's a warm human being, he's bright. I think he can be a success in anything he does."

Brokaw laid both hands flat on his desk in that signal that invariably means the interview is over. "I told you at the beginning that you might have a chance to meet Mark," he said. "You read where we keep him from the press and no one wants to talk about him. Well, you just walked in and got an appointment right away with me. And Mark is in the lobby right now."

Brokaw told me that I could say hello to Mark, but then I would have to leave. There was going to be a meeting, and of course, it would have to be a private one. I was somewhat stunned by the idea that Brokaw and I had been sitting there for several minutes talking about Mark Spitz while Mark Spitz sat in the lobby with nothing to do.

Brokaw brought them in and Mark was smiling. When he saw me, he stopped in his tracks, about two feet from the door. He wore a pair of artfully faded jeans and a red turtleneck sweater. Susan smiled contagiously. She wore a white sweater and slacks. Together they would not have looked out of place on any campus in the country, though they looked out of place in that office. Brokaw introduced us, and when my eyes met Mark's, he looked suddenly away, like a trapped animal. I stepped forward to shake his hand, and he literally flinched, finally taking my hand in a firm fraternity man's grip.

"I saw you on Bob Hope last night," I offered.

He stared at the floor.

"You got off one good line, I thought," I said.

He brightened instantly. "Which one was that?"

"The one where you pretended not to know who John Wayne was."

He smiled broadly—the poster smile—and in that moment, I found myself liking him immensely. "I know the one," he said. "Where I said, 'I can't remember your name.'"

"Yeah. Was that an ad lib?"

His eyes fell to the floor.

"Yes, that was an ad lib," Norman Brokaw said proudly.

I wondered how he knew. Susan continued to smile and Mark stared at the floor. "Well . . ." Brokaw said, and cleared his throat lightly. It was a polite signal for me to get my ass out of there.

* * *

On the plane back to San Francisco, I thought about the wise men in Mark's life. Arnold Spitz through Norman Brokaw. I thought about the specter of Johnny Weismuller that looms over the whole affair. I wondered if the next time Mark Spitz heard a high scratchy voice calling, "Mark, Mark, it's me, Johnny," he would stop. What would the two men talk about?

ON SET WITH 'THE GODFATHER':
Crime & Nostalgia

by Michael Zwerin

The law locks up the man or woman
Who steals the goose from off the
    common
But lets the greater villain loose
Who steals the common from the
    goose

—English proverb

Marlon Brando pulled his hair back into a tight pony-tail, grew a moustache with an eyebrow pencil, put powder on for pallor, stuffed toilet paper in his cheeks for jowls and . . . it was incredible . . . the imperious movement of the hands, eyes growing delicately from compassion to humor to murder and back again, his Sicilian manner with a cigar, the white shirt collar bent up and caught on his jacket just waiting for his favorite son Michael to smoothe back . . . one swell screen test. Instant God-father.

* * *

The taxi driver from the airport had arms like thighs and long white hair curling over his starched collar. He could be an unemployed stunt-man or maybe he played a good con in *Angels With Dirty Faces*. Anyway, he was mad: "Goddamn L.A. Yellow . . . first they rob the public of five million bucks and then what happens? They get rewarded with a fare increase. What a fuckin' system? Guy steals 75 bucks from a gas station and he gets three years, but if the heist is big enough they make you a judge or something."

Coming back to America—I live in London—is always an injection of energy, though too often negative. There's the violence, of course, but also a lot of that energy is greed. I always start hustling my "career" back here. Luxury items suddenly appear necessary. Survival level is too high. Everybody needs more toys.

Hollywood is even worse. Pools and limousines are staples, around movies even hippies require them. Having bread, or at least being near it, is an assumed goal. Whereas the Fabulous Furry Freak Brothers' philosophy is that dope will get you through times of no money better than money will get you through times of no dope, the requisite here is for both. Doesn't matter how you got the money, having it is enough. That's why there are so many good gangster movies.

Remember when crime didn't pay . . . when the bad man never got away? Jimmy Cagney, where are you? Pat O'Brien . . . we are in dire need of a blessing. Lenny Bruce said that if all politicians from the beginning were crooked, then there is no crooked. Well, once there were good bad guys and bad bad guys but the good guys were always just plain apple-pie good. Judge Hardy, for example, was *good*. Now we know that kindly old gentleman for what he is, Julius Hoffman, and in *The Godfather* there are no bad guys at all because organized crime is about power and power is shown for what it is—corruption—but if all power from the beginning corrupted then there is no corrupt.

Morality has become whatever we can get away with. On one hand you might say the new Hollywood ethic, where crime can pay, is more honest. The French heroin exporter in *The French Connection,* for example, would and does get away. One myth at least demystified. More likely though, it reflects the institutionalization of the ripoff.

In this scheme of things, who are you to say it's dishonest or unethical to review an unfinished film I snuck into. Are you kidding? Business is business.

Francis Ford Coppola's theory has been never to *ask* anybody if he can make a movie; he presents them with the fact. "This is a movie I'm going to make and if you're wise you'll get in on it." Hollywood can never resist something like that, they are afraid to be left out of something already going. At 32, Francis has a healthy gut, a full beard, his innocence and five pictures behind him. Plus an Oscar for the screenplay for *Patton*. And now *The Godfather*, the best screen adaptation of a best-seller I've ever seen. Whatever it takes to be a winner he's got it.

Francis once compared his career to that of Adolph Hitler: "The point I was trying to make was that all the young film students I knew who wanted to make films were just sitting up in the hills talking about it. While I went out into the Establishment—and I was very sharply criticized by my friends as being a total sellout. My allusion to Hitler was simply that, contrary to what a lot of people think, he wasn't a revolutionary who came down out of the hills and took the government over. He wormed his way into the government, became a part of it, and then used that to take it over. I was trying to say that it didn't matter that I became part of the Hindenburg Government, because I was going to make it on my own. The way to come to power is not always to challenge the Establishment, but first make a place in it and then double-cross them. Which is essentially what I've done."

Take *The Rain People*—a film about a housewife who runs away—he walked into Warner Brothers one Friday and said: "I'm going to Long Island on Monday and I'm going to start shooting a movie. I'm not going to tell you what it's about, or what the title is, or the script, because I haven't written the script yet." He left and shot. He's made films and he's making them.

Although he relates to clothes as a joke, drives a beat-up little Honda and uses his money for freedom, not slavery, he's got the toy syndrome pretty bad . . . a trombone, trumpet, harpsichord, a bass guitar, a tuba Fred Astaire laid on him after *Finian's Rainbow* ("I wish I had time to just stay at home and learn them all"), an Italian chestnut-cooker, an espresso machine with a gold eagle on top, a pool table, a zoetrope . . .

A zoetrope is an old circular drum with slits, and figures on the inside. When you spin the drum and look through the slits the figures move, like flipping the pages of those old big-little books. He named his production company after it, American Zoetrope . . . an expensive toy. When he moved to San Francisco and set it up this was to produce his own movies and free him from the Hollywood mill. Like Welles and De Sica, he works on commercial films for the money to invest on his own. And like them he adds quality those commercial films otherwise wouldn't have. He had directed *Finian's Rainbow* and wrote part of *Is Paris Burning* and then *Patton* and that would seem to be enough. What he wanted was to make personal films like *The Rain People,* but those who do not lust after money for its own sake generally have trouble amassing it and he was forced back to commodities.

The Godfather will cost $6½ million. Coppola has six percent of the action. Since $12 million in theater guarantees it already in, that percentage will buy some nice toys. But the trouble with people like Francis is they can't think in terms of commercialism even if that's all that's expected of them. They can't sell out even when they think they're doing it.

He wrote a three-inch-thick, 50-scene outline early on, a combination of his own prose and paste-ups from the book, copiously notated with exclamations, cautions and questions. Nobody required this; he just got involved. It led to writing the screenplay too. Which led to Marlon Brando. Paramount wanted no part of Brando . . . a trouble-maker, they said, too expensive and besides none of his pictures have made money in seven years. When Coppola insisted and insisted, they set what they considered impossible conditions: Brando must post a bond which would be forfeited if the picture went over budget because of him; he would receive much less than superstar salary, and he must make a screen test. Francis immediately agreed to all three. And then . . . holy shit! How do you ask Marlon Brando to take a screen test?

He called and they chatted. Brando was interested in playing Vito Corleone, in principle anyway. Let's have lunch, we'll talk about it. Great . . . Hey! I have an idea. Supposing I bring along a video camera or something and we'll play around a little . . . which turned out the very image of the Godfather.

372

It was hell for the six months' shooting in New York. Pressure from all over. The studio put a strict embargo on publicity because the press was too interested and the campaign peaking too early. All sorts of guys with hidden cameras and long lenses hovering around. And some of the extras, Francis noticed, were a bit too professional with their toy guns. Fortunately, Paramount had just made a killing on *Love Story* and was only nervous, rather than desperate, over its investment. But executives still hovered. Everybody had a suggestion or two. Francis is no Stanley Kubrick and he doesn't have the kind of leverage it takes to tell top executives to fuck off. Ironically, the easiest thing about shooting this picture was Brando, who was on time, creative and a total joy.

Francis tends to break out into some aria at any time. He's very Italian, got that operatic soul. He wrote the *Godfather* screenplay—in only three weeks—in a North Beach Italian coffee shop. Nino Rota was on the juke box. Rota writes music for Fellini . . . *La Strada, 8½, Giulietta, The Clowns* . . . and his simple fol-da-ra assumes the irony of the Berlin Theater Songs of Kurt Weill when composing for the Mafia (a word, by the way, never mentioned in the film).

Then some imaginative casting . . . Al Pacino (from *Panic in Needle Park)*—not a pretty-boy—as Michael Corleone, Bobby Duval as Tom Hagen, James Caan as Sonny, Sterling Hayden as the crooked cop McCloskey, Richard Conte as Barzini . . .

Conte had just finished dubbing . . . fast, businesslike, one-take. A guy I know, a technician on *The Godfather* —the guy who showed me Brando's test—took me into the Paramount lot with him and I'd been watching them dub all morning. Now it was Caan's turn. All morning he's been talking like a Brooklyn hood. Caan went cross-country with Coppola shooting *The Rain People* and, along with Bobby Duval, he's part of Francis' band of actors, kind of like John Wayne and Ben Johnson and those people were for John Ford. Caan and Francis had been playing a salty number: "Now listen . . ." Caan jammed a straight between his teeth. ". . . Ya remember dat scene when Brando's talkin' to Bobby . . . when Bobby looked to me and I went . . . [an elegant shrug]

. . . why'd ya cut dat out? All dat shit ya cut out 'cause ya got no taste. Five fuckin' yeahs I been tellin' him he got no taste. Ya figgah he'd learn, ya know. Excuse me. Let me study."

He studied the scrap of paper on which Francis had typed out some dialogue only that morning. This was to match his silent mouth on-screen to what it should be saying . . . no one was totally sure what that was and they were going by memory. The footage was run a few times and Caan missed some takes.

Francis let him work it out himself before his first instructions, *sotto voce:* "Jimmy, the thing is you're supposed to be very morose in this scene and I thought you should . . . well, be softer with it than . . . Hey! Can you let us hear this back with a filter?"

The boys in the control room said they could. First some blips and bleeps while the film ran backwards for 24 feet, then: "Hey kid. Where ya been? We been worried boutcha . . . " Not exactly filtered poetry but you can't always get what you want. These are professionals working at their craft and that's what professionals do . . . you're not a musician unless you're playing music, a writer writes every day or he isn't, an actor acts, a director directs . . . and if you can't do exactly what you like, you work with the best you can. . . . Love the one you're with, sort of thing.   Next, a kindly Italian actor who plays Bonasera the undertaker. He'd never been to a dubbing session before. It went slowly. His timing was poor and so was his English and he muffed lines. In the control room the engineers had plenty of time to show me, with some pride, their brand-new sophisticated computers . . . finds the frame immediately, no room for human error . . . banks and banks of buttons, dials, levers and knobs. They were straight-looking, professional and bored. After an almost perfect take, one of the engineers pointed out a not quite on-the-button "She . . . " The others looked over at him like he was crazy: "We're gonna be here till Christmas."

So it went . . . and went. Francis, having dubbed and looped all week, was past tired. He stretched out on a couch while they changed reels and lit a long Havana cigar. Indicating the big-time, union rule hard and software in the indirectly lit, carpeted studio, he moaned: "This is ridiculous. All I want to do is make personal movies."

They resumed. I wandered out looking for an open long-distance line. I found one and called a few friends back East. Then I found a Steinway grand and fooled around with some Monk for a while. It must have been more than an hour later . . . returning to the dubbing room, I passed a workman laboring under a big pile of reels: "Late day today," he said to his mate, "we're running *The Godfather*." He went into a projection room and on impulse I followed him, sat down and looked as official as possible. Soon three more guys came in, totally ignoring me. "Roll it," one of them shouted.

What we looked at was a fine cut without sound effects, not yet dubbed, one scene was missing, some were in black and white, it was not color-corrected and most of the music was provisional. But it was enough. The film lasts three hours but passed faster than most one-minute spots. This is a film, not a property, something to think about rather than pass some time with. Hollywood wanted only its usual rich shit and got ice cream, turned only by the slightly stale grade of the source.

The film is less romantic than the book, harder, and the women play smaller roles. In the visual medium, killers well-cast look like killers no matter how often and with what care they kiss their babies. It's set in the late Forties . . . all those wide-brimmed hats, zoot suits and beautiful old Lincoln Continentals . . . the nostalgia is heavy. The story is told cinematically with a minimum of dialogue and what there is is believable. The acting is believable. For those cineasts who feel that believability should be taken for granted, not worthy of compliments, let us not forget the type of plastic this sort of filmed best-seller epic usually sinks to. Remember *The Naked and the Dead*?

Pacino as Michael Corleone is particularly strong playing the war hero who comes into the family business reluctantly but dutifully when the father is sick and in trouble, clobbering the competition with youthful ruthlessness. Clemenza, the fat family lieutenant, tells Michael at one point how proud they all were of him as a war hero. He's a nice boy, this hero, who wants no part of his family's wars and at the end when he has proven his worth at urban guerrilla fighting, is he any less heroic? As he learns the business we see him mature through the burden not of blood but of increased responsibility. And through it we can infer our own brutalization. Good wars no longer exist, although we still kill in their name. Michael's assassination of the enemy families is no different in kind from what every government, the Peoples' Republic of China included, does every day . . . what they've always done. Michael is only another harried politician taking some calculated risks in order to diversify his peoples' economic interests, a man keeping up with changing times, trying to buy peace in his time. "They shoulda stopped Hitler at Munich," Clemenza says at another point, but they didn't and who are "they" anyway? Michael knows nice guys finish last if at all and we can imagine him now, 20 years after, sitting by his pool, proud of his children who have graduated from the best schools. He could even own Paramount.

The collage of images through a hazy lens which floats over bittersweet Italian ballads when the families go to the mattresses conveys the irony and stark absurdity of that bit of gangland choreography. Mattresses are as absurd as trenches. And the final strategy where Michael eliminates every enemy the family ever had while acting as Godfather at his nephew's baptism is accompanied by the priest's invocation and a pipe organ wailing. Michael's eyes have seen the devil, with whom he will not have too much trouble living. Maybe a bad night's sleep here and there, but that will be mostly fear and nothing serious. To understand how a man can live with that conscience imagine Milhouse or Mao. Sometimes these things are "necessary."

It comes to the same thing, murder by proxy. The Commander in Chief gives orders to his troops and they carry them out. It just so happens that in this case it's by dese, dems and dosers in white-on-white ties, not khaki. Nobody knows the slightest bit of emotion when they are ordered to rub out a guy who two seconds earlier was a faithful member of the boys. The Germans, after all, used to be the bad guys. When Sonny beats up his brother-in-law the crowd of sidewalk onlookers stands by impassively, like they're watching a game of touch football, not a flicker of horror on their faces. Of course nobody goes for the cops. The cops are just more killers in uniform. This impassivity to violence is too consistent to be accidental, although it is inherent in the story. In the film it becomes somehow *the* story.

There is violence only where the story demands it, but it *is* a violent story. And what there is is boss. This band knows how to die. In death, as in life, Marlon Brando is a man among boys. Stumbling around his garden towards the end . . . senile, overweight and clumsy, making funny faces with an orange peel in his mouth to amuse a grandson, Brando leaves as strong an image as Welles' aging Charles Foster Kane. Plus all the little things . . . disdainfully dusting an ash off the arm of Sollozo's chair as he refuses his request to bank a heroin deal . . . back home in bed after the assassination attempt, raising his arms in silent benediction to the visiting children and relatives . . . his voice becoming hoarse as he grows weaker through age . . . an actor, a star, a superstar, a household name and sight as himself, totally succeeding in making us forget him for the role. Class!

He assumes the character and as he died I marvelled not at the virtuoso performance but at a society which condemns murder in the name of morality but rewards it with wealth and natural death if on a large enough scale. I wondered whatever happened to "America never fought an unjust war," or to "Crime doesn't pay."

WHOSE FILM IS 'LAST TANGO,'
ANYWAY?

by Jon Landau

Last Tango in Paris
directed by
Bernardo Bertolucci
United Artists

    Last Tango in Paris unites the most appealing of sub-
jects, sex, with the most respected of actors, Marlon
Brando, under the guidance of the stylistically dazzling
young director Bernardo Bertolucci. As a prescription
for economic success, it is flawless; as a movie it is a
failure in which everyone concerned continually shows
us how hard he is working at achieving a profundity that,
by the film's end, is still nowhere in sight. In fact, the
deeper our immersion in the film, the more hollow it
seems, until its often dream-like aura has been transformed from mere self-consciousness into pure narcissism.
We are left wondering only whose narcissism we have
been watching.

    The film concerns four characters: Paul (Marlon
Brando), an aging American in Paris whose wife has just
committed suicide; Jeanne (Maria Schneider), a young
girl he meets while both are looking over the same vacant
apartment, and with whom Paul has a series of sexual
encounters during which he forbids the use of names or
any other social amenity; Tom (Jean-Pierre Leaud),

Jeanne's ingratiatingly eccentric filmmaker boyfriend, who is making a television show about her; and Rosa, Paul's dead wife. From these four characters Bertolucci contrives three types of scenes: Paul and Jeanne's explorations of sex in the apartment, Jeanne and Tom's continuing relationship outside the apartment, and Paul's search for the meaning of Rosa's death through encounters with her religious mother, her supercilious lover, the people in the flophouse she ran, and her embalmed corpse.

The narrative is rendered in a strictly tit-for-tat style —in fact, maddeningly so. For every choice offered one character, we are simplistically shown the counter-choice offered the other. Paul is crude, old, American and real; Tom is charming, young, European and naive. Jeanne must choose. Rosa is dead; Jeanne is alive. Paul must choose. During the course of the picture, Paul and Jeanne do choose each other, only—with convenient irony (or is it tragedy?)—always at different times.

Given the limited nature of Bertolucci's easy-does-it approach to allegory and the big subjects, the film would have been far better if at least his precious structure weren't so flawed. Given the symmetry that dominates the plot and style of the film, *Last Tango in Paris* could only have worked if Jeanne were a real match for Paul, and if Rosa were a comprehensible force from the past. Bertolucci fails on both counts.

In the director's vision, Paul's crudeness, his contemptuous demands on Jeanne and his apparent unconcern for anything that happens outside the apartment are justified by his need for emotional catharsis, and his search for a primal state of being. By comparison, Jeanne is a thrill seeker, willing to forget her romance with Tom in a matter of minutes, overwhelmed by desire for a not particularly attractive sexual boor twice her age. We are asked to accept this inexplicable relationship as a premise, but one can't watch the film without questioning it and everything that follows from it. Jeanne remains a child playing with the fire of Paul's private tragedy and who (as in the lyrics of a thousand pop songs) is inevitably burned when things get too hot. Paul is mythologized as the noble American savage, willing to risk freedom while she must rebel against it. It really is rather an old-fashioned view of the difference between man and woman.

As if the plot weren't weighted enough against our interest in, let alone sympathy for, Jeanne, there is the fact that she is played by a beautiful, talented but limited unknown, while Paul is played by the most generally admired of all American actors. Brando's performance is an enigma—one is continually wondering whether he is playing anyone but himself. His importance to the life of the film is most evident from the fact that when he disappears from the screen our interest virtually collapses. His absence is felt as dramatic, not emotional, loss. Without him up there, it is difficult to care about what happens to anyone.

And yet his performance is very soft. He throws away key lines, relies heavily on attempts at significant gestures, pauses, and what-have-you and, most surprisingly of all, vitiates his anger to the point where it seems more forced than anything else. I miss the sting of the Marlon Brando of my memories.

The better part of screen acting is in the reacting, and Brando's performance is clearly stifled by having so little to work against—a sketchily drawn young girl and a dead wife. Caught between such evanescent figures, his depictions of grief, anguish, despair and violence seem isolated and without any anchors outside his own personality. It is therefore unsurprising that his naturalism exists in a vacuum, and that his acting seems hollow compared with even his most mediocre Fifties performances. In *The Godfather* he was surrounded by interesting actors, his character firmly rooted in the stylized environment of the film. Forced to create an environment by sheer force of personality in *Last Tango,* he under-extends himself. His already famous soliloquy at Rosa's bedside doesn't have an iota of the force that made people remember whole scenes from *On The Waterfront* years after they saw it. At his worst—and the long monologues are it—we are left only with the voice and the arching brows.

And then there is the much discussed phenomenon of Paul—Brando making love mainly with his clothes on, while Maria Schneider is fully exposed. Some have cited this as an anachronistic bit of puritanism, outrageously out of place in a film with pretensions to cinematic sexual innovation. It is more than that. In the past, given accepted limits of censorship, audiences could accept stylized approaches to lovemaking that were suggestive without being realistic. But in the context of a film that is clearly aiming at sexual realism, it is an act of incalculable arrogance to portray a man given over to resolving his emotional crises through endless bouts of sexual debauchery as one who would fuck with his clothes on. This oppressively obvious departure from the general tone of the film renders several of the sexual sequences bizarre and comic, in a way that Bertolucci and Brando must never have intended. Even Brando at his best couldn't make anything so fake seem real. At his most mediocre he doesn't try, and is apparently content to let all of the sexual sequences stand as obvious bits of blatant simulation which, at the very least, make a complete mockery of any of the film's claims for cinematic sexual advance.

Is there nothing salvable in this film? It is becoming a commonplace observation that Bertolucci's style outdistances his themes, characters, narrative and ideas, and *Last Tango* is confirmation of that thought. The only thing of more than ephemeral interest in the film is how Bertolucci visualizes the story. For example, the credits are shown on a divided screen, with the alternate half taken up first with a painting of a man, and then with one of a woman. Finally the two paintings are joined together, just before the first frame of the film shatters the illusion of harmony. Then, as Paul begins to walk underneath an above-ground metro line, we see Jeanne, in soft focus, in the background. In the last shot of the picture we see Jeanne in the foreground and Paul, in soft focus, in the background, their roles and destinies reversed.

The first encounter under the metro foreshadows the beginning of their relationship. A second—this time with Jeanne walking in front of Paul—signifies its ending. By shooting both scenes in the same place, Bertolucci emphasizes his belief that events cannot repeat themselves, and that an opportunity was missed.

The train itself takes on symbolic importance, both through the meeting under it and the frequent quick cuts to it and its accompanying, horrifying noise, depicting the oppressive passage of time. It has a different meaning for

381

Jeanne and Tom's relationship as they find themselves on opposite sides of an underground metro. As they argue across the tracks a train rolls by, separating them. As it passes, Tom runs around to the other side and starts to fight with Jeanne. The scene ends in an embrace that reveals his innocent determination not to let anything come between them.

Bertolucci revels in traditional devices. Jeanne's relationship to Paul begins when she opens a shade in the apartment and the sudden rush of sunlight reveals Paul curled up on the floor. The relationship ends when Tom comes to the apartment, decides not to take it, and leaves. After he does, Jeanne lowers the shade, extinguishing the light of her relationship with Paul.

Bertolucci's use of color is no less stylized. He chose yellow as a basic motif for the life force represented by Paul and Jeanne's relationship, and he never misses an opportunity to underline its significance, as so much of the film is washed in that color.

Given the shortcomings of everything else, Bertolucci cannot be accused of soft-pedaling his point of view visually. Whatever force the film finally attains comes most often from his willingness to take his situation seriously, and to depict it with stylistic devices that are at least fascinating as evidences of misapplied talent. There is a lot more to be said for Bertolucci's device of having Paul face his wife's lover in the identical bathrobes she gave each one of them, than there is for Brando's of making Paul's last gesture sticking some chewing gum under a railing ledge. Bertolucci's style resonates; Brando's, in this instance, is hollow.

It is unfortunate that Brando's narcissism overwhelms Bertolucci's style; that his poorly defined presence throws the film so out of balance. But it is impossible to imagine *Last Tango in Paris* without him and therefore impossible to answer the question, whose film is this, anyway? If there were an answer, *Last Tango in Paris* would be much better than it is.

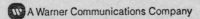